Second Edition

LITERATURE

Alive!

The Art
Of
Oral Interpretation

Teri Gamble
Michael Gamble

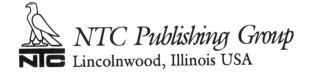

NTC Publishing Group
Lincolnwood, Illinois USA

Acknowledgments for literary material and photographs are on
pp. 471–472, which represent a continuation of the title page.

3 4 5 6 7 8 9 AG 9 8 7 6 5 4 3 2 1

CONTENTS

INTRODUCTION

In *Literature Alive!* you will explore oral interpretation, the art of performing literature. As you develop the physical and mental resources necessary for performing literature, you will come to know that analyzing a poem, prose, or drama selection and sharing your interpretation of it with others can be a rewarding experience—both for you and your audience. As you journey into different literary worlds, you will find a unique meeting of yourself and literature through oral interpretation, as well as the realization that you can affect others with your performance.

Literature Alive! is carefully structured to help you develop oral interpretation skills. In Part One you will focus on how to effectively use your body, voice, and all your senses in the oral interpretation process. In Part Two you will journey into the special worlds of narrative and descriptive prose, drama, and poetry, discovering the varying aspects of those literary genres in performance. In Part Three you will go beyond those worlds to chapters on documentary material as fuel for interpretation, performing literature for children, ensemble or group approaches to interpretation, and planning special programs.

Each of the eleven chapters in *Literature Alive!* contains a number of activities, as well as a wide range of literary selections—cuttings and complete works. "Getting Involved" activities are designed to help you discover and develop oral interpretation skills and become a performer of literature. These exercises do get you involved, and are fun as well as challenging. We ask you to approach each of the exercises with an open mind and a willingness to participate. As you move through each chapter, you will find that you can apply what you have learned in one exercise to what you are working on in another. Each "Getting Involved" exercise offers you "Reflections," questions that urge you to think about and discuss your experiences with the oral interpretation process and the literary selection at hand.

Another feature of this book is an exercise entitled "Performer's Journal." Beginning in Chapter Two, these exercises will encourage you to analyze and evaluate your interpretations—your performances—of literary selections through the keeping of a journal or notebook. You will be able to chart your personal growth as a performer and your interpretations of literature as you progress through *Literature Alive!*

PART ONE

Harnessing Your Resources

- **Awakening and Contacting Your Body**
- **Discovering and Developing Your Voice**
- **Training Your Sense Memory for Oral Interpretation**

CHAPTER ONE

Awakening and Contacting Your Body

Effective interpreters of literature are performers of literature. As a performer, your challenge is to transform the written words of literature into *behaved* words. As an oral interpreter, your responsibility is to make the words of an author live; your task is to breathe energy into each page of a selected script. How can you meet these responsibilities? How can you make the written words of a literary selection come alive for your audience?

Bringing Words Alive

First, think about the characteristics that all living things share. Ask yourself what it means to be alive, to be animate. Animate or living organisms are vital, functional, and flexible. Unlike dead organisms, which are rigid, nonfunctional, and inflexible, living organisms are always in a state of activity. If you hope to share a literary selection successfully—if you hope to make the words live for your audience—then you should be able to convey the sense of activity or movement that you discover within that selection. Doing so, however, is not as simple or straightforward as you might think. For, in order to find and activate movement, you first have to be able to use your whole body to understand and interpret the literature. In other words, you have to embody the literature. This means you must use your body to help you express the experiences literature contains. Keep in mind that using your body will help you to communicate the emotional and intellectual meanings of your work through performance. You can prepare it for this by helping your body be fully aware and elastic. This chapter will examine some of the techniques you can use in order to ready your body for this effort.

Body Language and Literature Performance

As a serious interpreter, you will be interested in work done recently in **kinesics**, or body language. Kinesiologists, those who study visible body behavior, regard the entire visible body as potentially communicative. Included under the general category of kinesics are the subcategories of posture and stance, muscle tension and gestures, facial expressions, and eye contact. These modes of behavior have long been recognized as carrying, clarifying, or enhancing meaning in performance situations. Indeed, the body of a performer or interpreter of literature is an essential part of that person's communication resource system. Effective interpreters speak not only with their voices, but with their faces, their necks, their shoulders, their torsos, their arms, and their legs, as well. Effective interpretations are not simply performances from the neck up. The entire body supports the dynamic experience of reading literature aloud.

How can you prepare your body to explore and communicate literature? Begin with a few body warm-ups. After all, a communicative body is an expressive body, and an expressive body is agile and aware. The following exercises should help you to physically experience, internalize, and perform literature. You should use them to approach a literary selection with your whole being.

GETTING INVOLVED
The Body Machine

This exercise will help you awaken and loosen the expressive parts of your body. The goal is to discover all the different body parts you can move separately, then in various combinations. As a partner or your instructor calls out a particular body part, begin to move and exercise it to the music or beat provided. Ready?

1. First, fingers. Move every joint on both hands. Now, shake your wrists. Turn them in circles. Next, bend your elbows; How many ways can you move your forearms? Concentrate on your shoulders; swing your arms in circles above your head. Now, experience silence and stillness. Feel your body at rest. Let your neck stretch upward toward the ceiling—up—up—up. Slowly, let it fall smoothly forward, until the tip of your chin touches your chest. Be careful not to force it.

    Next, slowly circle your head. Now, concentrate on your face. Exercise your facial muscles. Bat your eyelashes; pretend to chew a gigantic piece of bubble gum; scrunch your face up. How many different masks can you create with your face? Now let your face relax.

    Bend at your waist and at your knees. You have become a monkey, so let yourself sway side to side as you swish your monkey tail. Straighten now, and stand on one leg, taking care to keep your balance. Focus on your free leg; bend it at your knee; turn it at your ankle; let your toes wriggle. Now repeat this sequence using your other leg as the free leg. Finally, with both feet on the floor, use your legs together as the beat or music suggests.

2. Let's complicate this exercise a bit. Repeat the above sequence, only this time, after you start to move a body part, try not to let it stop moving. Think of your body as a machine being wound up—a machine that will not run down until it is told to do so.

Move your fingers.

Add your wrists, but keep your fingers moving.

Add your elbows; watch your fingers and wrists move.

Add your shoulders—really swing your arms.

Stretch, stretch, s-t-r-e-t-c-h your neck.

Keep the other parts of your machine moving and "start up" your face.

Add your legs, one at a time.

Add your ankles. Are your fingers still moving?

Finally, add your toes to your body machine.

3. When your partner or your instructor claps his or her hands twice, freeze in whatever position you find yourself. At the command "go," start everything moving again, all at once. Be sure to listen carefully to the leader's signals.

Reflections

1. How does your body machine feel now?

2. What clues do you have that your body can really work?

GETTING INVOLVED
Refining Body Awareness

A. As a class, stand in a large semicircle. Your instructor will provide you with sounds to move to, and your goal is simply to react physically to the vocal impulses. Listen to your leader and, after a while, to your fellow students. For example, what type of body reaction might result from a scream? a cry? a hearty laugh? a giggle? If you are fed the same vocal impulse more than once, alter your physical response to it.

Reflections

1. How did the students in your class react to each of the vocal stimuli? Were there a variety of responses? Why?

2. How did your body's reactions mirror the type of vocal stimuli provided? What happened to your body each time the vocal stimulus changed?

3. Were you able to respond with your entire body? For example, did you *feel* a scream with your neck and your back?

B. Working in small groups, use your body to simulate the motion of a machine—an engine, for example. To do this, have group members move in a sequence that you design. Think of the way an automobile engine operates. Its various parts function in sequence in order to propel the car. Start slowly and add power to your machine gradually. As your group gets going, speed up your movements and add sounds, as well.

Reflections

1. How did you use your body and voice to develop a machine that operated in a unique way?

2. How did you manage to solve the timing problem so all members of the group could perform in sequence as needed?

These preliminary exercises should serve to awaken your body machine. Do understand, however, that the goal of these activities is not simply to provide your body with physical stimulation. A flexible and energetic body is your starting point, but it is not your ultimate goal. As a performer you want to be able to harness all the energy your body possesses. You want to make your body's energy work for you.

The Conductor

As an interpreter, you want to be able to control your body's energy output effectively and efficiently. The type of energy expenditures you experienced in the preceding two exercises were, in fact, quite different from the type of energy expenditures you will experience in performance situations. Why? Because the amount of energy you expend in performing will be directly related to the content of your selection, your space limitations, and your ability to empathize or feel *with* and *for* characters in literature. When interpreting a selection, you are the "machine" and the literature is the "conductor"; in other words, literature fuels your machine—specifically, with the feelings, experiences, and attitudes that are the heart of the selection. In order to share the literature with your audience, your body needs to call on many of its expressive agents for help. Learn more about your body's expressive abilities in the next activity.

GETTING INVOLVED
The Body Talks

Your instructor will provide you with two envelopes. One will be labeled "Emotion" and the other will be labeled "Body Part." Class members will choose a slip of paper from each envelope and attempt to express the named emotion using the particular body part they drew.

When it is your turn, name the part of the body on which your fellow students should focus their attention, and they will attempt to identify the emotion you are "physicalizing." The following feelings are listed on slips in the Emotion envelope: happiness, sadness, jealousy, pride, sympathy, anger, hope, hatred, greed, scorn.

On the slips in the Body Parts envelope are listed the following: left arm, right arm, back, torso, face, whole body.

Reflections

1. Which emotions were easiest for you to portray? Which emotions were a greater challenge to convey?

2. Which parts of your body were more communicative than others? Why?

3. Is it possible for you to isolate one part of your body and allow it to speak?

4. Do you need your whole body to help you communicate or interpret literature?

Physicalizing Metaphors

The feelings and emotions you experience are closely linked with your body's behavior. In fact, emotional state or attitude is often described in terms of body parts or body movements. Think about the following **metaphors** or figures of speech often used in daily conversations to describe behavior: hair-raising; grit your teeth; pain in the neck; butterflies in your stomach; heart in your throat; white with fear; red with rage; frozen with terror; stiff upper lip; watery knees; under your skin; a cold shoulder; an itching palm; itching to do it; a bleeding heart; a heart of stone; an upstanding person; on your toes; turn your nose up; turn your nose down; swallow your tongue.

GETTING INVOLVED
Body Metaphors

Choose one of the preceding metaphors to portray to your class. Based on your performance, your fellow students will attempt to determine the expression you are embodying. After you perform and observe others' performances, answer these reflections.

Reflections

1. What metaphors were most easily shared with the audience?

2. What body parts did you and others use to help you communicate the metaphorical expressions?

These idiomatic expressions support the fact that your body reflects your emotions and/or your attitudes. Your body can indicate your moods and your feelings. In fact, as your state of being changes, the parts of your body serve to mirror this difference. A change in posture, gesture, facial expression, or general body tone usually indicates a corresponding change in emotional state. In the following activity, you will examine more closely the way your body fulfills its various expressive functions.

GETTING INVOLVED
Body Walks

Portray one of the following feelings while crossing from the left side to the right side of your classroom: happiness, sadness, jealousy, sympathy, outrage, warmth, cold, arrogance, timidity

Reflections

1. What happened to your posture as you expressed the particular feeling?

2. What type of path through space did you map out for yourself?

3. At what rate did you move?

4. How heavy were your steps?

5. What gestures did you use to support the feeling you portrayed?

6. What did your face say?

7. How would you describe the general feeling-tone of your body?

Your posture probably served to reinforce the feeling you chose to portray. **Posture** may be defined as the alignment of your body parts. The way you stand or sit helps to reveal to your audience an emotional or physical state of being. Body posture communicates everything from contentment and confidence to worry and discouragement. Your posture signals your intent to approach and meet the world or your wish to avoid and withdraw from it. Remember, you will add definition to your performance as an interpreter simply by the nature of your posture.

Gestures, Facial Expressions, and Body Tone

Gestures are motions of your limbs or body you can use to help you express or accentuate an idea. Mood values are inherent in certain gestures. For example, with your arms you can indicate approach or invitation, love or protection, avoidance or anger, jealousy or envy, nervousness or tension, comfort or relaxation. Even the absence of specific gestural signals may serve to enhance your communication effectiveness. Be certain, however, that you neither overuse nor extensively repeat certain gestures, unless your literary script specifically calls for such behavior. The gestures you employ should always reinforce your material; they should grow out of your response to your material. Understand that gestures are not used to call attention to an interpreter; rather, they are used to help an interpreter's audience concentrate on the performance of a piece of literature. Consequently, gestures need to be appropriate to the total effect an interpreter seeks to make.

In addition to gestures, the face is also rich in communicative potential. Facial expressions can help you indicate the impact upon you that certain experiences or feelings have. Truly remarkable qualities of the human face are its mobility and its elasticity. If used effectively, your **face-work** can provide a direct physical counterpart to the actions, feelings, or emotions expressed in your selection.

In addition, your general **body tone**—your overall degree of body tension or relaxation—should also be affected by the nature of your selection, and by your performance goals. Your body might be compared to a rubber band. Sometimes nerves are stretched, causing muscles to tense and tighten, veins to constrict, blood pressure to rise, and the heart to race. At other times, nerves are eased, so muscles relax, veins dilate, joints become more flexible, head and neck rest comfortably on the shoulders, and swallowing becomes easier. An interpreter needs to realize that body tension and relaxation are not separate, unrelated states. They are, in fact, opposite points on a continuum. The body can be stretched taut and the body can be at ease. It is important, however, to know how to discover and manifest the amount of body tension appropriate to a reading. With this in mind, during rehearsal periods you should experiment with various degrees of movement, continuing to make adjustments during the course of a single selection, passage, sentence, or phrase.

At this point, we want to emphasize that your body is not simply a collection of parts working independently. Instead, it works as a synchronized whole. Though it is helpful for our purposes to examine it part by part as we consider the body's communication potential, bear in mind it is the movements of the entire body that help to interpret literature and to enrich a performance.

Before you try to apply what you have learned about body expressiveness to specific literary selections, try this.

GETTING INVOLVED

Texture Movement

You are walking in space. What happens to your body? You are slogging through sticky taffy. How do your movement capabilities change? Now you are slipping on a floor slick with grease. How will you adapt your movements to this slithery situation? Finally, your sneakers are sinking into foam rubber. How does your body react?

GETTING INVOLVED

Move to the Music

Your instructor will play some musical selections that vary in rhythm, volume, and tone. Working alone or with a group, react with your body to each of the pieces of music. Then develop answers to the following reflections.

Reflections

1. How did the selection make you feel?

2. How did you choose to move to it?

3. Did your way of moving change during the course of a single selection? Why?

Your physical responses probably changed in the first exercise as the texture of the atmosphere changed and in the second exercise as the tempo and tone of the music changed. In effect, you reacted to the **moods** or "**feeling-tones**" ingrained in each of the atmospheric textures and musical compositions. Like the atmosphere and like music, literature also affects your whole body. In turn, you can use your whole body to respond to the mood changes of a literary selection. Tuning into music is enjoyable and fulfilling, and so is tuning into literature.

GETTING INVOLVED

Literary Tune-In: A

Your instructor will read "The Hat Act" aloud. This selection involves a presentation by an unusual magician who is constantly on the brink of giving a disastrous performance.

As your instructor reads "The Hat Act" aloud, half of the class should mime the movements it suggests and the remaining students should provide the required audience responses.

■ THE HAT ACT ■

ROBERT COOVER

In the middle of the stage: a plain table.

A man enters, dressed as a magician with black cape and black silk hat. Doffs hat in wide sweep to audience, bows elegantly.

Applause.

He displays inside of hat. It is empty. He thumps it. It is clearly empty. Places hat on table, brim up. Extends both hands over hat, tugs back sleeves exposing wrists, snaps fingers. Reaches in, extracts a rabbit.

Applause.

Pitches rabbit into wings. Snaps fingers over hat again, reaches in, extracts a dove.

Applause.

Pitches dove into wings. Snaps fingers over hat, reaches in, extracts another rabbit. No applause. Stuffs rabbit hurriedly back in hat, snaps fingers, reaches in, extracts another hat, precisely like the one from which it came.

Applause.

Places second hat alongside first one. Snaps fingers over new hat, withdraws a third hat, exactly like the first two.

Light applause.

Snaps fingers over third hat, withdraws a fourth hat, again identical. No applause. Does not snap fingers. Peers into fourth hat, extracts a fifth one. In fifth, he finds a sixth. Rabbit appears in third hat. Magician extracts seventh hat from sixth. Third hat rabbit withdraws a second rabbit from first hat. Magician withdraws eighth hat from seventh, ninth from eighth, as rabbits extract other rabbits from other hats. Rabbits and hats are everywhere. Stage is one mad turmoil of hats and rabbits.

Laughter and applause.

Frantically, magician gathers up hats and stuffs them into each other, bowing, smiling at audience, pitching rabbits three and four at a time into wings, smiling, bowing. It is a desperate struggle. At first, it is difficult to be sure he is stuffing hats and pitching rabbits faster than they are reappearing. Bows, stuffs, pitches, smiles, perspires.

Laughter mounts.

Slowly the confusion diminishes. Now there is one small pile of hats and rabbits. Now there are no rabbits. At last there are only two hats. Magician, perspiring from overexertion, gasping for breath, staggers to table with two hats.

Light applause, laughter.

Magician, mopping brow with silk handkerchief, stares in perplexity at two remaining hats. Pockets handkerchief. Peers into one hat, then into other. Attempts tentatively to stuff first into second, but in vain. Attempts to fit second into first, but also without success. Smiles weakly at audience. No applause. Drops first hat to floor, leaps on it until crushed. Wads crushed hat in fist, attempts once more to stuff it into second hat. Still, it will not fit.

Light booing, impatient applause.

Trembling with anxiety, magician presses out first hat, places it brim up on table, crushes second hat on floor. Wads second hat, tries desperately to jam it into first hat. No, it will not fit. Turns irritably to pitch second hat into wings.

Loud booing.

Freezes. Pales. Returns to table with both hats, first in fair condition brim up, second still in a crumpled wad, faces hats in defeat. Bows head as though to weep silently.

Hissing and booing.

Smile suddenly lights magician's face. He smoothes out second hat and places it firmly on his head, leaving first hat bottomside-up on table. Crawls up on table and disappears feet first into hat.

Surprised applause.

Moments later, magician's feet poke up out of hat on table, then legs, then torso. Last part to emerge is magician's head, which, when lifted from table, brings first hat with it. Magician doffs first hat to audience, shows it is empty. Second hat has disappeared. Bows deeply.

Enthusiastic and prolonged applause, cheers.

Magician returns hat to head, thumps it, steps behind table. Without removing hat, reaches up, snaps fingers, extracts rabbit from top of hat.

Applause.

Pitches rabbit into wings. Snaps fingers, withdraws dove from top of hat.

Sprinkling of applause.

Pitches dove into wings. Snaps fingers, extracts lovely assistant from top of hat.

Astonished but enthusiastic applause and whistles.

Lovely assistant wears high feathery green hat, tight green halter, little green shorts, black net stockings, high green heels. Smiles coyly at whistles and applause, scampers bouncily off stage.

Whistling and shouting, applause.

Magician attempts to remove hat, but it appears to be stuck. Twists and writhes in struggle with stuck hat.

Mild laughter.

Struggle continues. Contortions. Grimaces.

Laughter.

Finally, magician requests two volunteers from audience. Two large brawny men enter stage from audience, smiling awkwardly.

Light applause and laughter.

One large man grasps hat, other clutches magician's legs. They pull cautiously. The hat does not come off. They pull harder. Still, it is stuck. They tug now with great effort, their faces reddening, their thick neck muscles taut and throbbing. Magician's neck stretches, snaps in two: POP! Large men tumble apart, rolling to opposite sides of stage, one with body, other with hat containing magician's severed head.

Screams of terror.

Two large men stand, stare aghast at handiwork, clutch mouths.

Shrieks and screams.

Decapitated body stands.

Shrieks and screams.

Zipper in front of decapitated body opens, magician emerges. He is as before, wearing same black cape and same black silk hat. Pitches deflated decapitated body into wings. Pitches hat and head into wings. Two large men sigh with immense relief, shake heads as though completely baffled, smile faintly, return to audience. Magician doffs hat and bows.

Wild applause, shouts, cheers.

Reflections

1. How did the action of your body help you to appreciate the literature?

2. How did your movements serve to reinforce the ideas in the selection?

3. How did the amount of movement you mimed change as the reader progressed through the story?

GETTING INVOLVED
Literary Tune-In: B

Relax and close your mind to your immediate surroundings and all of your daily concerns. This is your chance to let your mind and your body rest—to let them ease into contentment. Feel your toes and your legs relax; let your arms go limp; breathe deeply.

Now, think about feeling pain. Think of pain as an extension of the sense of touch. Concentrate on the particular set of circumstances that originally caused you to experience intense physical pain. Recall the conditions that made you feel the pain. Was it a fire? Was it an illness? Was it a wound? Get in touch with the pain once again. Let your body react to the discomfort you are reexperiencing. Respond with your face, your back, your muscles. Close your eyes and let your entire body process this pain.

Reflections

1. What type of pain did you imagine?

2. What happened to your body as in your mind you re-created this pain? Be as specific as possible in describing the physical sensations you just experienced. For example, how did the calves of your legs feel? What did you do with your arms? How was your muscle tone affected?

3. Why do you think you needed to use your body in order to really "remember" your pain?

The mind and the body work together. Our physical responses make our mental and emotional reactions vivid and intense. Our thoughts affect us, and the effects of our ruminations are visible. In this way, the mind and the body are inextricably linked.

GETTING INVOLVED

Literary Tune-In: C

Now, read aloud to a group the following passage from "Flight" by John Steinbeck. In this passage Pepe is suffering from a wound that has become grossly infected. He has no choice but to treat it himself.

FROM

 FLIGHT

JOHN STEINBECK

When the dawn came, Pepe pulled himself up. His eyes were sane again. He drew his great puffed arm in front of him and looked at the angry wound. The black line ran up from his wrist to his armpit. Automatically he reached in his pocket for his big black knife, but it was not there. His eyes searched the ground. He picked up a sharp blade of stone and scraped at the wound, sawed at the proud flesh and then squeezed the green juice out in big drops. Instantly he threw back his head and whined like a dog. His whole right side shuddered at the pain, but the pain cleared his head.

Reflections

Be as specific as possible in answering the following questions.

1. What happened to your muscle tension as you read?

2. What happened to the muscle tone of your audience?

3. How, if at all, did your posture change? Did the listener/observers reflect this change?

4. What gestures did you use to reinforce meaning? What did these gestures communicate to the audience?

GETTING INVOLVED

Eye-openers

1. Your instructor or a partner will lead you in the next "eye-opening" exercise. First, close your eyes and relax as you clear your mind of all extraneous thoughts. When you open your eyes, "see" an imaginary caterpillar clinging to the palm of your left hand. Study the caterpillar. What does it look like? How does it feel to have a caterpillar crawling on your palm? Watch the caterpillar crawl off your hand and close your eyes again.

2. Open your eyes. This time, notice that a butterfly has just landed on your hand. Examine the patterns and colors of its wings. Touch it gently with your free hand. Watch it as it flies away. Use your face to reflect your feelings. Close your eyes again.

3. Now you are enclosed in a very small space from which you cannot escape. You try, but you cannot raise your hands or your head more than six inches. As you lie flat on your back you begin to have trouble breathing. How else is your body responding to being confined? Process the experience through each of your nerve centers.

4. The following passage focuses on a nightmarish experience in which the speaker wakes to find that he has been buried in a sealed coffin. Read aloud the excerpt from "The Premature Burial" by Edgar Allan Poe.

■ THE PREMATURE BURIAL ■
EDGAR ALLAN POE

I remained without motion . . . I could not summon courage to move. I dared not make the effort which was to satisfy me of my fate—and yet there was something at my heart which whispered to me *it was true*. Despair—such as no other species of wretchedness ever calls into being—despair alone urged me, after long irresolution, to uplift the heavy lids of my eyes. I uplifted them. It was dark—all dark. I knew that the fit was over. I knew that the crisis of my disorder had long passed. I knew that I had now fully recovered the use of my visual faculties—and yet it was dark—all dark—the intense and utter raylessness of the Night that endureth for evermore.

I endeavored to shriek; and my lips and my parched tongue moved convulsively together in the attempt—but no voice issued from the cavernous lungs, which, oppressed as if by the weight of some incumbent mountain, gasped and palpitated, with the heart, at every elaborate and struggling inspiration.

The movement of the jaws, in this effort to cry aloud, showed me that they were bound up, as is usual with the dead. I felt, too, that I lay upon some hard substance; and by something similar my sides were, also, closely compressed. So far, I had not ventured to stir any of my limbs—but now I violently threw up my arms, which had been lying at length with the wrists crossed. They struck a solid wooden substance, which extended above my person at an elevation of not more than six inches from my face. I could no longer doubt that I reposed within a coffin at last. . . .

As this awful conviction forced itself, thus, into the innermost chambers of my soul, I once again struggled to cry aloud. And in this second endeavor I succeeded. A long, wild, and continuous shriek, or yell, of agony resounded through the realms of the subterrene Night.

Reflections

1. How can your body help you to experience this selection imaginatively?

2. Is it necessary to lie down in order to present this passage effectively?

3. What body movements can you use instead of lying down?

You, Your Selection, and Your Audience

Your body helps you to sense all the experiences described in a selection of literature. It helps you to feel yourself move into a selection, or to project yourself imaginatively into the world of the selection. In other words, your body helps you to feel with or **empathize** with the persons and the things that inhabit the piece of literature you wish to interpret. It helps you to relate actively to the thoughts, emotions, and attitudes described in the literature. It also helps you to share these same thoughts, emotions, and attitudes with your audience.

As you read, your audience will probably unconsciously imitate your physical movement. Just as you tend to smile when you see a baby smile at his mother, to look up when you notice other people looking up, to clench your fists when one boxer punches another boxer, to stretch your neck when number nineteen aims for the basket, to mimic your friend's facial expression when she tells a joke or relates a sad tale, and to imitate a monkey's movements as you watch it swing in a cage at the zoo, so your audience tends to respond physically to your performance. If your performance is successful, you will find that your audience will duplicate the tensions, the emotions, and the general behavioral cues or motor adjustments that you externalize before them. Thus, empathy functions to guide your audience's responses to you. There is, consequently, a give-and-take relationship established between your selection, yourself, and your audience.

GETTING INVOLVED
The Body and Performance

Use the following selections to illustrate what you have learned about your body's expressive qualities. Assess the degree of body tension, gesture, and movement that each passage requires. Remember, let your muscles respond completely as you perform or interpret each piece of literature. For each selection, be prepared to answer the following questions.

Reflections

1. How did you use your body to reinforce the emotional and intellectual content of the material?

2. At which points in the selection did your muscle tone change? Why?

Selections for Body Work

In this excerpt from Ernest Hemingway's *The Old Man and the Sea*, we meet Santiago, an elderly man who has spent his life waging a constant tug of war with the sea.

■ THE OLD MAN ■
AND THE SEA
ERNEST HEMINGWAY

When the old man saw him coming he knew that this was a shark that had no fear at all and would do exactly what he wished. He prepared the harpoon and made the rope fast while he watched the shark come on. The rope was short as it lacked what he had cut away to lash the fish.

The old man's head was clear and good now and he was full of resolution but he had little hope. It was too good to last, he thought. He took one look at the great fish as he watched the shark close in. It might as well have been a dream, he thought. I cannot keep him from hitting me but maybe I can get him. *Dentuso,* he thought. Bad luck to your mother.

The shark closed fast astern and when he hit the fish the old man saw his mouth open and his strange eyes and the clicking chop of the teeth as he drove forward in the meat just above the tail. The shark's head was out of water and his back was coming out and the old man could hear the noise of skin and flesh ripping on the big fish when he rammed the harpoon down onto the shark's head at a spot where the line between his eyes intersected with the line that ran straight back from his nose. There were no such lines. There was only the heavy sharp blue head and the big eyes and the clicking, thrusting all-swallowing jaws. But that was the location of the brain and the old man hit it. He hit it with his blood mushed hands driving a good harpoon with all his strength. He hit it without hope but with resolution and complete malignancy.

The shark swung over and the old man saw his eye was not alive and then he swung over once again, wrapping himself in two loops of the rope. The old man knew that he was dead but the shark would not accept it. Then, on his back with his tail lashing and his jaws clicking, the shark plowed over the water as a speed-boat does. The water was white where his tail beat it and three-quarters of his body was clear above the water when the rope came taut, shivered, and then snapped. The shark lay quietly for a little while on the surface and the old man watched him. Then he went down very slowly.

In her powerful selection "For My People," African American poet Margaret Walker recounts the long struggle for freedom experienced by her people, calls for peace among humans, and asks that strength and healing lead the way into the future.

■ FOR MY PEOPLE ■

MARGARET WALKER

For my people everywhere singing their slave songs repeatedly:
    their dirges and their ditties and their blues and jubilees,
    praying their prayers nightly to an unknown god, bending their
    knees humbly to an unseen power;

For my people lending their strength to the years: to the gone
    years and the now years and the maybe years, washing ironing
    cooking scrubbing sewing mending hoeing plowing digging
    planting pruning patching dragging along never gaining never
    reaping never knowing and never understanding;

For my playmates in the clay and dust and sand of Alabama
    backyards playing baptizing and preaching, and doctor and jail
    and soldier and school and mama and cooking and playhouse
    and concert and store and Miss Choomby and hair and company;

For the cramped bewildered years we went to school to learn to
    know the reasons why and the answers to and the people who
    and the places where and the days when, in memory of the
    bitter hours we discovered we were black and poor and
    small and different and nobody wondered and nobody under-
    stood;

For the boys and girls who grew in spite of these things to be
    Man and Woman, to laugh and dance and sing and play and
    drink their wine and religion and success, to marry their play-
    mates and bear children and then die of consumption and
    anemia and lynching;

For my people thronging 47th Street in Chicago and Lenox Avenue
in New York and Rampart Street in New Orleans, lost dis-
inherited dispossessed and HAPPY people filling the cabarets
and taverns and other people's pockets needing bread and shoes
and milk and land and money and Something—Something
all our own;

For my people walking blindly, spreading joy, losing time being
lazy, sleeping when hungry, shouting when burdened, drinking
when hopeless, tied and shackled and tangled among ourselves
by the unseen creatures who tower over us omnisciently and
laugh;

For my people blundering and groping and floundering in the dark
of churches and schools and clubs and societies, associations
and councils and committees and conventions, distressed and
disturbed and deceived and devoured by money-hungry glory-
craving leeches, preyed on by facile force of state and fad and
novelty by false prophet and holy believer;

For my people standing staring trying to fashion a better way from
confusion from hypocrisy and misunderstanding, trying to
fashion a world that will hold all the people all the faces all
the adams and eves and their countless generations;

Let a new earth rise. Let another world be born. Let a bloody
peace be written in the sky. Let a second generation full of
courage issue forth, let a people loving freedom come to growth,
let a beauty full of healing and a strength of final clenching
be the pulsing in our spirits and our blood. Let the martial
songs be written, let the dirges disappear. Let a race of men
now rise and take control!

John Steinbeck took a commonplace situation that most of us would
overlook and describes it in a way that is unforgettable. In this excerpt from
his novel *The Grapes of Wrath*—a work that explores Oklahoma and its people
in the 1930s, during the Great Depression—Steinbeck describes the trials
of a turtle who desires simply to cross the road.

■ THE GRAPES OF WRATH ■
JOHN STEINBECK

The sun lay on the grass and warmed it, and in the shade under the grass
the insects moved, ants and ant lions to set traps for them, grasshoppers to
jump into the air and flick their yellow wings for a second, sow bugs like
little armadillos, plodding restlessly on many tender feet. And over the
grass at the roadside a land turtle crawled, turning aside for nothing, dragging his high-domed shell over the grass, not really walking, but boosting
and dragging his shell along. The barley beards slid off his shell, and the
clover burrs fell on him and rolled to the ground. His horny beak was partly
open, and his fierce, humorous eyes, under brows like fingernails, stared
straight ahead. He came over the grass leaving a beaten trail behind him,
and the hill, which was the highway embankment, reared up ahead of him.
For a moment he stopped, his head held high. He blinked and looked up
and down. At last he started to climb the embankment. Front clawed feet
reached forward but did not touch. The hind feet kicked his shell along, and
it scraped on the grass, and on the gravel. As the embankment grew steeper
and steeper, the more frantic were the efforts of the land turtle. Pushing
hind legs strained and slipped, boosting the shell along, and the horny head
protruded as far as the neck could stretch. Little by little the shell slid up the
embankment until at last a parapet cut straight across its line of march, the
shoulder of the road, a concrete wall four inches high. As though they
worked independently the hind legs pushed the shell against the wall. The
head upraised and peered over the wall to the broad smooth plain of cement. Now the hands, braced on top of the wall, strained and lifted, and the
shell came slowly up and rested its front end on the wall. For a moment the
turtle rested. A red ant was crushed between body and legs. And one head
of wild oats was clamped into the shell by a front leg. For a long moment the
turtle lay still, and then the neck crept out and the old humorous frowning
eyes looked about and the legs and tail came out. The back legs went to
work, straining like elephant legs, and the shell tipped to an angle so that

the front legs could not reach the level cement plain. But higher and higher the hind legs boosted it, until at last the center of balance was reached, the front tipped down, the front legs scratched at the pavement, and it was up. But the head of wild oats was held by its stem around the front legs.

Now the going was easy, and all the legs worked, and the shell boosted along, waggling from side to side. A sedan driven by a forty-year-old woman approached. She saw the turtle and swung to the right, off the highway, the wheels screamed and a cloud of dust boiled up. Two wheels lifted for a moment and then settled. The car skidded back onto the road, and went on, but more slowly. The turtle had jerked into its shell, but now it hurried on, for the highway was burning hot.

And now a light truck approached, and as it came near, the driver saw the turtle and swerved to hit it. His front wheel struck the edge of the shell, flipped the turtle like a tiddly-wink, spun it like a coin, and rolled it off the highway. The truck went back to its course along the right side. Lying on its back, the turtle was tight in its shell for a long time. But at last its legs waved in the air, reaching for something to pull it over. Its front foot caught a piece of quartz and little by little the shell pulled over and flopped upright. The wild oat head fell out and three of the spearhead seeds stuck in the ground. And as the turtle crawled on down the embankment, its shell dragged dirt over the seeds. The turtle entered a dust road and jerked itself along, drawing a wavy shallow trench in the dust with its shell. The old humorous eyes looked ahead, and the horny beak opened a little. His yellow toe nails slipped a fraction in the dust.

In this poem a daughter speaks to her mother. Let your body reflect the movement and emotion you feel as you read this poem aloud.

■ MY MOTHER ■
PIECED QUILTS
TERESA PALOMO ACOSTA

They were just meant as covers
in winter
as weapons
against pounding january winds

but it was just that every morning I awoke to these
october ripened canvases
passed my hand across their cloth faces
and began to wonder how you pieced
all these together
these strips of gentle communion cotton and
    flannel nightgowns
wedding organdies
dime store velvets

how you shaped patterns square and oblong and
    round
positioned
balanced
then cemented them
with your thread
a steel needle
a thimble

how the thread darted in and out
galloping along the frayed edges, tucking them in
as you did us at night
oh how you stretched and turned and re-arranged
your michigan spring faded curtain pieces
my father's santa fe work shirt
the sunnier denims, the tweeds of fall

in the evening you sat at your canvas
—our cracked linoleum floor the drawing board
me lounging on your arm
and you staking out the plan:
whether to put the lilac purple of easter against the
    red plaid of winter-going
into-spring
whether to mix a yellow with blue and white and
    paint the
corpus christi noon when my father held your
    hand
whether to shape a five-point star from the
somber black silk you wore to grandmother's
    funeral

you were the river current
carrying the roaring notes
forming them into pictures of a little boy reclining
a swallow flying
you were the caravan master at the reins
driving your threaded needle artillery across the
    mosaic cloth bridges
delivering yourself in separate testimonies.

oh mother you plunged me sobbing and laughing
into our past
into the river crossing at five
into the spinach fields
into the plainview cotton rows
into the tuberculosis wards
into braids and muslin dresses
sewn hard and taut to withstand the thrashings of
    twenty-five years

stretched out they lay
armed/ready/shouting/celebrating

knotted with love
the quilts sing on

The river Sumpul separates Salvador from Honduras. On May 14, 1980, six hundred men, women, and children were fleeing the Salvadoran army and trying desperately to get into Honduras. When they reached the river they thought that they had found safety. As they crossed the river, however, the Honduran army arrived, and all of the peasants were slaughtered as gunfire from both armies rained down on them.

José Alejandro Romero, a Salvadoran emigrant now living in New England, wrote this poem to protest against repression and barbarism.

■ SUMPUL ■

JOSÉ ALEJANDRO ROMERO

The afternoon has fallen into black dust,
and from the dust emerges death.
In the red river we swam, desperate to live.
We splashed in its waters and then,
bruised, we were floated by them.
From the river the massacred body arose.
Sumpul drowned in blood,
Sumpul deafened by the shots,
river turned red,
river swollen with anguish,
witnessing river, your hidden heart
containing the anonymous screams of martyrs—
of children, tender shoots,
of mothers, fruiting trees
and old ones ancient oaks.
Facing you is Yankee torture,
murderous sounds and the growl of the dog,
splattering this universe with shrapnel,
splitting open pregnant stars,
slashing the face of the peasant.

Beast, take note:
the worker's face will carry this scar.

River,
We seek your water made holy by force,
and with it anoint our arms,
with reddened eyes.
In a single, slaughtered droplet we watch
the sun, its hopeful yellow;
in its yellow is a future,
a victory, a triumph, a people.
In your winding current
We seek the wide and war-injured reflection of the people
confronting a vast machine;
their last words cursing despotism
their words like weapons, their body a shield,
their ideals, pure light.

I want to respond to the screams of the people,
to fixed eyes shooting off hatred,
to hoist your spirit in the fighting flag of guns.
I salute you with each shot aimed at the enemy
I swear to remember you in our future land,
and in the sky brimming with stars,
and in the first maize field of winter,
and in the waters of every river where I live.

Robert Benchley was an American humorist who always had a unique view of our culture. In this selection from a novel we meet the Twilly family. How would you like to have grown up among Wilbur, Grandma, Mable, Bernice, and the memory of the Grandfather with a mean face?

■ FAMILY LIFE IN AMERICA ■
ROBERT BENCHLEY

The living room in the Twilly's house was so damp that thick, soppy moss grew all over the walls. It dripped on the picture of Grandfather Twilly that hung over the melodeon, making streaks down the dirty glass like sweat on the old man's face. It was a mean face. Grandfather Twilly had been a mean man and had little spots of soup on the lapel of his coat. All his children were mean and had soup spots on their clothes.

Grandma Twilly sat in the rocker over by the window, and as she rocked the chair snapped. It sounded like Grandma Twilly's knees snapping as they did whenever she stooped over to pull the wings off a fly. She was a mean old thing. Her knuckles were grimy and she chewed crumbs that she found in the bottom of her reticule. You would have hated her. She hated herself. But most of all she hated Grandfather Twilly.

''I certainly hope you're frying good,'' she muttered as she looked up at his picture.

''Hasn't the undertaker come yet, Ma?'' asked young Mrs. Wilbur Twilly petulantly. She was boiling water on the oilheater and every now and again would spill a little of the steaming liquid on the baby who was playing on the floor. She hated the baby because it looked like her father. The hot water raised little white blisters on the baby's red neck and Mable Twilly felt short, sharp twinges of pleasure at the sight. It was the only pleasure she had had for four months.

''Why don't you kill yourself, Ma?'' she continued. ''You're only in the way here and you know it. It's just because you're a mean old woman and want to make trouble for us that you hang on.''

Grandma Twilly shot a dirty look at her daughter-in-law. She had always hated her. Stringy hair, Mabel had. Dank, stringy hair. Grandma Twilly thought how it would look hanging at an Indian's belt. But all that she did was to place her tongue against her two front teeth and make a noise like the bathroom faucet.

Wilbur Twilly was reading the paper by the oil lamp. Wilbur had watery blue eyes and cigar ashes all over his knees. The third and fourth buttons of his vest were undone. It was too hideous.

He was conscious of his family seated in chairs about him. His mother, chewing crumbs. His wife Mabel, with her stringy hair, reading. His sister Bernice, with projecting front teeth who sat thinking of the man who came every day to take away the waste paper. Bernice was wondering how long it would be before her family would discover that she had been married to this man for three years.

How Wilbur hated them all. It didn't seem as if he could stand it any longer. He wanted to scream and stick pins into every one of them and then rush out and see the girl who worked in his office snapping rubber bands all day. He hated her too, but she wore side-combs.

CHAPTER TWO

Discovering and Developing Your Voice

Your task as an oral interpreter is challenging. You are asked to share with your audience all the experiences that exist within a piece of literature, and you are expected to accomplish this using only the selection and your mind, body, and voice as tools. Indeed, your job of interpreter is not a simple one.

Consider the four resources available to you—the literary selection, your mind, your body, and your voice. With these, you will transform written words into performed words. In effect, these four resources combine to form the framework of an interpreter's performing system. Each component is related to and is interdependent with the other components in the system; a change in one component of the performing system should call forth corresponding changes in all other parts of the system.

Chapter 2 will focus on the vocal component of the interpreter's performing system. It is very important that you realize, however, that this aspect of interpreter behavior is isolated for purposes of examination only. In a performance situation, the interpreter's voice never functions alone; rather, it functions in relation to each of the three elements remaining. In effect, these four different components represent the four speakers of the interpreter's quadraphonic performing system. It is only by the successful interaction of selection, mind, body, and voice that literature will be fully revealed or communicated to an audience. To begin, how can an interpreter use his or her voice in order to maximize effectiveness as a performer of literature?

Levels of Meaning in Selections

First of all, you need to realize that every selection, printed page—in fact, every *word*—has two levels of meaning associated with it: its report or **content level**, and its command or **relationship level**. It is the relationship level that concerns you as an interpreter, because it is this level that helps to define the actual meaning of a word, phrase, or passage. The relationship level helps you, the reader, decide how to interpret the literal content, because as an interpreter you are concerned not only with the dictionary meaning of words, but also with the ways these words sound when read aloud. Thus, it remains for you to **restore the vocal cues** the words ''lost'' when the literature was originally transcribed.

The spoken word is rarely, if ever, neutral. It is, in fact, always affected by **paralinguistic**, or vocal, factors. Among these paralinguistic factors are speech intelligibility, time, volume and force, pitch, and vocal quality. Effective interpreters are able to use these basic elements of paralanguage to help them communicate both the emotional and intellectual meanings of their selections. In other words, trained readers know how to use vocal qualities to help their audiences appreciate and understand the content and mood-tones of their literature. Their voices are adaptable and tensile, responding totally to the literature. Now, how can you as an interpreter acquire this sought-after vocal flexibility and agility?

First you need to be willing to unleash your voice—to play with it freely. Try these exercises now.

GETTING INVOLVED
Freeing the Voice

A. Open your mouth wide and yawn. Try it again and really get into that yawn, stretching your arms and legs as an extension of it.

Reflections

1. What happens in the back of your mouth as you yawn?

2. What happens to your eyes?

B. This time, yawn with your mouth closed. Keeping your lips together, try to attain an open feeling in the back of your mouth.

Reflections

1. How do you feel now?

2. What has happened to the muscles in your throat and neck?

C. Now, sitting up straight in your chair, place your hand on your stomach, inhale through your nose, drop your jaw as you did in the open-mouth yawn, and use your stomach muscles or diaphragm to push the sound "Ha" up from within you. Try this several times; aim to create a full, resonant, unstrained tone.

Reflections

1. When you inhale through your nose, what happens to the hand resting on your stomach?

2. What surprised you about the tone of your voice?

D. Again, attain the open feeling of the yawn at the back of your throat and emit a "Ha," as you did in the preceding portion of this exercise. Now speed up the production of these sounds, until they gradually form a full-bodied, resonant laugh.

Reflections

1. What did your laugh sound like?

2. How did it differ from your normal laugh?

Now that your voice is partially freed, try channeling its effectiveness in new directions. Try this.

GETTING INVOLVED
Voice Orchestras

A. Your instructor will divide your class into five vocal sections. Each vocal section corresponds to an instrument in an orchestra: violins, clarinets, drums, tubas, and trumpets. Each instrument team will be given one of the following themes to perform vocally, as its members pantomime playing their instruments.

Violins: n

                                  n   n
                                        n

Clarinets: th

                                  th

                                        th

                                                th

Drums: broo-oom boom boom

Trumpets: tatatata ta ta

Tubas: omp pa omp pa omp pa pa

Your instructor will act as your orchestral conductor. He or she will warm up each instrument of the orchestra. When the rehearsal is finished, your conductor will mount an imaginary platform, raise his or her arms, and lead you in the musical piece you have prepared. Your group must be alert to the conductor's signals, for the instrument sections of the orchestra may be faded out, emphasized, or faded in at will.

B. Your instructor may now divide your class into new musical teams. It will be your team's goal to become a specific type of musical combo. You will use only your voices and bodies as tools; words are not necessary. For example, you might choose to become a rock group, a jazz combo, a classical combo, or a sound-effects studio. Do not be limited by the ideas you read here—conduct your own voice-combo explorations. When each group has prepared its musical presentation, perform the "opus" for the other combos in the class. Then, as a group, discuss answers to the following questions:

Reflections

1. What type of combo did your group choose to create?

2. How did you use your voices and your bodies to create this combo?

3. What expressive qualities did you discover in your own voice?

Learning to "play" your voice is akin to learning to play an instrument. In order to develop vocal skill, artistry, and dexterity, you have to play and practice your voice as you would play and practice the piano, the tuba, the violin, or the guitar. Like their musician relatives, interpreters are orchestrators. Instead of orchestrating a musical score, however, interpreters orchestrate a written script. Musical cues are replaced with paralinguistic or vocal cues. Now that your voice is warmed up, let us examine more closely some of these paralinguistic factors.

Speech Intelligibility

It is essential that you are able to communicate accurately your author's words to your audience. To do so, you must form the sounds of your script with *precision* and *control*. Just as musicians are careful not to play the note A when the note E is called for, so interpreters must be certain they play only the sounds their authors supply. If interpreters slur their words when they should not be slurred or mix their sounds when they should not be mixed, then their performances are liable to be called sloppy or lazy, rather than clean and precise. Thus, interpreters need to work to *develop distinct and accurate speech*. To refine and improve the way you form sounds and enunciate words, try the following exercise.

GETTING INVOLVED
Sound Combinations

As you read the following poem, pay careful attention to the sound combinations in it.

In his book *Through the Looking Glass*, Lewis Carroll provides this delightful poem of nonsense words. How can you use your voice to give meaning to it?

■ JABBERWOCKY ■
LEWIS CARROLL

'Twas brillig, and the slithy toves
   Did gyre and gimble in the wabe;
All mimsy were the borogoves,
   And the mome raths outgrabe.

"Beware the Jabberwock, my son!
   The jaws that bite, the claws that catch!
Beware the Jubjub bird, and shun
   The frumious Bandersnatch!"

He took his vorpal sword in hand;
   Long time the manxome foe he sought—
So rested he by the Tumtum tree,
   And stood awhile in thought.

And, as in uffish thought he stood,
   The Jabberwock, with eyes of flame,
Came whiffling through the tulgey wood,
   And burbled as it came!

One, two! One, two! And through and through
    The vorpal blade went snicker-snack!
He left it dead, and with its head
    He went galumphing back.

''And hast thou slain the Jabberwock?
    Come to my arms, my beamish boy!
O frabjous day! Callooh, Callay!''
    He chortled in his joy.

'Twas brillig, and the slithy toves
    Did gyre and gimble in the wabe;
All mimsy were the borogoves,
    And the mome raths outgrabe.

Reflections

1. How do the sounds within it affect the sense of the poem?

2. How did your vocal reading add definition to the nonsense words?

Besides transferring the sounds of their selections accurately, interpreters should also add clarity to a work by varying the way they play the sounds within it. In doing so, interpreters share the hidden meanings of a piece of literature. Thus, you can use each of the vocal attributes we will examine to help you reveal to your audience the thoughts and feelings contained in your selection.

Time

We all have a **habitual rate** of speaking, and this rate helps characterize each of us as individuals. Yet, though your normal speaking rate may be comfortable for you, as a performer you need to recognize that your usual speaking tempo may not match or be in accord with the speaking tempo called for by the literature. In other words, you should *be certain that your reading rate fits the sense of your selection.* You need to be aware of another fact, as well: Your reading rate should vary as the mood or the created atmosphere of your material varies. Consequently, when approaching a literary selection, your first task is to *analyze that selection's emotional and intellectual* content, and then to find a rate of speaking appropriate to it.

GETTING INVOLVED
The Beat Goes On

A. Tap out a beat suggested by the following poem. The beat should fall on each syllable of the piece. Use a pencil for tapping.

Richard Armour shows us that even light, humorous verse can share a meaning with which we can all identify.

■ MONEY ■
RICHARD ARMOUR

Workers earn it,
Spendthrifts burn it,
Bankers lend it,
Women spend it,
Forgers fake it,
Taxes take it,
Dying leave it,
Heirs receive it,
Thrifty save it,
Misers crave it,
Robbers seize it,
Rich increase it,
Gamblers lose it . . .
I could use it.

Reflections

1. At what rate did you tap your pencil?

2. How did your reading of the literature control that rate?
   B. Now speed up the tap. Try reading the poem at double or triple time. What happened?
   C. Now slow down the tap to half the rate of the original reading. How did this distort the meaning?

Let's move ahead to some more complex pieces of literature so you can develop your skills further.

GETTING INVOLVED

Tempo Tips

Read the following selections. What is the dominant tempo of each selection? That is, does it seem to be rapid or slow, a saunter or a jog? Where in each selection is it appropriate for you to vary your reading rate? Why?

In this selection, a poet offers descriptions of four different creatures. Use your voice and body to reflect each of the distinct images so that your audience can complete the pictures you present.

■ IMAGES ■

JOSÉ JUAN TABLADA

Although he never stirs from home
the tortoise, like a load of furniture,
jolts down the path.

The tiny monkey looks at me . . .
He would like to tell me something
that escapes his mind!

Lumps of mud, the toads
along the shady path
hop . . .

The dragonfly strives patiently
to fasten its transparent cross
to the bare and trembling bough.

—translated by Samuel Beckett

A child's vision of old age matures during this poem. Let your speaking
tempo slow when the mood changes.

■ CHILDHOOD ■

FRANCES CORNFORD

I used to think that grown-up people chose
To have stiff backs and wrinkles round their nose,
And veins like small fat snakes on either hand,
On purpose to be grand.
Till through the banisters I watched one day
My great-aunt Etty's friend who was going away,
And how her onyx beads had come unstrung.
I saw her grope to find them as they rolled;
And then I knew that she was helplessly old,
As I was helplessly young.

As the speaker in this cutting from Poe's famous tale lies strapped down, he observes a razor sharp pendulum descending slowly. Using tempo, indicate your lack of concern in the first paragraph, your anger at the rats in the second paragraph, and then allow your tempo to increase further as you realize what is about to happen.

■ THE PIT AND THE PENDULUM ■
EDGAR ALLAN POE

Looking upward, I surveyed the ceiling of my prison. It was some thirty or forty feet overhead, and constructed much as the side walls. In one of its panels a very singular figure riveted my whole attention. It was the painted figure of Time as he is commonly represented, save that, in lieu of a scythe, he held what, at a casual glance, I supposed to be the pictured image of a huge pendulum such as we see on antique clocks. There was something in the appearance of this machine which caused me to regard it more attentively. While I gazed directly upward at it (for its position was immediately over my own) I fancied that I saw it in motion. In an instant afterward the fancy was confirmed. Its sweep was brief, and of course slow. I watched it for some minutes, somewhat in fear, but more in wonder. Wearied at length with observing its dull movement, I turned my eyes upon the other objects in the cell.

A slight noise attracted my notice, and, looking to the floor, I saw several enormous rats traversing it. They had issued from the well, which lay just within view to my right. Even then, while I gazed, they came up in troops, hurriedly, with ravenous eyes, allured by the scent of the meat. From this it required much effort and attention to scare them away.

It might have been half an hour, perhaps even an hour (for I could take but imperfect note of time) before I again cast my eyes upward. What I saw confounded and amazed me. The sweep of the pendulum had increased in extent by nearly a yard. As a natural consequence, its velocity was also much greater. But what mainly disturbed me was the idea that it had perceptibly *descended*. I now observed—with what horror it is needless to say—that its nether extremity was formed of a crescent of glittering steel, about a foot in length from horn to horn; the horns upward, and the under edge evidently as keen as that of a razor. Like a razor also, it seemed massy and heavy, tapering from the edge into a solid and broad structure above. It was appended to a weighty rod of brass, and the whole *hissed* as it swung through the air.

I could no longer doubt the doom prepared for me. . . .

Words and Tempo

Usually, the heavier the content, the slower the interpreter's tempo; the "lighter" the content, the quicker the interpreter's pace. However, this is not a hard-set rule. For example, a rapid or a slow tempo may be used to create an atmosphere of suspense; a rapid or a slow tempo may be used to create a sense of fear. Practiced performers of literature use occasional changes in speaking rates to enhance the moods they are working to create. Often, interpreters find that a selection is characterized by a poetic beat, but they also discover that within that established "beat" there are fluctuations. You need to be sensitive to such fluctuations, matching your tempo to the ebb and flow of the beat of the literature. In addition, keep in mind that just as you can stretch or compress the tempo of a selection to enhance its meaning, so you can also stretch or compress a selection's key words to enhance their meaning.

GETTING INVOLVED
Word Work

Read the following poem. Let the tempo of your voice reflect the various images that the poet includes in his work.

■ SILVER ■
WALTER DE LA MARE

Slowly, silently, now the moon
Walks the night in her silver shoon;
This way, and that, she peers, and sees
Silver fruit upon silver trees;
One by one the casements catch
Her beams beneath the silvery thatch;
Couched in his kennel, like a log,
With paws of silver sleeps the dog;
From their shadowy cote the white breasts peep
Of doves in a silver-feathered sleep;
A harvest mouse goes scampering by,
With silver claws, and silver eye;
And moveless fish in the water gleam,
By silver reeds in a silver stream.

Reflections

1. Which words in the passage do you believe reinforce or add to the emotional impact of the selection?

2. How can you use your vocal rate to communicate this? For example, at what rate would you read words such as ''Slowly, silently''? Would your reading rate change for ''a harvest mouse goes scampering by''?

Have you ever considered that key words in a literary selection can have *flavor* values? As you read, should you savor this word, or only taste it? Should you prolong the vowels to slow tempo down, or should you only touch the consonants to increase speed? Never neglect to consider the flavor of a key word. Its flavor adds power to your interpretation. Words that help to create or sustain a mood are rarely, if ever, neutral in taste. Therefore, to emphasize this, you will want to vary the sound duration of certain words within your passage.

Pauses

Another useful instrument of time is the **pause**—an absence of sound that can emphasize or reinforce important ideas and feelings inherent in your selection. A pause gives you extra time to transmit a particular experience to your audience, and it gives your audience extra time to process and appreciate the experience. Pauses should not be randomly placed; rather, they should be carefully and thoughtfully planned. A **planned pause** is alive with meaning; it allows your audience to hear what is not actually said. A **random pause**, on the other hand, may detract from and destroy—rather than sustain—the emotional content of the work. Consequently, interpreters need to focus on varying the length of their pauses; they need to insure that the **silent seconds** of their performances are effectively placed and in accord with the meaning of their selection.

GETTING INVOLVED

To Pause or Not . . .

A. In this passage from Shakespeare's *King Lear*, Lear rages against the elements he feels are conspiring against him. As you read the passage, pause only at the end of lines.

■ KING LEAR ■

WILLIAM SHAKESPEARE

Blow, winds, and crack your cheeks! Rage! Blow!
You cataracts and hurricanoes, spout
Till you have drenched our steeples, drowned the cocks!
You sulphurous and thought-executing fires,
Vaunt-couriers to oak cleaving thunderbolts,
Singe my white head! And thou, all-shaking thunder,
Smite flat the thick rotundity o' the world!

B. Now read the passage again, pausing this time for meaning.

Reflections

1. How did the meaning of the selection change during your second reading of it?

2. How did pausing help to clarify the content?

GETTING INVOLVED

Place the Pause

Most of the written punctuation in the following selection has been removed for the purpose of this exercise. It is your task to determine where to place the pauses in the passage. Remember, a pause is one very specific type of oral punctuation. Mark a single slash line / in your passage to indicate a short silence and a double slash line // to indicate silence of a somewhat longer duration.

In the following poem, Whitman describes the coffin of Abraham Lincoln as it is taken to its burial place.

■ WHEN LILACS LAST IN ■
THE DOORYARD BLOOM'D

WALT WHITMAN

Coffin that passes through lanes and streets
Through day and night with the great cloud darkening
    the land
With the pomp of the inloop'd flags with the cities
    draped in black
With the show of the States themselves as crape-veiled
    women standing
With processions long and winding and the flambeaus
    of the night
With the countless torches lit with the silent sea
    of faces and the unbared heads
With the waiting depot the arriving coffin and the
    somber faces
With dirges through the night with the thousand
    voices rising strong and solemn
With all the mournful voices of the dirges pour'd
    around the coffin
The dim-lit churches and the shuddering organs—where
    amid these you journey
With the tolling bells' perpetual clang
Here coffin that slowly passes
I give you my sprig of lilac.

Reflections

1. What aspects of your material helped you to determine your pauses?

2. How did pausing help your audience understand?

3. How does the meaning of the selection change as the placement of pauses changes?

Thus, in reading aloud you can emphasize the important ideas or feeling of a selection by pausing either before or after, or both before and after, a key word or group of words. In this way the interpreter can more efficiently create for an audience a mood of suspense or surprise, a mood of fear or exhilaration.

Volume and Force

Volume refers to an interpreter's degree of loudness as he or she reads the words of a selection; **force** refers to the emphasis or weight that he or she gives the words of the selection. Determining the appropriate degree of volume or the appropriate amount of force is not easy. In order to make the proper decisions, an interpreter must be able to *touch the words of the literature*. After a "literary touch experience," an interpreter will probably be in a better position to determine which words in the passage are *warm words*, calling for an outward and open expression style, and which words in the passage are *cool words*, requiring a gentle or restrained expression style.

GETTING INVOLVED
Touching Emotion

What degree of volume might you use to express each of the following feelings:

excitement	depression	anger
terror	joy	anxiety

Reflections

1. For each feeling, why did you choose that particular volume level?

2. Could you express the same emotion with a different sound level? When? Try it.

Interpreters want to be able to determine which words in their selections should be spotlighted and given emphasis and which words should be used to carry the sense, but remain subordinate in their impact. Test your own talent for this with the following exercise.

Touching Meaning

How do different vocal emphases influence the meaning given to the following message?

He's giving this package to Morris.

He's **giving** this package to Morris.

He's giving **this** package to Morris.

He's giving this **package** to Morris.

He's giving this package **to** Morris.

He's giving this package to **Morris**.

Clearly, your vocal emphasis serves to influence the way a sentence or phrase is perceived. As an interpreter, be certain that a change in either force or volume will work to complement your literature; be certain that your motivation for making such changes is inherent in the sense of your selection.

Touching Literature

Where in the following poem would you increase or decrease your volume as you read aloud? Why? On which words would your touch be heaviest? Which words would receive the lightest touch? Why?

■ KNOXVILLE, TENNESSEE ■

NIKKI GIOVANNI

I always like summer
best
you can eat fresh corn
from daddy's garden
and okra
and greens
and cabbage
and lots of
barbecue
and buttermilk
and homemade ice-cream
at the church picnic
and listen to
gospel music
outside
at the church
homecoming
and go to the mountains with
your grandmother
and go barefooted
and be warm
all the time
not only when you go to bed
and sleep

Pitch in Performance

Pitch refers to the *highness or lowness* of an individual's voice; that is, its place on the musical scale, or its frequency level. An effective voice has an extensive pitch range and is consequently capable of expressing a large variety of tones. The following exercises will allow you to explore the use of pitch in your performance of literature.

GETTING INVOLVED
Playing with Pitch

1. Read the following sentence aloud:
   "Now is the time for all good men to come to the aid of their country."

2. Now read it as if you had the voice of the following:
   a piccolo
   a huge oboe
   a bass drum
   a violin

Your first reading represents your *habitual pitch*—the pitch level you use most frequently when speaking. Previous readings should have helped demonstrate to you your *pitch range*—the pitch tones you are able to produce that lie either above or below your habitual pitch level. The pitch levels you employed in this exercise were imposed on you from without, and were used simply to illustrate that you can use your voice to produce varied degrees of high or low tones. In performance situations, however, your pitch will be controlled by the intellectual and emotional content of your selection. Focus on your variation in pitch as you try the following exercise.

GETTING INVOLVED
All That Jazz

As you read the following poem, use your voice to reflect the sounds of the various instruments.

Sandburg has given us a poem designed to reflect an improvised jazz concert. It is almost an early version of today's rap music. Experiment with a variety of pitches and work to find a beat that holds the poem together.

◼ JAZZ FANTASIA ◼

CARL SANDBURG

Drum on your drums, batter on your banjoes, sob on
    your long cool winding saxophones,
Go to it, O jazzmen!
Sling your knuckles on the bottoms of the happy tin pans;
Let your trombones ooze, and go hush-a-hush-a-hush
    on the slippery sand paper.
Moan like an autumn wind high in the lonesome tree-tops;
Cry like a racing car slipping away from a motorcycle cop!
Bang, bang, you jazzmen! Bang all together, drums,
    traps, banjoes, horns, tin-cans!
Make two people fight on the top of a stairway and scratch
    each other's eyes in a clinch tumbling down the stairs.
Can the rough stuff!
Now a Mississippi steamboat pushes up the night river,
    with a hoo-hoo-hoo,
And the green lanterns calling to the high soft stars;
A red moon rides on the humps of the low river hills;
Go to it, O jazzmen!

Reflections

1. Where did you employ a relatively low pitch? Why? Where did your pitch rise?

2. How did pitch variation enhance the meaning of the poem?

GETTING INVOLVED
Pitch Practice

Read the following brief passage aloud. Pay careful attention to the different ideas expressed in each verse; use pitch variations to put emphasis on these changes in thought and feeling. In this poem we see that age can alter a person's view of life.

■ YOUNG AND OLD ■
CHARLES KINGSLEY

When all the world is young, lad,
    And all the trees are green;
And every goose a swan, lad,
    And every lass a queen;
Then hey for boot and horse, lad,
    And round the world away;
Young blood must have its course, lad,
    And every dog his day.

When all the world is old, lad,
    And all the trees are brown;
And all the sport is stale, lad,
    And all the wheels run down;
Creep home, and take your place there,
    The spent and maimed among:
God grant you find one face there,
    You loved when all was young.

Reflections

1. What clues did you find in the literature that helped you insure that your pitch level was appropriate?

2. In what ways did you vary your pitch as you attempted to bring forth the meaning?

Vocal Quality

Just as different rates, different vocal tones, and different degrees of volume help an interpreter suggest certain attitudes or emotions to an audience, so do different vocal qualities. The following exercise will help you focus your attention on the quality of people's voices.

GETTING INVOLVED
Animal Talk

Read the sentence below aloud in your normal voice:

"My voice is a flexible instrument."

Now read it as if you were the following:

a small breathy sparrow

a squeaky mouse

a husky grizzly bear

a neighing horse

a kingly lion

Reflections

1. What did you notice happening to your voice as you attempted to project the vocal qualities of these different animals?

2. Do you have a better understanding of vocal quality now than you did before this experience?

Of course, people have different vocal qualities as well. In fact, many stars and media personalities have quite distinctive and recognizable qualities. Try this.

GETTING INVOLVED

Voice Typing

Recall the voices of some famous people. In fact, can't you almost hear them right now? Your instructor may decide to have you listen to tapes of some famous or familiar voices gathered at random. They may include some of the following entertainers:

Roseanne Arnold

Billy Crystal

Whoopi Goldberg

James Earl Jones

Joan Rivers

Paul Rodriguez

Try your hand at re-creating voices of these or other famous people. How successful are you at doing it? Compete for the "great impersonator" award for the class member who can most closely re-create the vocal quality of a celebrity or noted person.

Each of the celebrities you tried to impersonate has a distinctive vocal quality or **timbre.** Your own voice communicates different things about you, in fact. Vocal quality yields clues regarding a speaker's health, emotions, and sociocultural circumstances. In effect, the distinctive sound of an individual's voice varies according to his or her age, health, mood, and attitude.

Your role as an interpreter is like that of a radio announcer or an actor in that you can develop different vocal qualities to reflect a wide range of communicative purposes. The announcer calling a baseball game uses a voice different from the one a reporter might use at a presidential press conference. An actor playing the part of a mobster would use a different voice altogether to play a suave society person. Your voice, too, should be used to mirror to your audience the nature and contents of various scripts. Like performers, interpreters need to work at adopting vocal qualities to suit or enhance their selected materials. What vocal qualities can an interpreter choose to help him or her perform literature?

A breathy vocal quality can suggest anything from a confidential manner or a seductive demeanor to fear and horror. A hoarse or throaty timbre can suggest roughness, crudity, or brusqueness. A shrill or **hypernasal** vocal quality, often used to create a character who habitually whines or nags, has also been used to suggest stupidity or a lack of breeding. A hollow or *barrel-sounding voice* is characterized by its use of rich, round tones; interpreters may use it to suggest remoteness, dignity, power, or even morbidity. They may use a *tremulous voice*, shaking with uncertainty, pain, or old age. Certainly, the list of vocal qualities interpreters may use to help them share selections of literature with an audience is practically endless: A broad voice, a passionate voice, a falsetto voice—even a normal, conversational voice—can be useful.

Increase your understanding of vocal quality by considering the following exercise.

GETTING INVOLVED
Pick a Voice

Read the following selections. What type of vocal quality would you use when performing each of the passages? Why?

In this excerpt from a Poe story, the speaker is just completing the construction of a wall that will become the living tomb of Lord Fortunato.

■ THE CASK OF AMONTILLADO ■
EDGAR ALLAN POE

I had scarcely laid the first tier of masonry when I discovered that the intoxication of Fortunato had in a great measure worn off. The earliest indication I had of this was a low moaning cry from the depth of the recess. It was *not* the cry of a drunken man. There was then a long and obstinate silence. I laid the second tier, and the third, and the fourth; and then I heard the furious vibrations of the chain. The noise lasted for several minutes, during which, that I might hearken to it with the more satisfaction, I ceased my labours and sat down upon the bones. When at last the clanking subsided, I resumed the trowel, and finished without interruption the fifth, the sixth, and the seventh tier. The wall was now nearly upon a level with my breast. I again paused, and holding the flambeaux over the masonwork, threw a few feeble rays upon the figure within.

A succession of loud and shrill screams, bursting suddenly from the throat of the chained form, seemed to thrust me violently back. For a brief moment I hesitated. . . . I reapproached the wall; I replied to the yells of him who clamored. I reechoed, I aided, I surpassed them in volume and in strength. I did this, and the clamorer grew still.

It was now midnight, and my task was drawing to a close. I had completed the eighth, the ninth, and the tenth tier. I had finished a portion of the last and the eleventh; there remained but a single stone to be fitted and plastered in. I struggled with its weight; I placed it partially in its destined position. But now there came from out the niche a low laugh that erected the hairs upon my head. It was succeeded by a sad voice, which I had difficulty in recognizing as that of the noble Fortunato. The voice said—

"Ha! ha! ha!—he! he! he!—a very good joke indeed—an excellent jest. We will have many a rich laugh about it at the palazzo—he! he! he!—over our wine—he! he! he!"

"The Amontillado!" I said.

"He! he! he!—he! he! he!—yes, the Amontillado. But is it not getting late? Will not they be awaiting us at the palazzo, the Lady Fortunato and the rest? Let us be gone."

"Yes," I said, "let us be gone."

"For the love of God, Montresor!"

"Yes," I said, "for the love of God!"

Explore ways to create the voices of three witches in this opening scene from Shakespeare's play *Macbeth*. You may want to experiment with the entire class chanting the "Double, double toil and trouble . . ." refrain.

■ MACBETH ■

WILLIAM SHAKESPEARE

FIRST WITCH. Round about the caldron go.
    In the poisoned entrails throw.
    Toad, that under cold stone
    Days and nights has thirty-one
    Sweltered venom sleeping got,
    Boil thou first i' the charmèd pot.
ALL. Double, double toil and trouble,
    Fire burn and caldron bubble.

SECOND WITCH. Fillet of a fenny snake,
    In the caldron boil and bake.
    Eye of newt and toe of frog,
    Wool of bat and tongue of dog,
    Adder's fork and blindworm's sting,
    Lizard's leg and howlet's wing,
    For a charm of powerful trouble,
    Like a Hell broth boil and bubble.
ALL. Double, double toil and trouble,
    Fire burn and caldron bubble.
THIRD WITCH. Scale of dragon, tooth of wolf,
    Witches' mummy, maw and gulf
    Of the ravined salt-sea shark,
    Root of hemlock digged i' the dark,
    Liver of blaspheming Jew,
    Gall of goat and slips of yew
    Slivered in the moon's eclipse,
    Nose of Turk and Tartar's lips,
    Finger of birth-strangled babe
    Ditch-delivered by a drab,
    Make the gruel thick and slab.
    Add thereto a tiger's chaudron,
    For the ingredients of our caldron.
ALL. Double, double toil and trouble,
    Fire burn and caldron bubble.

Did you ever walk along the sandy shore and collect shells? This cutting from a story by a Japanese writer reflects the simple charm and beauty of the inside of a highly polished shell.

■ ABALONE, ABALONE, ABALONE ■
TOSHIO MORI

Before Mr. Abe went away I used to see him quite often at his nursery. He was a carnation grower just as I am one today. At noontime I used to go to his front porch and look at his collection of abalone shells.

They were lined up side by side against the side of his house on the front porch. I was curious as to why he bothered to collect them. It was a lot of bother polishing them. I had often seen him sit for hours on Sundays and noon hours polishing each one of the shells with the greatest of care. Of course I knew these abalone shells were pretty. When the sun strikes the insides of these shells it is something beautiful to behold. But I could not understand why he continued collecting them when the front porch was practically full.

He used to watch for me every noon hour. When I appeared he would look out of his room and bellow, "Hello, young man!"

"Hello, Abe-*san*," I said. "I came to see the abalone shells."

Then he came out of the house and we sat on the front porch. But he did not tell me why he collected these shells. I think I have asked him dozens of times but each time he closed his mouth and refused to answer.

"Are you going to pass this collection of abalone shells on to your children?" I said.

"No," he said. "I want my children to collect for themselves. I wouldn't give it to them."

"Why?" I said. "When you die?"

Mr. Abe shook his head. "No. Not even when I die," he said. "I couldn't give the children what I see in these shells. The children must go out for themselves and find their own shells."

"Why, I thought this collecting hobby of abalone shells was a simple affair," I said.

"It is simple. Very simple," he said. But he would not tell me further.

For several years I went steadily to his front porch and looked at the beautiful shells. His collection was getting larger and larger. Mr. Abe sat and talked to me and on each occasion his hands were busy polishing shells.

"So you are still curious?" he said.

"Yes," I said.

One day while I was hauling the old soil from the benches and replacing it with new soil I found an abalone shell half buried in the dust between the benches. So I stopped working. I dropped my wheelbarrow and went to the faucet and washed the abalone shell with soap and water. I had a hard time taking the grime off the surface.

After forty minutes of cleaning and polishing the old shell it became interesting. I began polishing both the outside and the inside of the shell. I found after many minutes of polishing I could not do very much with the exterior side. It had scabs of the sea which would not come off by scrubbing and the surface itself was rough and hard. And in the crevices the grime stuck so that even with a needle it did not become clean.

But on the other side, the inside of the shell, the more I polished the more lustre I found. It had me going. There were colors which I had not seen in the abalone shells before or anywhere else. The different hues, running berserk in all directions, coming together in harmony. I guess I could say they were not unlike a rainbow which men once symbolized. As soon as I thought of this I thought of Mr. Abe.

I remember running to his place, looking for him. "Abe-*san!*" I said when I found him. "I know why you are collecting the abalone shells!"

He was watering the carnation plants in the greenhouse. He stopped watering and came over to where I stood. He looked me over closely for awhile and then his face beamed.

"All right," he said. "Do not say anything. Nothing, mind you. When you have found the reason why you must collect and preserve them, you do not have to say anything more."

"I want you to see it, Abe-*san*," I said.

"All right. Tonight," he said. "Where did you find it?"

"In my old greenhouse, half buried in the dust," I said.

He chuckled. "That is pretty far from the ocean," he said, "but pretty close to you."

At each noon hour I carried my abalone shell and went over to Mr. Abe's front porch. While I waited for his appearance I kept myself busy polishing the inside of the shell with a rag.

One day I said, "Abe-*san*, now I have three shells."

"Good!" he said. "Keep it up!"

"I have to keep them all," I said. "They are very much alike and very much different."

"Well! Well!" he said and smiled.

That was the last I saw of Abe-*san*. Before the month was over he sold his nursery and went back to Japan. He brought his collection along and thereafter I had no one to talk to at the noon hour. This was before I discovered the fourth abalone shell, and I should like to see Abe-*san* someday and watch his eyes roll as he studies me whose face is now akin to the collectors of shells or otherwise.

Be cautious in your creation of voices, however. Never impose a specific vocal quality on a selection; rather, explore the selection in order to discover the vocal quality appropriate to it—one that works to enhance its intellectual and emotional meaning. Now try to put together what you have learned about a performer's voice by working on the following materials.

GETTING INVOLVED
The John and Mary Show

Your instructor will divide you into pairs. The male member of that pair may use only the word "Mary" to communicate with his partner. The female member may use only "John." Conduct a conversation using only vocal qualities to create and communicate meaning, such as an emotion.

Performer's Journal
Voice Vigorizers

Read the following selections. For each, note in your journal how using the paralingual or vocal qualities presented in this chapter can help you to share meaning with an audience.

James Seilsopour, a student of Iranian heritage, was a California high school student when the Iranian Hostage Crisis erupted in 1979. In this selection from an essay, he describes his experiences.

■ I FORGOT THE WORDS TO THE ■
NATIONAL ANTHEM
JAMES SEILSOPOUR

To me, a fourteen-year-old living in Teheran, the Iranian revolution was nothing more than an inconvenience. Although the riots were just around the corner, although the tanks lined the streets, although a stray bullet went through my sister's bedroom window, I was upset because I could not ride at the Royal Stable as often as I used to. In the summer of 1979 my family—father, mother, brothers, sister, aunt, and two cousins—were forced into exile. We came to Norco, California.

In Iran, I was an American citizen and considered myself an American, even though my father was Iranian. I loved baseball and apple pie and knew the words to the "Star-Spangled Banner." That summer before high school, I was like any other kid my age; I listened to rock 'n' roll, liked fast cars, and thought Farrah Fawcett was a fox. Excited about going to high school, I was looking forward to football games and school dances. But I learned that it was not meant to be. I was not like other kids, and it was a long, painful road I traveled as I found this out.

The American embassy in Iran was seized the fall I started high school. I did not realize my life would be affected until I read that bumper sticker in the high school parking lot which read, "Piss on Iran." At that moment I knew there would be no football games or school dances. For me, Norco High consisted of the goat ropers, the dopers, the jocks, the brains, and one quiet Iranian.

I was sitting in my photography class after the hostages were taken. The photography teacher was fond of showing travel films. On this particular day, he decided to show a film about Iran, knowing full well that my father was Iranian and that I grew up in Iran. During the movie, this teacher encouraged the students to make comments. Around the room, I could hear "Drop the bomb" and "Deport the mothers." Those words hurt. I felt dirty, guilty. However, I managed to laugh and assure the students I realized they were just joking. I went home that afternoon and cried. I have long since forgiven those students, but I have not and can never forgive that teacher. Paranoia set in. From then on, every whisper was about me: "You see that lousy son of a bitch? He's Iranian." When I was not looking, I could feel their pointing fingers in my back like arrows. Because I was absent one day, the next day I brought a note to the attendance office. The secretary read the note, then looked at me. "So you're Jim Seilsopour?" I couldn't answer. As I walked away, I thought I heard her whisper to her coworker, "You see that lousy son of a bitch? He's Iranian." I missed thirty-five days of school that year.

My problems were small compared to those of my parents. In Teheran, my mother had been a lady of society. We had a palatial house and a maid. Belonging to the women's club, she collected clothes for the poor and arranged Christmas parties for the young American kids. She and my father dined with high government officials. But back in the States, when my father could not find a job, she had to work at a fast-food restaurant. She was the proverbial pillar of strength. My mother worked seventy hours a week for two years. I never heard her complain. I could see the toll the entire situation was taking on her. One day my mother and I went grocery shopping at Stater Brothers Market. After an hour of carefully picking our food, we proceeded to the cashier. The cashier was friendly and began a conversation with my mother. They spoke briefly of the weather as my mother wrote the check. The cashier looked at the check and casually asked, ''What kind of name is that?'' My mother said, ''Italian.'' We exchanged glances for just a second. I could see the pain in her eyes. She offered no excuses; I asked for none.

Because of my father's birthplace, he was unable to obtain a job. A naturalized American citizen with a master's degree in aircraft maintenance engineering from the Northrop Institute of Technology, he had never been out of work in his life. My father had worked for Bell Helicopter International, Flying Tigers, and McDonnell Douglas. Suddenly, a man who literally was at the top of his field was unemployable. There is one incident that haunts me even today. My mother had gone to work, and all the kids had gone to school except me. I was in the bathroom washing my face. The door was open, and I could see my father's reflection in the mirror. For no particular reason I watched him. He was glancing at a newspaper. He carefully folded the paper and set it aside. For several long moments he stared blankly into space. With a resigned sigh, he got up, went into the kitchen, and began doing the dishes. On that day, I know I watched a part of my father die.

My father did get a job. However, he was forced to leave the country. He is a quality control inspector for Saudi Arabian Airlines in Jeddah, Saudi Arabia. My mother works only forty hours a week now. My family has survived, financially and emotionally. I am not bitter, but the memories are. I have not recovered totally; I can never do that.

And no, I have never been to a high school football game or dance. The strike really turned me off to baseball. I have been on a diet for the last year, so I don't eat apple pie much anymore. And I have forgotten the words to the national anthem.

In this selection, a poet shows us how a single word can alter our perceptions. Work to let your voice reflect this change.

■ INCIDENT ■

COUNTEE CULLEN

Once riding in old Baltimore,
　　Heart-filled, head-filled with glee,
I saw a Baltimorean
　　Keep looking straight at me.

Now I was eight and very small,
　　And he was no whit bigger,
And so I smiled, but he poked out
　　His tongue, and called me, ''Nigger.''

I saw the whole of Baltimore
　　From May until December;
Of all the things that happened there
　　That's all that I remember.

CHAPTER THREE

Training Your Sense Memory for Oral Interpretation

Sense memory. What is it? Consciousness? Alertness? Perceptiveness? Yes, yes, and yes. Your senses help you to understand life's mysteries and secrets; they let you know the very significant reason you were born a human being rather than a rocking chair, an ashtray, or a bread box. Your sensory awareness allows things to affect you and encourages you to respond to stimuli. Your sense memory enables you to feel.

In Chapter 3, as a performer of literature you will come to your senses! You will explore ways to enlarge and extend your sense memory antennae. You will be asked to process and draw on everything you discover in your store of sensory experience, which will continually serve you as a sense memory resource center. As an interpreter you will use it to help you experience the literature you hope to share with your audience; you will also use it to make the literature live for your audience.

Coming to Your Senses

Your senses operate much like the theatrical or movie spotlight that highlights various areas of a darkened stage or screen. The senses, like the spotlight, focus only on specific aspects of an event at any given moment. How well can you focus your senses? Try this.

GETTING INVOLVED
Spotlight!

Divide the class into small groups and let each group choose an event to observe for a five-minute period. For example, your group may decide to go to a McDonald's to watch one particular employee as he or she serves customers. Or, your group might choose instead to observe a school-crossing guard or a marching band member.

Each group member is to make detailed notes of his or her observations. Caution: Do not compare notes or discuss your observations with each other until you return to class and are questioned by your instructor. Bring your written description of the event to class with you, and be prepared to answer the following questions.

Reflections

1. What event did your group choose to observe?

2. How did each member of the group describe the event?

3. How were each group member's observations similar?

4. How did they differ?

5. What "new" aspects of the event are you aware of now?

6. What does this exercise tell you about your sensory capabilities?

7. How do you believe this exercise relates to your task as a performer of literature?

An interpreter must be certain that his or her perceptual spotlight is "clean"—not soiled or colored by preconceptions. The spotlight must also be sufficiently wide in scope, rather than local or narrow. In other words, you must be open to the wide variety of stimuli an author provides.

Eventually, your concentration as an interpreter will be focused on the imaginary worlds and the imaginary people in literature. To respond effectively to literature, you must be able to respond sensitively to life, having developed your own sensory apparatus and sense memory. You have to be able to bring sights, sounds, tastes, smells, feelings, movements, and other sensations present in literature to your audience through your interpretation. If you are to develop the power to elicit imagined sensory perceptions in your audience, you need first to evoke sensory perceptions in yourself.

How can you refine your senses and sense memory to better respond to and perform literature? Try the following "Getting Involved" activities that will help you focus on cultivating each of your senses for controlled use in the performance of literature. The different senses to be explored are grouped into "departments": visual, olfactory (smell), gustatory (taste), touch, and kinesthetic (movement).

GETTING INVOLVED
Auditory Acres: Listen to the World

A. Listen to the world around you for one minute as you become aware of all the different sounds that "live" and "die" in your immediate world.

Compare the sounds you focused on with the sounds that were noticed by your fellow students. How were the sounds similar? How were they different?

B. Listen again, choosing one specific sound on which to focus. Close your eyes and immerse yourself in the private world of this particular sound. Then turn to a partner and take turns telling each other a story involving your specific sound. For example, if you had listened to rain falling, you might create an imaginary tale involving puddle jumping.

C. You are stretched out on a sandy beach, sending a Frisbee sailing at the park, or lazing by a smoky camp fire. Work with your group to create a *sound collage*, representative of all the auditory stimuli you might hear at your specific summer site. Be imaginative—lapping or splashing water is not the only sound you will hear. What other sounds are typical of your summer place? Weave them into your group's sound collage.

D. Working with your group, perform your created sound collage for the other groups. Let them attempt to identify your summer site and the specific sounds associated with it.

Reflections

1. What sounds were clearly identifiable? Why was this so?

2. What sound required the most audience effort to identify?

3. How could your group have made its sound collage even more effective?

E. Using what you have discovered about the nature of sound and your reactions to it, prepare to effectively perform the following passages aloud.

In this cutting from a famous poem by Poe, let your senses create two types of bells—small silver bells and large iron bells. How are they similar and how are they different?

■ THE BELLS ■

EDGAR ALLAN POE

Hear the sledges with the bells—
    Silver Bells!
What a world of merriment their melody foretells!
How they tinkle, tinkle, tinkle,
    In the icy air of night!
While the stars that oversprinkle
All the heavens, seem to twinkle
    With a crystalline delight.

Hear the tolling of the bells—
    Iron Bells!
What a world of solemn thought their monody compels!
    In the silence of the night
    How we shiver with affright
At the melancholy menace of their tone!

Have you heard the deafening crack of a sonic boom as a military jet or the Concorde breaks the sound barrier? Use your senses to create the sound of a sonic boom and the effect it would probably have on someone who was relaxing comfortably in his or her living room.

■ SONIC BOOM ■

JOHN UPDIKE

I'm sitting in the living room,
When, up above, the Thump of Doom
Resounds. Relax. It's a sonic boom.

Reflections

1. How can you create the feeling of a sonic boom during your performance?

2. What words should an interpreter choose to emphasize in this poem? Why?

F. In what ways will your knowledge of sound affect your reading of the next poem? Try to imagine a world without sound as you re-create it.

In this selection James Wright describes a parent pondering over the problems that will beset an infant who was born deaf. Will the adult pity the child or find ways for the child to live life to the fullest, even with this disability?

■ MUTTERINGS OVER THE CRIB ■ OF A DEAF CHILD

JAMES WRIGHT

"How will he hear the bell at school
Arrange the broken afternoon,
And know to run across the cool
Grasses where the starlings cry,
Or understand the day is gone?"

Well, someone lifting cautious brows
Will take the measure of the clock.
And he will see the birchen boughs
Outside the sagging dark from the sky,
And the shade crawling upon the rock.

"And how will he know to rise at morning?
His mother has other sons to waken,
She has the stove she must build to burning
Before the coals of night-time die,
And he never stirs when he is shaken."

I take it the air affects the skin,
And you remember when you were young,
Sometimes you could feel the dawn begin
And the fire would call you, by and by,
Out of the bed and bring you along.

''Well, good enough. To serve his needs
All kinds of arrangements can be made.
But what will you do if his finger bleeds?
Or a bobwhite whistles invisibly
And flutes like an angle off in the shade?''

He will learn pain. And, as for the bird,
It is always darkening when that comes out.
I will putter as though I had not heard,
And lift him into my arms and sing
Whether he hears my song or not.

Reflections

1. How does this poem help demonstrate that we all need to hear with more than our ears?

2. What sounds did you attempt to re-create for your audience?

GETTING INVOLVED

Visual Vibes

A. Bring to class an object from nature, such as a rock or a flower, place it on your desk, and observe it carefully. Examine it from different angles; note its numerous characteristics and qualities. List them. After fifteen minutes, trade objects with a classmate nearby and repeat the above process. Compare your lists.

Reflections

1. How were your observation lists similar?

2. In what ways did they differ?

B. Your instructor will divide the class into small groups. Each group will choose to visit an imagined environment such as a zoo or a toy shop. Members of each group should re-create or pantomime some of the sights that might be seen in the respective environments. Other groups will guess what those sights are. They may suggest additional sights that the group might re-create.

Reflections

1. What did you have to do in order to ''see'' the imagined environment?

2. What performances were most effective? Why?

C. Now, focusing on what you have internalized about sight, prepare to read the following poem aloud.

How does a cat move? Can you see fog moving in a similar fashion? Pretend you are the fog and move as the poem suggests as your partner reads it aloud.

■ Fog ■

CARL SANDBURG

The fog comes
on little cat feet.

It sits looking
over harbor and city
on silent haunches
and then moves on.

Reflections

1. Can you see the fog as it approaches the city?

2. What parts of the exercise were most effective for you?

3. What parts were difficult to perform? Why?

GETTING INVOLVED
Olfactory Oval: Nose-ings

A. Choose some members of your class to be blindfolded and seated before a table. Your instructor will present them with a series of objects such as food, perfumes, or flowers they will be asked to identify using only the sense of smell.

Reflections

1. Which items were easiest to identify?

2. Which items were most difficult to identify? Why?

3. What happened to an individual's face as he or she smelled a particular object?

B. Think of a place you have visited—a bakery, a musty attic, the circus—that had a specific aroma you can recall. Without naming the place, describe for the class the distinctive scents that might be found in this remembered environment. Give only one smell clue at a time, and let the class guess the place you are describing.

Reflections

1. What type of clue did you find worked most effectively?

2. What happened to each performer's body and facial expressions as he or she delivered the clues?

3. How did the audience members react to each of the clues?

C. How do these olfactory involvement exercises sharpen your appreciation of the following passage from *The Hills Beyond* by Thomas Wolfe?

A waft of air, warm, chocolate-laden, filled his nostrils. He tried to pass the white front of the little eight-foot shop; he paused, struggling with conscience; he could not go on. It was the little candy shop run by old Crocker and his wife. And Grover could not pass.

"Old stingy Crockers!" he thought scornfully. "I'll not go there any more. But—" as the maddening fragrance of rich cooking chocolate touched him once again—"I'll just look in the window and see what they've got." He paused a moment, looking with his dark and quiet eyes into the window of the little candy shop. The window, spotlessly clean, was filled with trays of fresh-made candy. His eyes rested on a tray of chocolate drops. Unconsciously he licked his lips. Put one of them upon your tongue and it just melted there, like honeydew. And then the trays full of rich homemade fudge. He gazed longingly at the deep body of the chocolate fudge, reflectively at maple walnut, more critically, yet with longing, at the mints, the nougatines, and all the other dainties.

GETTING INVOLVED
Gustatory Gems: Testing Taste

A. Members of your class will be divided into teams, seated before a table, and blindfolded. Your instructor will present each team with a series of foods they will be asked to sample and then identify. Each team's taste score will then be tallied.

B. Think of a food such as cotton candy, peanut butter, pizza, or even a lemon. Write the name of this food on a slip of paper and drop it on a food tray your instructor provides for this exercise. When your instructor calls on you, come to the front of the room, pick an entry from the tray, and pantomime eating this food for the rest of the class. The class will attempt to guess what you are eating.

Reflections

1. What does it feel like to eat _____?

2. What happens to the inside of your mouth as you eat this food?

3. What does it do to your eyes? your forehead? your neck? your fingers?

4. Did your sense of smell operate together with your sense of taste? How could you tell?

C. Now read and "taste" the following two poems. Which poem has a sweet taste? Which has a bitter taste? How can your readings reinforce these different flavors?

When was the last time you raided the refrigerator or the cookie jar? How much did you enjoy eating what you found? Let your audience know how very much the speaker in this poem enjoyed the plums he found in the ice box.

■ THIS IS JUST TO SAY ■
WILLIAM CARLOS WILLIAMS

I have eaten
the plums
that were in
the ice box

and which
you were probably
saving
for breakfast.

Forgive me
they were delicious
so sweet
and so cold.

Reflections

1. Can you taste the plums?

2. Show how the speaker might have looked when eating the plums.

What have you eaten lately that is really bitter? Can you recall that taste? Is it difficult to continue eating something bitter? Let your audience feel the surreal mood and taste bitterness as you read the following poem.

■ IN THE DESERT ■

STEPHEN CRANE

In the desert
I saw a creature, naked, bestial,
Who, squatting upon the ground,
Held his heart in his hands,
And ate of it.
I said, "Is it good, friend?"
"It is bitter—bitter," he answered,
"But I like it
Because it is bitter
And because it is my heart."

Reflections

1. How do you envision the creature sitting as he eats his heart?

2. How would you portray the creature?

3. What facial expressions can you imagine the creature making as he swallows a piece of his own heart? Show a classmate.

GETTING INVOLVED
Touch Town: A Thermal and Tactile Trip

A. Choose a partner for this exercise. The shorter member of each pair is blindfolded and led on a *silent* five-minute sensory journey by his or her partner. The goal of the journey is to allow the blindfolded member to touch various items in his or her immediate environment, such as the desk top, the wall, the windowpane, a pencil, fabric samples, cold water, and warm water. Remember, neither partner is to speak during the touch tour.

After five minutes, the leader and the blind partner are to trade roles. After five more minutes of a silent touch tour, remove your blindfold and travel the touch-sense trail alone. Try to re-examine carefully the items you just experienced.

Reflections

1. What did you learn from this exercise about your sense of touch?

2. When blindfolded, which items could you identify most easily?

3. Which items were difficult to name?

4. Which fabric did you find most pleasing to touch?

5. How did you react to the "cool" items? The "warm" ones?

B. Portray the following through pantomime, or through sound and movement:

frost	the fabric wool
the color red	the fabric silk
the color blue	the fabric velvet
the rising sun	

Reflections

1. What happened to your arms when you were _____?

2. How did _____ affect your face and neck?

3. Did you see _____ with your eyes? with your shoulders?

4. Which of your reactions worked against you becoming _____?

5. What emotions or feelings did you experience while portraying the various colors, objects, and fabrics?

Now read the following poem.

Were you ever in a particular mood that you could represent with a color? Your author Teri Gamble sums up a portion of her life which she represents with the color purple.

■ WHEN I WAS PURPLE ■
TERI GAMBLE

When I was purple—
Ice-cream wishes and
Milk-chocolate dreams
Always came true.

It was fun to play sunshine
And melt the sadness out of shadows
It was easy to be moonglow
And light the dark with laughter.

When I was purple—
Touching the morning
And coloring care
Always made me smile.

It was fun to play tipsy
And fill your heart with rainbows
It was easy to be sea-breeze
And blow the secrets from your eyes.

I won't forget having once been purple
It was one of the nicer things to be
Being purple was a lot of flowers
Being purple was a lot of love.

Reflections

1. What do you think it means to the author to be purple?

2. How can you reflect this feeling with your body and your voice?

GETTING INVOLVED

Kinesthetic Korners: Meeting Your Motor Sense

A. Listen to one member of your group squeak a piece of chalk or fingernails across the blackboard.

Reflections

1. What did you hear?

2. What did you feel?

3. What happened to your facial muscles as you experienced the sound? What happened to your shoulders? your stomach? your legs?

4. Did you hear the chalk or nails just with your ears?

5. What other parts of your body heard the squeak? How do you know?

B. Now imagine that, on a dark night, you are standing alone waiting for a bus. The street is absolutely deserted and is not well lit. Suddenly you hear a shrill scream behind you.

Reflections

1. Describe the scream as you just heard it in your mind's ear.

2. Describe how your body reacted to this imagined stimulus. Did you tense? Did you relax? What happened to your eyebrows? your mouth? your knees and fingers?

3. Is it possible that a piece of literature in performance might elicit similar responses from the interpreter or from the audience?

C. Your instructor may wish to use a drum to pace this section of the exercise. Imagine yourself taking a leisurely walk on a quiet night; now you increase your pace to a jog; suddenly, you discover you are being chased by a car. You dart back and forth across a narrow alley to avoid being hit. Suddenly you see a small gate at the end of the alley and you sprint for it. You are safe!

Reflections

Discuss how your body responded differently as the situation changed. Be specific in describing your actual body sensations. For example, what happened to your eyes? your lips? your knees? your rate of breathing? How did your sensory responses affect your overall muscle tone?

D. Read this passage from *Incidents in the Life of a Slave Girl*. In this part of her narrative, Harriet A. Jacobs tells of going into hiding to escape being abused by a master during the time of slavery in the United States.

A small shed had been added to my grandmother's house years ago. Some boards were laid across the joists at the top, and between these boards and the roof was a very small garret, never occupied by any thing but rats and mice. It was a pent roof, covered with nothing but shingles, according to the southern custom for such buildings. The garret was only nine feet long and seven wide. The highest part was three feet high, and sloped down abruptly to the loose board floor. There was no admission for either light or air. My uncle Phillip, who was a carpenter, had very skillfully made a concealed trap-door, which communicated with the storeroom. He had been doing this while I was waiting in the swamp. The storeroom opened upon a piazza. To this hole I was conveyed as soon as I entered the house. The air was stifling; the darkness total. A bed had been spread on the floor. I could sleep quite comfortably on one side; but the slope was so sudden that I could not turn on the other without hitting the roof. The rats and mice ran over my bed; but I was weary, and I slept such sleep as the wretched may, when a tempest has passed over them. Morning came. I knew it only by the noises I heard; for in my small den day and night were all the same. I suffered for air even more than for light. But I was not comfortless. I heard the voices of my children. There was joy and there was sadness in the sound. It made my tears flow. How I longed to speak to them! I was eager to look on their faces; but there was no hole, no crack, through which I could peep. This continued darkness was oppressive. It seemed horrible to sit or lie in a cramped position day after day, without one gleam of light. Yet I would have chosen this, rather than my lot as a slave, though white people considered it an easy one; and it was so compared with the fate of others. I was never cruelly overworked; I was never lacerated with the whip from head to foot; I was never so beaten and bruised that I could not turn from one side to the other; I never had my heel-strings cut to prevent my running away; I was never chained to a log and forced to drag it about, while I toiled in the fields from morning till night; I was never branded with hot iron, or torn by bloodhounds. On the contrary, I had always been kindly treated, and tenderly cared for, until I came into the hands of Dr. Flint. I had never wished for freedom till then. But though my life in slavery was comparatively devoid of hardships, God pity the woman who is compelled to lead such a life!

Reflections

1. How can your physical reactions help you to successfully perform this excerpt for an audience?

2. At what points in the passage will your muscle tone change?

3. At what point will your state of physical tension be greatest?

Feelings are universal—everyone has them. An interpretative performer uses methods to help audience members feel and understand literature in ways they could not simply by reading the piece themselves. An interpretative performer must be an expert on feelings and the descriptive words that convey them. The following exercise will help you to refine your descriptive talents.

GETTING INVOLVED
Descriptions

1. As a group, select one of the following images: clouds, fire, rain, a flower, a car, softball, football, hockey.

2. Working individually, visualize the chosen image. Write down as many descriptive words as you can think of to help paint a verbal picture.

3. Next, work with a team to devise a more extensive list of words to describe the chosen image. For example, if you had chosen "clouds," you might describe them as open, fluid, feathery, fleecy, threatening, light, magical, gloomy, ominous, rainbowlike, shadowy, and nebulous.

4. Now perform the description aloud. Each member of the team should select specific words to read. Working together, communicate the various meanings of your image through your performance.

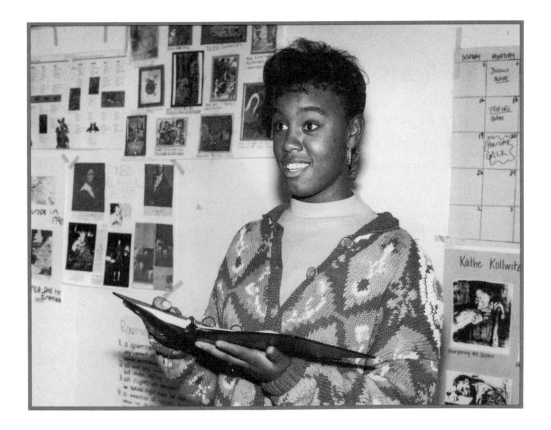

Reflections

1. How did the various images held by individuals in your group merge during the actual reading?

2. How did sense memory skills help you communicate your assigned descriptive words to your audience?

3. Given another opportunity, in what ways would you like to change your performance?

Performer's Journal

A Japanese American speaks of immigrating to America to join her husband. Analyze this poem, then answer the following questions before sharing your interpretation with your class.

■ MARRIAGE WAS A ■
FOREIGN COUNTRY
MITSUYE YAMADA

I come to be here
because
they say I must
follow my husband

so I come.

My grandmother cried:
you are not cripple
why
to America?

When we land the boat full
of new brides
lean over railing

with wrinkled glossy pictures
they hold inside hand
like this
so excited
down there a dock full of men
they do same thing
hold pictures
look up and down
like this
they find faces to
match pictures.

Your father I see him on the dock
he come to Japan to marry
and leave me
I was not a picture bride
I only was afraid.

1. What do the title of this poem and the term "picture bride" mean to you?

2. As you read the poem aloud, are you able to create the fear the speaker must have felt in coming to a strange place to meet her husband?

3. Do you let the grandmother's dislike for the idea come through in your reading?

In this excerpt from Alex Haley's Pulitzer Prize-winning novel, Kunta Kinte has been captured and placed on a slave ship bound from Africa for America. He and hundreds of other men are living in a stinking, filthy compartment of the ship.

■ Roots ■

ALEX HALEY

The stinging bites, then the itching of the body lice, steadily grew worse. In the filth, the lice as well as the fleas had multiplied by the thousands until they swarmed all over the hold. They were worst wherever the body crevices held any hair. Kunta's armpits, and around his foto, felt as if they were on fire, and his free hand scratched steadily wherever his shackled hand couldn't reach.

He kept having thoughts of springing up and running away; then, a moment later, his eyes would fill with tears of frustration, anger would rise in him, and he would fight it all back down until he felt again some kind of calm. The worst thing was that he couldn't *move* anywhere; he felt he wanted to *bite* through his chains. He decided that he must keep himself focused upon something, anything to occupy his mind or his hands, or else he would go mad—as some men in the hold seemed to have done already, judging from the things they cried out.

By lying very still and listening to the breathing sounds of the men on either side of him, Kunta had long since learned to tell when either of them was asleep or awake. He concentrated now upon hearing farther away from him. With more and more practice at listening intently to repeated sounds, he discovered that his ears after a while could discern their location almost exactly; it was a peculiar sensation, almost as if his ears were serving for eyes. Now and then, among the groans and curses that filled the darkness, he heard the thump of a man's head against the planks he lay on. And there was another odd and monotonous noise. It would stop at intervals, then resume after a while; it sounded as if two pieces of metal were being rubbed hard together, and after hearing more of it Kunta figured that someone was trying to wear the links of his chains apart. Kunta often heard, too, brief exclamations and janglings of chains as two men furiously fought, jerking their shackles against each other's ankles and wrists.

Kunta had lost track of time. The urine, vomit, and feces that reeked everywhere around him had spread into a slick paste covering the hard planking of the long shelves on which they lay. Just when he had begun to think he couldn't stand it any more, eight toubob came down the hatchway, cursing loudly. Instead of the routine food container, they carried what seemed to be some kind of long-handled hoes and four large tubs. And Kunta noticed with astonishment that they were not wearing any clothes at all.

Reflections

1. How can you demonstrate the feel and smell the stench of the ship in your interpretation?

2. In what ways can you convey to your audience the sense of being chained in one place for an extended period of time?

3. How ill is the speaker? Were you able to reflect his lack of physical stamina after days and weeks in the hold?

Your basic sense memory training is complete now. At this point you ought to be able to successfully work alone in each "department," with a new respect for the value of your sharpened senses. Use these exercises throughout the term to limber up your senses. Remember, like any performing artist, a performer of literature is constantly in training. Your senses are your avenues to appreciation; as an interpreter you will travel them continually.

PART TWO

Exploring Literary Worlds

- The Interpretation of Descriptive Prose

- The Interpretation of Narrative Prose

- The Interpretation of Drama

- The Interpretation of Poetry

CHAPTER FOUR

The Interpretation of Descriptive Prose

In Chapter 4 we will focus on descriptive prose—the type of prose that uses literary close-ups. Reflecting careful and deliberate thought, descriptive prose envelops and surrounds the action of a story.

Refreshing Your Senses

Before proceeding, read this passage. The excerpt from *Johnny Got His Gun* by Dalton Trumbo describes Joe, a human being whom war has turned into a living vegetable. Joe could be a soldier in any war we have waged—those a lifetime ago and those in our own lifetime.

■ JOHNNY GOT HIS GUN ■
DALTON TRUMBO

He began to resent the question itself and the way they asked it and the ignorance that lay behind it. Who did they think they were and what did they think he wanted that they could give him? Did they think he would ask for an ice-cream cone?

. . . Maybe they thought he would ask for a change of diet. The coffee you've been pouring into my tube lately needs a little more sugar; it tastes bitter to my intestines so add a half teaspoonful of sugar and stir it well please. . . .

They should know what he wanted . . . and they should know they couldn't give it to him. He wanted eyes to see with. Two eyes to see sunlight and moonlight and blue mountains and tall trees and little ants and houses that people live in and flowers opening in the morning and snow on the ground and streams running and trains coming and going and people walking and a puppy dog playing with an old shoe worrying it and growling at it and backing away from it and frowning and wiggling its bottom and taking the shoe very seriously. He wanted a nose so he could smell rain and burning wood and cooking food and the faint perfume that stays in the air after a girl has passed by. He wanted a mouth so he could eat and talk and laugh and taste and kiss. He wanted arms and legs so that he could work and walk and be like a man like a living thing.

Reflections

1. How do the ideas expressed in the above passage relate to you as a human being?

2. How do they relate to you as an interpreter?

3. Using what you've learned in Chapter 3, how can you relate to Joe's feelings?

   As an interpreter, you can use your senses as a kind of "open sesame" to literature. To review, your senses are the avenues you will travel in order to arrive at a satisfactory appreciation of the literature. In order to share a literary world with an audience, you must communicate the experience that resides within the literary selection, conveying its full meaning by embodying its emotional overtones. To accomplish this you will depend upon the inner resources of mind and body; they will help you to perceive the evocative elements a work contains. Only by using all your senses will you be able—first—to empathize with and—second—to re-create the fictional world an author has created with carefully selected words.

   An important part of an author's fictional world is presented through descriptive prose. Description introduces characters and setting; it creates suspense or sustains a mood; it gives a picture of something essential to a piece of literature. To understand its important role, let's examine how description works.

GETTING INVOLVED

Meeting Descriptive Prose

   Imagine having the same dream night after night. Pretend that in that dream you were to see your father, whom you had not seen in years, since he was imprisoned in a concentration camp. You are told one day that he is alive in a hospital—but that his mind has been destroyed. This is what faced Karen Clement, a character in *Exodus*, by Leon Uris. Read the following passage.

■ Exodus ■

LEON URIS

The doctor led them down a corridor and stopped before a door. A nurse unlocked it. He held the door open.

Karen walked into a cell-like room. The room held a chair, a stand and a bed. She looked around for a moment and then she stiffened. A man was sitting on the floor in a corner. He was barefooted and uncombed. He sat with his back against the wall and his arms around his knees and stared blankly at the opposite wall.

Karen took a step toward him. He was stubble-bearded and his face was scarred. Suddenly the pounding within Karen's heart eased. This is all a mistake, she thought . . . this man is a stranger . . . he is not my father . . . he cannot be. It is a mistake! A mistake! She was filled with the urge to turn around and scream out . . . *you see, you were wrong. He is not Johann Clement, he is not my father. My father is still alive somewhere and looking for me.* Karen stood before the man on the floor to assure herself. She stared into the crazed eyes. It had been so long . . . so very long, she could not remember. But the man she had dreamed about meeting again was not this man.

There was a fireplace and the smell of pipe tobacco. There was a big moppy dog. His name was Maximilian. A baby cried in the next room. "Miriam, see to Hans. I am reading a story for my girl and I cannot be disturbed."

Karen Hansen Clement slowly knelt before the hulk of mindless flesh.

Grandma's house in Bonn always smelled of newly baked cookies. She baked all week getting ready for the family on Sunday.

The insane man continued to stare at the opposite wall as though he were alone in the room.

Look how funny the monkeys are in the Cologne Zoo! Cologne has the most wonderful zoo. When will it be carnival time again?

She studied the man from his bare feet to his scarred forehead. Nothing . . . nothing she saw was like her father . . .

"Jew! Jew! Jew!" the crowd screamed as she ran into her house with the blood pouring down her face. "There, there, Karen don't you cry. Daddy won't let them hurt you."

Karen reached out and touched the man's cheek. "Daddy?" she said. The man did not move or react.

There was a train and lots of children around and they were talking of going to Denmark but she was tired. "Goodby, Daddy," Karen had said. "Here, you take my dolly. He will watch after you." She stood on the platform of the train and watched her Daddy on the platform as he grew smaller and smaller.

"Daddy! Daddy!" Karen cried. "It's Karen, Daddy! I'm your girl. I'm all grown up now, Daddy. Don't you remember me?"

The doctor held Kitty in the doorway as she shook from head to foot. "Let me help her, please," Kitty cried.

"Let it be done," he said.

And Karen was filled with remembering—"Yes! Yes! He is my father! He is my father!"

"Daddy!" she screamed and threw her arms around him. "Please talk to me. Please say something to me. I beg you . . . beg you!"

The man who was once the living human person of Johann Clement blinked his eyes. A sudden expression of curiosity came over his face as he became aware of a person clutching at him. He held the expression for a tense moment as though he were trying, in his own way, to allow something to penetrate the blackness—and then, his look lapsed back into lifelessness.

"Daddy!" she screamed. "Daddy! Daddy!"

And her voice echoed in the empty room and down the long corridor—"Daddy!"

The strong arms of the doctor pried her loose, and she was gently dragged from the room. The door was closed and locked and Johann Clement was gone from her—forever. The girl sobbed in anguish and crumpled into Kitty's arms. "He didn't even know me! Oh, my God . . . God . . . why doesn't he know me? Tell me, God . . . tell me!"

Reflections

1. What types of feelings did the preceding passage evoke in you?

2. Can you point to specific phrases in the passage that you find particularly effective?

3. Why do you believe these phrases affect you as they do?

As your answers and comments probably reveal, the word-pictures that the author created touched you; the images he evoked moved you.

One of the chief characteristics of descriptive prose is its reliance on imagery. An **image** is simply *a group of words that affects your senses so as to elicit an internal and external response* from you. As an interpreter, you ought to realize that the effectiveness of imagery and, consequently, the effectiveness of description, depend upon four things: the writer's ability to describe a sensory experience; the reader's ability to process the sensory experience by making associations from his or her own experience; the interpreter's ability to embody the sensory experience described in the literature; and, finally, the performer's ability to share the literature in a way that enlivens and communicates the emotional experience to the audience.

Thus, descriptive cues or images help you enter the literature; they sharpen your perception of the created world and the created characters of the literature. Description transforms the skeleton or plot of a tale into something that seems to live and breathe. As an interpreter, you can use the enrichment that description brings to literature to enhance your performance of it.

The following exercises will illustrate how authors use description to establish who the characters are and what they are like, as well as to establish the environment or setting of the selection.

GETTING INVOLVED
Character Descriptions

What do the following descriptions tell you about each of the characters in them?

In the first passage, the writer focuses on the face of a man in order to establish his personality traits for the reader.

■ ALL GOLD CANYON ■
JACK LONDON

He was a sandy-complexioned man in whose face geniality and humor seemed the salient characteristics. It was a mobile face, quick-changing to inward mood and thought. Thinking was in him a visible process. Ideas chased across his face like wind flows across the surface of a lake. His hair, sparse and unkempt of growth, was as indeterminate and colorless as his complexion. It would seem that all the color of his frame had gone into his eyes, for they were startlingly blue. Also, they were laughing and merry eyes, within them much of the naivete and wonder of the child; and yet in an unassertive way, they contained much of calm self-reliance and strength of purpose founded upon self-experience and experience of the world.

Dickens gives us a description of his character Scrooge in this excerpt from his famous tale.

■ A CHRISTMAS CAROL ■
CHARLES DICKENS

Oh! but he was a tight-fisted hand at the grindstone. Scrooge! a squeezing, wrenching, grasping, scraping, clutching, covetous, old sinner! Hard and sharp as flint, from which no steel had ever struck out generous fire; secret, and self-contained, and solitary as an oyster. The cold within him froze his old features, nipped his pointed nose, shrivelled his cheek, stiffened his gait; made his eyes red, his thin lips blue; and spoke out shrewdly in his grating voice. A frosty rime was on his head, and on his eyebrows, and his wiry chin. He carried his dog-days, and didn't thaw it one degree at Christmas.

External heat and cold had little influence on Scrooge. No warmth could warm, no wintry weather chill him. No wind that blew was bitterer than he, no falling snow was more intent upon its purpose, no pelting rain less open to entreaty. Foul weather didn't know where to have him. The heaviest rain, and snow, and hail, and sleet, could boast of the advantage over him in only one respect. They often ''came down'' handsomely, and Scrooge never did.

Nobody ever stopped him in the street to say, with gladsome looks, ''My dear Scrooge, how are you? When will you come to see me?'' No beggars implored him to bestow a trifle, no children asked him what it was o'clock, no man or woman ever once in all his life inquired the way to such and such a place, of Scrooge. Even the blind men's dogs appeared to know him; and when they saw him coming on, would tug their owners into doorways and up courts; and then would wag their tails as though they said, ''No eye at all is better than an evil eye, dark master!''

Reflections

1. How do the physical appearances and personalities of the characters in each cutting differ from each other?

2. What type of physical stance would you, as interpreter, assume when portraying these characters?

3. What mood-tones would you work to reinforce?

The descriptions of a character's physique or body shape, clothes or general style of dress, and attitude or general affective mood are written to influence and to determine response. As Sherlock Holmes said: "By a man's fingernails, by his coat sleeve, by his boots, by his trouser-knees, by the callosities of his forefinger and thumb, by his expression, by his shirtcuffs—by each of these things a man's calling is plainly revealed. That all united should fail to enlighten the competent inquirer in any case is almost inconceivable." Above all an interpreter must be a "competent inquirer."

An author uses descriptions of setting or environment in much the same way. Just as the details of character assist a reader in arriving at an effective interpretation, so the description of a city, a town, a home, a room, or an object may also be used to further refine a reader's perception. After all, the environments in which people find themselves compelled to communicate frequently contribute directly to the outcomes of their encounters. In other words, an author may use the location of a character and the objects that surround him or her to influence, either subtly or overtly, the character's attitudes and communicative behavior.

GETTING INVOLVED
Environmental Descriptions

Analyze the way environment is used in each of the following passages.

■ Fox and Swan ■
JOHN L'HEUREUX

It seemed the cold would never let up. For over a week the temperature had been below freezing and for most of that time it had hovered around zero. Francis hated cold weather, his long stringy body responding to it with unmanly shivers. Nor could he afford the winter coat he needed.

Christ, will it never end, he asked himself, and he pulled his scarf tighter. It was a long striped scarf worn like a college student's—outside the jacket, hanging down in front and in back—even though he knew he was too old for that sort of thing.

■ Sorrow-Acre ■

ISAK DINESEN (KAREN BLIXEN)

The low, undulating Danish landscape was silent and serene, mysteriously wide-awake in the hour before sunrise. There was not a cloud in the pale sky, not a shadow along the dim, pearly fields, hills and woods. The mist was lifting from the valleys and hollows, the air was cool, the grass and the foliage dripping wet with morning-dew. Unwatched by the eyes of man, and undisturbed by his activity, the country breathed a timeless life, to which language was inadequate.

All the same, a human race had lived on this land for a thousand years, had been formed by its soil and weather, and had marked it with its thoughts, so that now no one could tell where the existence of the one ceased and the other began. The thin grey line of a road, winding across the plain and up and down hills was the fixed materialization of human longing, and of the human notion that it is better to be in one place than in another.

A child of the country would read this open landscape like a book. The irregular mosaic of meadows and cornlands was a picture in timid green and yellow, of the people's struggle for its daily bread; the centuries had taught it to plough and sow in this way. On a distant hill the immovable wings of a windmill, in a small blue cross against the sky, delineated a later stage in the career of bread. The blurred outline of thatched roofs—a low, brown growth of the earth—where the huts of the village thronged together, told the history, from his cradle to his grave, of the peasant, the creature nearest to the soil and dependent on it, prospering in a fertile year and dying in years of drought and pests.

Reflections

1. How can you as interpreter help your audience to envision these environments?

2. What physical and vocal responses can you use to suggest the feelings associated with each environment?

As we have seen, description fills in the qualities of a person, a place, an object, or even an event in terms of the senses; it tells how something looks, sounds, smells, tastes, feels, or moves. To help you as an interpreter and performer, you will want to be able to detail completely the way a descriptive passage appeals to your senses, pointing to and identifying each type of image a selection contains. There are six basic image categories with which an interpreter of literature should be familiar. These six image categories correspond to the six senses explored in the preceding chapter.

Types of Images

Images that appeal primarily to the sense of sight are *visual images*; to the sense of hearing are *auditory images*; to the sense of taste are *gustatory images*; and to the sense of smell are *olfactory images*. The sense of touch is appealed to in either *tactile* or *thermal imagery* (tactile imagery evokes a sensation of physical contact, while thermal imagery refers to the feeling of cold or the feeling of heat).

In addition to the images that appeal to the five traditional senses, an interpreter is also concerned with images designed to appeal to his or her motor sense. These images are classified as **kinetic** in nature if they describe a large overt action of the muscles: "John ran and then he jumped." The images are **kinesthetic** in nature if they refer to degrees of muscular tension or relaxation: "John sat down nervously while Kevin smiled smugly." Consider some imagery examples from literature.

GETTING INVOLVED

Imagery

What are the predominant sensory responses evoked by each of the descriptions in the following cuttings? Carefully note them in your performer's journal.

■ LOOK HOMEWARD ANGEL ■

THOMAS WOLFE

The room was heavy with the rich odor of mellowing pears; an unaccustomed fire of pine sticks burned in the grate: he took up his place before it, and began to pare his nails.

■ THE RED BADGE OF COURAGE ■

STEPHEN CRANE

The youth tried to observe everything. He did not use care to avoid trees and branches, and his forgotten feet were constantly knocking against stones or getting entangled in briers. He was aware that these battalions with their commotions were woven red and startling into the gentle fabric of softened greens and browns. It looked to be a wrong place for a battle field.

The skirmishers in advance fascinated him. Their shots into thickets and at distant and prominent trees spoke to him of tragedies—hidden, mysterious, solemn.

Once the line encountered the body of a dead soldier. He lay upon his back staring at the sky. He was dressed in awkward suit of yellowish brown. The youth could see that the soles of his shoes had been worn to the thinness of writing paper, and from a great rent in one the dead foot projected piteously. And it was as if fate had betrayed the soldier. In death it exposed to his enemies that poverty which in life he had perhaps concealed from his friends.

■ IN BLACK AND WHITE ■
ANN JONES

Patricia walked through the empty house, finding herself alone in all of its comfort. She was the owner now, but loss surrounded her, footsteps echoed in her mind, eyes filled with patterns that were now a few ashes scattered over a mountain. Ben was gone, but the house didn't seem to know this. Objects waited for his touch. Clothes waited for his body. Cold white gin waited for his thirst. It was merciful that things could not talk. Although the real miracle, she decided, was that anything at all remained, as the day outside the house seemed to remain, warm and soft, edges shaped by morning shadow.

Another morning, other shadows had held the swift cutting of the catamaran through the gray ocean water, just beyond the breakers, parallel to where she was walking on the beach near the school she was attending. The fog was coming in, touching everything with light fingers, and there the boy was, seen through the mist, brown skin in bright yellow trunks, lying stretched out on his side beneath the small sail, waving to her as though he knew her and had expected, maybe even hoped to see her walking on this strip of sand between the water and the pressing rows of city houses. She had waved back, feeling something catch in her throat, surprised almost to the point of tears. And then he was gone, knifing through the gray water. It was right somehow that none of these actions had made any more sound than the fog touching the sand. She remembered hoping that he would turn around and come back, but he hadn't.

■ THE LESSON ■
TONI CADE BAMBARA

Back in the days when everyone was old and stupid or young and foolish, and me and Sugar were the only ones just right, this lady moved on our block with nappy hair and proper speech and no makeup. And quite naturally we laughed at her, laughed the way we did at the junk man who went about his business like he was some big-time president and his sorry horse his secretary. And we kinda hated her, too, hated the way we did the winos who cluttered up our parks . . . and stank up our hallways and stairs so you couldn't halfway play hide-and-seek without a gas mask. Miss Moore was her name. The only woman on the block with no first name. And she was black, cept for her feet, which were fish-white and spooky. And she was always planning these boring things for us to do, us being my cousin, mostly, who lived on the block cause we all moved North the same time and to the same apartment then spread out gradual to breathe. And our parents would yank our heads into some kinda shape and crisp up our clothes so we'd be presentable for travel with Miss Moore, who always looked like she was going to church, though she never did. Which is one of the things the grownups talked about when they talked behind her back like a dog.

■ LOOK HOMEWARD ANGEL ■
THOMAS WOLFE

Dusk came. The huge bulk of the hills was foggily emergent. Small smoky lights went up in the hillside shacks. The train crawled dizzily across high trestles spanning ghostly hawsers of water. Far up, far down, plumed with wisps of smoke, toy cabins stuck to bank and gulch and hillside. The train toiled sinuously up among gouged red cuts with slow labor. As darkness came, Oliver descended at the little town of Old Stockade where the rails ended. The last great wall of the hills lay stark above him. As he left the dreary little station and stared into the greasy lamplight of a country store, Oliver felt that he was crawling, like a great beast, into the circle of those enormous hills to die.

■ THE VENGEANCE OF NITOCRIS ■
TENNESSEE WILLIAMS

They all turned toward the mysteriously opened wall and gazed into its black depths.

A hush fell over them. And then became audible the mounting sound of rushing water. A shriek rose from the throat of a woman. And then terror took possession of all within the room. Panic like the burst of flames flared into their hearts. Of one accord, they rushed upon the stair. And it, being purposely made frail, collapsed before the foremost of the wildly screaming mob had reached its summit. Turbulently they piled over the tables, filling the room with a hideous clamor. But rising above their screams was the shrill roar of the rushing water, and no sound could be more provoking of dread and terror. Somewhere in its circuitous route from the pier to the chamber of its reception it must have met with temporary blockade; for it was several minutes after the sound of it was first detected that the first spray of that death-bringing water leapt into the faces of the doomed occupants of the room.

■ ''MEET ME IN THE ■ GREEN GLEN''
ROBERT PENN WARREN

He was a long time coming back. She was glad of that, for now everything was ready, the mashed potatoes, the two porkchops, canned peas. In his chair, he looked down at the food, making not the slightest preparatory move to touch it, then up at her as she stood above him to pour the coffee. He looked down at the coffee, while the vapor rose thinly into the blank whiteness of the light of the bulb that hung almost directly above him. She had gone back to stand near the range, watching him.

All at once, having touched nothing, he shoved back the chair, with a scraping noise on the boards, and rose. Ignoring her, he went to the old electric icebox in the corner beyond the sink, got a tray of ice, put three cubes into the glass, poured it two-thirds full of water, and carried it back to the table. He set it carefully beside his plate, sat down, and, never having looked at her, having in fact, mysteriously denied her presence, her very existence, by every motion made, drew a bottle of whiskey from his right hip pocket. He poured the glass nearly full.

■ A SEPARATE PEACE ■

JOHN KNOWLES

A little fog hung over the river so that as I neared it I felt myself becoming isolated from everything except the river and the few trees beside it. The wind was blowing more steadily here, and I was beginning to feel cold. I never wore a hat, and had forgotten gloves. There were several trees bleakly reaching into the fog. Any one of them might have been the one I was looking for. Unbelievable that there were other trees which looked like it here. It had loomed in my memory as a huge lone spike dominating the riverbank, forbidding as an artillery piece, high as the beanstalk. Yet here was a scattered grove of trees, none of them of any particular grandeur.

Reflections

1. How can you physically and vocally embody the sensory appeals?

2. How can you use your sensory responses to help make the literature live for your audience?

From your reading, you may have already realized that images do not reside in solely one sensory class or category. There is simply no such thing as a purely auditory image, a purely visual image, and so on. An image always stimulates more than one sense. While its emphasis may be in one area—that is, an appeal to a single sense—the image will also always contain secondary or subdominant sense appeals. Identifying both the primary and the secondary sense appeals that reside in a phrase is a critical skill for an interpreter, who must always be a thorough sensory tracker. How are your tracking skills? Try the following exercise.

GETTING INVOLVED

The Sense Search Game

Divide the class into a number of teams. Each team is to find and classify all the images contained in one of the following passages. Groups should note both primary (dominant) and secondary (subdominant) sense appeals.

After your group has completed its sense search, select one member to perform the passage for the rest of the class. Those who do not perform are to serve as their chosen performer's "training team," helping him or her to rehearse the passage, and being certain to communicate which images are being sent clearly and which images need further work or clarification. After the rehearsal period, your group's representative will perform the passage for the remaining class members, who will also have a chance to evaluate the clarity and effectiveness of the re-created images. (You may wish to use this group rehearsal method at various points during the semester. Performance exercises throughout this book may be easily adapted to include this type of preparation approach.) Now, for a complete sensory tracking experience. . . .

■ THE HOPELAND ■

K. KAM

I try to imagine my mother as a young girl, small and frail with a quiet heart, shiny black hair cropped to prevent her from indulging in hours of vanity before the mirror. I laugh when she tells me some pranksters in her village filled a large vat with dung and lit a fire under it, boiling the smelly contents until they exploded.

But the funny stories are always followed by somber ones that will not let me forget the horrors my parents must have endured. I hear only bits and pieces. My mother tells of drunken soldiers banging on the doors of houses nearby, dragging out screaming girls and raping them in the night. She watched an angry crowd of villagers haul a traitor to the top of a hill, where they hanged him for selling secrets to the enemy. There were the victims forced to kneel on broken glass and the hunted ones who chose suicide. During land raids, she stared mutely as soldiers smashed windows and shot down old women barricading doorways with their bodies to protect young ones inside. During one onslaught, she hid underneath the bed as a soldier entered her house and held a bayonet to her mother's throat.

I am disturbed, yet intrigued. I listen to the stories, casting the characters and writing the script, but my mental exercise is only a game. My parents' China still eludes me.

■ RAIN ■
W. SOMERSET MAUGHAM

He scratched his mosquito bites. He felt very short-tempered. When the rain stopped and the sun shone, it was like a hothouse, seething, humid, sultry, breathless, and you had a strange feeling that everything was growing with savage violence. The natives, blithe and childlike by reputation, seemed then, with their tattooing and their dyed hair, to have something sinister in their appearance; and when they pattered along at your heels with their naked feet you looked back instinctively. You felt they might at any moment come behind you swiftly and thrust a long knife between your shoulder blades. You could not tell what dark thoughts lurked behind their wide-set eyes. They had a little the look of ancient Egyptians painted on a temple wall, and there was about them the terror of what is immeasurably old.

■ PERSIMMONS FOR BREAKFAST ■
JOHN McPHEE

Unfortunately, Gibbons did not make pralines for breakfast. As unappealing as pralines might have been at that time of day, nothing edible could have been worse than what we had. The meal began with peppermint tea, which was very good in itself and was excellent with chunks of maple sugar in it. The substance of that breakfast, however, was a great mound of hot persimmons, which had been stewed in maple sugar and were now glued together with concentrated maple syrup. We stuffed them eagerly into our mouths, because they looked good, but we found that all the astringency of slightly unripe persimmons seemed to be brought out powerfully when they are stewed. They puckered not only our mouths, but also our throats. Gibbons observed without apparent alarm, that he thought that his esophagus was going to close. Nonetheless, he kept shovelling in the styptic persimmons, and I followed his lead. There was enough carbohydrate fuel in the stewed fruit to keep us going all day, and we needed it. Each mouthful tasted fine on entry but quickly turned into something like a glut of blotting paper, requiring a half dozen forced swallows to squeeze it down. Gibbons had told me that in all his experience of cooking wild food for others no one had ever got sick. In order to preserve his record, I excused myself and went for a walk, taking deep breaths, until I was sure that the persimmons were going to stay with me.

■ THE HUNTERS ■

HARRIS DOWNEY

He had traversed plow-furrowed fields when silence, imminent with violence, weighted him down like a pack. He had traversed shell-pelted fields when fear tangled his legs like a barricade. He had seen his enemy and his comrades sprawled grotesque and cold in the neutrality of death, as impersonal as the cows among them, angling stiff legs to the sky. He had thrown grenades at hidden men; and once, staring into wide, stark eyes down the bead of his aim, he had sighed out his breath toward a union more intimate than love—and more treacherous than its denial. He had seen a dog, tethered at the gate, howl at the noise of destruction and die in terror; had seen bees swarm from their hives at the ground of a cannon and hang in the air, directionless. He had seen Frenchmen return to their villages to gesticulate the glory of victory and, sobering, to peer from behind a silly grin at the rubbish that had been their homes. But these things had not touched him. He had left himself somewhere, and the farther he walked the terrain of war, the farther he went from himself.

He heard the spasmodic eruptions of war. He listened to silence hissing like the quick fuse of a bomb. Yet he felt nothing—unless it was weariness. He walked under the high fire of artillery as though it were a canopy against the rain. At first he had been unhappy and afraid; and perhaps, in the static musing, in the constant but unapprehended memory that was himself, he was yet unhappy and afraid.

■ Mark Twain's Autobiography ■

I can see the farm yet, with perfect clearness. I can see all its belongings, all its details; the family room of the house, with a ''trundle'' bed in one corner and a spinning-wheel in another—a wheel whose rising and falling wail, heard from a distance, was the mournfulest of all sounds to me and made me homesick and low spirited and filled my atmosphere with the wandering spirits of the dead; the vast fireplace, piled high on winter nights with flaming hickory logs from whose ends a sugary sap bubbled out but did not go to waste, for we scraped it off and ate it; the lazy cat spread out on the rough hearthstones; the drowsy dogs braced against the jambs and blinking; my aunt in one chimney corner, knitting; my uncle in the other, smoking his corn-cob pipe; the slick and carpetless oak floor faintly mirroring the dancing flame tongues and freckled with black indentations where fire coals had popped out and died a leisurely death; half a dozen children romping in the background twilight; ''split''-bottomed chairs here and there, some with rockers; a cradle—out of service but waiting with confidence; in the early cold mornings a snuggle of children in shirts and chemises, occupying the hearthstone and procrastinating—they could not bear to leave that comfortable place and go out on the windswept floor space between the house and kitchen where the general tin basin stood, and wash.

Along outside of the front fence ran the country road, dusty in the summertime and a good place for snakes—they liked to lie in it and sun themselves; when they were rattlesnakes or puff adders we killed them; when they were black snakes or racers or belonged to the fabled ''hoop'' breed we fled without shame; when they were ''house snakes'' or ''garters'' we carried them home and put them in Aunt Patsy's work basket for a surprise; for she was prejudiced against snakes, and always when she took the basket in her lap and they began to climb out of it it disordered her mind. She never could seem to get used to them. . . .

Beyond the road where the snakes sunned themselves was a dense young thicket and through it a dim-lighted path led a quarter of a mile; then out of the dimness one emerged abruptly upon a level great prairie which was covered with wild strawberry plants, vividly starred with prairie pinks and walled in on all sides by forests. The strawberries were fragrant and fine, and in the season we were generally there in the crisp freshness of the early morning, while the dew beads still sparkled upon the grass and the woods were ringing with the first songs of the birds. . . .

This type of sensory search experience should evoke certain *emotional* or *empathic responses* in you—responses that are essential if you hope to communicate word pictures effectively. Emotional responses help you create a meaningful *reflection of a literary world*. When you have fully processed the images of your selection, you are ready to re-create the literature physically and vocally, to interpret and perform the literature so that others may appreciate it.

GETTING INVOLVED
Performing Descriptive Prose

Choose a passage of descriptive prose to perform in class. This four-to-five-minute selection may include some dialogue, but it should be predominantly descriptive in nature. Because of the time limits, you may have to do some thoughtful cutting of the selection; however, be sure the lines you eliminate do not disturb the flow of the passage. Your deletions should not distort the picture your author has tried to create.

You may select your reading from end-of-the-chapter selections in this text or from literature you find on your own. Try to ensure that the piece you select is worthy of your time and study. Will its content appeal to and hold your audience's attention? Will the material provide you with a performance challenge, broadening your reading abilities?

When rehearsing and performing your selection, keep in mind your sensory education experiences. Work to fully capture and internalize the sensory qualities of the person, place, action, or object described. This is essential if you hope to communicate the word pictures, the mood, and the tone of the passage to your audience. Also, write a few sentences that will serve both to introduce your literature to the class and help your audience to empathize. Finally, as you rehearse, use *all* your senses to appreciate and fully understand what you hope to convey to your audience.

Performer's Journal

On the day you perform your selection, write in your responses to the following questions in your journal.

1. Why did you choose this selection? What about it appeals to you?

2. What is being described in the literature?

3. What is the speaker's attitude in the passage?

4. What types of sense images did the author use? Discuss how the imagery contributed to the development of mood.

5. What emotional values may be stimulated by an interpretation of your selection?

6. What would you like to impel your audience to imagine, feel, or know about your selection?

Selections for Further Work

Poe uses description and suspense in a manner that few writers can equal. Consider this passage.

■ THE TELL-TALE HEART ■

EDGAR ALLAN POE

True!—nervous—very, very dreadfully nervous I have been and am; but why *will* you say that I am mad? The disease had sharpened my senses— not destroyed—not dulled them. Above all was the sense of hearing acute. I heard all things in the heaven and in the earth. I heard many things in hell. How, then, am I mad? Hearken! and observe how healthily—how calmly I can tell you the whole story.

It is impossible to say how first the idea entered my brain; but once conceived, it haunted me day and night. Object there was none. Passion there was none. I loved the old man. He had never wronged me. He had never given me insult. For his gold I had no desire. I think it was his eye! Yes, it was this! He had the eye of a vulture—a pale blue eye, with a film over it. Whenever it fell upon me, my blood ran cold; and so by degrees—very gradually—I made up my mind to take the life of the old man and thus rid myself of the eye forever.

Now this is the point. You fancy me mad. Madmen know nothing. But you should have seen *me*. You should have seen how wisely I proceeded— with what caution—with what foresight—with what dissimulation I went to work! I was never kinder to the old man than during the whole week before I killed him. And every night about midnight, I turned the latch of his door and opened it—oh so gently! And then, when I had made an opening sufficient for my head, I put in a dark lantern, all closed, closed, so that no light shone out, and then I thrust in my head. Oh, you would have laughed to see how cunningly I thrust it in! I moved it slowly—very, very slowly, so that I might not disturb the old man's sleep. It took me an hour to place my whole head within the opening so far that I could see him as he lay upon his bed. Ha!—would a madman have been so wise as this? And then, when my head was well in the room, I undid the lantern cautiously—oh, so cautiously—cautiously (for the hinges creaked)—I undid it just so much that a single thin ray fell upon the vulture eye. And this I did for seven long nights—every night just at midnight—but I found the eye always closed; and so it was impossible to do the work; for it was not the old man who vexed me, but his Evil Eye. And every morning, when the day broke, I went boldly into the chamber, and spoke courageously to him, calling him by name in a hearty tone, and inquiring how he had passed the night. So you see he would have been a very profound old man, indeed, to suspect that every night, just at twelve, I looked in upon him while he slept.

Upon the eighth night I was more than usually cautious in opening the door. A watch's minute hand moves more quickly than did mine. Never before that night had I *felt* that extent of my own powers—of my sagacity. I could scarcely contain my feelings of triumph. To think that there I was, opening the door, little by little, and he not even to dream of my secret deeds or thoughts. I fairly chuckled at the idea; and perhaps he heard me; for he moved on the bed suddenly, as if startled. Now you may think that I drew back—but no. His room was as black as pitch with the thick darkness, (for the shutters were close fastened, through fear of robbers,) and so I knew that he could not see the opening of the door, and I kept pushing it on steadily, steadily.

I had my head in, and was about to open the lantern, when my thumb slipped upon the tin fastening, and the old man sprang up in bed, crying out—''Who's there?''

I kept quite still and said nothing. For a whole hour I did not move a muscle, and in the meantime I did not hear him lie down. He was still sitting up in the bed listening;—just as I have done, night after night, harkening to the death watches in the wall.

Presently I heard a slight groan, and I knew it was the groan of mortal terror. It was not a groan of pain or of grief—oh no!—it was the low stifled sound that arises from the bottom of the soul when over-charged with awe. I knew the sound well. Many a night, just at midnight, when all the world slept, it has welled up from my own bosom, deepening, with its dreadful echo the terrors that distracted me. I say I knew it well. I knew what the old man felt, and pitied him, although I chuckled at heart. I knew that he had been lying awake ever since the first slight noise, when he had turned in the bed. His fears had been ever since growing upon him. He had been trying to fancy them causeless, but could not. He had been saying to himself—''It is nothing but the wind in the chimney—it is only a mouse crossing the floor,'' or ''it is merely a cricket which has made a single chirp.'' Yes, he had been trying to comfort himself with these suppositions: but he had found all in vain. *All in vain*; because Death, in approaching him had stalked with his black shadow before him, and enveloped the victim. And it was the mournful influence of the unperceived shadow that caused him to feel—although he neither saw nor heard—to *feel* the presence of my head within the room.

When I had waited a long time, very patiently, without hearing him lie down, I resolved to open a little—a very, very little crevice in the lantern. So I opened it—you cannot imagine how stealthily, stealthily—until, at length a simple dim ray, like the thread of the spider, shot from out the crevice and fell full upon the vulture eye.

It was open—wide, wide open—and I grew furious as I gazed upon it. I saw it with perfect distinctness—all dull blue, with a hideous veil over it that chilled the very marrow in my bones; but I could see nothing else of the old man's face or person: for I had directed the ray as if by instinct, precisely upon the damned spot.

And I have not told you that what you mistake for madness is but overacuteness of the senses?—now, I say, there came to my ears a low, dull, quick sound, such as a watch makes when enveloped in cotton. I knew *that* sound well, too. It was the beating of the old man's heart. It increased my fury, as the beating of a drum stimulates the soldier into courage.

But even yet I refrained and kept still. I scarcely breathed. I held the lantern motionless. I tried how steadily I could maintain the ray upon the eye. Meantime the hellish tattoo of the heart increased. It grew quicker and quicker, and louder and louder every instant. The old man's terror *must* have been extreme! It grew louder, I say louder every moment!—do you mark me well? I have told you that I am nervous: so I am. And now at the dead hour of the night, amid the dreadful silence of that old house, so strange a noise as this excited me to uncontrollable terror. Yet, for some minutes longer I refrained and stood still. But the beating grew louder, louder! I thought the heart must burst. And now a new anxiety seized me— the sound would be heard by a neighbor! The old man's hour had come! With a loud yell, I threw open the lantern and leaped into the room. He shrieked once—once only. In an instant I dragged him to the floor, and pulled the heavy bed over him. I then smiled gaily to find the deed so far done. But for many minutes, the heart beat on with a muffled sound. This, however, did not vex me; it would not be heard through the wall. At length it ceased. The old man was dead. I removed the bed and examined the corpse. Yes, he was stone, stone dead. I placed my hand upon the heart and held it there many minutes. There was no pulsation. He was stone dead. His eye would trouble me no more.

In this passage Sherwood Anderson describes old people in a rural community. What age do you imagine the narrator is?

■ DEATH IN THE WOODS ■

SHERWOOD ANDERSON

She was an old woman and lived on a farm near the town in which I lived. All country and small-town people have seen such old women, but no one knows much about them. Such an old woman comes into town driving an old worn-out horse or she comes afoot carrying a basket. She may own a few hens and have eggs to sell. She brings them in a basket and takes them to a grocer. There she trades them in. She gets some salt pork and some beans. Then she gets a pound or two of sugar and some flour.

Afterward she goes to the butcher's and asks for some dog meat. She may spend ten or fifteen cents, but when she does she asks for something. In my day the butchers gave liver to anyone who wanted to carry it away. In our family we were always having it. Once one of my brothers got a whole cow's liver at the slaughter-house near the fair-grounds. We had it until we were sick of it. It never cost a cent. I have hated the thought of it ever since.

The old farm woman got some liver and a soup bone. She never visited with anyone, and as soon as she got what she wanted she lit out for home. It made quite a load for such an old body. No one gave her a lift. People drive right down a road and never notice an old woman like that.

There was such an old woman used to come into town past our house one summer and fall when I was sick with what was called inflammatory rheumatism. She went home later carrying a heavy pack on her back. Two or three large gaunt-looking dogs followed at her heels.

The old woman was nothing special. She was one of the nameless ones that hardly anyone knows, but she got into my thoughts. I have just suddenly now, after all these years, remembered her and what happened. It is a story. Her name was, I think, Grimes, and she lived with her husband and son in a small unpainted house on the bank of a small creek four miles from town.

The husband and son were a tough lot. Although the son was but twenty-one, he had already served a term in jail. It was whispered about that the woman's husband stole horses and ran them off to some other county. Now and then, when a horse turned up missing, the man had also disappeared. No one ever caught him. Once, when I was loafing at Tom Whitehead's livery barn, the man came there and sat on the bench in front. Two or three other men were there, but no one spoke to him. He sat for a few minutes and then got up and went away. When he was leaving he turned around and stared at the men. There was a look of defiance in his eyes. ''Well, I have tried to be friendly. You don't want to talk to me. It has been so wherever I have gone in this town. If, some day, one of your fine horses turns up missing, well then what?'' He did not say anything actually. ''I'd like to bust one of you on the jaw,'' was about what his eyes said. I remember how the look in his eyes made me shiver.

The old man belonged to a family that had had money once. His name was Grimes, Jake Grimes. It all comes back clearly now. His father, John Grimes, had owned a sawmill when the country was new and had made money. Then he got to drinking and running after women. When he died, there wasn't much left.

Life for some of our senior citizens is less rewarding than it should be. Have you seen the elderly sitting on park benches? Do some of them live in small rooms barely larger than a cupboard?

■ MISS BRILL ■

KATHERINE MANSFIELD

Although it was so brilliantly fine—the blue sky powdered with gold and great spots of light like white wine splashed over the Jardins Publiques— Miss Brill was glad that she had decided on her fur. The air was motionless, but when you opened your mouth there was just a faint chill, like a chill from a glass of iced water before you sip, and now and again a leaf came drifting—from nowhere, from the sky. Miss Brill put up her hand and touched her fur. Dear little thing! It was nice to feel it again. She had taken it out of its box that afternoon, shaken out the mothpowder, given it a good brush, and rubbed the life back into the dim little eyes. ''What has been happening to me?'' said the sad little eyes. Oh, how sweet it was to see them snap at her again from the red eiderdown! . . . But the nose, which was of some black composition, wasn't at all firm. It must have had a knock, somehow. Never mind—a little dab of black sealing-wax when the time came—when it was absolutely necessary. . . . Little rogue! Yes, she really felt like that about it. Little rogue biting its tail just by her left ear. She could have taken it off and laid it on her lap and stroked it. She felt a tingling in her hands and arms, but that came from walking, she supposed. . . .

Only two people shared her "special" seat: a fine old man in a velvet coat, his hands clasped over a huge carved walking-stick, and a big old woman, sitting upright, with a roll of knitting on her embroidered apron. This was disappointing, for Miss Brill always looked forward to the conversation. She had become really quite expert, she thought, at listening as though she didn't listen, at sitting in other people's lives just for a minute while they talked round her. . . .

The old people sat on the bench, still as statues. Never mind, there was always the crowd to watch. To and fro, in front of the flower-beds and the band rotunda, the couples and groups paraded, stopped to talk, to greet, to buy a handful of flowers from the old beggar who had his tray fixed to the railings. Little children ran among them, swooping and laughing; little boys with big white silk bows under their chins, little girls, little French dolls, dressed up in velvet and lace. And sometimes a tiny staggerer came suddenly rocking into the open from under the trees, stopped, stared, as suddenly sat down "flop" until its small high-stepping mother, like a young hen, rushed scolding to its rescue. Other people sat on the benches and green chairs, but they were nearly always the same, Sunday after Sunday, and—Miss Brill had often noticed—there was something funny about nearly all of them. They were odd, silent, nearly all old, and from the way they stared they looked as though they'd just come from dark little rooms or even—even cupboards! . . .

On her way home she usually bought a slice of honeycake at the baker's. It was her Sunday treat. Sometimes there was an almond in her slice, sometimes not. It made a great difference. If there was an almond it was like carrying home a tiny present—a surprise—something that might very well not have been there. She hurried on the almond Sundays and struck the match for the kettle in quite a dashing way.

But today she passed the baker's by, climbed the stairs, went into the little dark room—her room like a cupboard—and sat down on the red eiderdown. She sat there for a long time. The box that the fur came out of was on the bed. She unclasped the necklet quickly, quickly, without looking, laid it inside. but when she put the lid on she thought she heard something crying.

Childhood leaves us all many memories. Mark Twain used description to share some of his early memories with us, as in the following passage.

■ Mark Twain's Autobiography ■

. . . I spent some part of every year at the farm until I was twelve or thirteen years old. The life which I led there with my cousins was full of charm, and so is the memory of it yet. I can call back the solemn twilight and mystery of the deep woods, the earthy smells, the faint odors of the wild flowers, the sheen of rainwashed foliage, the rattling clapper of drops when the wind shook the trees, the far-off hammering of woodpeckers and the muffled drumming of wood pheasants in the remoteness of the forest, the snapshot glimpses of disturbed wild creatures scurrying through the grass—I can call it all back and make it as real as it ever was, and as blessed. I can call back the prairie, and its loneliness and peace, and a vast hawk hanging motionless in the sky, with his wings spread wide and the blue of the vault showing through the fringe of their end feathers. I can see the woods in their autumn dress, the oaks purple, the hickories washed with gold, the maples and the sumachs luminous with crimson fires, and I can hear the rustle made by the fallen leaves as we plowed through them. I can see the blue clusters of wild grapes hanging among the foliage of the saplings, and I remember the taste of them and the smell. I know how the wild blackberries looked, and how they tasted, and the same with the pawpaws, the hazelnuts, and the persimmons; and I can feel the thumping rain, upon my head, of hickory nuts and walnuts when we were out in the frosty dawn to scramble for them with the pigs, and the gusts of wind loosed them and sent them down. I know the stain of blackberries, and how pretty it is, and I know the stain of walnut hulls, and how little it minds soap and water, also what grudged experience it had of either of them. I know the taste of maple sap, and when to gather it, and how to arrange the troughs and the delivery tubes, and how to boil down the juice, and how to hook the sugar after it is made, also how much better hooked sugar tastes than any that is honestly come by, let bigots say what they will. I know how a prize watermelon looks when it is sunning its fat rotundity among pumpkin vines and ''simblins''; I know how to tell when it is ripe without "plugging" it; I know how inviting it looks when it is cooling itself in a tub of water under the bed, waiting; I know how it looks when it lies on the table in the sheltered great floor space between house and kitchen, and the children gathered for the sacrifice and their mouths watering; I know the crackling sound it makes when the carving knife enters its end, and I can see the split fly along in front of the blade as the knife cleaves its way to the other end; I can see its halves fall apart and display the rich red meat and the black seeds, and the heart standing up, a luxury fit for the elect; I know how a boy looks behind a yard-long slice of that melon, and I know how he feels; for I have been there. I know the taste of the watermelon which has been honestly come by, and I know the taste of the watermelon which has been acquired by art. Both taste good, but the experienced know which tastes best.

Joyce Carol Oates is one of America's most prolific writers. In this passage from *I Lock My Door Upon Myself,* she combines calm descriptive prose with a surprise ending.

■ I Lock My Door Upon Myself ■

JOYCE CAROL OATES

. . . there on the river, the Chautauqua, in a sepia sun, the rowboat bucking the choppy waves with a look almost of gaiety, defiance. And in the boat the couple: the man, rowing, a black man, the woman a white woman whose face is too distant to be seen. The man is rowing the boat downstream in a slightly jagged course yet with energy, purpose, the oars like blades rising and dropping and rising and again dropping, sinking into the water only to emerge again dripping and impatient; the woman is facing him, close, their knees touching, or so it appears from shore . . . the woman sits straight, ramrod straight, in a posture of extreme attentiveness to the man's and the boat's every move. With one hand she clutches the lurching side of the boat to steady herself, the other hand is shut into a fist, white-knuckled, immobile, in her lab.

. . . past Milburn, past Flemingville, past Shaheen, and then they begin to be seen, to be remarked upon . . . but only when they are a mile above Tintern Falls do people begin to shout in warning and now even the cries of birds at the river's edge lift sharp and piercing with warning. Then about a half-mile above Tintern the rowboat is taken by the swift-flowing current as by a giant hand and now it would require the black man's most strenuous and desperate exertions to steer it from its course yet he lifts the oars and rests them calmly in place as the woman sits continuing to watch him closely, possibly smiling, are the two of them smiling?—talking together?—hearing nothing of the shouts from shore and nothing of the increasing roar of the falls ahead, the sixty-foot drop on the other side of the bridge and the churning white water beyond. . . .

CHAPTER FIVE

The Interpretation of Narrative Prose

Oral Interpretation As Storytelling

In Chapter 5, you will turn your attention to **narrative prose**—prose that tells a story. To prepare, try the following exercise.

GETTING INVOLVED
Animalizing

Think of three of your favorite animals and choose one you would like to portray. In your own small space—even seated at your desk—try to assume all the physical and vocal characteristics of your animal. Do not talk to any other "animals" at this point, but instead consider the following questions. What is your animal's attitude toward life? Is it fearful? lazy? aggressive? restless? bored? proud? jaunty? Why does your animal act the way he or she does? Think carefully about your answers to these questions. Next, repeat the process for your other two animal choices.

To build on this exercise, choose one of the three animals you portrayed. Assuming its physical and vocal characteristics once again, interact with one other animal in the classroom—preferably one seated close to you. Now ask yourself the following questions. Do you know the type of animal you are interacting with? How can you tell? Why do you react the way you do to this animal? What happens to your animal's dominant characteristics when you are relating to another animal character?

Still in character, include at least two additional animals in your interaction group. Relate to the others, but this time as you start to interact, allow yourself to become more and more human. Begin to straighten up, assuming the posture of a human, but retain your animal's dominant characteristics and traits as you gradually change.

Reflections

1. What happened as you started to relate to the other animals in your group?

2. Were you able to interact meaningfully with each other? Why or why not?

3. What was said? What action occurred? Did a *story* begin to evolve?

As you interacted with the other animals, probably a story *did* begin to evolve among you. Storytelling is, after all, an important part of our heritage, and for many people it's an enjoyable activity, as well. Given its importance in shaping our culture, let's focus on the story in literature.

GETTING INVOLVED
A Fable for Our Time

■ THE OWL WHO WAS GOD ■
JAMES THURBER

Once upon a starless midnight there was an owl who sat on the branch of an oak tree. Two ground moles tried to slip quietly by, unnoticed. "You!" said the owl. "Who?" they quavered in fear and astonishment, for they could not believe it was possible for anyone to see them in that thick darkness. "You two!" said the owl. The moles hurried away and told the other creatures of the field and forest that the owl was the greatest and wisest of all animals because he could see in the dark and because he could answer any question. "I'll see about that," said a secretary bird, and he called on the owl one night when it was again very dark. "How many claws am I holding up?" said the secretary bird. "Two," said the owl, and that was right. "Can you give me another expression for 'that is to say,' or 'namely'?" asked the secretary bird. "To wit," said the owl. "Why does a lover call on his love?" asked the secretary bird. "To woo," said the owl.

The secretary bird hastened back to the other creatures and reported that the owl was indeed the greatest and wisest animal in the world because he could see in the dark and because he could answer any question. "Can he see in the daytime too?" asked the red fox. "Yes," echoed a dormouse and a French poodle. "Can he see in the daytime too?" All the other creatures laughed loudly at this silly question, and they set upon the red fox and his friends and drove them out of the region. Then they sent a messenger to the owl and asked him to be their leader.

When the owl appeared among the animals it was high noon and the sun was shining brightly. He walked very slowly, which gave him an appearance of great dignity, and he peered about him with large, staring eyes, which gave him an air of tremendous importance. "He's God!" screamed a Plymouth Rock hen. And others took up the cry. "He's God!" So they followed him wherever he went and when he began to bump into things, they began to bump into things too. Finally, he came to a concrete highway and he started up the middle of it and all the other creatures followed him. Presently a hawk, who was acting as outrider, observed a truck coming toward them at fifty miles an hour, and he reported to the secretary bird and the secretary bird reported to the owl. "There's danger ahead," said the secretary bird. "To wit?" said the owl. The secretary bird told him. "Aren't you afraid?" he asked. "Who?" said the owl calmly, for he could not see the truck. "He's God!" cried all the creatures again, and they were still crying "He's God!" when the truck hit them and ran them down. Some of the animals were merely injured, but most of them, including the owl, were killed.

Moral: *You can fool too many of the people too much of the time.*

Your instructor will either divide the class into small groups or select one demonstration group to perform. The group or groups will act out the story by James Thurber. What preparation will be necessary? You may want to refer to the following work outline for assistance.

Begin by casting the fable, then dividing it into its component incidents. At what point should your action begin? Where should it end? Secondly, improvise each incident or scene and then rework the plot. Remember, just as in the "Animalizing" exercise, you must try to assume all the attributes of your assigned specific character in the fable. After a brief rehearsal, perform your version of "The Owl Who Was God" for the rest of the class.

Reflections

1. What similarities do you note between the fable and your first animal improvisations?

2. What additional elements does the Thurber fable include that your initial skits did not?

James Thurber's fable is an example of narrative prose. Let's examine more closely the characteristics of this particular prose form. *Narrative prose tells a story and involves action or experience.* The action or experience it details occurs in an imaginary world—the world of literature. It is to this literary world that you, as a performer of literature, must be able to respond.

The world in your mind must merge with the world of the story. What creative processes can you use to allow this to happen? You can begin by building on the experiences you have already had with descriptive prose. Use the setting, the time, and the character pictures to help you tell your author's tale. With these elements, you create the appropriate mood or atmosphere. Narrative prose involves a greater number of elements than does descriptive prose, however, and you should become familiar with them. Whether a simple fable, a short story, or a portion of a complex novel, narrative prose involves a number of elements. Let's examine them further.

GETTING INVOLVED
A Closer Look

Reread "The Owl Who Was God" and answer the following questions with your instructor.

1. What is happening in the story? (the plot)

2. Where and when is it happening? (the setting)

3. To whom is it happening? (the characters)

4. Why is it happening? (the motivation)

5. How is it happening? (the author's attitude)

6. Who is telling what is happening? (speaker or narrator) From what perspective or point of view does he or she speak?

A Close Look at the Narrator

The narrator is the person who tells what happens in a story. This person establishes the point of view or perspective from which the story is detailed. Like tour guides, narrators lead you skillfully through a world of the author's choosing. The narrator's angle of vision, decided by the author, will determine the details the author chooses to include and how these details will be used within the story. Learn more about the importance of perspective in the following exercise.

GETTING INVOLVED
Room Tour

A. You will have three minutes to guide your classmates through a room that is real for you—one that lives in your imagination. It can be a room you have actually experienced or one you invent. Your goal is to make that room visible to the other members of your class. You may not use any props to do this, but you may walk around as you describe the various qualities of the room that lives in your mind.

B. Now change your perspective. Pretend you are extremely nearsighted. How does this modify your view of the room? What would you notice if you looked at the room through the eyes of a farsighted person? Through the eyes of a very short person? a giant? a busybody? an interior decorator? Do the things you notice or describe change depending on who you are? How? Why?

GETTING INVOLVED
Picture Taking

A. Take some photographs with a camera held at waist level rather than at the customary eye level. If possible, use a Polaroid so you can see your results developed immediately.

B. If you have access to a camcorder, try the same exercise with the camcorder held at waist level as you walk through both familiar and unfamiliar territory.

Reflections

1. What did you notice about the pictures or the videos taken from this angle of vision?

2. How does the world look different when seen from waist level?

3. How does this experience relate to the experiences you had during the prior "Room Tour" exercise?

Many Voices

In both of the preceding "Getting Involved" exercises, you were asked to adopt different perspectives. Each perspective you adopted determined both the organization and your perception of the world around you. Actually, each time you changed your angle of vision, you became a somewhat different narrator. As interpreters, remember *it is always the "I" behind the eye that is in control.* That is, it is always the narrator—the person telling the story—who determines the way the story is revealed. Let's examine more fully the form of control that may be exerted by various types of narrative voices.

The "I" Behind the Eye

A narrator may function as a character in the story. He or she may be either intimately involved in the action, or an outsider who views firsthand the occurrences in the story's imaginary world. In either case, this particular type of narrator would use the personal pronoun "*I*" as the story is told, and we can recognize him or her by the presence of such phrases as "I saw" or "I heard."

The following version of Aesop's fable "Slow But Sure" is told from the *first-person point of view*; that is, it is told from the point of view of the hare.

First-Person Point of View

■ SLOW BUT SURE ■

One day I noticed a tortoise resting in the middle of the road. I tapped him on the shell to get his attention. "Anyone home in there?" I inquired. The tortoise tentatively stuck his head out of his shell and stared me up and down. Then he slowly drew his head back in to its natural resting place. I knew that I was far superior to that lazy tortoise, so I could not allow him to simply retreat; instead, I started an argument with him. "Bet I could run the pants off you in a race," I interjected. "Why that old shell is just too heavy for you to bear." I was quite sure that I had duly insulted his ego, and I was right, for he ever so tentatively stuck his head out again. I knew he would hear me out.

"Well, there you are," I said rather innocently as I looked him in the eye. "What do you say, is it a race?"

"I meet your challenge, sir," he said. I knew, however, that he would never measure up to it. He was much too hesitant.

We set a time and a place for the race. After a few laps I knew I could afford to give the slowpoke a break, so I laid down to take a nap. I must have overslept, however, because the next thing I heard was the voice of the tortoise gleefully calling from the finish line, "I won! I won!" He was darn smug about it, too.

Moral: *He Who Rests Assured On His Laurels Is Often Overtaken By A Plodder.*

A story may also be recounted by various *third person points of view.* The narrator may be omniscient: In telling the story, he or she moves from one character's mind to another character's mind. Such narrators have complete access to the motivations, thoughts, and feelings of all the characters. They are free to introduce information to the reader when and where they choose. The following is the fable "Slow But Sure" told from an omniscient point of view.

Omniscient Narrator Point of View

■ Slow But Sure ■

A tortoise awoke one afternoon after being tapped on the shell by a hare. "Anyone home in there?" The tortoise tentatively stuck his head out of his shell and stared at the hare standing before him. He gazed at him a while but then he slowly drew his head back into its natural resting place. The hare, however, was quite eager to prove that he was superior to his fellow creature, so he started an argument with him. "Bet I could run the pants off you in a race," he chortled. "Why that old shell of yours is just too heavy for you to bear."

The hare, full of pride, grinned contentedly. He was quite sure that the tortoise would not dare meet his challenge. The tortoise, however, ever so tentatively stuck his head out again. I THINK I'LL JUST HEAR HIM

OUT. ''Well, there you are,'' said the cocky hare, as he looked the tortoise in the eye. ''What do you say, is it a race?''

The tortoise looked the hare up and down. I KNOW HIS KIND. ''I meet your challenge, sir.''

So a time and place for the race was agreed. The hare began the race, but had such confidence in his natural fleetness that he did not trouble about it, and instead lay down by the roadside and went to sleep. I'LL JUST REST FOR A WHILE AND EASILY OVERTAKE MR. SLOWPOKE IN A FEW MINUTES. He was quite unaware of what was about to happen to him; he was too busy snoring.

The tortoise, acutely conscious of its slow movements, simply plodded along continuously until it passed the still napping hare and won the race.

Moral: *He Who Rests Assured On His Laurels Is Often Overtaken By A Plodder.*

A third-person narrator may possess what is termed *limited omniscience*. This type of narrator closely identifies with only one character, and that particular character is known as the narrator's **sentient center.** The narrator journeys with, or resides within, that character, following him or her throughout the story and restricting the reader to that character's range of knowledge and angle of vision solely. Once again, Aesop's fable is used to illustrate this concept. ''Slow But Sure'' is told in the third person from the point of view of the tortoise.

Limited Omniscient Narrator Point of View

■ Slow But Sure ■

A tortoise awoke one afternoon after being tapped on the shell by a hare. ''Anyone home in there?'' he heard the hare ask. The tortoise tentatively stuck his head out of his shell and stared at the hare standing before him. Then he slowly drew his head back into its natural resting place.

''Bet I could run the pants off you in a race,'' he heard the hare cry. ''Why that old shell of yours is just too heavy for you to bear.'' The tortoise saw the hare grin much too contentedly. Ever so tentatively he stuck his head out again. I THINK I'LL JUST HEAR HIM OUT.

''Well, there you are,'' said the hare. ''What do you say, is it a race?''

The tortoise looked the hare up and down. I KNOW HIS KIND. ''I'll meet your challenge, sir.''

So a time and place for the race was agreed.

The hare started the race, but soon lay down by the roadside and went to sleep.

The tortoise, acutely conscious of its slow movements, simply plodded along continuously until he passed the still napping hare and won the race.

Moral: *He Who Rests Assured On His Laurels Is Often Overtaken By A Plodder.*

Notice that a third-person narrator usually includes some passages of interior speech or indirect discourse. In this way the reader is allowed to move into the character's mind and hear his or her unspoken thoughts.

An author may also endow his narrator with an *objective* rather than a subjective point of view. Such a narrator lets the characters speak for themselves through dialogue or direct discourse. In this case, the narrator does not overtly tell us whether he or she approves or disapproves of a character's actions or thoughts. Notice how "Slow But Sure" changes when told from the perspective of an objective narrator.

Objective Narrator Point of View

■ SLOW BUT SURE ■

A tortoise was awakened one afternoon by a hare who tapped him on his shell. The tortoise stuck his head out of his shell, looked at the hare, and then drew his head back in to its natural resting place.

The hare, however, did not give up his attempt to communicate with the tortoise. "Bet I could run the pants off you in a race," he said. "Why that old shell of yours is just too heavy for you to bear." The tortoise stuck his head out of his shell again.

"Well, there you are," said the hare as he looked the tortoise in the eye. "What do you say, is it a race?"

The tortoise looked the hare up and down. "I meet your challenge, sir," he said.

So a time and place for the race was agreed.

The hare began the race, but soon after lay down by the roadside to rest. The tortoise, however, persevered and crossed the finish line first. "I won, I won," he called back to the napping hare.

Moral: *He Who Rests Assured On His Laurels Is Often Overtaken By A Plodder.*

Notice that at no point in the last version did you actually enter into the thoughts or feelings of either of the characters.

In order to solidify your conceptualization of the narrative point of view, imagine you are flying in an airplane that suddenly experiences engine difficulty. The plane must make an emergency landing, and you escape from the crash unscathed. Now, how would you tell your friends about your close call? You would probably use the first-person point of view—you were directly involved in the events that occurred. On the other hand, if you were waiting at the airport and a close friend was in that airplane when it experienced difficulty, you might choose to tell the story from the point of view of a third person with limited omniscience. Your friend would serve as your sentient center.

If you were at the airport gathering research for a report to be given in class and suddenly heard news that a plane was about to crash-land, which angle of vision might you adopt in relating the story? If you acted as a newspaper reporter, you would present your story from the objective point of view. You would become a completely omniscient narrator only if you wished to hover inside the mind of each panicky occupant in the cabin, to share the desperate determination of the pilot, and to pace up and down the aisles with each fearful flight attendant. It is only with this point of view that you would be in a position to see and report on the true feelings, experiences, and behavior of all persons involved in the incident.

GETTING INVOLVED
Determining the Point of View

A. Check your understanding by selecting a recent news item such as a sports story or national or local event that caught your attention. Work individually or with others to tell the story from several of the following different points of view.

first person

omniscient third person

limited omniscient third person

objective third person

Be sure you select and maintain a point of view throughout the telling of the story.

B. Check your understanding by determining the type of narrative control found in each of the following passages from literary works.

■ HILLS LIKE WHITE ELEPHANTS ■

ERNEST HEMINGWAY

The hills across the valleys of the Ebro were long and white. On this side there was no shade and no trees and the station was between two lines of rails in the sun. Close against the side of the station there was the warm shadow of the building and a curtain, made of strings of bamboo beads, hung across the open door into the bar, to keep out the flies. The American and the girl with him sat at a table in the shade, outside the building. It was very hot and the express from Barcelona would come in forty minutes. It stopped at this junction for two minutes and went on to Madrid.

"What should we drink?" the girl asked. She had taken off her hat and put it on the table.

"It's pretty hot," the man said.

Let's drink beer."

"Dos cervezas," the man said into the curtain.

"Big ones?" a woman asked from the doorway.

"Yes. Two big ones."

The woman brought two glasses of beer and two felt pads. She put the felt pads and the beer glasses on the table and looked at the man and the girl. The girl was looking off at the line of hills. They were white in the sun and the country was brown and dry.

"They look like white elephants," she said.

"I've never seen one," the man drank his beer.

■ THE CARIBOO CAFE ■

HELENA MARIA VIRAMONTES

He's got lice. Probably from living in the detainers. Those are the rooms where they round up the children and make them work for their food. I saw them from the window. Their eyes are cut glass, and no one looks for sympathy. They take turns, sorting out the arms from the legs, heads from the torsos. Is that one your mother? one guard asks, holding a mummified head with eyes shut tighter than coffins. But the children no longer cry. They just continue sorting as if they were salvaging cans from a heap of trash. They do this until time is up and they drift into a tunnel, back to the womb of sleep, while a new group comes in. It is all very organized. I bite my fist to keep from retching. Please God, please don't let Geraldo be there.

For you see, they took Geraldo. By mistake, of course. It was my fault. I shouldn't have sent him out to fetch me a mango. But it was just to the corner. I didn't even bother to put his sweater on. I hear his sandals flapping against the gravel. I follow him with my eyes, see him scratching his buttocks when the wind picks up swiftly, as it often does at such unstable times, and I have to close the door.

The darkness becomes a serpent's tongue, swallowing us whole. It is the night of La Llorona. The women come up from the depths of sorrow to search for their children. I join them, frantic, desperate, and our eyes become scrutinizers, our bodies opiated with the scent of their smiles. Descending from door to door, the wind whips our faces. I hear the wailing of the women and know it to be my own. Geraldo is nowhere to be found.

Dawn is not welcomed. It is a drunkard wavering between consciousness and sleep. My life is fleeing, moving south towards the sea. My tears are now hushed and faint.

The boy, barely a few years older than Geraldo, lights a cigarette, rests it on the edge of his desk, next to all the other cigarette burns. The blinds are down to keep the room cool. Above him hangs a single bulb that shades and shadows his face in such a way as to mask his expressions. He is not to be trusted. He fills in the information, for I cannot write. Statements delivered, we discuss motives.

''Spies,'' says he, flicking a long burning ash from the cigarette onto the floor, then wolfing the smoke in as if his lungs had an unquenchable thirst for nicotine. ''We arrest spies. Criminals.'' He says this with cigarette smoke spurting out from his nostrils like a nosebleed.

"Spies? Criminals?" My shawl falls to the ground. "He is only five and a half years old." I plead for logic with my hands. "What kind of crimes could a five-year-old commit?"

"Anyone who so willfully supports the contras in any form must be arrested and punished without delay." He knows the line by heart.

I think about moths and their stupidity. Always attracted by light, they fly into fires, or singe their wings with the heat of the single bulb and fall on his desk, writhing in pain. I don't understand why nature has been so cruel as to prevent them from feeling warmth. He dismisses them with a sweep of a hand. "This," he continues, "is what we plan to do with the contras, and those who aid them." He inhales again.

"But, Señor, he's just a baby."

"Contras are tricksters. They exploit the ignorance of people like you. Perhaps they convinced your son to circulate pamphlets. You should be talking to them, not us." The cigarette is down to his yellow fingertips, to where he can no longer continue to hold it without burning himself. He throws the stub on the floor, crushes it under his boot. "This," he says, screwing his boot into the ground, "is what the contras do to people like you."

"Señor. I am a washerwoman. You yourself see I cannot read or write. There is my X. Do you think my son can read?" How can I explain to this man that we are poor, that we live as best we can? "If such a thing has happened, perhaps he wanted to make a few centavos for his mamá. He's just a baby."

"So you are admitting his guilt?"

"So you are admitting he is here?" I promise, once I see him, hold him in my arms again, I will never, never scold him for wanting more than I can give. "You see, he needs his sweater . . ." The sweater lies limp on my lap.

"Your assumption is incorrect."

"May I check the detainers for myself?"

"In time."

"And what about my Geraldo?"

"In time." He dismisses me, placing the forms in a big envelope crinkled by the day's humidity.

"When?" I am wringing the sweater with my hands.

"Don't be foolish, woman. Now off with your nonsense. We will try to locate your Pedro."

"Geraldo."

■ METAMORPHOSIS ■

FRANZ KAFKA

As Gregor Samsa awoke one morning from uneasy dreams he found himself transformed in his bed into a gigantic insect. He was lying on his hard, as it were armor-plated, back, and when he lifted his head a little he could see his dome-like belly divided into stiff arched segments on top of which the bed quilt could hardly keep in position and was about to slide off completely. His numerous legs, which were pitifully thin compared to the rest of his bulk, waved helplessly before his eyes.

What happened to me? he thought. It was no dream. His room, a regular human bedroom, only rather too small, lay quiet between the four familiar walls. . . .

Gregor's eyes turned next to the window, and the overcast sky—one could hear raindrops beating on the window gutter—made him melancholy. What about sleeping a little longer and forgetting all this nonsense, he thought, but it could not be done, for he was accustomed to sleeping on his right side, and in his present condition he could not turn himself over.

■ HOW LIGHT BELIEF ■
BRINGETH DAMAGE

BIDPAI

Two skillful thieves one night entered the house of a wealthy knight, no less wise than worshipped in the community. The gentleman, hearing the noise of their feet in the house, awakened and suspected that they were thieves. They were upon the point of opening the door of the chamber wherein he lay, when he jogged his wife, awakened her, and whispered, ''I hear the noise of thieves who have come to rob us. I would have you, therefore, ask me straight, and with great insistence, whence and by what means I came by all I own. Ask me loudly and earnestly, and, as I shall appear reluctant, you must plead and whiddle until, at length, I shall succumb and tell you.'' The Lady, his wife, being wise and subtle, began in this manner to question her husband—''O, dear sir. Grant me one thing this night that I have for so long desired to know. Tell me how you have come by all these goods you now possess.'' He, speaking at random and carelessly, scarce answered. Finally, after she kept pleading, he said, ''I can but wonder, Madam, at what moves you to know my secrets. Be contented then, to live well, to dress well, and to be waited upon and served. I have heard that all things have ears, and that many things are spoken which are later repented. Therefore, I pray you, hold your peace.''

But even this did not deter the Lady. Sweetly and lovingly enticing, she besought him to tell her. Finally, wearying of her speech, the knight said, ''All we have—and I charge you to say nothing of this to anyone—is stolen. Indeed, of all I own I got nothing truly.'' The Lady, unbelieving, so berated her husband that he answered farther, ''You think what I have already told you is a wonder. Listen then. Even in my cradle, I delighted in stealing and filching. And I lived among thieves so that my fingers might never be idle. One friend among them loved me so well that he taught me a rare and singular trick. He taught me a conjuration which I made to the moonbeams—enabling me to embrace them suddenly. Thus I sometimes came down upon them from a high window—or served myself with them to go up again to the top of the house. So I used them as I would. The Moon, hearing my conjuration seven times, showed me all the money and treasure of the house and with her beams I flew up and down. And thus, good wife, I made me rich. Now, no more.''

One of the thieves, listening at the door, heard all that was said and bore it away. Because the knight was known to be a man of credit and integrity, the thieves believed his story. The chief thief, desirous to prove in deeds what he had heard in words, repeated the conjuration seven times, and then, embracing the moonbeams, he cast himself upon them thinking to go from window to window, and he fell headlong to the ground. The Moon, however, favored him so that he was not killed, but broke his legs and one arm. He cried aloud in his pain and at his stupidity in trusting too much to another's words.

In short, the ''teller'' of a story may be designated as ''I'' and speak from the first-person point of view. He or she may be either a fully revealed character or a minor character. The third-person point of view may reside in either an omniscient, all-seeing, faceless narrator, or in a narrator with a somewhat limited field of vision. In addition, a narrator may adopt an objective, rather than a subjective, perspective.

It is not unusual to find modern writers shifting their point of view during the course of a single story. Examine such a change in the next selection.

GETTING INVOLVED
Shifting Point of View

Determine where and why the author shifts his point of view in the following story.

■ My Son the Murderer ■
BERNARD MALAMUD

He wakes to a feeling his father is in the hallway, listening. Listening to what? Listening to him sleep and dream. To him get up and fumble for his pants. To him not going to the kitchen to eat. Staring with shut eyes in the mirror. Sitting an hour on the toilet. Flipping the pages of a book he can't read. To his rage, anguish, loneliness. The father stands in the hall. The son hears him listen.

My son the stranger, he tells me nothing.

I open the door and see my father in the hall.

Why are you standing there, why don't you go to work?

I took my vacation in the winter instead of the summer like I usually do.

What the hell for if you spend it in this dark smelly hallway watching my every move. Guessing for what you don't see. Why are you spying on me?

My father goes to his room and after a while comes out in the hallway again, listening.

I hear him sometimes in his room but he don't talk to me and I don't know what's what. It's a terrible feeling for a father. Maybe someday he'll write me a nice letter, My dear father. . . .

My dear son Harry, open up your door.

My son the prisoner.

My wife leaves in the morning to be with my married daughter who is having her fourth child. The mother cooks and cleans for her and takes care of the children. My daughter is having a bad pregnancy, with high blood pressure, and is in bed most of the time. My wife is gone all day. She knows something is wrong with Harry. Since he graduated college last summer he is nervous, alone, in his own thoughts. If you talk to him, half the time he yells. He reads the papers, smokes, stays in his room. Once in a while he goes for a walk.

How was the walk, Harry?

A walk.

My wife told him to go look for work and a few times he went, but when he got some kind of offer he didn't take the job.

It's not that I don't want to work. It's that I feel bad.

Why do you feel bad?

I feel what I feel. I feel what is.

Is it your health, sonny? Maybe you ought to go to a doctor?

Don't call me by that name. It's not my health. Whatever it is I don't want to talk about it. The work wasn't the kind I want.

So take something temporary in the meantime, she said.

He starts to yell. Everything is temporary. Why should I add more to what is already temporary? My guts feel temporary. The world is temporary. On top of that I don't want temporary work. I want the opposite of temporary, but where do you look for it? Where do you find it?

My father temporarily listens in the kitchen.

My temporary son.

She said I'd feel better if I work. I deny it. I'm twenty-two, since last December, a college graduate and you know where you can stick that. At night I watch the news broadcasts. I watch the war from day to day. It's a large war on a small screen. I sometimes lean over and touch the war with the flat of my hand. I'm waiting for my hand to die.

My son with the dead hand.

I expect to be drafted any day but it doesn't bother me so much anymore. I won't go. I'll go to Canada or somewhere, though the idea is a burden to me.

The way he is frightens my wife and she is glad to go off to my daughter's house in the morning to take care of the three children. I'm left alone, but he don't talk to me.

You ought to call up Harry and talk to him, my wife says to my daughter.

I will sometimes, but don't forget there's nine years difference between our ages. I think he thinks of me as another mother around and one is enough. I used to like him, but it's hard to deal with a person who won't reciprocate.

She's got high blood pressure. I think she's afraid to call.

I took two weeks off from work. I'm a clerk at the stamps window in the Post Office. I told the superintendent I wasn't feeling so good, which is no lie, and he said I should take sick leave, but I said I wasn't that sick. I told my friend Moe Berk I was staying out because Harry had me worried.

I know what you mean, Leo. I got my own worries and anxieties about my kids. If you have two girls growing up you got hostages to fortune. Still in all, we got to live. Will you come to poker Friday night? Don't deprive yourself of a good form of relaxation.

I'll see how I feel by then, how it's coming. I can't promise.

Try to come. These things all pass away. If it looks better to you, come on over. Even if it don't look so good, come on over anyway because it might relieve the tension and worry that you're under. It's not good for your heart at your age if you carry that much worry around.

This is the worst kind of worry. If I worry about myself I know what the worry is. What I mean, there's no mystery. I can say to myself, Leo, you're a fool, stop worrying over nothing—over what, a few bucks? Over my health that always stood up pretty good although I've had my ups and downs? Over that I'm now close to sixty and not getting any younger? Everybody that don't die by age fifty-nine gets to be sixty. You can't beat time if it's crawling after you. But if the worry is about somebody else, that's the worst kind. That's the real worry because if he won't tell you, you can't get inside the other person and find out why. You don't know where's the switch to turn off. All you can do is worry more.

So I wait in the hallway.

Harry, don't worry about the war.

Don't tell me what to worry about.

Harry, your father loves you. When you were a little boy, every night when I came home you used to run to me. I picked you up and lifted you to the ceiling. You liked to touch it with your small hand.

I don't want to hear about that anymore. It's the very thing I don't want to hear about. I don't want to hear about when I was a child.

Harry, we live like strangers. All I'm saying is I remember better days. I remember when we weren't afraid to show we loved each other.

He says nothing.

Let me cook you an egg.

I don't want an egg. It's the last thing in the world I want.

So what do you want?

He put his coat on. He pulled his hat off the clothes tree and went downstairs into the street. Harry walked along Ocean Parkway in his long coat and creased brown hat. He knew his father was following him and it filled him with rage.

He didn't turn around. He walked at a fast pace up the broad avenue. In the old days there was a bridle path at the side of the walk where the concrete bicycle path was now. And there were fewer trees now, their black branches cutting the sunless sky. At the corner of Avenue X just about where you begin to smell Coney Island, he crossed over and began to walk home. He pretended not to see his father cross over, although he was still infuriated. The father crossed over and followed his son home. When he got to the house he figured Harry was already upstairs. He was in his room with the door shut. Whatever he did in his room he was already doing.

Leo took out his key and opened the mailbox. There were three letters. He looked to see if one of them was by any chance, from his son to him. My dear father, let me explain myself. The reason I act as I do is. . . . But there was no such letter. One of the letters was from the Post Office Clerks Benevolent Society, which he put in his pocket. The other two letters were for his son. One was from the draft board. He brought it up to his son's room, knocked on the door and waited.

He waited for a while.

To the boy's grunt he said, There is a draft board letter for you. He turned the knob and entered the room. Harry was lying on the bed with his eyes shut.

You can leave it on the table.

Why don't you open it? Do you want me to open it for you?

No, I don't want you to open it. Leave it on the table. I know what's in it.

What's in it?

That's my business.

The father left it on the table.

The other letter to his son he took into the kitchen, shut the door and boiled up some water in a kettle. He thought he would read it quickly and then seal it carefully with a little paste so that none leaked over the edge of the flap, then go downstairs and put it back in the mailbox. His wife would take it out with her key when she returned from their daughter's house and bring it up to Harry.

The father read the letter. It was a short letter from a girl. The girl said Harry had borrowed two of her books more than six months ago and since she valued them highly she would like him to send them back to her. Could he do that as soon as possible so that she wouldn't have to write again?

As Leo was reading the girl's letter Harry came into the kitchen and when he saw the surprised and guilty look on his father's face, he tore the letter out of his hands.

I ought to kill you the way you spy on me.

Leo turned away, looking out of the small kitchen window into the dark apartment-house courtyard. His face was a mottled red, his eyes dull, and he felt sick.

Harry read the letter at a glance and tore it up. He then tore up the envelope marked personal.

If you do this again don't be surprised if I kill you. I'm sick of you spying on me.

Harry left the house.

Leo went into his room and looked around. He looked in the dresser drawers and found nothing unusual. On the desk by the window was a paper Harry had written on. It said: Dear Edith, If you write another such letter I'll murder you.

The father got his hat and coat and left the house. He ran for a while, running then walking, until he saw Harry on the other side of the street. He followed him a half block behind.

He followed Harry to Coney Island Avenue and was in time to see him board a trolleybus going toward the Island. Leo had to wait for the next bus. He thought of taking a taxi and following the bus, but no taxi came by. The next bus came by fifteen minutes later and he took it all the way to the Island. It was February and Coney Island was cold and deserted. There were few cars on Surf Avenue and few people on the streets. It looked like snow. Leo walked on the boardwalk, amid snow flurries, looking for his son. The grey sunless beaches were empty. The hot-dog stands, shooting galleries, and bathhouses were shuttered up. The gunmetal ocean, moving like melted lead, looked freezing. There was a wind off the water and it worked its way into his clothes so that he shivered as he walked. The wind white-capped the leaden waves and the slow surf broke on the deserted beaches with a quiet roar.

He walked in the blow almost to Sea Gate, searching for his son, and then walked back. On his way toward Brighton he saw a man on the beach standing in the foaming surf. Leo went down the boardwalk stairs and onto the ribbed-sand beach. The man on the shore was Harry, standing in water up to his ankles.

Leo ran to his son. Harry, it was my mistake, excuse me. I'm sorry I opened your letter.

Harry did not turn. He stayed in the water, his eyes on the leaden waves.

Harry, I'm frightened. Tell me what's the matter. My son, have mercy on me.

It's not my kind of world, Harry thought. It fills me with terror.

He said nothing.

A blast of wind lifted his father's hat off his head and carried it away over the beach. It looked as if it were going to land in the surf but then the wind blew it toward the boardwalk, rolling like a wheel along the ground. Leo chased after his hat. He chased it one way, then another, then toward the water. The wind blew the hat against his legs and he caught it. He pulled the freezing hat down tight on his head until it bent his ears. By now he was crying. Breathless, he wiped his eyes with icy fingers and returned to his son at the edge of the water.

He is a lonely man. This is the type he is, Leo thought. He will always be lonely.

My son who became a lonely man.

Harry, what can I say to you? All I can say to you is who says life is easy? Since when? It wasn't for me and it isn't for you. It's life, what more can I say? But if a person don't want to live what can he do if he's dead? If he doesn't want to live, maybe he deserves to die.

Come home, Harry, he said. It's cold here. You'll catch a cold with your feet in the water.

Harry stood motionless and after a while his father left. As he was leaving, the wind plucked his hat off his head and sent it rolling along the sand.

My father stands in the hallway. I catch him reading my letter. He follows me at a distance in the street. We meet at the edge of the water. He is running after his hat.

My son stands with his feet in the ocean.

Why Is the Narrator So Important?

Why is it important for a performer of literature to understand the role the narrator plays in a story? As oral readers, you must use this information to help you know when to adjust your tone, attitude, and degree of openness. Only by making adaptations will a performance be truly effective.

As a performer, you should think of yourself as similar to a moving television camera. Why? An interpreter has the ability psychologically and physically to back up and look at a scene from a distance, or to pan in for a close-up of one particular individual or event. You can view a scene through the eyes of a single character. Or, like a television camera, you can *juxtapose two images* and allow your audience to attain the subjective vision of a number of characters. If you think of your job as interpreter as functioning as a television camera, you will not allow yourself to become static; instead, you will move smoothly and efficiently through the varied incidents of your story, adjusting your focus as needed.

GETTING INVOLVED
I Am a Camera

Close one eye. Now cup your hand into a cylinder shape and hold it over the other eye. The opening in your hand represents your camera lens. Using that opening, scan the entire room. Experiment with the concept by making the "lens" wider and more narrow.

Reflections

1. How many different objects or people can you fit into your camera's eye during a single shot?

2. What happens to your field of vision if you back up? if you move in for a close-up?

3. Why does an experienced camera operator usually vary the number of long or short shots?

4. How do you think this variation could affect the detailing of a story?

Narrative Prose Presentation Techniques

As an interpreter, you sometimes speak directly to your audience as if you were the narrator, while at other times you allow this narrator to disappear for a while and permit your audience to hear the story's characters speak. Adapting your perspective in a manner such as this is a crucial aspect of performance. There are other techniques you will need to master, as well. You should be able to communicate those portions of your selection that are predominantly **scene**, that is, those primarily written in dialogue form. The units of the story that are treated as scene give you the greatest opportunity to suggest and delineate the characters in the story. Unless both you and your audience are aware of the type of people involved in the action of your story, the material will not come alive fully. Let's examine some techniques that you can use to re-create a character.

What should you, as interpretative performer, consider when deciding how to play a character? What methods or strategies do you think you could use to help suggest the qualities of the people who reside in the imaginary world of your selection? Begin by seeking to build in your mind an image of each character you have to interpret. Try this now.

GETTING INVOLVED
Image Building

Read the following literary excerpts, concentrating on the character pictures that emerge.

■ THE GOD-SEEKER ■
SINCLAIR LEWIS

The reverend Mr. Chippler, who had organized the revival which would wind up this afternoon, was a leaping little man, fuller of friendliness, optimism, go, zip, imagination, ingenuity, cheeriness and oratory than the nobler and slower animals. In joy over his camp meeting, he was jammed with exuberant wrath at sinners, this bountiful June morning. His text was from Job: "For the arrows of the Almighty are within me, the poison whereof drinketh up my spirit: the terrors of God do set themselves in array against me."

■ THE ADVENTURES OF ■ HUCKLEBERRY FINN
MARK TWAIN

Well, I got a good going-over in the morning from old Miss Watson on account of my clothes; but the widow she didn't scold, but only cleaned off the grease and clay, and looked so sorry that I thought I would behave awhile if I could. Then Miss Watson she took me in the closet and prayed, but nothing came of it. She told me to pray every day, and whatever I asked for I would get it. But it warn't so. I tried it. Once I got a fish-line but no hooks; it warn't any good to me without hooks. I tried for the hooks three or four times, but somehow I couldn't make it work. By and by, one day, I asked Miss Watson to try for me, but she said I was a fool. She never told me why, and I couldn't make it out no way.

■ SOAP AND WATER ■

ANZIA YEZIERSKA

What I so greatly feared, happened! Miss Whiteside, the dean of our college, withheld my diploma. When I came to her office, and asked her why she did not pass me, she said that she could not recommend me as a teacher because of my personal appearance.

She told me that my skin looked oily, my hair unkempt, and my fingernails sadly neglected. She told me that I was utterly unmindful of the little niceties of the well-groomed lady. She pointed out that my collar did not set evenly, my belt was awry, and there was a lack of freshness in my dress. And she ended with: "Soap and water are cheap. Anyone can be clean."

In those four years while I was under her supervision, I was always timid and diffident. I shrank and trembled when I had to come near her. When I had to say something to her, I mumbled and stuttered, and grew red and white in the face with fear.

Every time I had to come to the dean's office for a private conference, I prepared for the ordeal of her cold scrutiny, as a patient prepares for a surgical operation. I watched her gimlet eyes searching for a stray pin, for a spot on my dress, for my unpolished shoes, for my uncared-for fingernails, as one strapped on the operating table watches the surgeon approaching with his tray of sterilized knives.

She never looked into my eyes. She never perceived that I had a soul. She did not see how I longed for beauty and cleanliness. How I strained and struggled to lift myself from the dead toil and exhaustion that weighed me down. She could see nothing in people like me, except the dirt and the stains on the outside.

But this last time, when she threatened to withhold my diploma because of my appearance, this last time when she reminded me that "Soap and water are cheap. Anyone can be clean," this last time, something burst within me.

I felt the suppressed wrath of all the unwashed of the earth break loose within me. My eyes blazed fire. I didn't care for myself, nor the dean, nor the whole laundered world. I had suffered the cruelty of their cleanliness and the tyranny of their culture to the breaking point. I was too frenzied to know what I said or did. But I saw clean, immaculate, spotless Miss Whiteside shrivel and tremble and cower before me, as I had shriveled and trembled and cowered before her for so many years.

Why did she give me my diploma? Was it pity? Or can it be that in my outburst of fury, at the climax of indignities that I had suffered, the barriers broke, and she saw into the world below from where I came?

■ TEARS, IDLE TEARS ■

ELIZABETH BOWEN

Frederick burst into tears in the middle of Regent's Park. His mother, seeing what was about to happen, had cried: "Frederick, you can't—in the middle of Regent's Park!" Frederick, knees trembling, butted towards his mother a crimson convulsed face, as though he had the idea of burying himself in her. She whipped out a handkerchief and dabbed at him with it under his grey felt hat, exclaiming meanwhile in fearful mortification: "You really haven't got to be such a baby!" Her tone attracted the notice of several people, who might otherwise have thought he was having something taken out of his eye.

He was too big to cry: the whole scene was disgraceful. He wore a grey flannel knickerbocker suit and looked like a schoolboy; though in fact he was seven, still doing lessons at home. . . . His tears were a shame of which she could speak to no one; no offensive weakness of body could have upset her more.

■ SLIPPING BEAUTY ■

JEROME WEIDMAN

He was a little man with an untidy beard and a prominent paunch that seemed startlingly out of place because of his emaciated appearance. Winter and summer he wore a battered cap, a leather vest, and a look of indifferent resignation, well seasoned with disgust, that gave no hint of the almost violent loquacity he could attain without even a moment of preparation. In a world of trucks and automobiles he drove a flat, open wagon behind a huge, drooping horse. And although his seltzer bottles came in neatly cased boxes of ten, he preferred to carry them by their spouts, five in each hand, like clusters of grapes, and take his chances on opening doors with shoulder shoves and kicks.

■ A Worn Path ■

EUDORA WELTY

It was December—a bright frozen day in the early morning. Far out in the country there was an old Negro woman with her head tied in a red rag, coming along a path through the pinewoods. Her name was Phoenix Jackson. She was very old and small and she walked slowly in the dark pine shadows, moving a little from side to side in her steps, with the balanced heaviness and lightness of a pendulum in a grandfather clock. She carried a thin, small cane made from an umbrella, and with this she kept tapping the frozen earth in front of her. This made a grave and persistent noise in the air that seemed meditative, like the chirping of a solitary little bird. . . . Everytime she took a step she might have fallen over her shoelaces, which dragged from her unlaced shoes. She looked straight ahead. Her eyes were blue with age. . . . Now and then there was a quivering in the thicket. Old Phoenix said, ''Out of my way, all you foxes, owls, beetles, jack rabbits, coons, and wild animals! Keep out from under these feet.'' The path ran up a hill. ''Seems like there is chains about my feet, time I get this far,'' she said, in the voice of argument old people keep to use with themselves. ''Something always takes a hold of me on this hill—pleads I should stay.''

■ The Bride Comes to ■
Yellow Sky

STEPHEN CRANE

A man in a maroon-colored flannel shirt rounded a corner and walked into the middle of the main street of Yellow Sky. In either hand the man held a long, heavy, blue-black revolver. Often he yelled, and these cries rang through a semblance of a deserted village, shrilly flying over the roofs in a volume that seemed to have no relation to the ordinary vocal strength of a man. It was as if the surrounding stillness formed the arch of a tomb over him. These cries of ferocious challenge rang against the walls of silence. . . .

The man's face flamed in a rage begot of whisky. His eyes, rolling, and yet keen for ambush, hunted the still doorways and windows. He walked with the creeping movement of the midnight cat. As it occurred to him, he roared menacing information.

Reflections

Now try to demonstrate your feel for each of the described characters by responding to the following prompts. Work on only one character sketch at a time.

A. Draw a line graph that represents your feel for the character's way of moving. For example, do you perceive this particular character as tense? Does he or she have sudden spurts of activity? If so, your graph might look something like this:

On the other hand, if you see your character as graceful and fluid, the graph you draw might resemble this one:

Also, draw a line graph that represents your feel for your own way of moving. How do these graphs differ?

B. Move across the room as you believe your personal graph directs you to move.

C. Now, move as you believe your character's graph directs. What movement adaptation must you make to embody the character? Allow your body to show what your mind has conceptualized or perceived about your character's rhythm in motion.

D. Create a mood simile to represent the character you are describing. In other words, how would you complete the following sentence:

"This character is like a _____."

Try to determine what you associate with this specific character. If he or she were a particularly dull individual, he or she might remind you of mashed potatoes without salt. What does the character make you feel or make you want to do?

Create a mood simile to represent your own feelings about yourself. What performance adaptation does this call for you to make?

E. Now, put an imaginary mask on your face; this mask should symbolically represent your view of your character's face and attitude toward life. Can you allow your face to help you experience this?

F. Stand as your character would stand; walk as you imagine your character would walk. Are you allowing yourself to see your character with your arms and legs as well as with your eyes?

G. Try to contact the person next to you by using the letters or sounds of the alphabet to suggest the tone of voice, speaking rate, and vocal quality you perceive your character has. How did your voice sound?

These exercises are part of your rehearsal repertoire for any character you perform. If you use them properly, they will allow you to share in the physical and mental world of various fictional characters. The system suggested above should permit you to know the character you choose to interpret with your whole being, rather than with only your mind.

Revealing Characters to Audiences

Having clarified the image of a particular character for yourself while rehearsing, how will you reveal this character to your audience during performance? First, you can use all the affective and cognitive information you gained during your rehearsal sessions. Use *visible action* to suggest your character's traits or moods. Indicate speech habits by *changing your own voice pattern*. Use *muscle memory* to convey your character's degree of tension or relaxation.

Keep in mind that many times an oral interpreter will be called on to assume more than one character during a single presentation. Thus, another technique we have not yet mentioned might also prove useful to you. It is certainly a convention about which all beginning interpreters should be aware, and it is termed **character placement.** The following passage and diagram will help explain this tool.

■ A VISIT OF CHARITY ■

EUDORA WELTY

Marian stood enclosed by a bed, a washstand, and a chair; the tiny room had altogether too much furniture. Everything smelled wet—even the bare floor. She held onto the back of the chair, which was wicker and felt soft and damp. Her heart beat more and more slowly, her hands got colder and colder, and she could not hear whether the old women were saying anything or not. She could not see them very clearly. How dark it was! The window shade was down, and the only door was shut. Marian looked at the ceiling. . . . It was like being caught in a robber's cave, just before one was murdered.

"Did you come to be our little girl for a while?" the first robber asked.

Then something was snatched from Marian's hand—the little potted plant.

"Flowers!" screamed the old woman. She stood holding the pot in an undecided way. "Pretty flowers," she added.

Then the old woman in bed cleared her throat and spoke. "They are not pretty," she said, still without looking around, but very distinctly.

Marian suddenly pitched against the chair and sat down in it.

"Pretty flowers," the first woman insisted. "Pretty—pretty. . . ."

Marian wished she had the little pot back for just a moment—she had forgotten to look at the plant herself before giving it away. What did it look like?

"Stinkweeds," said the other woman sharply.

Now, study the character placement diagram below.

The diagram demonstrates how the interpreter can use *placement* to create the illusion that more than one speaker is involved in the performed reading. When re-creating a selection in which more than one character speaks, the interpreter simply *establishes his or her eye focus for each character at a specific position on the back wall of the performing area.*

For example, whenever Old Lady #1 speaks, the interpreter's angle of address would be along the line labeled #1; when the speaker looks along this position, he or she is Old Lady #1 and no one else. Likewise, when Old Lady #2 converses, the interpreter's angle of address would now move along the line labeled #2. Similar adaptations would be made for each additional character. The interpreter must concentrate on keeping the essential locations of each character clear, but at the same time he or she must *be careful not to exaggerate the shift in eye focus* in moving from one character to another.

Using this performance technique, you will make it clear which character is speaking, thus helping your audience to differentiate one character from another. Even more significant, however, is that in choosing a concentrated location, you can imagine the character whom you are addressing at that moment. The audience, too, will learn to expect a character to direct his or her words to a specifically defined area.

Though this technique is not as subtle as others we have explored thus far, do not underestimate its value. Be careful, however, not to overemphasize your changes in eye focus: avoid a ''tennis match.'' Overly wide visual placement, as shown in the diagram below, will contribute to a back-and-forth effect. Try to be natural in your eye shifts. For best results, combine this strategy with those discussed previously to bring characters to life for your audience.

GETTING INVOLVED
Using Character Placement

Concentrating on character placement only, prepare to read one or more of the versions of ''Slow But Sure'' presented earlier in this chapter.

Reflections

1. What does your placement diagram look like?

2. In what ways does your approach differ from others created by your classmates?

Have you perfected your ability to create and suggest a character? Try the following activity to check your skills.

GETTING INVOLVED

Refining Character Suggestion

Bring to class a picture of an individual you find particularly interesting. This picture may be cut from a newspaper or magazine.

When you get to class, study the picture. Then, on a separate sheet of paper, write down the age you perceive the character in the picture to be. Also write down two or three adjectives you believe describe your character's personality or attitude—lazy, bored, furious, shy, or any other adjectives that seem appropriate.

Next, standing at the front of the room and using only the letters of the alphabet as your script and your body and your voice as instruments, communicate your image of your character to the audience. Remember, we are not using existing literature, so there is no need to focus on creating actual dialogue.

Reflections

1. What devices did the performer use to create his or her character?

2. How old do you believe the character was?

3. What do you believe to be this character's attitude toward life? What distinguishable traits does he or she have?

4. What adjectives describe the character? Do they correspond with those planned by the performer?

5. After seeing the picture of the character, how do you think the projected character image could have been further clarified or refined?

Keep in mind this situation is artificial, but useful for training. You should realize, however, that in performance your characters must be created from information the author supplies. Now, on to the next step. . . .

GETTING INVOLVED
Putting It All Together

Choose a selection of narrative prose to interpret before the class. If you wish, select one of those provided at the end of this chapter. Carefully rehearse your material, combining all the techniques you have learned thus far. Focus on the literature and prepare to give a really fine performance!

Performer's Journal

As you prepare your performance, write a brief analysis of your selection and interpretation of it as part of your Performer's Journal. Cover these questions.

1. Why did you choose this particular piece of literature? Why do you think it will appeal to your audience? Why is it worth your preparation time and effort?

2. What type of narrator is involved? What are the dominant ideas and actions within your selection?

3. What types of characters are included in your passage? How do the characters relate to each other?

4. What kind of posture will you assume? How and where will you stand? Draw a character placement diagram for your performance.

5. Describe the physical sensations you experienced during your rehearsal period. How can you use your body to help you express the literature?

6. As a result of your performance, what would you like your audience to feel, know, or imagine?

A Narrative Prose Trip

Have you ever been bothered or tormented by a little brother, sister, or other child? In this excerpt a Russian writer shows such annoyances are universal.

■ A WICKED BOY ■

ANTON CHEKHOV

Ivan Ivanych Lapkin, a young man of nice appearance, and Anna Semionovna Zamblitskaia, a young girl with a little turned-up nose, went down the steep bank and sat down on a small bench. The bench stood right by the water among some thick young osier bushes. What a wonderful little place! Once you'd sat down, you were hidden from the world—only the fish saw you, and the water-tigers, running like lightning over the water. The young people were armed with rods, nets, cans of worms, and other fishing equipment. Having sat down, they started fishing right away.

"I'm glad we're alone at last," Lapkin began, looking around. "I have to tell you a lot of things, Anna Semionovna . . . an awful lot . . . when I saw you the first time. . . . You've got a bite . . . when I saw you for the first time . . . then I understood what I'm living for, understood where my idol was— to whom I must devote my honest, active life . . . that must be a big one that's biting. . . . Seeing you, I feel in love for the first time, feel passionately in love! Wait before you give it a jerk . . . let it bite harder. . . . Tell me, my darling, I adjure you, may I count on—not on reciprocity, no! I'm not worthy of that, I dare not even think of that—may I count on . . . Pull!"

Anna Semionovna raised her hand with the rod in it, yanked, and cried out. A little silvery-green fish shimmered in the air.

"My Lord, a perch! Ah, ah. . . . Quickly! It's getting free!"

The perch got free of the hook, flopped through the grass toward its native element . . . and plopped into the water!

In pursuit of the fish, Lapkin somehow inadvertently grabbed Anna Semionovna's hand instead of the fish, inadvertently pressed it to his lips. . . . She quickly drew it back, but it was already too late; their mouths inadvertently merged in a kiss. It happened somehow inadvertently. Another kiss followed the first, then vows and protestations. . . . What happy minutes! However, in this earthly life there is no absolute happiness. Happiness usually carries a poison in itself, or else is poisoned by something from outside. So this time, too. As the young people were kissing, a laugh suddenly rang out. They glanced at the river and were stupefied: a naked boy was standing in the water up to his waist. This was Kolia, a schoolboy, Anna Semionovna's brother. He was standing in the water, staring at the young people and laughing maliciously.

"Ah-ah-ah . . . you're kissing?" he said. "That's great! I'll tell Mama."

"I hope that you, as an honest young man . . . ." muttered Lapkin, blushing. "It's low-down to spy, and to tell tales is foul and detestable. . . . I assume that you, as an honest and noble young man . . . ."

"Give me a ruble and then I won't tell!" said the noble young man. "Or else I will."

Lapkin pulled a ruble out of his pocket and gave it to Kolia. Kolia squeezed the ruble in his wet fist, whistled, and swam off. And the young people didn't kiss any more that time.

The next day Lapkin brought Kolia some paints and a ball from town, and his sister gave him all her empty pill-boxes. After that they had to give him some cuff-links with dogs' heads on them. The wicked boy obviously liked all these things very much and, in order to get still more, he started keeping his eye on them. Wherever Lapkin and Anna Semionovna went, he went too. He didn't leave them alone for a minute.

"The bastard!" Lapkin gnashed his teeth. "So little and already such a real bastard! What's he going to be like later?"

All through June, Kolia made life impossible for the poor lovers. He threatened to tell on them, kept his eye on them, and demanded presents; it all wasn't enough for him, and he finally started talking about a pocket watch. And what then? They had to promise the watch.

One time at dinner when the waffle cookies were being passed, he suddenly burst out in a guffaw, winked an eye, and asked Lapkin:

"Shall I tell? Huh?"

Lapkin blushed terribly and started eating his napkin instead of the cookie. Anna Semionovna jumped up from the table and ran into the other room.

And the young people found themselves in this position until the end of August, until the very day when, at last Lapkin proposed to Anna Semionovna. Oh what a happy day that was! Having talked to the parents of his bride, and having received their consent, Lapkin first of all ran out into the garden and started looking for Kolia. Once he had found him, he almost sobbed from delight and seized the wicked boy by the ear. Anna Semionovna, who had also been looking for Kolia, ran up, and seized him by the other ear. And you really ought to have seen what joy was written all over the lovers' faces as Kolia cried and begged them:

"Dearest, darling, angels, I'll never do it again! Ow, ow! Forgive me!"

And afterwards they both admitted that during the whole time they had been in love with each other they had never once felt such happiness, such breath-taking bliss as during those moments when they were pulling the wicked boy's ears.

Meeting new people socially is sometimes difficult. In "The Waltz," Dorothy Parker showed that the dance can add to the difficulties.

■ THE WALTZ ■

DOROTHY PARKER

Why, thank you so much. I'd adore to.

I don't want to dance with him. I don't want to dance with anybody. And even if I did, it wouldn't be him. . . . Just think, not a quarter of an hour ago, here I was sitting, feeling so sorry for the poor girl he was dancing with. And now I'm going to be the poor girl . . .

And I had to go and tell him that I'd adore to dance with him. I cannot understand why I wasn't struck dead. Yes, and being struck dead would look like a day in the country, compared to struggling out a dance with this boy. But what could I do? Everyone else at the table had got up to dance, except him and me. There I was, trapped. Trapped like a trap in a trap.

What can you say, when a man asks you to dance with him? . . . Oh, yes, *do* let's dance together—it's so nice to meet a man who isn't a scaredy-cat about catching my beriberi. No. There was nothing for me to do, but say I'd adore to . . .

Why, I think it's more of a waltz, really. Isn't it? We might just listen to the music a second. Shall we? Oh yes, it's a waltz. Mind? Why, I'm simply thrilled. I'd love to waltz with you.

I'd love to waltz with you. I'd love to waltz with you. I'd love to have my tonsils out, I'd love to be in a midnight fire at sea. Well, it's too late now. We're getting under way. *Oh.* Oh, dear. Oh, dear, dear, dear. Oh, this is even worse than I thought it would be. I suppose that's the one dependable law of life—everything is always worse than you thought it was going to be. Oh, if I had any real grasp of what this dance would be like, I'd have held out for sitting it out. Well, it will probably amount to the same thing in the end. We'll be sitting it out on the floor in a minute if he keeps this up . . .

Why can't we stay in one place just long enough to get acclimated? It's this constant rush, rush, rush, that's the curse of American life. That's the reason that we're all of us so—*OW!* For heaven's sake don't *kick,* you idiot, this is only the second down. Oh, my shin. My poor shin that I've had ever since I was a little girl!

Oh, no, no, no. Goodness no. It didn't hurt the least little bit. And anyway it was my fault. Really it was. Truly. Well, you're just being sweet, to say that. It really was all my fault.

I wonder what I'd better do—kill him this instant, with my naked hands, or wait and let him drop in his traces. Maybe it's best not to make a scene . . .

Maybe he didn't do it maliciously. Maybe it's just his way of showing his high spirits. I suppose I ought to be glad that one of us is having such a good time. I suppose I ought to think myself lucky if he brings me back alive . . .

Yes, it's lovely, isn't it? It's simply lovely. It's the loveliest waltz. Isn't it. Oh, I think it's lovely, too.

OW! Get off my instep, you hulking peasant! What do you think I am, anyway—a gangplank? *OW!*

No, of course it didn't hurt. Why, it didn't a bit. Honestly. And it was my fault. You see that little step of yours—well, it's perfectly lovely, but it's just a tiny bit tricky to follow at first. Oh, did you work it up yourself? You really did? Well, aren't you amazing! Oh, now I think I've got it. Oh, I think it's lovely. I was watching you do it when you were dancing before. It's awfully effective when you look at it.

It's awfully effective when you look at it. I bet I'm awfully effective when you look at me. My hair is hanging along my cheeks, my skirt is swaddled about me, I can feel the cold damp of my brow. I must look like something out of the "Fall of the House of Usher." Is that orchestra never going to stop playing? Or must this obscene travesty of a dance go on until hell burns out?

Oh, they're going to play another encore. Oh, goody. Oh, that's lovely. Tired? I should say I'm not tired. I'd like to go on like this forever.

I should say I'm not tired. I'm dead, that's all I am. . . . I wonder why I didn't tell him I was tired. I wonder why I didn't suggest going back to the table. . . .

Still, if we were back at the table, I'd probably have to talk to him. Look at him—what could you say to a thing like that! Did you go to the circus this year, what's your favorite kind of ice cream, how do you spell *cat*? I guess I'm as well off here. As well off as if I were in a cement mixer in full action.

I'm past feeling now. The only way I can tell when he steps on me is that I can hear the splintering of bones. And all the events of my life are passing before my eyes. There was a time I was in a hurricane in the West Indies, there was the day I got my head cut open in the taxi smash, there was the night the drunken lady threw a bronze ash tray at her own true love and got me instead, there was that summer that the sailboat kept capsizing. Ah, what an easy, peaceful time was mine, until I fell in with Swifty, here. . . . I think my mind is beginning to wander. It almost seems to me as if the orchestra were stopping. It couldn't be, of course; it could never be. . . .

Oh, they've stopped, the mean things. They're not going to play any more. Oh, darn. Oh, do you think they would? Do you really think so, if you gave them twenty dollars? Oh, that would be lovely. And look, do tell them to play this same thing. I'd simply adore to go on waltzing.

Is it ever appropriate to fabricate a story or situation? In "Snake Dance," Jerry thinks that he must do just that. What do you think?

■ SNAKE DANCE ■
COREY FORD

"Hello. That you, Mom? . . . Oh, I'm sorry, operator, I thought I was connected with . . . No, I'm trying to get long distance . . . What? Centerville, Ohio, ring five. I told that other operator . . . What? . . . I *am* holding it."

He fished nervously in his pocket for a pack of cigarettes, pulled one cigarette out of the pack with his thumb and forefinger, and stuck it swiftly between his lips. He glanced at his watch and scowled. The game had been over for half an hour. The snake dance would be coming down the street this way any minute now. With his free hand he tore a match from the paper safe, and propped the telephone receiver for a moment between shoulder and ear while he struck the match on the flap. As he put the match to the tip of the cigarette, a thin voice rasped vaguely inside the receiver, and he whipped out the match.

"Hello. Mom? . . . Oh, I'm sorry," he mumbled. "How much?" He took a handful of silver from his pocket and began to drop the coins into the slot of the pay telephone. He could hear someone speaking above the echoing reverberations inside the phone.

"What? Oh, Mom? Hello, Mom. This is Jerry. I say, this is—Can you hear me now? . . . Sure, I can hear you fine . . . Sure, I'm all right. I'm fine. And you? . . . That's fine.

"Mom"—and his voice seemed to falter for a fraction of a second. Then: "How is he? Is there any change?"

There was a tiny silence.

"Oh." His voice was a little duller when he spoke again. "I see. Yeh. This afternoon, eh? And that other specialist, he said the same thing? Um-hummm . . . Oh, sure, sure. No, of course, Mom, there's nothing to worry about. No, I'm not worried; I only just called to find out if there was any change, that was all. . . . Did they say he could ever—I mean, can he move his arms any yet?" He gulped. "Well, that doesn't mean anything, really . . . No, of course, all those things take time. Sure, a year, maybe less . . . What?"

He took a second cigarette out of his pocket and thrust it between his lips nervously. He lit it from the stub of the first one and ground out the stub beneath his heel.

"What money? Oh, you mean I sent you last week? Now, Mom," impatiently, "I told you all about that already in the letter, didn't I? . . . Sure it's a scholarship. I got it for playing football. And so naturally I didn't need all that money you and Pop had been saving up for me to go to college, and so I just thought maybe with Pop being laid up now for a while and all . . .

"Where? Why right here." He frowned. "No, this isn't exactly a dormitory; it's—I live here in the fraternity house, you see. Sure I'm in a fraternity. It's the one Pop wanted me to join, too, tell him . . . No, honest, Mom, it doesn't cost me a cent for my room. It's on account of my football."

He opened the folding door a little. He thought he could hear the band in the distance.

"Who, me? Homesick? Not so you'd notice it." He laughed. "I'm having the time of my life here. Everybody's so swell. I know practically everybody here at Dover already. They even call me by my first name. Say, if you don't think I'm sitting pretty, you ought to see my fraternity house here." He gazed out through the glass door of the phone booth.

"Every night the fellows sit around and we . . . go down to Semple's for a milk shake . . . No, that's only the drugstore . . . No." He smiled slowly. "I promised you I wouldn't drink, Mom."

In the distance now he could hear the sound of the band approaching.

"Well, Mom, I gotta hang up now. The gang'll be here in a minute. We're having a celebration after the game today. We played Alvord—took 'em sixteen to nothing. . . . Sure I did, the whole game; you oughta seen me in there. I made two touchdowns. Everybody's going down to Semple's after the game, and I gotta be ready, because of course they'll all want me to be there too. Can you hear the band now?"

It was growing louder, and the eager voices in the snake dance could be heard above the brasses, chanting the score of the game in time with the band.

"Now, listen, Mom. One other thing before they get here. Mom, see, I'm going to be sending you about ten or twelve dollars or so each week from now on until Pop is better. . . . No, Mom. Heck, I got plenty. Sure they always fix you up with a soft job if you're a good enough player. The alumni do it. . . . Here they are now. Hear them?"

The band had halted outside. Someone led a cheer.

"That's for me, Mom. . . . Sure. Didn't I practically win the game for them today? Hear that?" He kicked open the door of the phone booth.

He held the receiver toward the open door of the phone booth. They were calling, ''Jerry! Hey Jerry, hang up on that babe!''

''Hear that, Mom? Now goodby. And look, by the way, if you should ever happen to see Helen,'' he added carelessly, ''tell her I couldn't ask her up to the freshman dance like I planned, but with the football season and my scholarship and all—tell her, Mom. She—she didn't answer my last letter. O.K. Mom. Tell Pop everything's O.K., see? Now don't worry . . . , Bye.''

He replaced the receiver slowly on the hook and stared at the mouthpiece a moment. As he opened the door and stepped out of the booth, he could see his reflection for a moment in the tall mirror behind the soda fountain—the familiar white cap, the white jacket with ''Semple's'' stitched in red letters on the pocket. The crowd was lined along the soda fountain, shouting, ''Jerry!'' ''Milk shake, Jerry!''

American humorist James Thurber created Walter Mitty—a character who has come to symbolize daydreaming. Mitty is always lost in a dream. When was the last time you were drifting in a daydream?

■ THE SECRET LIFE OF ■ WALTER MITTY
JAMES THURBER

''We're going through!'' The Commander's voice was like thin ice breaking. He wore his full-dress uniform, with the heavily braided white cap pulled down rakishly over one cold gray eye. ''We can't make it, sir. It's spoiling for a hurricane, if you ask me.'' ''I'm not asking you, Lieutenant Berg,'' said the Commander. ''Throw on the power lights! Rev her up to 8,500! We're going through!'' The pounding of the cylinders increased; ta-pocketa-pocketa-pocketa-*pocketa-pocketa*. The Commander stared at the ice forming on the pilot window. He walked over and twisted a row of complicated dials. ''Switch on No. 8 auxiliary!'' he shouted. ''Switch on No. 8 auxiliary!'' repeated Lieutenant Berg. ''Full strength in No. 3 turret!'' shouted the Commander. ''Full strength in No. 3 turret!'' The crew, bending to their various tasks in the huge, hurtling eight-engined Navy hydroplane, looked at each other and grinned, ''The Old Man ain't afraid of Hell!'' . . .

"Not so fast! You're driving too fast!" said Mrs. Mitty. "What are you driving so fast for?"

"Hmm?" said Walter Mitty. He looked at his wife, in the seat beside him, with shocked astonishment. She seemed grossly unfamiliar, like a strange woman who had yelled at him in a crowd. "You were up to fifty-five," she said. "You know I don't like to go more than forty. You were up to fifty-five." Walter Mitty drove on toward Waterbury in silence, the roaring of the SN202 through the worst storm in twenty years of Navy flying fading in the remote, intimate airways of his mind. "You're tensed up again," said Mrs. Mitty. "It's one of your days. I wish you'd let Dr. Renshaw look you over."

Walter Mitty stopped the car in front of the building where his wife went to have her hair done. "Remember to get those overshoes while I'm having my hair done," she said. "I don't need overshoes," said Mitty. She put her mirror back into her bag. "We've been all through that," she said, getting out of the car. "You're not a young man any longer." He raced the engine a little. "Why don't you wear your gloves? Have you lost your gloves?" Walter Mitty reached in a pocket and brought out the gloves. He put them on, but after she had turned and gone into the building and he had driven on to a red light, he took them off again. "Pick it up brother!" snapped a cop as the light changed, and Mitty hastily pulled on his gloves and lurched ahead. He drove around the streets aimlessly for a time, and then he drove past the hospital on his way to the parking lot.

. . . "It's the millionaire banker, Wellington McMillan," said the pretty nurse. "Yes?" said Walter Mitty, removing his gloves slowly. "Who has the case?" "Dr. Renshaw and Dr. Benbow, but there are two specialists here, Dr. Remington from New York and Dr. Pritchard-Mitford from London. He flew over." A door opened down a long, cool corridor and Dr. Renshaw came out. He looked distraught and haggard. "Hello, Mitty," he said. "We're having the devil's own time with McMillan, the millionaire banker and close personal friend of Roosevelt. Obstreosis of the ductal tract. Tertiary. Wish you'd take a look at him." "Glad to," said Mitty.

In the operating room there were whispered introductions: "Dr. Remington, Dr. Mitty, Dr. Pritchard-Mitford, Dr. Mitty." "I've read your book on streptothricosis," said Pritchard-Mitford, shaking hands. "A brilliant performance, sir." "Thank you," said Walter Mitty. "Didn't know you were in the States, Mitty," grumbled Remington. "Coals to Newcastle, bringing Mitford and me up here for a tertiary." "You are very kind," said Mitty. A huge, complicated machine, connected to the operating table, with many tubes and wires, began at this moment to go pocketa-pocketa-pocketa. ''The new anaesthetizer is giving away!'' shouted an intern. ''There is no one in the East who knows how to fix it!'' ''Quiet, man!'' said Mitty, in a low, cool voice. He sprang to the machine, which was now going pocketa-pocketa-pocketa-queep-pocketa-queep. He began fingering delicately a row of glistening dials. ''Give me a fountain pen!'' he snapped. Someone handed him a fountain pen. He pulled a faulty piston out of the machine and inserted the pen in its place. ''That will hold for ten minutes,'' he said. ''Get on with the operation.'' A nurse hurried over and whispered to Renshaw, and Mitty saw the man turn pale. ''Coreopsis has set in,'' said Renshaw nervously. ''If you would take over, Mitty?'' Mitty looked at him and at the craven figure of Benbow, who drank, and at the grave, uncertain faces of the two great specialists. ''If you wish,'' he said. They slipped a white gown on him; he adjusted a mask and drew on thin gloves; nurses handed him shining . . . .

''Back it up, Mac! Look out for that Buick!'' Walter Mitty jammed on the brakes. ''Wrong lane, Mac,'' said the parking-lot attendant, looking at Mitty closely. ''Gee. Yeh,'' muttered Mitty. He began cautiously to back out of the lane marked ''Exit Only.'' ''Leave her sit there,'' said the attendant. ''I'll put her away.'' Mitty got out of the car. ''Hey, better leave the key.'' ''Oh,'' said Mitty, handing the man the ignition key. The attendant vaulted into the car, backed it up with insolent skill, and put it where it belonged.

They're so damn cocky, thought Walter Mitty, walking along Main Street; they think they know everything. Once he had tried to take his chains off, outside New Milford, and he had got them wound around the axles. A man had had to come out in a wrecking car and unwind them, a young, grinning garage man. Since then Mrs. Mitty always made him drive to a garage to have the chains taken off. The next time, he thought, I'll wear my right arm in a sling; they won't grin at me then. I'll have my right arm in a sling and they'll see I couldn't possibly take the chains off myself. He kicked at the slush on the sidewalk. ''Overshoes,'' he said to himself, and he began looking for a shoe store.

When he came out into the street again, with the overshoes in a box under his arm, Walter Mitty began to wonder what the other thing was his wife had told him to get. She had told him, twice before they set out from their house for Waterbury. In a way he hated these weekly trips to town— he was always getting something wrong. Kleenex, he thought, Squibb's, razor blades? No. Toothpaste, toothbrush, bicarbonate, carborundum, initiative and referendum? He gave it up. But she would remember it. "Where's the what's-its-name?" she would ask. "Don't tell me you forgot the what's-its-name." A newsboy went by shouting something about the Waterbury trial.

. . . "Perhaps this will refresh your memory." The District Attorney suddenly thrust a heavy automatic at the quiet figure on the witness stand. "Have you ever seen this before?" Walter Mitty took the gun and examined it expertly. "This is my Webley-Vickers 50.80," he said calmly. An excited buzz ran around the courtroom. The judge rapped for order. "You are a crack shot with any sort of firearms, I believe?" said the District Attorney, insinuatingly. "Objection!" shouted Mitty's attorney. "We have shown the defendant could not have fired the shot. We have shown that he wore his right arm in a sling on the night of the fourteenth of July." Walter Mitty raised his hand briefly and the bickering attorneys were stilled. "With any known make of gun," he said evenly, "I could have killed Gregory Fitzhurst at three hundred feet *with my left hand.*" Pandemonium broke loose in the courtroom. A woman's scream rose above the bedlam and suddenly a lovely, dark-haired girl was in Walter Mitty's arms. The District Attorney struck at her savagely. Without rising from his chair, Mitty let the man have it on the point of the chin. "You miserable cur!" . . .

"Puppy biscuit," said Walter Mitty. He stopped walking and the buildings of Waterbury rose up out of the misty courtroom and surrounded him again. A woman who was passing laughed. "He said 'Puppy biscuit,' " she said to her companion. "That man said 'Puppy biscuit' to himself!" Walter Mitty hurried on. He went into an A&P, not the first one he came to but a smaller one farther up the street. "I want some biscuit for small, young dogs," he said to the clerk. "Any special brand, sir?" The greatest pistol shot in the world thought a moment. "It says 'Puppies Bark for It' on the box," said Walter Mitty.

His wife would be through at the hairdresser's in fifteen minutes, Mitty saw in looking at his watch, unless they had trouble drying it; sometimes they had trouble drying it. She didn't like to get to the hotel first; she would want him to be there waiting for her as usual. He found a big leather chair in the lobby, facing a window, and he put the overshoes and the puppy biscuit on the floor beside it. He picked up an old copy of *Liberty* and sank down into the chair. "Can Germany Conquer the World through the Air?" Walter Mitty looked at the pictures of bombing planes and of ruined streets.

. . . "The cannonading has got the wind up in young Raleigh, sir," said the sergeant. Captain Mitty looked up at him through tousled hair. "Get him to bed,'' he said wearily, ''with the others. I'll fly alone.'' ''But you can't, sir,'' said the sergeant anxiously. ''It takes two men to handle that bomber and the Archies are pounding hell out of the air. Von Richtman's circus is between here and Saulier.'' ''Somebody's got to get that ammunition dump,'' said Mitty. ''I'm going over. Spot of brandy?'' He poured a drink for the sergeant and one for himself. War thundered and whined around the dugout and battered at the door. There was a rending of wood and splinters flew through the room. ''A bit of a near thing,'' said Captain Mitty carelessly. ''The box barrage is closing in,'' said the sergeant. ''We only live once, sergeant,'' said Mitty, with his faint, fleeting smile. ''Or do we?'' He poured another brandy and tossed it off. ''I never see a man would hold his brandy like you, sir,'' said the sergeant. ''Begging your pardon, sir.'' Captain Mitty stood up and strapped on his huge Webley-Vickers automatic. ''It's forty kilometers through hell, sir,'' said the sergeant. Mitty finished one last brandy. ''After all,'' he said softly, ''what isn't?'' The pounding of the cannon increased; there was the rat-tat-tatting of machine guns, and from somewhere came the menacing pocketa-pocketa-pocketa of the new flame-throwers. Walter Mitty walked to the door of the dugout humming ''*Après de Ma Blonde.*'' He turned and waved to the sergeant. ''Cheerio!'' he said. . . .

Something struck his shoulder. ''I've been looking all over this hotel for you,'' said Mrs. Mitty. ''Why do you have to hide in this old chair? How did you expect me to find you?'' ''Things close in,'' said Walter Mitty vaguely. ''What?'' Mrs. Mitty said. ''Did you get the what's-its-name? The puppy biscuit? What's in that box?'' ''Overshoes,'' said Mitty. ''Couldn't you have put them on in the store?'' ''I was thinking,'' said Walter Mitty. ''Does it ever occur to you that I am sometimes thinking?'' She looked at him. ''I'm going to take your temperature when I get you home,'' she said.

They went out through the revolving doors that made a faintly derisive whistling sound when you pushed them. It was two blocks to the parking lot. At the drugstore on the corner she said, ''Wait here for me. I forgot something. I won't be a minute.'' She was more than a minute. Walter Mitty lighted a cigarette. It began to rain, rain with sleet in it. He stood up against the wall of the drugstore, smoking. . . . He put his shoulders back and his heels together. ''To hell with the handkerchief,'' said Walter Mitty scornfully. He took one last drag on his cigarette and snapped it away. Then, with that faint, fleeting smile playing about his lips, he faced the firing squad; erect and motionless, proud and disdainful, Walter Mitty the Undefeated, inscrutable to the last.

A driver's test is a stressful experience under the best of circumstances. Writer Angelica Gibbs shows us a situation in which bigotry makes it impossible.

■ THE TEST ■

ANGELICA GIBBS

On the afternoon Marian took her second driver's test, Mrs. Ericson went with her. "It's probably better to have someone a little older with you," Mrs. Ericson said as Marian slipped into the driver's seat beside her. "Perhaps the last time your Cousin Bill made you nervous, talking too much on the way."

"Yes, Ma'am," Marian said in her soft unaccented voice. "They probably do like it better if a white person shows up with you."

"Oh, I don't think it's *that*," Mrs. Ericson began, and subsided after a glance at the girl's set profile. Marian drove the car slowly through the shady streets. It was one of the first hot days in June, and when they reached the boulevard they found it crowded with cars headed for the beaches.

"Do you want me to drive?" Mrs. Ericson asked. "I'll be glad to if you're feeling jumpy." Marian shook her head. Mrs. Ericson watched her dark, competent hands and wondered for the thousandth time how the house had ever managed to get along without her, or how she had lived through those earlier years when her household had been presided over by a series of slatternly white girls who had considered housework demeaning and the care of children an added insult. "You drive beautifully, Marian," she said. "Now don't think of the last time. Anybody would slide on a steep hill on a wet day like that."

"It takes four mistakes to flunk you," Marian said. "I don't remember doing all the things the inspector marked down on my blank."

"People say that they only want you to slip them a little something," Mrs. Ericson said doubtfully.

"*No*," Marian said. "That would only make it worse, Mrs. Ericson, I know."

The car turned right, at a traffic signal, into a side road and slid up to the curb at the rear of a short line of parked cars. The inspectors had not arrived yet.

"You have the papers?" Mrs. Ericson asked. Marian took them out of her bag: her learner's permit, the car registration, her birth certificate. They settled down to the dreary business of waiting.

"It will be marvellous to have someone dependable to drive the children to school every day," Mrs. Ericson said.

Marian looked up from the list of driving requirements she had been studying. "It'll make things simpler at the house, won't it?" she asked.

"Oh, Marian," Mrs. Ericson exclaimed, "if I could only pay you half of what you're worth!"

"Now, Mrs. Ericson," Marian said firmly. They looked at each other and smiled with affection.

Two cars with official insignia on their doors stopped across the street. The inspectors leaped out, very brisk and military in their neat uniforms. Marian's hands tightened on the wheel. "There's the one who flunked me last time," she whispered, pointing to a stocky, self-important man who had begun to shout directions at the driver at the head of the line. "Oh, Mrs. Ericson."

"Now Marian," Mrs. Ericson said. They smiled at each other again, rather weakly.

The inspector who finally reached their car was not the stocky one, but a genial, middle-aged man who grinned broadly as he thumbed over their papers. Mrs. Ericson started to get out of the car. "Don't you want to come along?" the inspector asked. "Mandy and I don't mind company."

Mrs. Ericson was bewildered for a moment. "No," she said, and stepped to the curb. "I might make Marian self-conscious. She's a fine driver, Inspector."

"Sure thing," the inspector said, winking at Mrs. Ericson. He slid into the seat beside Marian. "Turn right at the corner, Mandy Lou."

From the curb, Mrs. Ericson watched the car move smoothly up the street.

The inspector made notations in a small black book. "Age?" he inquired presently, as they drove along.

"Twenty-seven."

He looked at Marian out of the corner of his eye. "Old enough to have quite a flock of pickaninnies, eh?"

Marian did not answer.

"Left at this corner," the inspector said, "and park between that truck and the green Buick."

The cars were very close together, but Marian squeezed in between them without too much maneuvering. "Driven before, Mandy Lou?" the inspector asked.

"Yes, sir. I had a license for three years in Pennsylvania."

"Why do you want to drive a car?"

"My employer needs me to take her children to and from school."

"Sure you don't really want to sneak out nights to meet some young blood?" the inspector asked. He laughed as Marian shook her head.

"Let's see you take a left at the corner and then turn around in the middle of the next block," the inspector said. He began to whistle "Swanee River." "Make you homesick?" he asked.

Marian put out her hand, swung around neatly in the street, and headed back in the direction from which they had come. "No," she said. "I was born in Scranton, Pennsylvania."

The inspector feigned astonishment. "You-all ain't Southern?" he said. "Well dog my cats if I didn't think you-all came from down yondah."

"No, sir," Marian said.

"Turn onto Main Street and let's see how you-all does in heavier traffic."

They followed a line of cars along Main Street for several blocks until they came in sight of a concrete bridge which arched high over the railroad tracks.

"Read that sign at the end of the bridge," the inspector said.

"Proceed with caution. Dangerous in slippery weather," Marian said.

"You-all sho can read fine," the inspector exclaimed. "Where'd you learn to do that, Mandy?"

"I got my college degree last year," Marian said. Her voice was not quite steady.

As the car crept up the slope of the bridge the inspector burst out laughing. He laughed so hard he could scarcely give his next direction. "Stop here," he said, wiping his eyes, "then start 'er up again. Mandy got her degree, did she? Dog my cats!"

Marian pulled up beside the curb. She put the car in neutral, pulled on the emergency, waited a moment, and then put the car into gear again. Her face was set. As she released the brake her foot slipped off the clutch pedal and the engine stalled.

"Now, Mistress Mandy," the inspector said, "remember your degree."

"*Damn* you!" Marian cried. She started the car with a jerk.

The inspector lost his joviality in an instant. "Return to the starting place, please," he said, and made four very black crosses at random in the squares on Marian's application blank.

Mrs. Ericson was waiting at the curb where they had left her. As Marian stopped the car, the inspector jumped out and brushed past her, his face purple. "What happened?" Mrs. Ericson asked, looking after him with alarm.

Marian stared down at the wheel and her lip trembled.

"Oh, Marian, *again*?" Mrs. Ericson said.

Marian nodded. "In sort of a different way," she said, and slid over to the right-hand side of the car.

War is painful. In a story written in 1925, an Irish writer narrates a story that could and does still happen every day.

■ THE SNIPER ■
LIAM O'FLAHERTY

The long June twilight faded into night. Dublin lay enveloped in darkness but for the dim light of the moon that shone through fleecy clouds, casting a pale light as of approaching dawn over the dark waters of the Liffey. Around the beleaguered Four Courts the heavy guns roared. Here and there through the city, machine guns and rifles broke the silence of the night, spasmodically, like dogs barking on lone farms. Republicans and Free Staters were waging civil war.

On a rooftop near O'Connell Bridge, a Republican sniper lay watching. Beside him lay his rifle and over his shoulders were slung a pair of field glasses. His face was the face of a student, thin and ascetic, but his eyes had the cold gleam of the fanatic. They were deep and thoughtful, the eyes of a man who is used to looking at death.

He was eating a sandwich hungrily. He had eaten nothing since morning. He had been too excited to eat. He finished the sandwich, and, taking a flask of whisky from his pocket, he took a short draught. Then he returned the flask to his pocket. He paused for a moment, considering whether he should risk a smoke. It was dangerous. The flash might be seen in the darkness, and there were enemies watching. He decided to take the risk.

Placing a cigarette between his lips, he struck a match, inhaled the smoke hurriedly and put out the light. Almost immediately, a bullet flattened itself against the parapet of the roof. The sniper took another whiff and put out the cigarette. Then he swore softly and crawled away to the left.

Cautiously he raised himself and peered over the parapet. There was a flash and a bullet whizzed over his head. He dropped immediately. He had seen the flash. It came from the opposite side of the street.

He rolled over the roof to a chimney stack in the rear, and slowly drew himself up behind it, until his eyes were level with the top of the parapet. There was nothing to be seen—just the dim outline of the opposite house-top against the blue sky. His enemy was under cover.

Just then an armored car came across the bridge and advanced slowly up the street. It stopped on the opposite side of the street, fifty yards ahead. The sniper could hear the dull panting of the motor. His heart beat faster. It was an enemy car. He wanted to fire, but he knew it was useless. His bullets would never pierce the steel that covered the gray monster.

Then round the corner of a side street came an old woman, her head covered by a tattered shawl. She began to talk to the man in the turret of the car. She was pointing to the roof where the sniper lay. An informer.

The turret opened. A man's head and shoulder appeared, looking toward the sniper. The sniper raised his rifle and fired. The head fell heavily on the turret wall. The woman darted toward the side street. The sniper fired again. The woman whirled round and fell with a shriek into the gutter.

Suddenly from the opposite roof a shot rang out and the sniper dropped his rifle with a curse. The rifle clattered to the roof. The sniper thought the noise would wake the dead. He stopped to pick the rifle up. He couldn't lift it. His forearm was dead. ''I'm hit,'' he muttered.

Dropping flat onto the roof, he crawled back to the parapet. With his left hand he felt the injured right forearm. The blood was oozing through the sleeve of his coat. There was no pain—just a deadened sensation, as if the arm had been cut off.

Quickly he drew his knife from his pocket, opened it on the breastwork of the parapet, and ripped open the sleeve. There was a small hole where the bullet had entered. On the other side there was no hole. The bullet had lodged in the bone. It must have fractured it. He bent the arm below the wound. The arm bent back easily. He ground his teeth to overcome the pain.

Then taking out his field dressing, he ripped open the packet with his knife. He broke the neck of the iodine bottle and let the bitter fluid drip into the wound. A paroxysm of pain swept through him. He placed the cotton wadding over the wound and wrapped the dressing over it. He tied the ends with his teeth.

Then he lay still against the parapet, and, closing his eyes, he made an effort of will to overcome the pain.

In the street beneath all was still. The armored car had retired speedily over the bridge, with the machine gunner's head hanging lifeless over the turret. The woman's corpse lay still in the gutter.

The sniper lay for a long time nursing his wounded arm and planning escape. Morning must not find him wounded on the roof. The enemy on the opposite roof covered his escape. He must kill that enemy and he could not use his rifle. He had only a revolver to do it. Then he thought of a plan.

Taking off his cap, he placed it over the muzzle of his rifle. Then he pushed the rifle slowly upward over the parapet, until the cap was visible from the opposite side of the street. Almost immediately there was a report, and a bullet pierced the center of the cap. The sniper slanted the rifle forward. The cap slipped down into the street. Then catching the rifle in the middle, the sniper dropped his left hand over the roof and let it hang lifelessly. After a few minutes he let the rifle drop to the street. Then he sank to the roof, dragging his arm with him.

Crawling quickly to the left, he peered up at the corner of the roof. His ruse had succeeded. The other sniper, seeing the cap and rifle fall, thought that he had killed his man. He was now standing before a row of chimney pots, looking across, with his head clearly silhouetted against the western sky.

The Republican sniper smiled and lifted his revolver above the edge of the parapet. The distance was about fifty yards—a hard shot in the dim light, and his right arm was paining him like a thousand devils. He took a steady aim. His hand trembled with eagerness. Pressing his lips together, he took a deep breath through his nostrils and fired. He was almost deafened with the report and his arm shook with the recoil.

Then when the smoke cleared he peered across and uttered a cry of joy. His enemy had been hit. He was reeling over the parapet in his death agony. He struggled to keep his feet, but he was slowly falling forward, as if in a dream. The rifle fell from his grasp, hit the parapet, fell over, bounded off the pole of a barber's shop beneath and then clattered on the pavement.

Then the dying man on the roof crumpled up and fell forward. The body turned over and over in space and hit the ground with a thud. Then it lay still.

The sniper looked at his enemy falling and he shuddered. The lust of battle died in him. He became bitten by remorse. The sweat stood out in beads on his forehead. Weakened by his wound and the long summer day of fasting and watching on the roof, he revolted from the sight of the shattered mass of his dead enemy. His teeth chattered, he began to gibber to himself, cursing the war, cursing everybody.

He looked at the smoking revolver in his hand, and with an oath he hurled it to the roof at his feet. The revolver went off with the concussion and the bullet whizzed past the sniper's head. He was frightened back to his senses by the shock. His nerves steadied. The cloud of fear scattered from his mind and he laughed.

Taking the whisky flask from his pocket, he emptied it at a draught. He felt reckless under the influence of the spirit. He decided to leave the roof now and look for his company commander to report. Everywhere around was quiet. There was not much danger in going through the streets. He picked up his revolver and put it in his pocket. Then he crawled down through the skylight to the house underneath.

When the sniper reached the laneway on the street level, he felt a sudden curiosity as to the identity of the enemy sniper whom he had killed. He decided that he was a good shot, whoever he was. He wondered did he know him? Perhaps he had been in his own company before the split in the army. He decided to risk going over to have a look at him. He peered around the corner to O'Connell Street. In the upper part of the street there was heavy firing, but around here all was quiet. The sniper darted across the street. A machine gun tore up the ground around him with a hail of bullets, but he escaped. He threw himself face downward beside the corpse. The machine gun stopped.

Then the sniper turned over the dead body and looked into his brother's face.

Pulitzer Prize-winner Russell Baker reflects on his mother's aging process and how it affected him as an adult.

■ GROWING UP ■

RUSSELL BAKER

At the age of eighty my mother had her last bad fall, and after that her mind wandered free through time. Some days she went to weddings and funerals that had taken place half a century earlier. On others she presided over family dinners cooked on Sunday afternoons for children who were now gray with age. Through all this she lay in bed but moved across time, traveling among the dead decades with a speed and ease beyond the gift of physical science.

"Where's Russell?" she asked one day when I came to visit at the nursing home.

"I'm Russell," I said.

She gazed at this improbably overgrown figure out of an inconceivable future and promptly dismissed it.

"Russell's only this big," she said, holding her hand, palm down, two feet from the floor. That day she was a young country wife with chickens in the backyard and a view of hazy blue Virginia mountains behind the apple orchard, and I was a stranger old enough to be her father.

Early one morning she phoned me in New York. "Are you coming to my funeral today?" she asked.

It was an awkward question with which to be awakened. "What are you talking about, for God's sake?" was the best reply I could manage.

"I'm being buried today," she declared briskly, as though announcing an important social event.

"I'll phone you back," I said and hung up, and when I did phone back she was all right, although she wasn't all right, of course, and we all knew she wasn't.

She had always been a small woman—short, light-boned, delicately structured—but now, under the white hospital sheet, she was becoming tiny. I thought of a doll with huge, fierce eyes. There had always been a fierceness in her. It showed in that angry, challenging thrust of the chin when she issued an opinion, and a great one she had always been for issuing opinions.

"I tell people exactly what's on my mind," she had been fond of boasting. "I tell them what I think, whether they like it or not." Often they had not liked it. She could be sarcastic to people in whom she detected evidence of the ignoramus or the fool.

"It's not always good policy to tell people exactly what's on your mind," I used to caution her.

"If they don't like it, that's too bad," was her customary reply, "because that's the way I am."

And so she was. A formidable woman. Determined to speak her mind, determined to have her way, determined to bend those who opposed her. In that time when I had known her best, my mother had hurled herself at life with chin thrust forward, eyes blazing, and an energy that made her seem always on the run.

CHAPTER SIX

The Interpretation of Drama

This chapter focuses on the interpretation of drama. Your class will be transformed into a series of drama workshops exploring the nature of dramatic literature and the unique challenges this art form presents to the interpretative performer.

Like the other forms of literature we have explored thus far, dramatic literature also functions to exhibit human nature and the human experience. Reading plays allows you to learn about people—to listen and to watch them as they go about the business of being human. The plays that succeed reveal something about the human predicament; successful plays widen our understanding and appreciation of the way human beings interact, the way they affect each other psychologically, and the way they cope with the external and internal forces that affect them.

Drama is a literary cousin of narrative prose. Like narrative prose, a dramatic work includes the elements of plot (a series of incidents), setting (a location), time (a point in past, present, or future history), and characters (individuals to people the literary world). Consequently, much of what you learned while studying narrative prose may also be applied here.

Transpositions

Compare and contrast the following two versions of *One Flew Over the Cuckoo's Nest*. One version is in narrative form, written by Ken Kesey; the other version is in play form, adapted from the novel by Dale Wasserman. In each version we are given a look at life inside a particular mental institution.

■ ONE FLEW OVER THE ■ CUCKOO'S NEST

KEN KESEY

I'm the last one. Still strapped in the chair in the corner. McMurphy stops when he gets to me and hooks his thumbs in his pockets again and leans back to laugh, like he sees something funnier about me than about anybody else. All of a sudden I was scared he was laughing because he knew the way

I was sitting there with my knees pulled up and my arms wrapped around them, staring straight ahead as though I couldn't hear a thing, was all an act.

"Hooeee," he said, "look what we got here."

I remember all this part real clear. I remember the way he closed one eye and tipped his head back and looked down across that healing wine-colored scar on his nose, laughing at me. I thought at first that he was laughing because of how funny it looked, an Indian's face and black, oily Indian's hair on somebody like me. I thought maybe he was laughing at how weak I looked. But then's when I remember thinking that he was laughing because he wasn't fooled for one minute by my deaf-and-dumb act; it didn't make any difference *how* cagey the act was, he was onto me and was laughing and winking to let me know it.

"What's your story, Big Chief? You look like Sittin' Bull on a sitdown strike." He looked over to the Acutes to see if they might laugh about his joke; when they just sniggered he looked back to me and winked again. "What's your name, Chief?"

Billy Bibbit called across the room. "His n-n-name is Bromden. Chief Bromden. Everybody calls him Chief Buh-Broom, though, because the aides have him sweeping a l-large part of the time. There's not m-much else he can do, I guess. He's deaf." Billy put his chin in his hands. "If I was d-d-deaf"—he sighed—"I would kill myself."

McMurphy kept looking at me. "He gets his growth, he'll be pretty good-sized, won't he? I wonder how tall he is."

"I think somebody m-m-measured him once at s-six feet seven; but even if he is big, he's scared of his own sh-sh-shadow. Just a bi-big deaf Indian."

"When I saw him sittin' here I *thought* he looked some Indian. But Bromden ain't an Indian name. What tribe is he?"

"I don't know," Billy said. "He was here wh-when I c-came."

"I have information from the doctor," Harding said, "that he is only half Indian, a Columbia Indian, I believe. That's a defunct Columbia Gorge tribe. The doctor said his father was the tribal leader, hence this fellow's title, 'Chief.' As to the 'Bromden' part of the name, I'm afraid my knowledge in Indian lore doesn't cover that."

McMurphy leaned his head down near mine where I had to look at him. "Is that right? You deaf, Chief?"

"He's de-de-deef and dumb."

McMurphy puckered his lips and looked at my face a long time. Then he straightened back up and stuck his hand out.

"Well, what the hell, he can shake hands can't he? Deef or whatever. By God, Chief, you may be big, but you shake my hand or I'll consider it an insult. And it's not a good idea to insult the new bull goose loony of the hospital."

When he said that he looked back over to Harding and Billy and made a face, but he left that hand in front of me, big as a dinner plate.

I remember real clear the way that hand looked: there was carbon under the fingernails where he'd worked once in a garage; there was an anchor tattooed back from the knuckles; there was a dirty Band-Aid on the middle knuckle, peeling up at the edge. All the rest of the knuckles were covered with scars and cuts, old and new. I remember the palm was smooth and hard as bone from hefting the wooden handles of axes and hoes, not the hand you'd think could deal cards. The palm was callused, and the calluses were cracked, and dirt was worked in the cracks. A road map of his travels up and down the West. That palm made a scuffing sound against my hand. I remember the fingers were thick and strong closing over mine, and my hand commenced to feel peculiar and went to swelling up out there on my stick of an arm, like he was transmitting his own blood into it. It rang with blood and power. It blowed up near as big as his, I remember. . . .

"Mr. McMurry."

It's the Big Nurse.

"Mr. McMurry, could you come here please?"

It's the Big Nurse. That black boy with the thermometer has gone and got her. She stands there tapping that thermometer against her wrist watch, eyes whirring while she tries to gauge this new man. Her lips are in that triangle shape, like a doll's lips ready for a fake nipple.

"Aide Williams tells me, Mr. McMurry, that you've been somewhat difficult abut your admission shower. Is this true? Please understand, I appreciate the way you've taken it upon yourself to orient with the other patients on the ward, but everything in its own good time, Mr. McMurry. I'm sorry to interrupt you and Mr. Bromden, but you do understand: *everyone* . . . must follow the rules."

He tips his head back and gives that wink that she isn't fooling him any more than I did, that he's onto her. He looks up at her with one eye for a minute.

"Ya know, ma'am," he says, "ya know—that is the ex-*act* thing somebody *always* tells me about the rules. . . ."

He grins. They both smile back and forth at each other, sizing each other up.

" . . . just when they figure I'm about to do the dead opposite."

Then he lets go my hand.

■ One Flew Over the ■ Cuckoo's Nest The Play

DALE WASSERMAN

MC MURPHY   (*Stops short at* CHIEF BROMDEN *strapped in the chair.*) Hooee! What have we got here?

CHESWICK   That's Chief Bromden.

MC MURPHY   What's your story, Big Chief?

BILLY   He can't hear you. He's duh-deaf and dumb.

MC MURPHY   Well, what they got him strapped down for? I don't like that, no, *sir*. (*As he unstraps the Chief.*) It just ain't dignified. (CHIEF BROMDEN *rises.* MC MURPHY *whistles.*) Say, you get your full growth you're gonna be pretty good-sized. (*Circles* CHIEF BROMDEN *on a tour of inspection.*) What tribe is he?

BILLY   I don't know. He was here when I c-came.

HARDING   According to the doctor, he's a Columbia River Indian . . . one of those who lived up on the water falls? But I believe the tribe is now defunct.

MC MURPHY   That right, Chief? You defunct?

BILLY   He c-can't hear a word you say. (NURSE RATCHED *has entered on this, followed by* WILLIAMS. WARREN *comes out of the Station and joins them.*)

NURSE RATCHED   (*Holding out her hand.*) Mr. McMurphy.

MC MURPHY   (*Shaking hands with her.*) Howdy, Ma'am!

NURSE RATCHED   I'll take that. (*She takes the strap from him, hands it to* WARREN.) Aide Williams tells me you are being difficult.

MC MURPHY   (*Pained.*) Me?

NURSE RATCHED   I understand you refused to take your admission shower?

MC MURPHY   Well, as to that, ma'am, they showered me at the courthouse and last night at the jail, and I swear they'd of washed my ears for me on the way over if they coulda found the facilities. (*Explodes into laughter.*)

NURSE RATCHED   That's quite amusing, Mr. Murphy. But you must realize that our policies are engineered for *your cure*. Which means cooperation.

MC MURPHY   Ma'am, I'll cooperate from hell to Thursday, but you wouldn't want me to be unpolite? I mean, had to get acquainted with my new buddies?

NURSE RATCHED   (*Ever-smiling.*) Please understand, I *do* appreciate the way you've taken it upon yourself to . . . orient with other patients? But everything in its own time. You *must* follow the *rules*.

MC MURPHY   (*Face close to* NURSE RATCHED's, *smiling brightly.*) Ya know, ma'am—that is the *exact* thing somebody *always* tells me about the rules—just when I'm thinkin' a breakin' every one of 'em. (*Lights down fast.*) . . .

Next compare and contrast the narrative excerpt from *The Grapes of Wrath* by John Steinbeck with the following play script by Frank Galati. Both deliver moving portraits of people hit hard and mercilessly by the Great Depression.

■ THE GRAPES OF WRATH ■
JOHN STEINBECK

The preacher, staring off across the fields, said, "Somebody's coming. Look! Down there, right through the cotton."

Joad looked where Casy's finger pointed. "Comin' afoot," he said. "Can't see 'im for the dust he raises. . . ." They watched the figure approaching in the evening light, and the dust it raised was reddened by the setting sun. "Man," said Joad. The man drew closer, and as he walked past the barn, Joad said, "Why, I know him. You know him—that's Muley Graves." And he called, "Hey, Muley! How ya?"

The approaching man stopped, startled by the call, and then he came on quickly. He was a lean man, rather short. His movements were jerky and quick. He carried a gunnysack in his hand. His blue jeans were pale at knee and seat, and he wore an old black suit coat, stained and spotted, the sleeves torn loose from the shoulders in back, and ragged holes worn through at the elbows. His black hat was as stained as his coat, and the band, torn half

free, flopped up and down as he walked. Muley's face was smooth and un-
wrinkled, but it wore the truculent look of a bad child's, the mouth held
tight and small, the little eyes half scowling, half petulant.

"You remember Muley," Joad said softly to the preacher.

"Who's that?" the advancing man called. Joad did not answer. Muley
came close, very close, before he made out the faces. . . . "It's Tommy
Joad. When'd you get out, Tommy?"

"Two days ago," said Joad. "Took a little time to hitchhike home. An'
look here what I find. Where's my folks, Muley? What's the house all
smashed up for, an' cotton planted in the dooryard?"

"It's lucky I come by!" said Muley. "Cause ol' Tom worried himself.
When they was fixin to move I was settin' in the kitchen there. I jus' tol'
Tom I wasn't gonna move. . . . I tol' him that, an' Tom says, 'I'm wor-
ryin' myself about Tommy. S'pose he comes home an' they ain't nobody
here. What'll he think?' I says, 'Whyn't you write down a letter?' And
Tom says, 'Maybe I will. I'll think about her. But if I don't, you keep your
eye out for Tommy if you're still aroun'.' 'I'll be aroun',' I says. 'I'll be
aroun' till hell freezes over. There ain't nobody can run a guy name of
Graves outa this country.' An' they ain't done it, neither."

Joad said impatiently, "Where's my folks? Tell about you standin' up to
'em later, but where's my folks?"

"Well, they was gonna stick her out when the bank come to tractorin' off
the place. Your grampa stood out here with a rifle, and blowed the head-
lights off that cat', but she come on just the same. Your grampa didn't
wanta kill the guy drivin' that cat', an' that was Willy Feeley, an' Willy
knowed it, so he jus' come on, an' bumped the hell outa the house, an' give
her a shake like a dog shakes a rat. Well, it took somepin outa Tom. Kinda
got into 'im. He ain't been the same ever since."

"Where is my folks?" Joad spoke angrily.

"What I'm tellin' you. Took three trips with your Uncle John's wagon.
Took the stove an' the pump an' the beds. You should a seen them beds go
out with all them kids an' your granma an' granpa settin' up against the
headboard, an' your brother Noah settin' there smokin' a cigareet, an'
spittin' la-de-da over the side of the wagon." Joad opened his mouth to
speak. "They're all at your Uncle John's," Muley said quickly.

"Oh! All at John's. Well, what they doin' there? Now stick to her for a
second, Muley. Jus' stick to her. In jus' a minute you can go on your own
way. What they doin' there?"

"Well, they been choppin' cotton, all of 'em, even the kids an' your
grampa. Gettin' money together so they can shove on west. Gonna buy a car

and shove on west where it's easy livin'. There ain't nothin' here. Fifty cents a clean acre for choppin' cotton, an' folks beggin' for the chance to chop.''

''An' they ain't gone yet?''

''No,'' said Muley. ''Not that I know. Las' I heard was four days ago when I seen your brother Noah out shottin jackrabits, an' he says they're aimin' to go in about two weeks. John got his notice he got to get off. You jus' go on about eight miles to John's place. You'll find your folks piled in John's house like gophers in a winter burrow.''

''O.K.,'' said Joad. ''Now you can ride on your own way. You ain't changed a bit, Muley. If you want to tell about somepin off northwest, you point your nose straight southeast.''

Muley said truculently, ''You ain't changed neither. You was a smart-aleck kid, an' you're still a smart aleck. You ain't tellin' me how to skin my life, by any chancet?''

Joad grinned. ''No, I ain't. If you wanta drive your head into a pile of broken glass, there ain't nobody can tell you different. You know this here preacher, don't you, Muley? Rev. Casy.''

''Why, sure, sure. Didn't look over. Remember him well.'' Casy stood up and the two shook hands. ''Glad to see you again,'' said Muley. ''You ain't been aroun' for a . . . long time.''

''I been off a-askin' questions,'' said Casy. ''What happened here? Why they kickin' folks off the lan'?''

Muley's mouth snapped shut so tightly that a little parrot's beak in the middle of his upper lip stuck down over his under lip. He scowled. . . . ''I ain't a-goin'. My paw come here fifty hears ago. an' I ain't a-goin'.''

■ THE GRAPES OF WRATH ■

FRANK GALATI

(An expanse of weathered wood blown over with dust. A frail barbed wire fence. . . .)

First Narrator: The dawn came, but no day.

(Particles of dust hang in the air as feeble light spreads up into the sky.)

In the morning the dust hung like fog. Men stood by their fences and looked at the ruined corn, drying fast now, only a little green showing through the film of dust. . . .

MULEY   Tommy?

TOM   Muley!

MULEY   When'd you get out, Tommy?

TOM   Two days ago. Took a little time to hitchhike home. An' lik here what I find. Where's my folks, Muley?

MULEY   They're all at your Uncle John's. The whole brood. Gettin' money together so they can shove on west. Uncle John got his notice, too.

TOM   You know this here preacher, don't you Muley? Rev. Casy.

MULEY   Why, sure, sure. Didn't look over. Remember him well.

TOM   What happened here?

MULEY   Well, your folks was gonna stick her out when the bank came to tractorin' off the place. Bumped the house, an' give her a shake like a dog shakes a rat.

CASY   Why they kickin' folks off the lan'?

MULEY   Bank can't afford to keep no tenants. . . . I tell ya, men, I'm stayin'. They ain't gettin' rid a me.

TOM   Sure. I wonder Pa went so easy. I wonder Grampa didn't kill nobody. *(Casy begins gathering splinters of wood and dry twigs. He builds and lights a fire.)* Nobody ever tol' Grandpa where to put his feet. An' Ma ain't nobody you can push aroun' neither. I seen her beat . . . a tin peddler with a live chicken one time 'cause he give her an argument. She had the chicken in one han', and the ax in the other, about to cut its head off. She aimed to go for that peddler with the ax, but she forgot which hand was which an' she takes after him with the chicken. Couldn't even eat that chicken when she got done. They wasn't nothin' but a pair a legs in her hand. Grandpa throwed a hip outa joint laughin'.

Reflections

1. What similarities do the works contain?

2. What differences are evident?

3. What purpose did the narrator serve in each of the novels?

4. How is the narrator's function fulfilled in each of the dramas?

Of course *Cuckoo's Nest* and *Grapes of Wrath* were also movies. You may want to watch the film versions and compare them to the novels and plays.

Unlike its close relative narrative prose, a play does not usually employ a narrator to summarize events, to tell how a character looks or moves, or to tell how other characters respond. A playwright, unlike a prose writer, cannot comment overtly on either the behavior of the characters or the actions that occur. Instead, the playwright simply shows us people in action. Thus, a play is composed of scene, rather than a mixture of scene and narration; a play is a story told in dialogue form. Before going on, try the following.

GETTING INVOLVED
Charting a Play

Divide the class into small groups. Each group chooses from the following chart: a number of characters (the number you select should equal the number of people in your group), a time, and a place.

Time	Place	Characters
morning	at the zoo	grandparent
afternoon	in a park	teacher
lunchtime	in school	bus driver
dinnertime	on the street	police officer
evening	in a restaurant	cat
midnight	at a circus	monkey
dawn	at a doctor's office	shopkeeper
twilight	in a store	salesperson
breakfast	in a bus	clown
		dentist
		patient
		dog
		beggar
		millionaire
		movie star
		first-grader
		parent
		waiter/waitress

Your group's goal is to combine your choices and to improvise or spontaneously enact a short play. Present it to the other members of your class.

Reflections

1. What type of action did your group evolve?

2. How did the characters in your group's improvisation relate to each other?

3. How did time and place affect the developments?

GETTING INVOLVED
All the World's a Stage

Now create an entire story you can turn into an improvisation. In other words, help your group create its own chart. Again, as a group, perform your spontaneous work for your classmates.

The elements you used in your improvisations are the same elements a writer uses to create a play. Let's look more closely at some of those elements.

Plot: What's Happening?

A playwright's *plot* is in many ways equivalent to the backbone of one's body, in that it supports his or her work. The plot usually consists of five main parts: exposition, conflict, crisis, climax, and denouement.

Exposition

Playwrights use *exposition* to provide their audiences with background information about setting, characters, or significant past and present happenings. Dramatists may use a number of means to transfer expository material to an audience: a prologue, a chorus, a soliloquy, a talkative servant or friend, a telephone conversation, or a character who returns after a lengthy absence. Whatever device is selected, however, the goal is always to ensure audiences have enough information to appreciate and understand fully the unfolding of the play's events.

GETTING INVOLVED

Exposition

Read the following expository passages carefully. Be aware of the information that is being revealed and how the playwright has chosen to reveal it.

■ RIDERS TO THE SEA ■

JOHN MILLINGTON SYNGE

NORA   *(In a low voice)* Where is she?

CATHLEEN   She's lying down, God help her, and may be sleeping, if she's able.

(NORA *comes in slowly, and takes a bundle from under shawl*)

CATHLEEN   *(Spinning the wheel rapidly)* What is it you have?

NORA   The young priest is after bringing them. It's a shirt and a plain stocking were got off a drowned man in Donegal.

(CATHLEEN *stops her wheel with a sudden movement, and leans out to listen*)

NORA   We're to find out if it's Michael's they are, some time herself will be down looking by the sea.

CATHLEEN   How would they be Michael's, Nora? How would he go the length of that way to the far north?

NORA   The young priest says he's known the like of it. "If it's Michael's they are," says he, "you can tell herself he's got a clean burial by the grace of God, and if they're not his, let no one say a word about them, for she'll be getting her death," says he, "with crying and lamenting."

   (*The door which* NORA *half closed is blown open by a gust of wind*)

CATHLEEN   *(Looking out anxiously)* Did you ask him would he stop Bartley going this day with the horses to the Galway fair?

NORA   "I won't stop him," says he, "but let you not be afraid. Herself does be saying prayers half through the night, and the Almighty God won't leave her destitute," says he, "with no son living."

CATHLEEN   Is the sea bad by the white rocks, Nora?

NORA   Middling bad, God help us. There's a great roaring in the west, and it's worse it'll be getting when the tide's turned to the wind. (*She goes over to the table with the bundle*) Shall I open it now?

CATHLEEN   Maybe she'd wake up on us, and come in before we'd done. (*Coming to the table*) It's a long time we'll be, and the two of us crying.

NORA   (*Goes to the inner door*) She's moving about on the bed. She'll be coming in a minute.

CATHLEEN   Give me a ladder, and I'll put them up in the turf-loft, the way she won't know of them at all, and maybe when the tide turns she'll be going down to see would he be floating from the east.

(*They put the ladder against the gable of the chimney:* CATHLEEN *goes up a few steps and hides the bundle in the turf-loft.* MAURYA *comes from the inner room*)

■ THE LARK ■

JEAN ANOUILH

(WARWICK *enters and moves through the crowd*)

WARWICK   Everybody here? Good. Let the trial begin at once. The quicker the judgment and the burning, the better for all of us.

CAUCHON   No, sire. The whole story must be played. Domremy, the Voices, Chinon—

WARWICK   I am not here to watch that children's story of the warrior virgin, strong and tender, dressed in white armor, white standard streaming in the wind. If they have time to waste, they can make the statues that way, in days to come. Different politics may well require different symbols. We might even have to make her a monument in London. Don't be shocked at that, sire. The politics of my government may well require it one day, and what's required, Englishmen supply. That's our secret, sire, and a very good one, indeed. (*Moves downstage to address the audience*) Well, let's worry about only this minute of time. I am Beauchamp, Earl of Warwick. I have a dirty virgin witch girl tucked away on a litter of straw in the depths of a prison here in Rouen. The girl has been an expensive nuisance. Your Duke of Burgundy sold her high. You like money in France, Monseigneur, all of you. That's the French secret, sire, and a very good one, indeed. (*He moves toward* JOAN) And here she is. The Maid. The famous Joan the Maid. Obviously, we paid too much. So put her on trial, and burn her, and be finished.

Reflections

1. What expository information is provided in these excerpts?

2. What are the characters in *Riders to the Sea* concerned about? Who are they seeking to protect?

3. Why does Beauchamp directly address the audience in *The Lark*?

Just as a dramatist uses exposition to set the stage for his or her play, so you as an interpreter can use exposition to set the stage for your reading. As in descriptive prose, narrative prose, or poetry, your introduction to a dramatic reading should serve to involve the audience in the world of your selection. It should include important facts about your dramatist, your play, the characters, and/or the setting; also, it should prepare your audience for the performance by creating a mood that echoes the intent of your literature.

Conflict

A *conflict* in drama is opposition that gives rise to the dramatic action. A disagreement or argument between persons or forces propels the story line and the actions of the characters. How are your arguing skills? Try this.

GETTING INVOLVED
Clash!

A. Pantomime a recent internal argument you had with yourself, such as, "I have to study, but I'd rather watch television." Show us which part of you won the struggle.

B. With a partner, improvise a two-person scene in which one person tries to persuade the other to do something against his or her will. For example, one wants to go to the movie theater, while the other wants to stay home and watch a video.

C. In groups of three, improvise a scene in which two people are competing for the attention of the third individual. What decision does the third individual make?

You should realize that a play often contains a number of conflicts, and each conflict serves to alter the direction of the action. Consider the following possible sources of conflict.

First, conflict may develop from a clash of personalities, wills, ideas, or actions. Second, conflict may develop because of a character's involvement or concern with outside forces. Third, conflict may develop because of a character's involvement or concern with himself or herself. Thus, dramatic conflict may have either a physical or emotional source. The central character in a conflict is referred to as the play's **protagonist**; the forces or people united against the protagonist are the **antagonists**.

A conflict leads to a crucial situation—a crisis. As an interpreter, you will want to use your voice and your body to reflect growing tension as a conflict builds to a crisis; likewise, you will want to use your voice and body to mirror the release in tension that accompanies the resolution of a conflict or crisis.

GETTING INVOLVED
Play Graphings

A. Looking at the voice graph that follows, reflect vocally the rises and falls in the graph's pattern. Use only the sound "mmm."

B. Use your arm to trace in space the movement pattern of the graph.

Reflections

1. What happened to your voice at the graph's lowest point? the graph's highest point?

2. In what position was your arm at the highest point? at the lowest point?

If you pause to think about it, you will realize that a play works in much the same way as the arm-tracing exercise, moving up and down in tension and conflict as it moves through a number of crises. After a series of crises, a decisive situation or a final climax usually emerges. This climax represents the apex or peak of intensity in the work—the highest point on the "graph" of the play. This is the point at which the conflict between the protagonist and the forces that oppose him or her has become so intense, a final solution must be determined. The solution your dramatist decided upon results in either success or defeat for the central character. The climax also leads to the play's final portion, known as the resolution or denouement. In this section, the dramatist usually untangles and ties off each strand of the plot in order to resolve the questions in the play.

Character—Who's Involved?

Characters make a play come alive; they are the primary means a playwright has to shape a plot. The characters manifest certain physical and verbal behaviors that a playwright uses to shape the action in the work. Thus, plot and character share a symbiotic relationship—that is, each one exists to fulfill the needs of the other.

When creating a character, the interpreter of drama relies on the same methods, the same type of literary fuel, as the actor of drama. However, the interpreter's task is further complicated by the nature of the art. Unlike the typical actor, the interpreter is expected to embody not one character, but an entire cast of characters. Thus, rather than getting to know and feel for a single character, interpreters need to know and feel for all the characters that inhabit their selected scripts. How can you go about this? Consider the following methods interpreters can use to portray an array of dramatic personages successfully.

You need to begin by discovering the predominant traits, motives, and moods of each character you hope to create. You want to communicate each character's degree of maturity and to re-create each character's style of verbal, vocal, and physical expression. Most of all, you want to use everything the author reveals about a character's attitude toward self, attitude toward surroundings, and attitude toward other individuals who share those surroundings.

Language and Character

Playwrights divulge information about their characters in a number of different ways. One way is through language—a character reveals a great deal about attitudes and background by what he or she says.

GETTING INVOLVED
Meeting a Character Through Language

Read the following passages carefully. What do each character's utterances reveal about who they are?

■ PYGMALION ■
BERNARD SHAW

DOOLITTLE   I ask you, what am I? I'm one of the undeserving poor, that's what I am. Think of what that means to a man. It means that he's up agen middle class morality all the time. If there's anything going, and I put in for a bit of it, it's always the same story: "You're undeserving: so you can't have it." But my needs is as great as the most deserving widow's that ever got money out of six different charities in one week for the death of the same husband. I don't need less than a deserving man: I need more. I don't eat less hearty than him; and I drink a lot more. I want a bit of amusement, cause I'm a thinking man. I want cheerfulness and a song and a band when I feel low. Well, they charge me just the same for everything as they charge the deserving. What is middle class morality? Just an excuse for never giving me anything. Therefore, I ask you, as two gentlemen, not to play that game on me. I'm playing straight with you. I ain't pretending to be deserving. I'm undeserving; and I mean to go on being undeserving. I like it; and that's the truth. Will you take advantage of a man's nature to do him out of the price of his own daughter what he's brought up and fed and clothed by the sweat of his brow until she's growed big enough to be interesting to you two gentlemen? Is five pounds unreasonable? I put it to you; and I leave it to you.

Reflections

1. To what social class does the speaker belong?

2. At what rate do you believe these lines should be delivered? What vocal qualities can you use to help you re-create Doolittle?

3. What physical gestures could you use to help characterize the man?

■ MORE PYGMALION . . . ■

BERNARD SHAW

There seems to be some curiosity as to what Higgins's lessons to Eliza were like. Well, here is a sample: the first one.

Picture Eliza, in her new clothes, and feeling her inside put out of step by a lunch, dinner, and breakfast of a kind to which it is unaccustomed, seated with Higgins and the Colonel in the study, feeling like a hospital outpatient at a first encounter with the doctors.

HIGGINS   Say your alphabet.

LIZA   I know my alphabet. Do you think I know nothing? I don't need to be taught like a child.

HIGGINS   (*Thundering*) Say your alphabet.

PICKERING   Say it, Miss Doolittle. You will understand presently. Do what he tells you; and let him teach you in his own way.

LIZA   Oh well, if you put it like that—Ahyee, Bayee, Cayee, Dayee—

HIGGINS   (*With the roar of a wounded lion*) Stop. Listen to this, Pickering. This is what we pay for as elementary education. This unfortunate animal has been locked up for nine years in school at our expense to teach her to speak and read the language of Shakespeare and Milton. And the result is Ahyee, Bayee, Ca-yee, Dayee. (*To* ELIZA) Say A, B, C, D.

LIZA   (*Almost in tears*) But I'm saying it. Ahyee, Bayee, Cayee—

HIGGINS   Stop. Say a cup of tea.

LIZA   A Capp ta-ee.

HIGGINS   Put your tongue forward until it squeezes against the top of your lower teeth. Now say cup.

LIZA   C-c-c—I can't. C-cup.

PICKERING   Good. Splendid, Miss Doolittle.

HIGGINS   By Jupitor. she's done it the first shot. Pickering, we shall make a duchess of her. (*To* ELIZA) Now do you think you could possibly say tea? Not Ta-ee, mind, if you ever say ba-ee, ca-yee, da-yee again you shall be dragged round the room three times by the hair of your head. (*Fortissimo*) T, T, T, T.

LIZA   (*Weeping*) I can't hear no difference cep that it sounds more genteel-like when you say it.

HIGGINS   Well, if you can hear that difference, what the devil are you crying for? Pickering, give her a chocolate.

PICKERING   No, no. Never mind crying a little, Miss Doolittle. You are doing very well; and the lessons won't hurt. I promise you I won't let him drag you round the room by your hair.

HIGGINS   Be off with you to Mrs. Pearce and tell her about it. Think about it. Try to do it by yourself; and keep your tongue well forward in your mouth instead of trying to roll it up and swallow it. Another lesson at half-past four this afternoon. Away with you.

Reflections

1. How are the differences among Liza. Higgins. and Pickering emphasized by their language and diction?

2. What speaking rates and mannerisms characterize each of the dramatic personages in this excerpt?

■ THE VISIT ■
FRIEDRICH DUERRENMATT

CLAIRE   Mike—Max! (*She claps her hands. Two huge bodyguards come in, left, carrying a sedan chair. She sits in it.*) I travel this way—a bit antiquated, of course. But perfectly safe. Ha! Ha! Aren't they magnificent? Mike and Max. I bought them in America. They were in jail, condemned to the chair. I had them pardoned. Now, they're condemned to my chair. I paid fifty thousand dollars apiece for them. You couldn't get them now for twice the sum. The sedan chair comes from the Louvre. I fancied it so much that the President of France gave it to me. The French are so impulsive, don't you think so, Anton? Go!

(MIKE and MAX *start to carry her off*)

Reflections

1. How do you imagine Claire as she speaks these lines?
2. What type of vocal quality would you attempt to suggest?
3. What gestures could enhance your verbalization?

■ A RAISIN IN THE SUN ■
LORRAINE HANSBERRY

MAMA   (*Still quietly*) Walter, what is the matter with you?

WALTER   Matter with me? Ain't nothing the matter with *me*!

MAMA   Yes there is. Something eating you up like a crazy man. Something more than me not giving you this money. The past few years I been watching it happen to you. You get all nervous acting and kind of wild in the eyes—(WALTER *jumps up impatiently at her words*) I said sit there now, I'm talking to you!

WALTER   Mama—I don't need no nagging at me today.

MAMA   Seem like you getting to a place where you always tied up in some kind of knot about something. But if anybody ask you 'bout it you just

yell at 'em and bust out of the house and go out and drink some-
wheres. Walter Lee, people can't live with that. Ruth's a good, patient girl in her way—but you getting to be too much. Boy, don't
make the mistake of driving that girl away from you.

WALTER   Why—what she do for me?

MAMA   She loves you.

WALTER   Mama—I'm going out. I want to go off somewhere and be by
myself for a while.

MAMA   I'm sorry 'bout your liquor store, son. It wasn't the thing for us to
do. That's what I want to tell you about—

WALTER   I got to go out, Mama—

(*He rises.*)

MAMA   It's dangerous, son.

WALTER   What's dangerous?

MAMA   When a man goes outside his home to look for peace.

WALTER   (*Beseechingly*) Then why can't there never be no peace in this
house then?

MAMA   You done found it in some other house?

WALTER   NO—there ain't no woman! Why do women always think
there's a woman somewhere when a man gets restless. (*Coming to her*)
Mama—Mama—I want so many things . . .

MAMA   Yes, son—

WALTER   I want so many things that they are driving me kind of crazy . . .
Mama—look at me.

MAMA   I'm looking at you. You are a good-looking boy. You got a job, a
nice wife, a fine boy—

WALTER   A job. (*Looks at her*) Mama, a job? I open and close car doors all
day long. I drive a man around in his limousine and I say, "Yes, sir;
no, sir! very good, sir; shall I take the Drive, sir?" Mama, that ain't
no kind of a job . . . that ain't nothing at all. (*Very quietly*) Mama, I
don't know if I can make you understand.

MAMA   Understand what, baby?

WALTER   (*Quietly*) Sometimes it's like I can see the future stretched out in
front of me—just as plain as day. The future, Mama. Hanging over
there at the edge of my days. Just waiting for me—a big, looming
blank space—full of *nothing*. Just waiting for *me*. (*Pause*) Mama—
sometimes when I'm downtown and I pass them cool, quiet looking

restaurants where them white boys are sitting and talking 'bout things
. . . sitting there turning deals worth millions of dollars . . . sometimes I see guys don't look much older than me—

MAMA   Son—how come you talk so much 'bout money?

WALTER   (*With immense passion*) Because it is life, Mama!

MAMA   (*Quietly*) Oh—(*Very quietly*) So now it's life. Money is life. Once upon a time freedom used to be life—now it's money. I guess the world really do change. . . .

WALTER   No—it always was money, Mama. We just didn't know about it.

MAMA   No . . . something has changed. (*She looks at him.*) You something new, boy. In my time we was worried about not being lynched and getting to the North if we could and how to stay alive and still have a pinch of dignity too . . . Now here come you and Beneatha—talking 'bout things we ain't even thought about hardly, me and your daddy. You ain't satisfied or proud of nothing we done. I mean that you had a home; that we kept you out of trouble till you was grown; that you don't have to ride to work on the back of nobody's streetcar—You my children—but how different we done become.

WALTER   You just don't understand, Mama, you just don't understand.

MAMA   Son—do you know your wife is expecting another baby? (WALTER *stands, stunned, and absorbs what his mother has said.*) That's what she wanted to talk to you about. (WALTER *sinks down into a chair*) This ain't for me to be telling—but you ought to know. (*She waits*) I think Ruth is thinking 'bout getting rid of that child.

WALTER   (*Slowly understanding*) No—no—Ruth wouldn't do that.

MAMA   When the world gets ugly enough—a woman will do anything for her family. *The part that's already living.*

WALTER   You don't know Ruth, Mama, if you think she would do that.

(RUTH *opens the bedroom door and stands there, a little limp*)

RUTH   (*Beaten*) Yes I would too, Walter. (*Pause*) I gave her a five dollar down payment.

(*There is total silence as the man stares at his wife and the mother stares at her son*)

MAMA   (*Presently*) Well—(*Tightly*) Well—son, I'm waiting to hear you say something . . . I'm waiting to hear you say something . . . I'm waiting to hear how you be your father's son. Be the man he was . . .

(*Pause*) Your wife say she going to destroy your child. And I'm waiting to hear you talk like him and say we a people who give children life, not who destroys them—(*She rises*) I'm waiting to see you stand up and look like your daddy and say we done give up one baby to poverty and that we ain't going to give up nary another one . . . I'm waiting.

WALTER   Ruth—

MAMA   If you are a son of mine, tell her! (WALTER *turns, looks at her and can say nothing. She continues bitterly*) You . . . you are a disgrace to your father's memory. Somebody get me my hat.

Reflections

1. What mood-tones characterize the speeches of each character?

2. What attitudes do the characters' words and actions reveal about them? How would you characterize their relationships with others and their relationships to their surroundings?

3. What speaking rhythms would you associate with each of the characters?

Playwrights use language in much the same way artists use paint, adding color and definition to their characters as they create clear portraits for their audiences. In giving life to a playwright's language, characters wear their speech styles almost visibly. Just as wearing distinctive clothing makes one recognizable, so does speech style. Pay careful attention to each character's speech pattern as you read, study, and prepare to perform a play. Consider the author's word choices and speech rhythms for the character, as well as the ideas the author has the character express. These attributes help communicate a character's basic traits.

Interpreters also need to appreciate and internalize the emotions and the attitudes characters display. These mood-cues serve to distinguish one character from another and to detail each character's mood range. Consequently, you need to be alert to words that indicate mood-tone and to recognize when a character's mood-tone changes. Using these skills, you will empathize with the author's characters, making them live for your audience.

Clues for Performance

Sometimes a playwright provides stage directions regarding the delivery of certain lines—that is, the kind of feelings the actor or interpreter of literature should experience and relay during the performance. These directions (phrases like "shouted angrily" or "whispered gently") are inserted in parentheses before the character's lines. The oral interpreter, as well as the actor in a production, should internalize the playwright's instructions and demonstrate in performance that these prompts were understood and applied.

GETTING INVOLVED

Taking Direction

Using the directions provided in parentheses, read the following sentences aloud. Demonstrate your understanding of these directions verbally and physically.

(*with an hysterical giggle*) Look what the monkey's doing!

(*harshly*) I don't want to go with you. I would not go with you if my life depended upon it.

(*as if to a baby*) Don't you want to go and get some ice cream?

(*with a tinge of sarcasm*) You're just so clever; you ought to be on a quiz show.

(*very quietly*) You can almost hear the sun rise; the day is starting so peacefully.

Reflections

1. What vocal actions did you use to support your reading of each sentence?

2. What physical actions did you use to support your interpretations?

The Art of Suggestion and Remembered Action

A character's personality is also revealed to us through his or her actions, physical behavior, and tension state. Naturally, as an interpreter you cannot mimic a character's every move during a performance, but certainly you can work to *suggest* to your audience the important movements a character makes.

Just how much does a suggestion involve, and how does the interpreter learn to suggest? Test your own instincts by answering the following questions. As an interpreter, what would you do if, during the scene you chose to perform, one character was supposed to throw a punch at another character? What would you do if, during a scene, one character was supposed to embrace another character?

During your performance, would you stand there and whack at the air or attempt to embrace empty space? Obviously, you would not. But in your rehearsals you might profit by carrying out these precise actions.

A preliminary use of literal action will aid you later in making the transfer to suggested or remembered action. It is this *remembered action* that an interpreter relies on during a performance. In other words, once you have "acted out" the action, it is expected that your muscles will be able to recall the dynamic movements they made originally during your literal enactment, and that you will experience the emotional tension you first felt at that time. Thus, you and your muscles work together in a performance, even if you choose to muffle their primary reactions. Through *physical suggestion*, you will allow audience members to complete the action in their minds. Try this now.

GETTING INVOLVED
The Road to Suggestion

Read the following passages from dramas aloud. In the first passage by Strindberg, we are introduced to two women who are rivals: Mrs. X and Miss Y.

■ THE STRONGER ■
JOHAN AUGUST STRINDBERG

SCENE. *The corner of a ladies' cafe. Two little iron tables, a red velvet sofa, several chairs. Enter* MRS. X, *dressed in winter clothes, carrying a Japanese basket on her arm.*

MISS Y (*Sits with a half-empty beer bottle before her, reading an illustrated paper, which she changes later for another.*)

MRS. X   Good afternoon, Amelia. You're sitting here alone on Christmas eve like a poor bachelor!

MISS Y (*Looks up, nods, and resumes her reading.*)

MRS. X   Do you know it really hurts me to see you like this, alone, in a cafe, and on Christmas eve, too. It makes me feel as I did one time when I saw a bridal party in a Paris restaurant, and the bride sat reading a comic paper, while the groom played billiards with the witnesses. Huh, thought I, with such a beginning, what will follow, and what will be the end? He played billiards on his wedding eve! (MISS Y *starts to speak*) And she read a comic paper, you mean? Well, they are not altogether the same thing.

(A WAITRESS *enters, places a cup of chocolate before* MRS. X *and goes out.*)

MRS. X   You know what, Amelia! I believe you would have done better to have kept him! Do you remember, I was the first to say "Forgive him?" Do you remember that? You would be married now and have a home. Remember that Christmas when you went out to visit your fiance's parents in the country? How you gloried in the happiness of home life and really longed to quit the theatre forever? Yes, Amelia dear, home is the best place of all—next to the theatre—and as for children—well, you don't understand that.

MISS Y (*Looks up scornfully.*)

MRS. X   (*Sips a few spoonfuls out of the cup, then opens her basket and shows Christmas presents.*) Now you shall see what I bought for my piggy-wigs. (*Takes up a doll.*) Look at this! This is for Lisa, ha! Do you see how she can roll her eyes and turn her head, eh? And here is Maja's popgun.

(*Loads it and shoots at* MISS Y.)

MISS Y (*Makes a startled gesture.*)

MRS. X   Did I frighten you? Do you think I would like to shoot you, eh? On my soul, if I don't think you did! If you wanted to shoot *me* it wouldn't be so surprising, because I stood in your way—and I know you can never forget that—although I was absolutely innocent. You still believe I intrigued and got you out of the Stora theatre, but I didn't. I didn't do that, although you think so. Well, it doesn't make any difference what I say to you. You still believe I did it. (*Takes up a pair of embroidered slippers.*)

And these are for my better half. I embroidered them myself—I can't bear tulips, but he wants tulips on everything.

MISS Y   (*Looks up ironically and curiously.*)

MRS. X   (*Putting a hand in each slipper.*) See what little feet Bob has! What? And you should see what a splendid stride he has! You've never seen him in slippers! (MISS Y *laughs aloud.*) Look! (*She makes the slippers walk on the table.*) (MISS Y *laughs loudly.*) And when he is grumpy he stamps like this with his foot. "What! damn those servants who can never learn to make coffee. Oh, now those creatures haven't trimmed the lamp wick properly!" And then there are draughts on the floor and his feet are cold. "Ugh, how cold it is; the stupid idiots can never keep the fire going." (*She rubs the slippers together, one sole over the other.*)

MISS Y   (*Shrieks with laughter.*)

MRS. X   And then he comes home and has to hunt for his slippers which Marie has stuck under the chiffonier—oh, but it's sinful to sit here and make fun of one's husband this way when he is kind and a good little man. You ought to have had such a husband, Amelia. What are you laughing at? What? What? And you see he's true to me. Yes, I'm sure of that, because he told me himself—what are you laughing at?— that when I was touring in Norway that brazen Frederika came and wanted to seduce him! Can you fancy anything so infamous? (*pause*) It was lucky that Bob told me about it himself and that it didn't reach me through gossip. (*pause*) But would you believe it, Frederika wasn't the only one! I don't know why, but the women are crazy about my husband. They must think he has influence about getting them theatrical engagements, because he is connected with the government. Perhaps you were after him yourself. I didn't use to trust you any too much. But now I know he never bothered his head about you, and you always seemed to have a grudge against him some way.

(*Pause. They look at each other in a puzzled way.*)

MRS. X   Come and see us this evening, Amelia, and show us that you're not put out with us—not put out with me at any rate. I don't know, but I think it would be uncomfortable to have you for an enemy. Perhaps it's because I stood in your way (*more slowly*) or—I really don't know why—in particular.

(*Pause.* MISS Y *stares at* MRS. X *curiously.*)

MRS. X (*thoughtfully*) Our acquaintance has been so queer. When I saw you for the first time I was afraid of you, so afraid that I didn't dare let you out of my sight; no matter when or where, I always found myself near you—I didn't dare have you for an enemy, so I became your friend. But there was always discord when you came to our house, because I saw that my husband couldn't endure you, and the whole thing seemed as awry to me as an ill-fitting gown—and I did all I could to make him friendly toward you, but with no success until you became engaged. Then came a violent friendship between you, so that it looked all at once as though you both dared show your real feelings only when you were secure—and then—how was it later? I didn't get jealous—strange to say! And I remember at the christening, when you acted as godmother, I made him kiss you—he did so, and you became so confused—as it were; I didn't notice it then—didn't think about it later, either—have never thought about it until—now! (*Rises suddenly.*) Why are you silent? You haven't said a word this whole time, but you have let me go on talking! You have sat there, and your eyes have reeled out of me all these thoughts which lay like raw silk in its cocoon—thoughts—suspicious thoughts, perhaps. Let me see— why did you break your engagement? Why do you never come to our house any more? Why won't you come to see us tonight?

(MISS Y *appears as if about to speak.*)

MRS. X Hush, you needn't speak—I understand it all! It was because— and because—and because! Yes, yes! Now all the accounts balance. That's it. Fie, I won't sit at the same table with you. (*Moves her things to another table.*) That's the reason I had to embroider tulips—which I hate—on his slippers, because you are fond of tulips; that's why (*throws slippers on the floor*) we go to Lake Malarn in the summer, because you don't like salt water; that's why my boy is named Eskil— because it's your father's name; that's why I wear your colors, read your authors, eat your favorite dishes, drink your drinks—chocolate, for instance; that's why—oh—my God—it's terrible, when I think about it; it's terrible. Everything, everything came from you to me, even your passions. Your soul crept into mine, like a worm into an apple, ate and ate, bored and bored, until nothing was left but the rind and a little black dust within. I wanted to get away from you, but I couldn't; you lay like a snake and charmed me with your black eyes; I felt that when I lifted my wings they only dragged me down; I lay in the water with bound feet, and the stronger I strove to keep up the deeper I worked myself down, down, until I sank to the bottom, where you lay like a giant crab to clutch me in your claws—and there I am lying now.

I hate you, hate you, hate you! And you only sit there silent—silent and indifferent; indifferent whether it's new moon or waning moon, Christmas or New Year's, whether others are happy or unhappy; without power to hate or to love; as quiet as a stork by a rat hole—you couldn't scent your prey and capture it, but you could lie in wait for it! You sit here in your corner of the cafe—did you know it's called "The Rat Trap" for you? And read the papers to see if misfortune hasn't befallen someone, to see if someone hasn't been given notice at the theatre, perhaps; you sit here and calculate about your next victim and reckon on your chances of recompense like a pilot in a shipwreck. Poor Amelia. I pity you, nevertheless, because I know you are unhappy, unhappy like one who has been wounded, and angry because you are wounded. I can't be angry with you, no matter how much I want to be—because you come out the weaker one. Yes, all that with Bob doesn't trouble me. What is that to me, after all? And what difference does it make whether I learned to drink chocolate from you or some one else? (*Sips a spoonful from her cup.*) Besides, chocolate is very healthful. And if you taught me how to dress—tant mieux!—that has only made me more attractive to my husband; so you lost and I won there. Well, judging by certain signs, I believe you have already lost him; and you certainly intended that I should leave him—so as you did with your fiance and regret as you now regret; but, you see, I don't do that— we mustn't be too exacting. And why should I take only what no one else wants?

Perhaps, take it all in all, I am at this moment the stronger one. You received nothing from me, but you gave me much. And now I seem like a thief since you have awakened and find I possess what is your loss. How could it be otherwise when everything is worthless and sterile in your hands? You can never keep a man's love with your tulips and your passions—but I can keep it. You can't learn how to live from your authors, as I have learned. You have no little Eskil to cherish, even if your father's name was Eskil. And why are you always silent, silent, silent? I though that was strength, but perhaps it is because you have nothing to say! Because you never think about anything! (*Rises and picks up slippers.*) Now I'm going home—and take the tulips with me—*your* tulips! You are unable to learn from another; you can't bend—therefore, you broke like a dry stalk. But I won't break! Thank you, Amelia, for all your good lessons. Thanks for teaching my husband how to love. Now I'm going home to love him. (*Goes.*)

Reflections

1. Which character does the title of the play allude to?

2. How will you reflect this fact in your interpretation?

Continue with the next passage, which takes a humorous look at an odd couple.

■ THE ODD COUPLE ■
NEIL SIMON

(FELIX *comes out of the kitchen carrying a tray with steaming dish of spaghetti. As he crosses behind* OSCAR *to the table, he smells it "deliciously" and passes it close to* OSCAR *to make sure* OSCAR *smells the fantastic dish he's missing. As* FELIX *sits and begins to eat,* OSCAR *takes can of aerosol spray from the bar, and circling the table sprays all about* FELIX, *puts can down next to him and goes back to his newspaper.*)

FELIX   (*Pushing spaghetti away.*) All right, how much longer is this gonna go on?

OSCAR   (*Reading his paper.*) Are you talking to me?

FELIX   That's right, I'm talking to you.

OSCAR   What do you want to know?

FELIX   I want to know if you're going to spend the rest of your life not talking to me. Because if you are, I'm going to buy a radio. (*No reply.*) Well? (*No reply.*) I see. You're not going to talk to me. (*No reply.*) All right. Two can play at this game. (*Pause.*) If you're not going to talk to me, I'm not going to talk to you. (*No reply.*) I can act childish too, you know. (*No reply.*) I can go on without talking just as long as you can.

OSCAR   Then why the hell don't you shut up?

FELIX   Are you talking to me?

OSCAR   You had your chance to talk last night. I begged you to come up-stairs with me. From now on I never want to hear a word from that shampooed head as long as you live. That's a warning, Felix.

FELIX   (*Stares at him.*) I stand warned. . . . Over and out!

OSCAR   (*Gets up, taking key out of his pocket and slams it on the table.*) There's a key to the back door. If you stick to the hallway and your room, you won't get hurt. (*Sits back down on couch.*)

FELIX   I don't think I gather the entire meaning of that remark.

OSCAR   Then I'll explain it to you. Stay out of my way.

FELIX   (*Picks up key and moves to couch.*) I think you're serious. I think you're really serious. . . . Are you serious?

OSCAR   This is my apartment. Everything in my apartment is mine. The only thing here that's yours is you. Just stay in your room and speak softly.

FELIX   Yeah, you're serious. . . . Well, let me remind you that I pay half the rent and I'll go into any room I want. (*He gets up angrily and starts towards hallway.*)

OSCAR   Where are you going?

FELIX   I'm going to walk around your bedroom.

OSCAR   (*Slams down newspaper.*) You stay out of there.

FELIX   (*Steaming.*) Don't tell me where to go. I pay a hundred and twenty dollars a month.

OSCAR   That was off-season. Starting tomorrow the rates are twelve dollars a day.

FELIX   All right. (*He takes some bills out of his pocket and slams them down on table.*) There you are. I'm paid up for today. Now I'm going to walk in your bedroom. (*He starts to storm off.*)

OSCAR   Stay out of there! Stay out of my room! (*He chases after him.* FELIX *dodges around the table as* OSCAR *blocks the hallway.*)

FELIX   (*Backing away, keeping table between them.*) Watch yourself! Just watch yourself, Oscar!

OSCAR   (*With a pointing finger.*) I'm warning you. You want to live here, I don't want to see you, I don't want to hear you and I don't want to smell your cooking. Now get this spaghetti off my poker table.

FELIX   Ha! Haha!

OSCAR   What the hell's so funny!

FELIX   It's not spaghetti. It's linguini! (OSCAR *picks up the plate of linguini, crosses to the doorway, and hurls it into the kitchen.*)

OSCAR   Now it's garbage! (*Paces around the couch.*)

FELIX   (*Looks at* OSCAR *unbelievingly.*) What an insane thing to do. You are crazy! . . . I'm a neurotic nut but *you are crazy!*

OSCAR   *I'm* crazy, heh? That's really funny coming from a fruitcake like you.

FELIX   (*Goes to kitchen door and looks in at the mess. Turns back to* OSCAR.) I'm not cleaning that up.

OSCAR   Is that a promise?

FELIX.   Did you hear what I said? I'm not cleaning it up. It's your mess. (*Looking into kitchen again.*) Look at it. Hanging all over the walls.

OSCAR   (*Crosses up on landing and looks at kitchen door.*) I like it. (*Closes door and paces right.*)

FELIX   (*Fumes.*) You'd just let it lie there, wouldn't you? Until it turns hard and brown and . . . yich. . . It's disgusting. . . . . I'm cleaning it up. (*He goes into the kitchen.* OSCAR *chases after him. There is the sound of a struggle and falling pots.*)

OSCAR   (*Off.*) Leave it alone. . . . . You touch one strand of that linguini— and I'm gonna punch you right in your sinuses.

FELIX   (*Dashes out of kitchen with* OSCAR *in pursuit. Stops and tries to calm* OS-CAR *down.*) Oscar . . . I'd like you to take a couple of phenobarbital.

OSCAR   (*Points.*) Go to your room! . . . Did you hear what I said? Go *to your room!*

Reflections

1. What adjectives would you use to describe Felix and Oscar?

2. How could you embody these adjectives during a performance?

Now, do the following exercises for the main characters in both of the preceding examples.

A. Walk across the room as you imagine the characters would walk if they were visiting your class. How do their walks differ?

B. Count from one to twenty as you imagine each of the characters in the passages would count. Give special attention to pitch, rate, volume, and quality.

C. Now, read the passages again, this time taking all the stage directions and dialogue literally. For example, when "Felix gets up angrily and starts towards hallway," get up angrily and start toward the hallway.

D. Read the passages for a third time. This time let your muscles recall where they have just been and what they have just experienced; use the medium of suggestion, rather than the medium of overt or literal action.

As an interpreter, you are expected to project your empathy for a character through your stance, your muscle tone, and your voice. With these tools you can suggest the degree of physical and vocal tension implied in your script. More than simply yourself, as an interpreter you can perform a play—with no need for a supporting cast!

Character Differentiation

The preceding techniques should help you to understand, to visualize, and to present the characters in your play. Once you develop a feel for each character's age, voice tone, health state, mood intensities, and movement rhythms, then you are ready to help your audience distinguish one character from another in a performance. In addition, you may reinforce the preceding techniques of character differentiation with the recognized technique of character placement.

As we discussed in the chapter on narrative prose, an interpreter using the device of character placement identifies a constant angle of address with a specific character. In other words, each character in a scene speaks in a predetermined direction, no matter whom he or she is addressing. This directional technique, when used in conjunction with the other methods we have discussed, enables the audience members to identify the character who is speaking; it also helps them to visualize and to hear the character from their own perceptions. Thus, a working understanding of character placement, together with the posture, facial expression, muscle tone, and vocal cues techniques we have already discussed, is an asset to the interpretative performer.

Setting and Time

Playwrights, like writers of narrative prose, also use setting and time to further enrich and define their works. Unlike the narrative prose writer, however, a dramatist usually places this kind of information in the *stage directions* that precede each act or scene of the play. This practice further complicates the task of the interpreter because, unlike actors who often work within an artificially created set, the oral interpreter usually works only with the set that exists in his or her mind.

To help re-create this set for an audience and to be sure the audience experiences the desired atmosphere, an interpreter should relate a portion of the stage directions provided by the author. To accomplish this, the oral reader may simply incorporate parts of these descriptions into his or her introduction and transitions. In this way, you can help your audience to internalize the scenic embellishments of the play. You can help them etch the important aspects of time and place into their imaginations and to appreciate the ways time and location affect the mood-tones that color each of the play's characters. Thus, like playwrights, oral interpreters of plays may also use setting to let their audiences know how environment and atmosphere pervade and permeate a drama.

GETTING INVOLVED
Stage Directions

What purposes are fulfilled by the following stage directions excerpted from *Long Day's Journey into Night* by Eugene O'Neill?

> It is around half past six in the evening. Dusk is gathering in the living room, an early dusk due to the fog which has rolled in from the Sound and is like a white curtain drawn down outside the windows. From a lighthouse beyond the harbor's mouth, a foghorn is heard at regular intervals, moaning like a mournful whale in labor, and from the harbor itself, intermittently, comes the warning ringing of bells on yachts at anchor.

Reflections

1. What kind of atmosphere has the author created in this passage?

2. Why do you think he uses the foghorn sound?

Styles of Drama

Styles of drama, like styles of architecture, painting, or dress, have changed and evolved through the centuries. In fact, it is this constant change in style that makes drama seem new from age to age.

During various periods, different dramatic elements have received emphasis. For example, the dramatic pendulum swings from simple and sparse plots to extensively developed plots, then back again. Similarly, we find the dramatic pendulum swinging from character types to detailed individuals and back again. In terms of dialogue, the pendulum has swung from verse dialogue to prose dialogue to no dialogue, then back again. Each age develops its own method of dramatically exhibiting the human condition. Our concern is with how the frequent change in dramatic style affects the oral interpreter. How does the oral interpreter approach the problem of style?

In order for you fully to suggest a specific character to an audience, you have to first immerse yourself into the dramatic period in which the character lives. To do so, you will want to familiarize yourself with the manner and customs of the period. Also, you should attempt to find out how and why the author's characters act, speak, and think as they do. At this point, let us briefly explore a number of different dramatic styles and periods.

The Greek Period

The tragic plays of the Greek period are elevated by verse and formalized by the use of a chorus. Unlike those in other dramatic periods, the characters in a Greek play are not surrounded by furniture, nor do they involve themselves in idle or unimportant conversations. Characters in Greek plays simply do not have time to involve themselves in inconsequential activities—these characters have been placed in the midst of mind-boggling crises.

Thus, when reading Greek tragedy aloud, you will want to communicate these dramatic qualities to your audiences. In order to do this, you will need to exhibit movements characterized by *dramatic economy;* that is, your movements should be slow, formal, and broad, rather than small, casual, and realistic. You will also want your voice to suit the roles you are portraying; for this you will need to work to capture vocally the rhythmic chants, the lamentations, and the exalted nature of the poetry.

GETTING INVOLVED

Brown Paper Movement

A. Your instructor will provide you with large sheets of brown wrapping paper. Your goal is to hold the wrapping paper so it is completely extended as you move about your classroom to the slow music provided. The real challenge though, is to move with the paper without making a sound. Do not allow that paper to crinkle. This is best accomplished by extending your arms completely.

B. Next, without breaking the silence, fold the sheet of brown paper into a very small package.

Reflections

1. To keep it silent, what type of movements did you have to make with the paper?

2. Were you successful in keeping the paper still while you moved about the classroom? Why?

You probably discovered that the previous task required some concentration. Did you find the exercise easier to do when your movements were large, slow, and stately? Challenge your abilities with the next exercise.

GETTING INVOLVED
Masks, Voice, and Movement

Wearing a mask you create from cardboard, posterboard, or a paper bag, express the following emotions using physical and vocal cues:

love, hate, fury, horror, hope, arrogance

Reflections

1. What happened to the size of your physical actions when you donned the mask? Did they become more sweeping and more majestic?

2. How did your voice differ from its normal conversational tone?

The wrapping paper and mask exercises were designed to give you the opportunity to internalize the types of body and vocal cues you must send your audience in order for them to understand the magnitude of the tragedies developed by the ancient Greeks. Try this now.

GETTING INVOLVED
Meet the Greeks

A. Read aloud the following passage from *Antigone* by the Greek playwright Sophocles. In this excerpt, Creon, the uncle of Antigone, has denied her brother Polynices the rite of burial. Antigone risked her life to see that Polynices was properly buried.

■ ANTIGONE ■
SOPHOCLES

CREON   You, you whose face is bent to earth, do you avow, or disavow, this deed?

ANTIGONE   I avow it; I make no denial.

CREON   (*To Guard*) You can go wherever you will, free and clear of a grave charge. (*Exit Guard*) (*To* ANTIGONE) Now, tell me, not in many words but briefly, did you know that an edict had forbidden this?

ANTIGONE   I knew it; could I help it? It was public.

CREON   Did you then dare transgress that law?

ANTIGONE   Yes, for it was not Zeus who had published that edict; not such are the laws set among men by the Justice who dwells with the gods below. Nor did I deem that your decrees were of such force that a mortal could override the unwritten and unfailing statutes of heaven. For their life is not of today or yesterday, but from all time; no man knows when they were first put forth.

Not through dread of any human pride could I answer to the gods for breaking *these*. Die I must; that I knew well (how should I not?) even without your edicts. But if I am to die before my time I count that a great gain. If anyone lives as I do, compassed about with evils, could he find anything but gain in death?

So for me to meet this doom is trifling grief. But if I had suffered my mother's son to lie in death an unburied corpse, that would have grieved me; for this I am not grieved. And if my present deeds are foolish in your sight, it may be that a foolish judge arraigns my folly.

CREON   Yet I would have you know that overstubborn spirits are most often humbled. It is the stiffest iron, baked to hardness in the fire, that you will most often see snapped and shivered; and I have known horses that show temper brought to order by a little curb. There is no room for pride when you are your neighbor's slave. This girl was already versed in insolence when she transgressed the laws that had been set forth; that now done, look, a second insult, to boast of it and exult in her deed.

Now truly I am no man, she is the man, if this victory shall rest with her and bring no penalty. No! though she is my sister's child or nearer to me in blood than any that worships Zeus at the altar of our house, she and her kinsfolk shall not avoid a doom most dire; for I charge that other with a like share in the plotting of this burial.

Summon her; I saw her within just now, raving and not mistress of her wits. So often before the deed, when people plot mischief in the dark, the mind stands self-convicted in its treason. But this too is hateful, when one who has been caught in wickedness then seeks to make the crime a glory.

ANTIGONE   Would you do more than take and slay me?

CREON   No, no more; having that I have all.

ANTIGONE   Why then do you delay? In your discourse there is nothing that pleases me—may there never be—and so my words must needs be unpleasing to you. And yet for glory—how could I have won a nobler than by giving burial to my own brother? All here would own that they thought it well, if their lips were not sealed by fear. Royalty, blessed in so much besides, has the power to do and say what it will.

CREON   In that view you differ from all these Thebans.

ANTIGONE   They also share it, but they curb their tongues for you

CREON   And are you not ashamed to act apart from them?

ANTIGONE   No; there is nothing shameful in piety to a brother.

CREON   Was it not a brother too that died in the opposite cause?

ANTIGONE   Brother by the same mother and the same sire.

CREON   Why then do you render a grace that is impious in his sight?

ANTIGONE   The dead man will not say that he so deems it.

CREON   Yes, if you make him but equal in honor with the wicked.

ANTIGONE   It was his brother, not his slave, that perished.

CREON   Wasting this land; while *he* fell as its champion.

ANTIGONE   Nevertheless Hades desires these rites.

CREON   But the good does not desire a like portion with the evil.

ANTIGONE   Who knows but this seems blameless in the world below.

CREON   A foe is never a friend—not even in death.

ANTIGONE   It is not my nature to join in hating, but in loving.

CREON   Pass then to the world of the dead, and if you must needs love, love them. While I live no woman shall rule me.

Reflections

1. What kind of characters are you asked to portray?

2. What type of language does each character use?

3. What are each character's chief concerns?

4. With what type of force is each character in conflict?

5. How do you visualize each character's movements?

6. How do you imagine each character's speaking voice?

B. Read the passage aloud again; this time wear your mask.

Reflections

1. How did wearing the mask change your reading, if at all? Was your reading faster? slower? louder? softer?

2. Did the gestures you employed alter? Why?

C. Remove the mask and read the passage aloud for a third time, attempting to maintain the style you attained previously when you were masked.

The Roman Period

While Greek tragedies are usually presented in a slow and stately style, Roman comedies have a rapid and conversational style. The plays in this period were comprised of loosely plotted domestic situations; in fact, the situation comedies we watch on television or see in movies are patterned after them.

The language of the characters in Roman comedies sparkles with wit and humor; the scripts abound in opportunities for expressive gestures or pantomime such as stock comic poses. When reading plays from this period, therefore, you will do well to think of yourself as a clown without make-up, a vaudeville comic, an animated stand-up comic, or a situation comedy star. You will want to utilize a wide variety of facial expressions to help you communicate to your audience the farcical nature of the material. Loosen up and give the following exercise a try.

GETTING INVOLVED
Let's Go Roman

Prepare to perform the following passage.

■ THE GHOST ■

PLAUTUS; translated by E. F. WATLING

(Outside the house of Theopropides an elderly and bucolic slave named Grumio is hammering at the door.)

GRUMIO   Hey there, Tranio! Come out of that kitchen, will you! . . . Come out, young whipper-snapper! . . . Up to some saucy tricks among the saucepans, I'll be bound . . . Come out here, you master's ruin! By gum, I'll give you what you deserve if I get you out on the farm, may I die if I don't. What are you hiding in there for, you smelly scullion? Come out here, I tell you!

(At last Tranio appears—a young and rather elegant slave.)

TRANIO   Now then, pig, what's all this clatter about? Out in the street too? Where do you think you are? This isn't the country, you know. Get away from this house, please. Go back to your farm. Go and hang yourself, if you like, only stay away from this door. . . . What are you waiting for? *(Starting to pummel him) This?*

GRUMIO   Hey, hey, steady on. What's that for?

TRANIO   For being alive.

GRUMIO   I can bear it. I only wish the old master would come home—if he ever does come home again, with you eating the life out of him while he's away.

TRANIO   That's a lie—and it doesn't make sense either, woodenhead. How can a person eat the life out of a person when that person's somewhere else?

GRUMIO   You think me a country bumpkin, I dare say—witty city chap that you are—pretty witty city chit. I expect you know you're going to be sent out to the mill yourself before long. Yes, any day now you'll be joining the outdoor staff—the ironclads. Better make the most of your time now, my lad. Drink and be merry, waste your master's goods and make a ruin of your master's fine young son. Drink with your friends all day and night, Greek fashion. Buy your women and set them free. Live like lords, with hangers-on feeding their bellies at your expense. Was this what your master told you to do when he went away? Is this the way he expects to find his house looked after when he comes back? Is this what you call being a good servant, playing fast and loose with your master's property and corrupting your master's son? Corrupted he surely is, for what I know the way he's going on.

Not so long ago he was known for the steadiest and best-behaved young man in all Athens; now he's top of a very different class. And that's thanks to your example and teaching.

TRANIO   Is it any business of yours what I am or what I do, damn you? Haven't you got any cattle to look after in the country? If I like drinking and wenching, that's my affair; it's my skin I'm risking, not yours.

GRUMIO   Bold as brass, ain't he?

TRANIO   Jupiter and all the gods strike you dead! Phew, you stink—mud-begotten clod of goat and pig dung; you stink of dog and goat garlic.

GRUMIO   What do you expect? We can't all stink of perfumes like you. We can't all lie on the best couches or feed on the finicky fodder you get. All right—keep your pigeons and poultry and game fish, and let me enjoy the fare that comes my way. You're the lucky one; I'm not. We must take as we find—as long as I can have what good I've got, and you the trouble you're going to get.

TRANIO   You're jealous, Grumio, if you ask me; jealous because I'm doing well and you're not. It's only natural. It's natural for me to keep women and you to keep cows; me to have a good life, you to have a mucky one.

GRUMIO   Gallows-meat, that's what you are, and what you soon will be, if I know anything about it—hustled through the streets under a yoke, with goads through your guts, when the master comes home.

TRANIO   Who knows? It might be you sooner than me.

GRUMIO   It won't because I've not deserved it, as you have and still do.

TRANIO   Cut it out, will you, if you don't want to be exterminated on this spot.

GRUMIO   (*Changing the subject*) Have you got any greenstuff for me to take out to the cattle? If so, let's have it . . . if you're not eating it . . . (*Tranio disdains to answer this*) Oh go to hell then; go on the way you're going; drink, eat your fancy Greek food, fill your bellies with slaughtered flesh—

TRANIO   Shut your mouth and get back to the farm. I have to go to Piraeus for some fish for supper. I'll get some fodder sent over to the farm tomorrow. . . . What are you standing staring at me now for, crossbones?

GRUMIO   That's what they'll be calling you before long, damn me if they won't.

TRANIO ''Before long'' they can do what they like, provided things can stay as they are for the present.

GRUMIO Have it your own way. I know one thing—what's coming to you always comes quicker than what you're looking for.

TRANIO Leave me alone, will you, and get back to the farm. Remove yourself. I can't waste any more time on you. (TRANIO *goes off along the street*)

GRUMIO Off he goes; and don't give tuppence for my warnings. Oh, gods, help me. Let the master come back soon!

Reflections

1. What characteristics serve to distinguish Tranio and Grumio from each other?

2. How can you suggest these characteristics vocally and physically during your performance?

3. If you were to cast popular comic actors in these parts, whom would you cast and why?

The Middle Ages

The life of the peasant in medieval times was one of struggle and hardship, while the life of the nobility was one of festivity and amusement. Both types of individuals, however, found joy in drama. Drama in the Middle Ages came out of the church; consequently, the subject matter of plays from this period is usually biblical or ethical in nature.

One type of play prominent in medieval times is the *morality drama*. In it, characters such as Vice, Death, Good Deeds, and Riches are personified. The purpose of the morality play is to teach or demonstrate a lesson. The characters in these plays are representative of types rather than individuals; thus, the interpreter should approach these roles with broad or exaggerated body and voice movements.

GETTING INVOLVED
Mingling in Medieval Times

Read the following passage from the morality play *Everyman*. In this play God sends Death to deliver a summons for Everyman. Everyman pleads for more time or for the right to have friends accompany him on his last journey. However, with the exception of Good Deeds, all of his friends (Good Fellowship, Kindred and Goods, Strength, Discretion, and Five Wits) desert him.

■ EVERYMAN ■
ANONYMOUS

MESSENGER   I pray you all give your audience,
    And hear this matter with reverence,
    By figure a moral play—
    The *Summoning of Everyman* called it is,
    That of our lives and ending shows
    How transitory we be all day.

DEATH   I am Death, that no man dreadeth.
    For every man I 'rest, and no man spareth;
    For it is God's commandment
    That all to me should be obedient.

EVERYMAN   O Death! thou comest when I had thee least in mind.
    In thy power it lieth me to save.
    Yet of my goods will I give thee, if thou will be kind;
    Yea, a thousand pounds shalt thou have,
    If thou defer this matter till another day.

DEATH   Everyman, it may not be, by no way!
    I set not by gold, silver, nor riches,
    Nor by pope, emperor, king, duke, nor princes.
    For, and I would receive gifts great,
    All the world I might get;
    But my custom is clean contrary.
    I give thee no respite. Come hence, and not tarry.

EVERYMAN   Alas! shall I have no longer respite?
      I may say Death giveth no warning.
      To think on thee, it maketh my heart sick,
      For all unready is my book of reckoning.
      But twelve year and I might have abiding,
      My counting-book I would make so clear,
      That my reckoning I should not need to fear.
      Wherefore, Death, I pray thee, for God's mercy,
      Spare me till I be provided of remedy.

DEATH   Thee availeth not to cry, weep, and pry;
      But haste thee lightly that thou were gone that journey,
      And prove thy friends if thou can.
      For wete thou well the tide abideth no man;
      And in the world each living creature
      For Adam's sin must die of nature.

EVERYMAN   Death, if I should this pilgrimage take,
      And my reckoning surely make,
      Show me, for saint charity,
      Should I not come again shortly?

DEATH   No, Everyman; and thou be once there,
      Thou mayest never more come here,
      Trust me verily.

EVERYMAN   O gracious God, in the high seat celestial,
      Have mercy on me in this most need!
      Shall I have no company from this vale terrestrial
      Of mine acquaintance that way me to lead?

DEATH   Yea, if any be so hardy,
      That would go with thee and bear thee company.
      Hie thee that thou were gone to God's magnificence,
      Thy reckoning to give before his presence.
      What! Weenest thou thy life is given thee,
      And thy worldly goods also?

EVERYMAN   I had weened so, verily.

DEATH   Nay, nay; it was but lent thee;
      For, as soon as thou art gone,
      Another a while shall have it, and then go therefrom
      Even as thou hast done.
      Everyman, thou art mad! Thou hast they wits five,
      And here on earth will not amend they life;
      For suddenly I do come.

EVERYMAN   O wretched caitiff! whither shall I flee,
        That I might 'scape endless sorrow?
        Now, gentle Death, spare me till tomorrow,
        That I may amend me
        With good advisement.

DEATH   Nay, thereto I will not consent,
        Nor no man will I respite,
        But to the heart suddenly I shall smite
        Without any advisement.
        And now out of thy sight I will me hie;
        See thou make thee ready shortly,
        For thou mayst say this is the day
        That no man living may 'scape away. (*Exit* DEATH.)

Reflections

1. How can you characterize Death and distinguish him from Everyman?

2. Why do you think the play was called *Everyman* rather than *Every person*?

3. What type of voice will you use for each of the characters?

4. How will Death and Everyman stand and move?

The Elizabethan Age

Whereas in ancient times, people believed that fate controlled them, the Renaissance people believed they were free to choose their own paths. Therefore, the plays of this period reflect the vitality that characterized the Elizabethan age. Rather than types, individuality of character and humanistic meaning now moved to the forefront.

Characters in Renaissance dramas are seen struggling to actualize their sense of value; sometimes their struggle gets out of hand. When rehearsing scenes from these plays, you will want to emphasize speech, because you will probably wish to communicate both the meaning and the music of the lines. *Soliloquies*, prompted by a character's psychological tensions, were also a common convention of this age. They act much as a flashback would in a film today. When performing a soliloquy, you will want to work to make both visible and audible the inner tensions experienced by the character in order to convince your audience that the words you speak actually live in your mind.

GETTING INVOLVED
Meet the Bard

A. Prepare to read the following soliloquy from *Hamlet*, by William Shakespeare. In this play, Hamlet, the royal Prince of Denmark, mourns the death of his father and the overhasty remarriage of his mother Gertrude to Claudius, Hamlet's uncle.

HAMLET   O that this too too solid flesh would melt,
     Thaw, and resolve itself into a dew!
     Or that the Everlasting had not fixed
     His canon 'gainst self-slaughter! Oh, God! God!
     How weary, stale, flat and unprofitable
     Seem to me all the uses of this world!
     Fie on 't, ah, fie! 'Tis an unweeded garden
     That grows to seed, things rank and gross in nature
     Possess it merely. That it should come to this!
     But two months dead! Nay, not so much, not two.
     So excellent a King, that was, to this,
     Hyperion to a satyr. So loving to my mother

That he might not beteem the winds of heaven
Visit her face too roughly. Heaven and earth!
Must I remember? Why, she would hang on him
As if increase of appetite had grown
By what it fed on. And yet within a month—
Let me not think on 't.—Frailty, thy name is woman!—
A little month, or ere those shoes were old
With which she followed my poor father's body,
Like Niobe, all tears.—Why she, even she—
Oh, God! A beast that wants discourse of reason
Would have mourned longer—married with my uncle,
My father's brother, but no more like my father
Than I to Hercules. Within a month,
Ere yet the salt of most unrighteous tears
Had left the flushing in her galled eyes,
She married. Oh, most wicked speed, to post
With such dexterity to incestuous sheets!
It is not, nor it cannot, come to good.
But break, my heart, for I must hold my tongue!

Reflections

1. What attitudes does Hamlet display in this soliloquy?

2. How can you use your voice and your body to suggest these feelings to your audience?

3. What words will you emphasize? Where will you pause?

4. Where will you direct your eye focus? When will you change the direction of your gaze? Why?

B. Now read this excerpt from *Macbeth*. In this scene, a doctor and a gentlewoman watch as Lady Macbeth enters sleepwalking, after having helped her husband murder King Duncan.

■ MACBETH ■

WILLIAM SHAKESPEARE

GENTLEWOMAN   Lo you, here she comes! This is her very guise, and upon my life, fast asleep. Observe her. Stand close.

DOCTOR   How came she by that light?

GENTLEWOMAN   Why, it stood by her. She has light by her continually, 'tis her command.

DOCTOR   You see, her eyes are open.

GENTLEWOMAN   Aye, but their sense is shut.

DOCTOR   What is it she does now? Look how she rubs her hands.

GENTLEWOMAN   It is an accustomed action with her to seem thus washing her hands. I have known her continue in this a quarter of an hour.

LADY MACBETH   Yet, here's a spot.

DOCTOR   Hark! She speaks. I will set down what comes from her, to satisfy my remembrance the more strongly.

LADY MACBETH   Out, damned spot! Out I say! One, two—why, then 'tis time to do 't. Hell is murky. Fie, my lord, fie! A soldier, and afeard? What need we fear who knows it, when none can call our power to account? Yet who would have thought the old man to have had so much blood in him?

DOCTOR   Do you mark that?

LADY MACBETH   The Thane of Fife had a wife. Where is she now? What, will these hands ne'er be clean? No more o' that, my lord, no more o' that. You mar all with this starting.

DOCTOR   Go to, go to. You have known what you should not.

GENTLEWOMAN   She has spoke what she should not, I am sure of that. Heaven knows what she has known.

LADY MACBETH   Here's the smell of the blood still. All the perfumes of Arabia will not sweeten this little hand. Oh, oh, oh!

DOCTOR   What a sigh is there! The heart is sorely charged.

GENTLEWOMAN   I would not have such a heart in my bosom for the dignity of the whole body.

DOCTOR   Well, well, well—

GENTLEWOMAN   Pray God it be, sir.

DOCTOR   This disease is beyond my practice. Yet I have known those which have walked in their sleep who have died holily in their beds.

LADY MACBETH   Wash your hands, put on your nightgown, look not so pale. I tell you yet again, Banquo's buried, he cannot come out on 's grave.

DOCTOR   Even so?

LADY MACBETH   To bed, to bed, there's knocking at the gate. Come, come, come, come, give me your hand. What's done cannot be undone. To bed, to bed, to bed. (*Exit*)

Reflections

1. Why does Lady Macbeth rub her hands?

2. What voice quality will you use to characterize her?

3. How will you use your body to express her tensions?

4. How will you change your eye focus for each of the characters?

The Restoration

The Restoration was an ostentatious and exuberant period. The comedies of this age were written for a small and sophisticated social set of English ladies and gentlemen. They gorged themselves with fine food and clothes, indulged themselves in love intrigues, and complimented themselves on being skilled in the arts of petty conversation and precise etiquette.

The plots of most of the Restoration comedies mirrored the love triangles and gaudy behavior of the audiences who originally viewed them. Thus, as an interpreter you want to capture the comic atmosphere of the plays, the graceful surface mannerisms of the characters, and the caprices and inclinations of the times. Most Restoration men and women would have compared themselves to peacocks. Interpreters should bear this in mind and take a moment to consider how peacocks move and sound. Variation in stance, posture, and voice quality will add to your re-creation.

GETTING INVOLVED

Restoration Feathers

Prepare to read aloud the following excerpt from William Congreve's *The Way of the World*. In this scene, Mirabell and Mrs. Millamant are two lovers who strike a bargain that allows them to base their forthcoming marriage on mutual respect, understanding, and equality.

Through their discussion we learn how real love was able to grow and prosper within the fashionable and sophisticated Restoration society. Note that Mirabell and Mrs. Millamant are well aware of the way of their world, and thus they are able to rise above it.

■ THE WAY OF ■
THE WORLD

WILLIAM CONGREVE

MRS. MILLAMANT   Ah! I'll never marry unless I am first made sure of my will and pleasure.

MIRABELL   Would you have 'em both before marriage? or will you be contented with the first now, and stay for the other till after grace?

MRS. MILLAMANT   Ah! don't be impertinent.—My dear liberty, shall I leave thee? my faithful solitude, my darling contemplation, must I bid you then adieu? Ay-hadieu—my morning thoughts, agreeable wakings, indolent slumbers, all *ye douceurs, ye sommeils du matin, adieu.*—I can't do't, 'tis more than impossible.—Positively, Mirabell, I'll lie abed in a morning as long as I please.

MIRABELL   Then I'll get up in a morning as early as I please.

MRS. MILLAMANT   Ah? Idle creature, get up when you will—and d'ye hear, I won't be called names after I'm married; positively, I won't be called names.

MIRABELL   Names!

MRS. MILLAMANT   Aye, as wife, spouse, my dear, joy, jewel, love, sweetheart, and the rest of that nauseous cant, in which men and their wives are so fulsomely familiar—and I shall never bear that. Good

Mirabell, don't let us be familiar or fond, nor kiss before folks, like my Lady Fadler and Sir Francis; nor go to Hyde Park together the first Sunday in a new chariot, to provoke eyes and whispers, and then never be seen there together again, as if we were proud of one another the first week, and ashamed of one another ever after. Let us never visit together, nor go to a play together, but let us be very strange and well-bred. Let us be as strange as if we had been married a great while, and as well-bred as if we were not married at all.

MIRABELL   Have you any more conditions to offer? Hitherto your demands are pretty reasonable.

MRS. MILLAMANT   Trifles—as liberty to pay and receive visits to and from whom I please; to write and receive letters, without interrogatories or wry faces on your part; to wear what I please, and choose conversation with regard only to my own taste; to have no obligation upon me to converse with wits that I don't like, because they are your acquaintance; or to be intimate with fools, because they may be your relations. Come to dinner when I please; dine in my dressing-room when I'm out of humor, without giving a reason. To have my closet inviolate; to be sole empress of my tea-table, which you must never presume to approach without first asking leave. And lastly, wherever I am, you shall always knock at the door before you come in. These articles subscribed, if I continue to endure you a little longer, I may by degrees dwindle into a wife.

MIRABELL   Your bill of fare is something advanced in this latter account. Well, have I liberty to offer conditions—that when you are dwindled into a wife, I may not be beyond measure enlarged into a husband?

MRS. MILLAMANT   You have free leave. Propose your utmost; speak and spare not.

MIRABELL   I thank you. *Imprimis* then, I convenant that your acquaintance be general; that you admit no sworn confidante or intimate of your own sex—no she-friend to screen her affairs under your countenance, and tempt you to make a trial of a mutual secrecy. No decoy-duck to wheedle you a fop-scrambling to the play in a mask, then bring you home in a pretended fright, when you think you shall be found out, and rail at me for missing the play and disappointing the frolic which you had, to pick me up and prove my constancy.

MRS. MILLAMANT   Detestable *imprimis*! I go to the play in a mask!

MIRABELL   Item, I article that you continue to like your own face as long as I shall; and while it passes current with me, that you endeavor not to new-coin it. To which end, together with all vizards for the day, I prohibit all masks for the night, made of oiled-skins and I know not what—hog's bones, hare's gall, pig-water, and the marrow of a roasted cat. In short, I forbid all commerce with the gentlewoman in what-d'ye-call-it Court. Item, I shut my doors against all bawds with baskets, and pennyworths of muslin, china, fans, atlases, etc.—Item, when you shall be breeding—

MRS. MILLAMANT   Ah! name it not.

MIRABELL   Which may be presumed, with a blessing on our endeavors—

MRS. MILLAMANT   Odious endeavors!

MIRABELL   I denounce against all strait lacing, squeezing for a shape, till you mould my boy's head like a sugar-loaf, and instead of a man-child, make me a father to a crooked billet. Lastly, to the dominion of the tea-table I submit—but with proviso, that you exceed not in your province, but restrain yourself to native and simple tea-table drinks, as tea, chocolate, and coffee; as likewise to genuine and authorized tea-table talk—such as mending of fashions, spoiling reputations, railing at absent friends, and so forth—but that on no account you encroach upon the men's prerogative, and presume to drink healths, or toast fellows; for prevention of which I banish all foreign forces and all auxiliaries to the tea-table, as orange-brandy, all aniseed, cinnamon, citron, and Barbadoes waters, together with ratafia, and the most noble spirit of clary, but for cowslip wine, poppy water, and all dormitives, those I allow. These provisos admitted, in other things I may prove a tractable and complying husband.

MRS. MILLAMANT   O horrid provisos! filthy strong-waters! I toast fellows! odious men! I hate your odious provisos.

MIRABELL   Then we're agreed. Shall I kiss your hand upon the contract?

Reflections

1. What interpretation techniques will you use to suggest the physical and vocal qualities of Mirabell and Mrs. Millamant?

2. How will you differentiate the lady from the gentleman while maintaining a Restoration demeanor?

Realism

The drama of this period requires very little elaboration or description. The actor in a realistic play is not supposed to be aware of the audience. Unlike the actor, the oral reader can never fully realize this ideal; the nature of the art form of interpretation simply prevents it.

On the other hand, as an interpreter of literature, you can use your voice and body to suggest the little physical and vocal gestures that identify each of the characters you portray. Concentrate on determining the mood and the movement intensities that distinguish your characters from one another. Carefully observe reality so you are able to re-create characters as truthfully as possible by painstakingly selecting details of action and speech to incorporate into your performance.

GETTING INVOLVED
Reaching for Realism

Prepare to read aloud the following passage from *A Doll's House* by Henrik Ibsen. In this play, Ibsen addresses the question of a woman's rights and social position. Specifically, the work introduces us to Nora, a wife who is treated like a child by her husband, Torvald Helmer.

■ A DOLL'S HOUSE ■
HENRIK IBSEN

NORA   (*Looking at her watch.*) It's not so late yet. Sit down, Torvald; you and I have much to say to each other. (*She sits at one side of the table.*)

HELMER   Nora—what does this mean? Your cold, set face—

NORA   Sit down. It will take some time. I have much to talk over with you. (HELMER *sits at the other side of the table.*)

HELMER   You alarm me, Nora. I don't understand you.

NORA   No, that is just it. You don't understand me; and I have never understood you—till tonight. No, don't interrupt. Only listen to what I say.—We must come to a final settlement, Torvald.

HELMER   How do you mean?

NORA   (*After a short silence.*) Does not one thing strike you as we sit here?

HELMER   What should strike me?

NORA   We have been married eight years. Does it not strike you that this is the first time we two, you and I, man and wife, have talked together seriously?

HELMER   Seriously! What do you call seriously?

NORA   During eight whole years, and more—ever since the day we first met—we have never exchanged one serious word about serious things.

HELMER   Was I always to trouble you with the cares you could not help me to bear?

NORA   I am not talking of cares. I say that we have never yet set ourselves seriously to get to the bottom of anything.

HELMER   Why, my dearest Nora, what have you to do with serious things?

NORA   There we have it! You have never understood me—I have had great injustice done me, Torvald; first by father, and then by you.

HELMER   What! By your father and me?—By us, who have loved you more than all the world?

HELMER   And you can say that?

NORA   And I—how have I prepared myself to educate the children?

HELMER   Nora!

NORA   Did you not say yourself, a few minutes ago, you dared not trust them to me?

HELMER   In the excitement of the moment! Why should you dwell upon that?

NORA   No—you were perfectly right. That problem is beyond me. There is another to be solved first—I must try to educate myself. You are not the man to help me in that. I must set about it alone. And that is why I am leaving you.

HELMER   (*Jumping up.*) What—do you mean to say—?

NORA   I must stand quite alone if I am ever to know myself and my surroundings; so I cannot stay with you.

HELMER   Nora! Nora!

NORA   I am going at once. I daresay Christina will take me in for tonight—

HELMER   You are mad! I shall not allow it! I forbid it!

NORA   It is of no use your forbidding me anything now. I shall take with me what belongs to me. From you I will accept nothing, either now or afterwards.

HELMER   What madness this is!

NORA   Tomorrow I shall go home—I mean to what was my home. It will be easier for me to find some opening there.

HELMER   Oh, in your blind inexperience—

NORA   I must try to gain experience, Torvald.

HELMER   To forsake your home, your husband, and your children! And you don't consider what the world will say.

NORA   I can pay no heed to that. I only know that I must do it.

HELMER   This is monstrous! Can you forsake your holiest duties in this way?

NORA   What do you consider my holiest duties?

HELMER   Do I need to tell you that? Your duties to your husband and your children.

NORA   I have other duties equally sacred.

HELMER   Impossible! What duties do you mean?

NORA   My duties towards myself.

NORA   (*Shaking her head.*) You have never loved me. You only thought it was amusing to be in love with me.

HELMER   Why, Nora, what a thing to say!

NORA   Yes, it is so, Torvald. While I was at home with father, he used to tell me all his opinions, and I held the same opinions. If I had others I said nothing about them, because he wouldn't have liked it. He used to call me his doll-child, and played with me as I played with my dolls. Then I came to live in your house—

HELMER   What an expression to use about our marriage!

NORA   (*Undisturbed.*) I mean I passed from father's hands into yours. You arranged everything according to your taste; and I got the same tastes as you; or I pretended to—I don't know which—both ways, perhaps; sometimes one and sometimes the other. When I look back on it now, I seem to have been living here like a beggar, from hand to mouth. I lived by performing tricks for you, Torvald. But you would have it so. You and father have done me a great wrong. It is your fault that my life has come to nothing.

HELMER   Why, Nora, how unreasonable and ungrateful you are! Have you not been happy here?

NORA   No, never. I thought I was; but I never was.

HELMER   Not—not happy!

NORA   No; only merry. And you have always been so kind to me. But our house has been nothing but a playroom. Here I have been your doll-wife, just as at home I used to be papa's doll-child. And the children, in their turn, have been my dolls. I thought it fun when you played with me, just as the children did when I played with them. That has been our marriage, Torvald.

HELMER   There is some truth in what you say, exaggerated and over-strained though it be. But henceforth it shall be different. Play-time is over; now comes the time for education.

NORA   Whose education? Mine, or the children's?

HELMER   Both, my dear Nora.

NORA   Oh, Torvald, you are not the man to teach me to be a fit wife for you.

Reflections

1. How will you re-create the character of Nora? What attitudes will you try to suggest?

2. How will you re-create the character of Helmer? How does he relate to Nora?

3. What is the main conflict between husband and wife in this scene?

Expressionism

A play that is expressionistic relies on a distortion of its prominent features for effect. In other words, the world is transformed or rearranged by the author. Through expressionistic plays, many authors hope to communicate their loathing for materialism and industrialism—forces they view as the major warpers and destroyers of humanity.

For example, in Elmer Rice's *The Adding Machine*, the depersonalization and mechanization of people is illustrated by characters who are known by numbers and who conduct themselves as machines. Thus, in interpreting this work, the mechanical quality essential to the author's attitude should be reflected in your vocal and physical behaviors.

GETTING INVOLVED
Expressionistic Expression

As you read the following passage, think about the ways in which the author has distorted reality.

■ THE ADDING MACHINE ■
ELMER RICE

BOSS (*Calling*) Oh—er—Mister—er— (ZERO *turns in surprise, sees who it is and trembles nervously.*)

ZERO (*Obsequiously.*) Yes, sir. Do you want me, sir?

BOSS Yes. Just come here a moment, will you?

ZERO Yes, sir. Right away, sir. (*He fumbles his hat, picks it up, stumbles, recovers himself, and approaches the* BOSS, *every fibre quivering.*)

BOSS Mister—er—er—

ZERO Zero.

BOSS Yes, Mr. Zero. I wanted to have a little talk with you.

ZERO (*With a nervous grin.*) Yes, sir, I been kinda expectin' it.

BOSS (*Staring at him.*) Oh, have you?

ZERO Yes, sir.

BOSS How long have you been with us, Mister—er—Mister—

ZERO Zero.

BOSS Yes, Mister Zero.

ZERO Twenty-five years today.

BOSS Twenty-five years! That's a long time.

ZERO Never missed a day.

BOSS And you've been doing the same work all the time?

ZERO Yes, sir. Right here at this desk.

BOSS Then, in that case, a change probably won't be unwelcome to you.

ZERO No, sir, it won't. And that's the truth.

BOSS We've been planning a change in this department for some time.

ZERO   I kinda thought you had your eye on me.

BOSS   You were right. The fact is that my efficiency experts have recommended the installation of adding machines.

ZERO   (*Staring at him.*) Addin' machines?

BOSS   Yes, you've probably seen them. A mechanical device that adds automatically.

ZERO   Sure. I've seen them. Keys—and a handle that you pull. (*He goes through the motions in the air.*)

BOSS   That's it. They do the work in half the time and a high-school girl can operate them. Now, of course, I'm sorry to lose an old and faithful employee—

ZERO   Excuse me, but would you mind sayin' that again?

BOSS   I say I'm sorry to lose an employee who's been with me for so many years—But of course, in an organization like this, efficiency must be the first consideration. You will draw your salary for the full month. And I'll direct my secretary to give you a letter of recommendation—

ZERO   Wait a minute, boss. Let me get this right. You mean I'm canned?

BOSS   I'm sorry—no other alternative—greatly regret—old employee—efficiency—economy—business—*business*—BUSINESS!

Reflections

1. What adjectives would you use to describe the boss?

2. How can you re-create these adjectives in your performance?

3. What kind of person is Zero? How can you suggest his traits during your performance?

Theatre of the Absurd

Absurdist plays, often referred to as the Theatre of the Absurd, emphasize the absurdity of existence. The works suggest that it is impossible to be certain about anything: truth is forever elusive and there are no absolutes on which to base behavior. Such a view grew out of post–World War II disillusionment. In absurdist plays, language and dialogue are often reduced to empty clichés, and people are replaced by material objects or are dehumanized in other ways. When interpreting an absurdist play for an audience, you will once again be called upon to represent types rather than individuals. You will be called upon to mirror the disorder of the world with your voice and your body.

GETTING INVOLVED
Adventure in the Absurd

Read the following passage from *The Sandbox* by Edward Albee. In it, the author relates how a family has chosen to treat the grandmother. How does this compare with the treatment some senior citizens receive in our society?

■ THE SANDBOX ■
EDWARD ALBEE

The Scene: The YOUNG MAN *is alone on stage to the rear of the sandbox. He is doing calisthenics* . . . MOMMY *and* DADDY *enter from stage left.*

MOMMY   (*motioning to* DADDY) Well, here we are; this is the beach.

DADDY   (*whining*) I'm cold.

MOMMY   (*dismissing him with a little laugh*) Don't be silly; it's as warm as toast. Look at that nice young man over there: *he* doesn't seem to think it's cold. (*Waves to the* YOUNG MAN) Hello.

YOUNG MAN   (*with an endearing smile*) Hi!

MOMMY   (*looking about*) This will do perfectly . . . don't you think so, Daddy? There's sand there . . . and the water beyond. What do you think, Daddy?

DADDY   (*vaguely*) Whatever you say, Mommy.

MOMMY   (*with the same little laugh*) Well, of course . . . whatever I say. Then it's settled, is it?

DADDY   (*shrugs*) She's *your* mother, not mine.

MOMMY   I know she's my mother. What do you take me for? (*A pause*) All right, now; let's get on with it . . . Are you ready, Daddy? Let's go get Grandma.

DADDY   Whatever you say, Mommy.

MOMMY   Of course, whatever I say. . . . (*After a moment* MOMMY *and* DADDY *reenter, carrying* GRANDMA. *She is borne in by their hands under her armpits; she is quite rigid; her legs are drawn up, her feet do not touch the ground; the expression on her ancient face is that of puzzlement and fear.*)

MOMMY   Don't look at her. Just sit here . . . be very still . . . and wait . . .

GRANDMA   Ah-haaaaaa! Graaaaa! (*Looks for reaction; gets none. Now . . . directly to the audience*) Honestly! What a way to treat an old woman! Drag her out of the house . . . stick her into a car . . . bring her out here from the city . . . dump her in a pile of sand . . . and leave her here to set. I'm eighty-six years old! I was married when I was seventeen. To a farmer. He died when I was thirty . . . I'm a feeble old woman . . . There's no respect around here! There's no respect around!

Reflections

1. How do the characters treat the grandmother?

2. How do the characters communicate with each other?

3. What vocal qualities and physical cues will you use to help you express Mommy, Daddy, and Grandma in your interpretation?

Now apply what you have learned about play analysis, characterization, and dramatic style to a reading that you choose. You should be able to analyze a scene, adapt it to an oral interpretation situation, identify and empathize with each of the characters, and find creative ways to present them to your audience.

Performer's Journal
The Play's the Thing

Choose a five-minute scene from a play involving no more than three characters to perform for your class. On the day you re-create your scene, hand in an analysis to your instructor. In your discussion, include answers to the following questions.

1. What is happening in your scene?

2. Where is the scene set? How does the atmosphere affect the action?

3. What is the main conflict in the scene?

4. What characters are involved in the scene?

5. How old are they?

6. How does each character see himself or herself?

7. How do each of the characters relate to the other characters in the play?

8. At what tempo does each character move and speak?

9. What adjectives would you use to describe each of the characters?

10. What physical and vocal gestures will you use to re-create the scene for your audience?

You may choose to perform the following scene from Marsha Norman's play 'Night, Mother. In this cutting, Mama tries to convince her daughter Jessie not to kill herself.

■ 'NIGHT, MOTHER ■
MARSHA NORMAN

MAMA   Everything you do has to do with me, Jessie. You can't do *anything*, wash your face or cut your finger, without doing it to me. That's right! You might as well kill me as you, Jessie, it's the same thing. This has to do with me, Jessie.

JESSIE   Then what if it does! What if it has everything to do with you! What if you are all I have and you're not enough? What if I could take all the rest of it if only I didn't have you here? What if the only way I can get away from you for good is to kill myself? What if it is? I can *still* do it!

MAMA   (*In desperate tears.*) Don't leave me, Jessie! (JESSIE *stands for a moment, then turns for the bedroom.*) No! (MAMA *grabs her arm.*)

JESSIE   (*Carefully takes her arm away.*) I have a box of things I want people to have. I'm just going to get it for you. You . . . just rest a minute. (*And* JESSIE *is gone and* MAMA *heads for the telephone, but she can't even pick up the receiver this time, and instead stoops to clean up the bottles that have spilled out of the tray.* JESSIE *returns carrying a box that groceries were delivered in. It probably says Hershey Kisses or Starkist Tuna.* MAMA *is still down on the floor cleaning up, hoping that maybe if she just makes it look nice enough,* JESSIE *will stay.*)

MAMA   Jessie, how can I live here without you? I need you! You're supposed to tell me to stand up straight and say how nice I look in my pink dress and drink my milk. You're supposed to go around and lock up so I know we're safe for the night, and when I wake up, you're supposed to be out there making the coffee and watching me get older every day and you're supposed to help me die when the time comes. I can't do that by myself, Jessie. I'm not like you, Jessie. I hate the quiet and I don't want to die and I don't want you to go, Jessie. How can I . . . (*Has to stop a moment.*) How can I get up every day knowing you had to kill yourself to make it stop hurting and I was here all the time and I never even saw it. And then you gave me this chance to make it better, convince you to stay alive, and I couldn't do it. How can I live with myself after this, Jessie?

JESSIE   I only told you so I could explain it, so you wouldn't blame yourself, so you wouldn't feel bad. There wasn't anything you could say to change my mind. I didn't want you to save me. I just wanted you to know.

MAMA   Stay with me just a little longer. Just a few more years. I don't have that many more to go, Jessie. And as soon as I'm dead, you can do whatever you want. Maybe with me gone, you'll have all the quiet you want, right here in the house. And maybe one day you'll put in some begonias up the walk and get just the right rain for them all summer. And Ricky will be married by then and he'll bring your grandbabies over and you can sneak them a piece of candy when their Daddy's not looking and then be real glad when they've gone home and left you to your quiet again.

JESSIE   Don't you see, Mama, everything I do winds up like this. How could I think you would understand? How could I think you would want a manicure? We could hold hands for an hour and then I could go shoot myself? I'm sorry about tonight, Mama, but it's exactly why I'm doing it.

MAMA   If you've got the guts to kill yourself, Jessie, you've got the guts to stay alive.

CHAPTER SEVEN

The Interpretation of Poetry

Poetry. What does it involve? How does it involve you? Poetry describes experience and allows you to share and understand experience. Poetry helps you develop a clearer perception of life. In fact, you can use poetry to concentrate and intensify your experience, as you use the metallic surface of a reflector to concentrate and intensify light. A poem may help you explore your own contacts with existence; it may help you live more fully and with greater awareness.

> *Poetry is the spontaneous overflow of*
> *powerful feelings; it takes its origin*
> *from emotion recollected in tranquility.*
>
> *—William Wordsworth*

Practically every culture from around the world, throughout history, has used poetry in one form or another to express every emotion and experience imaginable. Poetry, combined with music and dance, is often a part of cultural rituals. Early tribal groups encountered poetry as you will want to encounter poetry—from the inside, with their whole beings. They worked to establish a congruence between their poetic rites or chants and their inner selves; they participated in the life of a poem by dynamically embodying the poem. Ancient tribes first used poetry for what they considered to be important life functions: Poetry praised their gods, incited warriors to battle, celebrated war victories, taunted the defeated, and lamented their dead. Poetry was and still is the voice for desires, fears, prayers, joys, and despairs.

GETTING INVOLVED

Class Chants

Divide the class into small groups. Your group's goal is to create a poetic chant or rite that relates to a class experience. For example, your group might decide to create a chant to praise your instructor, to urge that a test not be given, or to lament a grade. Each person in the group should add a line to the chant, and the whole group, working together, should orchestrate the movement that accompanies the words—is it time for a wave? a raised fist? a pleading gesture?

Reflections

1. What type of chant did your group develop?

2. How did your group use sound and movement to add to the impact of the chant?

3. What repetitive patterns, if any, emerged?

Today, poetry is still an art form that is central to our existence. It serves as a funnel through which all types of impressions and sensations may be filtered—beautiful and ugly, strong and weak, common and proud. Poetry does not discriminate as to subject; it feeds on everything that is of interest or concern to humanity. In fact, the caldron of poetry brims with descriptions of myriad firsthand, observed, or imagined experiences. However, it does remain for a skilled poet to select, unite, and restructure the contents of the poetic pot. The poet does this by utilizing certain artistic resources. Let us examine these resources now.

Rhythm

The first of these artistic resources is *rhythm*. The following exercise should help to improve your understanding of rhythm and its function in poetry.

GETTING INVOLVED
Feeling Rhythm

A. Feel your own heart beat. What do you notice about it?

B. Take your own pulse. What is its rate per minute?

C. Relax a minute and become aware of your rate of breathing.

Like the universe, the human body is constantly engaged in different rhythmic activities. Just as the ocean tides roll in and away from the shore, just as birds seasonally migrate, just as day follows night, so your lungs inflate and deflate, so your heart beats steadily, and so your blood pulses. It is in death that life rhythms cease.

Think for a moment about the class chants you did in the previous exercise. What type of beat did each created chant have? Do you remember how the beat of your chant caused you to speak, move, and feel? Probably it helped your group to build emotional intensity. Think of the beat of your chant as a heartbeat—the pulse of a poem.

Rap music brought chanted poetry very much to the forefront of today's popular culture. Rap artists combine rhythmic poetry with music—a heavy beat and sound—to create an original art form. Come on now, don't be shy. You can learn how—just give rap a try!

GETTING INVOLVED
Rap Performance

A. Have class members who enjoy rap music bring samples to class. If possible, videotape some samples from MTV or similar sources. (Be sure to select segments that contain language you believe is appropriate to your educational setting.)

B. Working in groups, listen closely to one rap performance. Write out the lyrics and distribute them to group members.

C. Working with your group, reproduce the rap sound and the actions that go with it. Perform as if yours was the featured MTV video.

Reflections

1. Were you able to reproduce the feeling of the recording?

2. How did the rhythm work for you as you performed?

3. Are you surprised to learn that poetry—in the form of rap—has become very big business in this country today?

As a person, you walk and breathe rhythmically, with certain recurrent or characteristic patterns. So does a poem. Yet, just as the rhythm of one individual is somewhat different from the rhythm of another, so the rhythm of one poem varies from the rhythm of another. In some poems, the rhythm is so unpatterned or slight that a reader may scarcely be aware of it, while in other poems the rhythm is so pronounced or overt that feet are practically forced to tap and hands to clap to it. Poems with such dominant rhythms are probably written in one of four standard meters or patterns: *iambic, trochaic, anapestic,* or *dactylic.*

Meter

To clarify, **meter** refers to the type of rhythm that can be scanned for stressed and unstressed syllables and then divided into patterned feet, poetic rhythm units. A line in a poem that contains meter is measured by the number of metrical feet it contains. Thus, in metrical poetry a line may be monometer (one foot), dimeter (two feet), trimeter (three feet), tetrameter (four feet), pentameter (five feet), and so on. What are some of the characteristics of these four basic metrical patterns?

GETTING INVOLVED
Meeting Meters

A. The meter most commonly used is iambic or ˘´. In poetry that is predominantly *iambic*, a stressed syllable usually follows an unstressed syllable. The most common iambic line length is pentameter, or five feet. Thus, a line of five iambic feet is called *iambic pentameter*. Iambic is the meter that most nearly approximates the rhythm of ordinary speech. It is the rhythm commonly used by rap artists. It is also the meter Shakespeare used most often. Copy the poem and scan it, placing unstress (˘) and stress (´) marks appropriately above the syllables in Shakespeare's Sonnet 73.*

That time of year thou mayst in me behold
When yellow leaves, or none, or few, do hang
Upon those boughs which shake against the cold,
Bare ruin'd choirs, where late the sweet birds sang.
In me thou see'st the twilight of such day
As after sunset fadeth in the west;
Which by and by black night doth take away,
Death's second self, that seals up all in rest.
In me thou see'st the glowing of such fire,
That on the ashes of his youth doth lie,
As the death-bed whereon it must expire
Consum'd with that which it was nourish'd by.
   This thou perceiv'st, which makes thy love more strong,
   To love that well which thou must leave ere long.

*Note that a sonnet is a poetic form—14 lines of verse.

Reflections

1. Does the poet depart from the predominant iambic pattern at any point(s)? Where?

2. How does this change affect the mood of the poem?

   B. *Trochaic* rhythm is the reverse of iambic rhythm. It is ' ˘ rather than ˘ '. It tends to slow the poem's action or thought. Poe's "The Raven" is predominantly trochaic in rhythm. Scan this excerpt from it now.

■ THE RAVEN ■

EDGAR ALLAN POE

Once upon a midnight dreary, while I pondered, weak and
    weary,
Over many a quaint and curious volume of forgotten lore—
While I nodded, nearly napping, suddenly there came a
    tapping,
As of some one gently rapping, rapping at my chamber door—
" 'Tis some visitor," I muttered, "tapping at my chamber door—
            Only this and nothing more."

Presently my soul grew stronger; hesitating then no longer,
"Sir," said I, "or Madam, truly your forgiveness I implore;
But the fact is I was napping, and so gently you came rapping;
And so faintly you came tapping, tapping at my chamber door,
That I scarce was sure I heard you"—here I opened wide the door;—
            Darkness there and nothing more.

   C. The third standard rhythm is *anapestic* (˘ ˘ '). Each line of an anapestic poem is composed of a foot or number of feet that usually contain two unstressed syllables followed by a stressed syllable. The most usual home of the anapest is in light verse. It works there to create a fast-moving effect— almost a gallop. The limerick relies on anapestic meter.

■ A LIMERICK ■
ANONYMOUS

A staid schizophrenic named Struther,
When told of the death of his brother,
    Said: ''Yes, I am sad;
    It makes me feel bad,
But then, I still have each other.''

The anapest, however, may also be found in serious verse. For example, this excerpt from ''The Destruction of Sennacherib'' by Lord Byron is written in anapestic meter.

■ THE DESTRUCTION ■
OF SENNACHERIB
LORD BYRON

For the Angel of Death spread his wings on the
    blast,
And breathed in the face of the foe as he passed;
And the eyes of the sleepers waxed deadly and
    chill,
And their hearts but once heaved, and forever
    grew still!

D. The least used of the four standard rhythms is the *dactylic* ('˘˘). Unlike the anapestic pattern, it works to produce a monotonous, continuous, steady effect as in the following cutting.

■ Evangeline ■

HENRY WADSWORTH LONGFELLOW

It was the month of May. Far down the Beautiful
    River,
Past the Ohio shore and past the mouth of the
    Wabash,
Into the golden stream of the broad and swift
    Mississippi,
Floated a cumbrous boat, that was rowed by
    Acadian boatmen.

Take a few minutes to scan some of the lyrics in the rap music you examined previously. What poetic patterns are used there?

Besides using meter to provide a background, the poet also employs meter to control the speed and feeling of the lines of the poem. In fact, the poet usually works to match the speed of the poem to the sense of the poem. Consequently, when reading poetry aloud, you need to work to make the basic meter enhance the poem; however, you do *not* want to exaggerate it. The cost of metrical exaggeration might well be a loss of poetic meaning. When reading or performing poetry, you should permit the meter to provide you with a supportive rhythmic accompaniment, but you should not permit it to dominate or overpower your reading.

Regardless of whether you scan a poem methodically or not, as an interpreter you should always aim to feel the "beat" of your poem, to internalize the rhythm of your poem. Eventually, your rhythm and the rhythm of your selection should match.

In order to assure this, you will want to know where the pulse of your poem quickens and where it ebbs. You will want to know at what points you should experience tension and at what points you should experience release. If you cannot mirror these changes in movement, then the poem will not come alive for your audience.

GETTING INVOLVED
Rhythm Operations

Read aloud the following poem.

■ TARANTELLA ■
HILLAIRE BELLOC

Do you remember an Inn,
Miranda?
Do you remember an Inn?
And the tedding and the spreading
Of the straw for a bedding,
And the fleas that tease in the High Pyrenees,
And the wine that tasted of the tar?
And the cheers and the jeers of the young muleteers
(Under the vine of the dark verandah)?

Do you remember an Inn, Miranda,
Do you remember an Inn?
And the cheers and jeers of the young muleteers
Who hadn't got a penny,
And who weren't paying any,
And the hammer at the doors and the din?
And the *hip! hop! hap!*
Of the clap

Of the hands to the twirl and the swirl
Of the girl gone chancing,
Glancing,
Dancing,
Backing and advancing,
Snapping of the clapper to the spin
Out and in—
And the *ting, tong, tang* of the guitar!
Do you remember an Inn,
Miranda?
Do you remember an Inn?

Never more;
Miranda,
Never more.
Only the high peaks hoar:
And Aragon a torrent at the door
No sound
In the walls of the halls where falls
The tread
Of the feet of the dead to the ground,
No sound:
But the boom
Of the far waterfall like doom

Reflections

1. Where does the pulse of this poem quicken?

2. Where does it ebb? How do you know?

3. Why do you think the poet abruptly changed the rhythm of the work?

4. How can you reflect this change in your performance of the selection before an audience?

Tempo

Some lines in poetry speed and excite, while other lines seem to idle and calm. Like music, poetry possesses both crescendos and diminuendos; thus, you can learn to play the poem as you would learn to play a piece of music. A musician reads the time value—full beat, quarter beat, and so on— that a composer has accorded to each note of a composition; an interpreter should read to reflect the time value accorded to an author's words. Ask yourself whether your poem abounds in long or in short sounds, which words or syllables deserve emphasis or stress, and which words or syllables should be left unstressed.

Where has the poet placed rests, or sense pauses? Remember that the absence of sound may also contribute to the creation of a rhythm. By asking and answering such questions, you will discover and reveal the predominant tempo of the poem to your audience.

GETTING INVOLVED

Discovering Tempo

A. Read aloud the following poem.

■ DREAM BOOGIE ■

LANGSTON HUGHES

Good morning, daddy!
Ain't you heard
The boogie-woogie rumble
Of a dream deferred?

Listen closely:
You'll hear their feet
Beating out and beating out a—

> *You think*
> *It's a happy beat?*

Listen to it closely:
Ain't you heard
like a—

> *What did I say?*

Sure,
I'm happy!
Take it away!

> *Hey, pop!*
> *Re-bop!*
> *Mop!*
>
> *Y-e-a-h!*

Reflections

1. What type of beat does this poem have? How do you know?

2. Where does the poet accelerate his pace? How can you as an inter-
    preter indicate this acceleration?

3. How can you use the poem's rhythm to reinforce its meaning during
    performance?

    B. Now read this poem.

■ LINES FOR AN ALBUM ■
WELDON KEES

Over the river and through the woods
To grandmother's house we go . . .

She waits behind the bolted door,
Her withered face in thirty pieces,
While blood runs thin, and memory,
An idiot without a name,
Recalls the snows of eighty years,
The daughter whose death was unexplained,
Darkness, blue veins, and broken leases.
Grandmother waits behind the door
(Sight dims beyond the curtain folds)
With her toothless smile and enuresis.

Over the river and through the woods
To grandmother's house we go . . .

Reflections

1. How does the rhythm of this poem work to reinforce its meaning and feeling?

2. How can you as an interpreter vary your tempo or pace to help you effectively perform the poem?

Other Language Tools

Besides using rhythm as a resource, poets also use a number of specific language tools. These tools cause the words of an effective poem to seem to explode with inner meaning. The first language resource we will consider is **connotation**—the overtones of meaning that surround a word.

GETTING INVOLVED

Connotation

Physically portray each word in the following six word groups. In other words, pantomime your intellectual and emotional responses to each word.

1. firm, stubborn, obstinate

2. neat, fastidious, super-clean

3. slender, skinny, svelte

4. candid, honest, blunt

5. stare, gaze, glare

6. whimper, cry, wail

Reflections

1. What do your pantomimes tell you about your reactions to each word in a word group?

2. How were your reactions similar to those of your classmates? How were they different?

Clearly, the meaning of a word goes beyond its dictionary definition. The meaning also resides in the interpreter's mind and in the minds of each person in his or her audience. It is extremely important that you let the audience understand what the poet had in mind in selecting a particular term. At least convey what *you* have decided the word means. You can use more than just your voice to make this meaning clear. Try to move meaningfully in the exercise that follows.

GETTING INVOLVED
Moving into Meaning

A. Move to the following words and phrases. When your instructor tells you to freeze, momentarily hold the position in which you find yourself. To benefit most from this exercise, work to internalize the feeling of your position and the meaning the associated concept has for you.

1. tired and weary

2. drooping eyelids

3. dropping eyelids open wide

4. eyes wide open

5. shadow

6. jewels

7. ghastly night

Reflections

1. What did each word or phrase make you feel? What images were called to mind? What did you think about?

2. How did you choose to react to each of the word prompts? What do your physical reactions tell you? What did your freeze position tell you about your personal reaction to each word or phrase?

B. Now, read Sonnet 27 by Shakespeare.

Weary with toil, I haste me to my bed,
The dear repose for limbs with travel tired;
But then begins a journey in my head
To work my mind when body's work's expir'd:
For then my thoughts—from far where I
    abide—
Intend a zealous pilgrimage to thee,
And keep my dropping eyelids open wide,
Looking on darkness which the blind do see:
Save that my soul's imaginary sight
Presents thy shadow to my sightless view,
Which, like a jewel hung in ghastly night,
Makes black night beauteous and her old face
    new.
Lo! thus, by day my limbs, by night my mind,
For thee and for myself no quiet find.

Reflections

1. How did your exercise in turning movement into meaning prepare you to experience this literature?

2. How did it help to prepare you to interpret or perform the poem?

3. What movement adaptations did you make once the poetic context of the word or phrase was revealed?

The meaning you give to a word is based on your background, your experience, and the context of the word. In fact, it is context that serves to refine and alter your verbal perception. Accordingly, by their choice and arrangement of words, poets partially control your affective or emotional responses to their words. They actually channel your defining capabilities in specific directions. They encourage you to make certain mental associations.

Poets are thus concerned with more than the dictionary meaning of words. Of interest to them are the nuances of meaning, the associations, and the variations of mood evoked by specific words placed in specific contexts. Further your understanding by trying the following exercise.

GETTING INVOLVED
Word Choices

Read the following poem, giving careful attention to the word and phrase choices provided. In each case, the word or phrase the poet actually employed is placed first; the second word, in italics, was added for this exercise.

■ OZYMANDIAS ■
PERCY BYSSHE SHELLEY

I met a traveller/*voyager* from an antique/*old* land
Who said: Two vast/*large* and trunkless legs of stone/*rock*
Stand/*are* in the desert . . . Near them, on the sand,
Half sunk/*buried*, a shattered/*broken* visage lies, whose frown,
And wrinkled/*torn* lip, and sneer/*look* of cold command,
Tell that its sculptor/*artist* well those passions/*feelings* read
Which yet survive/*live on*, stamped on these lifeless/*dead* things,
The hand that mocked/*laughed at* them, and the heart that fed:
And on the pedestal/*base* these words appear:
''My name is Ozymandias/*Fred*, king of kings:
Look on my works, ye Mighty/*Strong*, and despair/*cry*!''
Nothing beside remains/*is left*. Round the decay/*rot*
Of that colossal wreck/*mess*, boundless and bare/*empty*
The lone and level/*barren* sands stretch far away.

Reflections

1. Why do you believe the poet chose the first word or phrase rather than the hypothetical alternative provided?

2. What does the first word or phrase suggest that the second does not?

You can see that the creative poet is as deliberate about selection of words as a songwriter is about selecting notes. The poet's words must work within the context of the entire piece. Try the next exercise to further solidify your understanding of word choices in poetry.

GETTING INVOLVED
Effective Words

Read the following poem carefully. Note the words and phrases you find particularly effective.

■ FACE OF POVERTY ■
LUCY SMITH

No one can communicate to you
The substance of poverty—
Can tell you either the shape,
   or the depth,
      or the breadth
Of poverty—
Until you have lived with her intimately.

No one can guide your fingers
Over the rims of her eye sockets,
Over her hollow cheeks—
Until perhaps one day
In your wife's once pretty face
You see the lines of poverty;
Until you feel
In her now skinny body,
The protruding bones,
The barely covered ribs,
The shrunken breasts of poverty,

Poverty can be a stranger
In a far-off land:

An alien face
Briefly glimpsed in a newsreel,
An empty rice bowl
In a skinny brown hand,
Until one bleak day
You look out the window—
And poverty is the squatter
In your own backyard.

Poverty wails in the night for milk,
Not knowing the price of a quart.
It is desperation in your teen-ager's face,
Wanting a new evening gown for the junior prom,
After going through school in rummage store clothes.
It is a glass of forgetfulness sold over the bar.
And poverty's voice is a jeer in the night—
   "You may bring another child
   Into the rat race that is your life;
   You may cut down on food
   To buy contraceptives;
   You may see your wife walk alone
   Down some back alley route
   To a reluctant appointment
   With an unsterile knife—
   Or you may sleep alone."
And one morning shaving
You look in the mirror—
And never again will poverty be alien,
For the face of poverty is not over your shoulder,
The face of poverty is your own.
And hearing the break in your wife's voice
At the end of a bedtime story,
You realize that somewhere along the way
The stock ending in your own story went wrong.
And now you no longer ask
That you and your wife
Will live happily ever after—
But simply that you
And your wife
And your children
Will live.

Reflections

1. What associations or overtones adhere to the words you noted? What types of images do these words provoke? How do the words help you experience the poem through your senses?

2. What kind of mood do these words help create?

3. How can you as interpreter harness the suggestive power of these words to enrich your performance of the poem?

Sense Imagery

Poets choose language rich in sense imagery because the words' fresh and vivid images help poets control their impact on readers. As you read more poetry, you will discover that effective poems abound in words relating to the senses.

The poet wants us to hear the words of the poem, to see the experiences they describe, to smell their nature, to taste their poignancy, to touch their core, to feel their warmth or coolness, and to process them physically with our muscles. The poet asks us to respond to the sensory appeals of the poem and, in doing so, to exist in the poem. Ready your senses for the following exercise.

GETTING INVOLVED

Processing Sense Imagery

Read the following poem.

■ MY FATHER'S GARDEN ■

DAVID WAGONER

On his way to the open hearth where white-hot steel
Boiled against furnace walls in wait for his lance
To pierce the fireclay and set loose demons
And dragons in molten tons, blazing
Down to the huge satanic caldrons,
Each day he would pass the scrapyard, his kind of garden.

In rusty rockeries of stoves and brake drums,
In grottoes of sewing machines and refrigerators,
He would pick flowers for us: small gears and cogwheels
With teeth like petals, with holes for anthers,
Long stalks of lead to be poured into toy soldiers,
Ball bearings as big as grapes to knock them down.

He was called a melter. He tried to keep his brain
From melting in those tyger-mouthed mills
Where the same steel reappeared over and over
To be reborn in the fire as something better
Or worse: cannons or cars, needles or girders,
Flagpoles, swords, or plowshares.

But it melted. His classical learning ran
Down and away from him, not burning bright.
His fingers culled a few cold scraps of Latin
And Greek, *magna sine laude*, for crosswords
And brought home lumps of tin and sewer grills
As if they were his ripe prize vegetables.

magna sine laude: without great praise.

Now, on a separate sheet of paper, list the following senses. Next to each sense, write the words or phrases in the poem that appeal to that sense. Be certain to include both primary (most prominent) and secondary appeals (those that are implied).

Sight	Touch
Hearing	Thermal
Smell	Kinetic
Taste	Kinesthetic

How can this exercise help you to effectively re-create literature in performance?

Already you have discovered that poetry overflows with vivid imagery. It abounds in sense appeals. It is up to the interpreter, however, to make these images live in performance. As the oral reader, you will discover and process the images that exist in the work. When performing poetry, use the sense impressions provided to guide you in communicating the total experience of the poem.

Figures of Speech

Poets also use figures of speech to enrich the meaning and impact of their poems. Figurative language functions as a type of *poetic shorthand*: In a brief, economical manner the word phrases convey a broader meaning than the words do when used singly. A figure of speech says something in a round-about way. A figure of speech provides an alternative to literal statement by allowing people to say one thing and mean something else. Some common word figures are *simile, metaphor, personification, hyperbole, paradox,* and *irony.* Let's look at each of these devices.

The Simile

A **simile** is easily identified because it makes an explicit comparison, generally using either the word *like* or *as.* It simply compares the qualities of one thing to the qualities of another, as in the following poem about a guitarist.

GETTING INVOLVED
The Simile

■ THE GUITARIST TUNES UP ■
FRANCES CORNFORD

With what attentive courtesy he bent
Over his instrument;
Not as a lordly conquerer who could
Command both wire and wood,
But as a man with a loved woman might,
Inquiring with delight
What slight essential things she had to say
Before they started, he and she, to play.

Reflections

1. What two things are compared in this poem?

2. Is the comparison a particularly effective one? Why?

3. What performance or behavioral clues does the poet provide the interpreter?

   B. Now read this poem.

■ SAYING GOODBYE ■
TERI GAMBLE

Saying goodbye
    is like crying a rainbow of feeling
      and hoping no.

Wanting to stay
    is like finding a cloud that's been emptied
      with nowhere to go.

But looking away
    is tearing a smile from the face of a rose
      and holding its thorn.

Reflections

1. What comparisons are made in this poem?

2. How can you use your voice and your body to reflect these comparisons?

The Metaphor

A **metaphor** functions like the simile, except it omits the words *like* or *as*. For example, the metaphorical equivalent of the simile ``that dog looks like a toad'' is simply ''that dog is a toad.'' By relating two hitherto unrelated objects, the poet widens the reader's perception of his or her subject. In the preceding poem, which verse contained a metaphor? How did the impact of the metaphor differ from the impact of the similes?

GETTING INVOLVED
The Metaphor

A. Can you identify the metaphor in this poem title: ''The Pretzel Is a Mrs. Weiner''?

Reflections

1. How do you imagine Mrs. Weiner looks when she sits or stands? Show your classmates.

2. What type of voice do you think Mrs. Weiner would have? Why?

B. What metaphor is contained in the following short verse by Teri Gamble?

War is a razor
That cuts into the heart
And makes it d
                    r
                     i
                   p
                     blood.

Reflections

1. What does this poem say about war?

2. How can you embody the metaphor?

C. What does this statement—''Anonymous was a woman.''—by writer Virginia Woolf tell you about women?

Personification

The attributing of human qualities to an object, an animal, or an idea is called **personification.** This device enables poets to add vividness and clarity to their creations. It is sometimes difficult to relate to an object, an animal, or an idea. Personification gives it life by giving it human characteristics. Check your understanding of this figure of speech with the next exercise.

GETTING INVOLVED
Personification

Read this poem aloud.

■ MIRROR ■
SYLVIA PLATH

I am silver and exact. I have no preconceptions.
Whatever I see I swallow immediately
Just as it is, unmisted by love or dislike.
I am not cruel, only truthful—
The eye of a little god, four-cornered.
Most of the time I meditate on the opposite wall.
It is pink, with speckles. I have looked at it so long
I think it is a part of my heart. But it flickers.
Faces and darkness separate us over and over.

Now I am a lake. A woman bends over me,
Searching my reaches for what she really is.
Then she turns to those liars, the candles or the moon.
I see her back, and reflect it faithfully.
She rewards me with tears and an agitation of hands.
I am important to her. She comes and goes.
Each morning it is her face that replaces the darkness.
In me she has drowned a young girl, and in me an old woman
Rises toward her day after day, like a terrible fish.

Reflections

1. What objects are personified in the poem?

2. How can this language device be used by interpreters to help them fulfill the task of poetic visualization?

Hyperbole

Overstatement, or **hyperbole,** is the figure of speech poets employ when they make gross exaggerations. These overstatements make a point more vivid in the mind of your audience. Try this.

GETTING INVOLVED
Hyperbole

■ THE EAGLE ■

ALFRED, LORD TENNYSON

He clasps the crag with crooked hands;
Close to the sun in lonely lands,
Ringed with the azure world, he stands.

The wrinkled sea beneath him crawls;
He watches from his mountain walls,
AND LIKE A THUNDERBOLT HE FALLS.

Reflections

1. What use of hyperbole does Tennyson make in this poem?

2. How does it aid you in formulating a more precise picture of the eagle?

3. How can you apply this understanding to a performance?

Paradox

Poets use **paradox** to point out apparent contradictions that somehow are true. Thus, this figure of speech allows poets to hint at additional meanings that lie beyond the surface level of their words. In this way, writers prod readers into making fresh connections.

GETTING INVOLVED

Paradox

Identify the paradox in the following lines from the Bible.

> Verily, verily, I say unto you, except a
> corn of wheat fall into the ground and
> die, it abideth alone: but if it die, it
> bringeth forth much fruit.

> (John 12:24)

Irony

Irony is simply a language device used by writers to imply the opposite of what they really say in words. You can find examples of irony in the two poems that follow. You can find examples of irony in the routines of many stand-up comics, as well.

GETTING INVOLVED

Irony

Read the following poem carefully, noting how the poet uses irony. How does the poet imply the opposite of what he is saying?

■ THE UNKNOWN CITIZEN ■

W. H. AUDEN

(To JS/07/M/378
This Marble Monument
Is Erected by the State)
He was found by the Bureau of Statistics to be
One against whom there was no official complaint,
And all the reports on his conduct agree
That, in the modern sense of an old-fashioned word, he was
                    a saint,
For in everything he did he served the Greater Community.
Except for the War till the day he retired
He worked in a factory and never got fired
But satisfied his employers, Fudge Motors Inc.
Yet he wasn't a scab or odd in his views,
For his Union reports that he paid his dues,
(Our report on his Union shows it was sound)
And our Social Psychology workers found
That he was popular with his mates and liked a drink.
The Press are convinced that he bought a paper every day
And that his reactions to advertisements were normal in
                    every way.
Policies taken out in his name prove that he was fully
                    insured,
And his Health-card shows he was once in hospital but left
                    it cured.
Both Producers Research and High-Grade Living declare
He was fully sensible to the advantages of the Installment
                    Plan
And had everything necessary to the Modern Man,
A phonograph, a radio, a car and a frigidaire.
Our researchers into Public Opinion are content
That he held the proper opinions for the time of year;
When there was peace, he was for peace; when there was
                    war, he went.
He was married and added five children to the population,
Which our Eugenist says was the right number for a parent
                    of his generation.
Was he free? Was he happy? The question is absurd:
Had anything been wrong, we should certainly have heard.

Reflections

1. How is irony used in this poem? What is literally expressed in it?

2. What attitudes lie beneath the surface of the lines?

3. How can you as an interpreter use your body and your voice to reflect the irony in the selection?

   By using the preceding language devices in various combinations, poets are able to chart verbal maps of experience. It is up to you as an interpretive artist to explore these verbal maps fully. In understanding how poets have used their words to sketch pictures, you will also understand how poets have used their words to touch men and women.

Sound Resources

In order to communicate their works effectively, poets also utilize sound resources with which you will want to familiarize yourself. These sound resources serve to reinforce the tone and meaning of a poem. How may a poet use sound as a medium of meaning?

Onomatopoeia

First of all, the poet may use words that sound like their meaning: flush, hiss, bark, crash, boom, and bubble. This technique is called **onomatopoeia.**

GETTING INVOLVED

Onomatopoeia

Which words in the following poem reinforce their meaning by their sound?

■ FLOOD ■

TERI GAMBLE

I can hear
The rush and surge of raging waters from far off mouths
The groan of the rising stream
The gurgle of river-banks dying,
Trees ravaged and drowning.

I can hear
The crash and thud of wailing rocks from bruised
mountains,
The whines of the crashing stones,
The brutal blasts of plunging pebbles
Gasping for unfound air.

Reflections

1. How can you use the sounds in the poem to clarify the meaning of the poem?

2. How can you use the sounds to strengthen the impact of your performance?

Rhyme

Another important sound resource—**rhyme**—is useful to poets. Besides creating a rich auditory effect through repetition, rhyme adds emphasis to chosen words. Rhyme may be internal, occurring in the middle of a line as it does in this excerpt from ''Tarantella'' by Belloc:

''And the fleas that tease in the high Pyrenees''

Or it may occur, as is customary, at the ends of lines. Poe uses rhyme in this way in ''Annabel Lee.''

It was many and many a year ago
In a kingdom by the sea
That a maiden there lived whom you may know
By the name of Annabel Lee;
And this maiden she lived with no other thought
Than to love and be loved by me.

Thus, besides pleasing our ears, rhyme also helps to organize thoughts and feelings in the poem. Can you think of examples from popular music in which the poet/songwriter uses rhyme to make the music come alive?

Alliteration, Assonance, and Consonance

Poets use the sound tools of alliteration, assonance, and consonance as unifying devices. **Alliteration** is the repetition of initial consonant sounds, as in "flakes fly faster"; **assonance** is the repetition of identical or closely similar vowel sounds, as in "waste no grave"; **consonance** involves the repetition of final consonant sounds, as in "odds and ends," "friend and fiend."

GETTING INVOLVED
Sound Surgery

Divide the class into Sound Surgery Teams. Each team has fifteen minutes to "cut into" a portion of this poem to "take out" examples of end rhyme, internal rhyme, alliteration, assonance, and consonance. After your exploratory operation, be prepared to answer how these sound devices help to carry the meaning of the poem.

■ THE PRINCESS ■
ALFRED, LORD TENNYSON

The splendor falls on castle walls
   And snowy summits old in story;
The long light shakes across the lakes
   And the wild cataract leaps in glory.
Blow, bugle, blow, set the wild echoes flying.
Blow, bugle; answer, echoes, dying, dying, dying.

> O, hark, O, hear! how thin and clear,
>   And thinner, clear, farther going!
> O, sweet and far from cliff and scar
>   The horns of Elfland faintly blowing!
> Blow, let us hear the purple glens replying,
> Blow, bugle: answer, echoes, dying, dying, dying.
>
> O love, they die in yon rich sky,
>   They faint on hill or field or river;
> Our echoes roll from soul to soul,
>   And grow for ever and for ever.
> Blow, bugle, blow, set the wild echoes flying.
> Blow, bugle; answer, echoes, dying, dying, dying.

In the previous exercises in this chapter, you performed rhythm, language, and sound operations. Notice the use of *operations*. Your interpreter's job is, in fact, rather like the job of a surgeon in that you perform an exploratory operation to discover what is inside the poem. During this process you examine the organs that comprise the body of the poem and feel the natural rhythm that flows through the poem. And, like a doctor, you should never simply abandon the poem, untreated, to its audience. You are there to breathe life into it as you help it to live for your audience.

Types of Poems

You will need to know, as an interpreter, the types of poems on which you may be asked to operate. Basically, there are three types: the *lyric* type, the *narrative* type, and the *dramatic* type.

In a **lyric** poem a writer describes and shares an intense subjective emotional experience, picture, or search with a general audience. The poet discloses personal feelings, thoughts, and fears. In effect, the inner self of the poet reaches out to touch the inner self of each reader or auditor of a lyric poem. When performing a lyric poem, make the poet's emotion, picture, or experience visible. Respond to the content of the poem to move your audience. Traditionally, lyric poems are classified as reflective poems, elegies, odes, or sonnets.

The **narrative** poem, like narrative prose, tells a story or details action that leads to a climax. The structure of this kind of poetry allows the poet to speak through specific characters as well as through a narrator. A performer of narrative poetry has a threefold task: first, you want to instill in your audience an understanding of and feeling for the poem's setting. Second, you want to transfer the plot to your audience. And third, you want to reveal the psychological and physical traits of the poem's characters and narrator. Ballads, metrical tales, and epics are three common types of narrative poetry.

Dramatic poetry is related to drama. The ideas, emotions, and action living in this kind of poetry are expressed through words and behaviors of the characters within. Thus, the dramatic poem is revealed without the aid of a third-person narrator.

GETTING INVOLVED
Body Type

Label each of the following poems as either lyric, narrative, or dramatic in nature. Be able to state how the "body type" of each poem helps you determine the way you will perform it. How does knowing the "body type" help you to refine your interpretations of the literature?

■ MY LAST DUCHESS ■
ROBERT BROWNING

That's my last Duchess painted on the wall,
Looking as if she were alive. I call
That piece a wonder, now; Fra Pandolf's hands
Worked busily a day, and there she stands.
Will't please you sit and look at her? I said
"Fra Pandolf" by design, for never read
Strangers like you that pictured countenance,
The depth and passion of its earnest glance,
But to myself they turned (since none puts by
The curtain I have drawn for you, but I)
And seemed as they would ask me, if they durst
How such a glance came there; so, not the first
Are you to turn and ask thus. Sir, 'twas not
Her husband's presence only, called that spot
Of joy into the Duchess' cheek. Perhaps
Fra Pandolf chanced to say, "Her mantle laps

Over my lady's wrist too much,'' or ''Paint
Must never hope to reproduce the faint
Half-flush that dies along her throat.'' Such stuff
Was courtesy, she thought, and cause enough
For calling up that spot of joy. She had
A heart—how shall I say?—too soon made glad,
Too easily impressed; she liked whate'er
She looked on, and her looks went everywhere.
Sir, 'twas all one! My favor at her breast,
The dropping of the daylight in the West,
The bough of cherries some officious fool
Broke in the orchard for her, the white mule
She rode with round the terrace—all and each
Would draw from her alike the approving speech,
Or blush, at least. She thanked me—good! but thanked
Somehow—I know not how—as if she ranked
My gift of a nine-hundred-years-old name
With anybody's gift. Who'd stoop to blame
This sort of trifling? Even had you skill
In speech—which I have not—to make your will
Quite clear to such a one, and say, ''Just this
Or that in you disgusts me; here you miss,
Or there exceed the mark''—and if she let
Herself be lessoned so, nor plainly set
Her wits to yours, forsooth, and made excuse—
E'en then would be some stooping; and I choose
Never to stoop. Oh, sir, she smiled, no doubt,
Whene'er I passed her; but who passed without
Much the same smile? This grew; I gave commands;
Then all smiles stopped together. There she stands
As if alive. Will't please you rise? We'll meet
The company below, then. I repeat,
The Count your master's known munificence
Is ample warrant that no just pretense
Of mine for dowry will be disallowed;
Though his fair daughter's self, as I avowed
At starting, is my object. Nay, we'll go
Together down, sir. Notice Neptune, though,
Taming a sea-horse, thought a rarity,
Which Claus of Innsbruck cast in bronze for me!

■ CONSOLING MEDITATION ON THE ■ GREAT MAJORITY: FATHERS

DON GEIGER

I saw my father rolled away
in a casket too expensive for my means
(I lived in another town, and somebody else
placed the rush order, but of course I agreed,
so much is our love victim of our fears
that somehow we will have made the dead uncomfortable).
His hair had been darkened nicely and,
stuffed to perfection with embalming fluid,
he made, as the funeral parlor hostess said,
the best prepared one that month.
The men from the office walked up quietly to shake my hand.
I do not think they meant, precisely, to congratulate me,
but it was the only way remaining for them
to show their genuine appreciation of my father.
Two or three of them said they would have known me anywhere,
that I looked just like him,
though I do not know if they meant before or after.
A pastor, seemingly somewhat bewildered
by his own presence in the mortuary chapel,
was nevertheless kindly and general,
as one ought to be in speaking of strangers.
He summarized matters swiftly,
giving a nice account of death's importance to us all,
and stumbling only once in need of some fact
tieing my father's case into basic principles.
Challenged by the occasion, he could not resist
reaching for one rapidly disappearing high note,
but at the graveside he glanced at me uneasily,
as if to wonder if I knew that, as my father taught me,
since only the solitary heart can know its reasons
for the random wailing, the gnashing, the spitting of fingernails,
these miseries, like visions, are most profitable when private.
But insistences in these affairs are many:
making a mawkish scene, it began to rain,
and the thing was done.

The dead gone quick, you might say.
I heard the wet tires roll back like paper horns.
Refusing someone's invitation,
I dined alone and late at my hotel,
to enjoy my rage and fear without interruption.
Feeding relentlessly, I tried to dispel the vision
of water squiggling in the banked earth,
of my father lying alone in the dark
a mountain of menus, welcoming strangers.
I told myself that for him it would be but an episode
in a lifetime of fresh starts from the horizontal position.
I told myself how much he would have enjoyed
our spirited attempts to give him a good send-off.
I told myself that never had he shown such composure in a tight place.
I told myself to go ahead and tell myself
what a ruinous old mess he had been for twenty years.
I told myself just as much of a conversation
as I could have without my father there to join in.
The next day, the rain had stopped, the sun rose,
and I with it—to wash, shave, eat, get going.
Outside, a steady wind swept yesterday's litter.
Where they waited for me, I once more shook hands
all the way around, paid everybody off,
and then, as we had done so many times together,
too many times together, too infrequently together,
my father and I moved off together,
shaking the dust of one more friendly town.

Remember, when preparing to interpret any poem, the first step is to determine the type of poem that it is. Then, to ensure the success of your interpreting operation, examine the resources the poet used to reveal the meaning of his or her work. When you have accomplished these tasks, you are ready to perform.

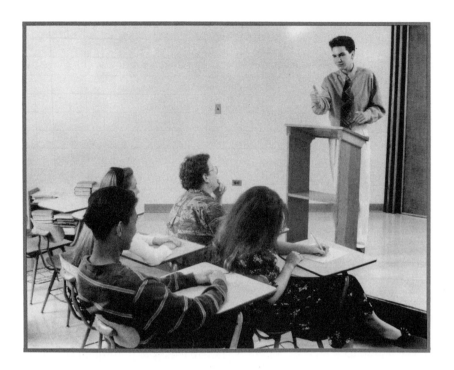

Performer's Journal
A: *Poem Gallery*

Choose a poem to interpret before the class. Select the poem from among those included in this chapter, from the "Poem-Pourri" at the end of this chapter, or from some you find on your own. Be certain to examine your poem thoroughly before attempting to perform it. On the day you are scheduled to read, hand in your analysis, following this format:

1. Why did you choose this poem? What about it appeals to you?

2. What type of experience is described in the poem?

3. What types of language resources does the poet employ? Give specific examples.

4. What is the poet's attitude?

5. How does the sound pattern help to support the meaning?

6. How does the rhythm help to support the meaning?

7. What physical responses are called for in the poem?

8. What vocal responses does the poem provoke?

9. In your presentation, what do you want to stimulate your audience to think and feel?

10. What portions of the poem do you feel will be a particular challenge to perform effectively?

B: Meet the Poets Convention

Choose one poet whose work particularly appeals to and interests you. Once again, it may be a work included in this chapter, a work from the "Poem-Pourri" that follows this chapter, or a work you discovered on your own.

Do some research on your poet. Where did he or she live, and in what lifestyle? What was the poet's ambition or personal cause? Your goal in the "Meet the Poets Convention," to be held in class, is to share your understanding of the poet and at least three of his or her works that you select.

C: Theme Forum

Try to increase your insight into poetry by comparing how a variety of poets treat similar themes. Use at least three selections on one theme in your presentation to the class. You may choose from the following poems or from poems you have encountered in other sources.

A Poem-Pourri

■ To a Daughter Leaving Home ■

LINDA PASTAN

When I taught you
at eight to ride
a bicycle, loping along
beside you
as you wobbled away
on two round wheels,
my own mouth rounding
in surprise when you pulled

ahead down the curved
path of the park,
I kept waiting
for the thud
of your crash as I
sprinted to catch up,
while you grew
smaller, more breakable
with distance,
pumping, pumping
for your life, screaming
with laughter,
the hair flapping
behind you like a
handkerchief waving
goodbye.

■ GENTLE COMMUNION ■

PAT MORA

Even the long-dead are willing to move.
Without a word, she came with me from the desert.
Mornings she wanders through my rooms
making beds, folding socks.

Since she can't hear me anymore,
Mamande ignores the questions I never knew
to ask, about her younger days, her red
hair, the time she fell and broke her nose
in the snow. I will never know.

When I try to make her laugh,
to disprove her sad album face, she leaves
the room, resists me as she resisted
grinning for cameras, make-up, English.

While I write, she sits and prays,
feet apart, legs never crossed,
the blue housecoat buttoned high
as her hair dries white, girlish
around her head and shoulders.

She closes her eyes, bows her head,
and like a child presses her hands together,
her patient flesh steeple, the skin
worn, like the pages of her prayer book.

Sometimes I sit in her wide-armed
chair as I once sat in her lap.
Alone, we played a quiet I Spy.
She peeled grapes I still taste.

She removes the thin skin, places
the luminous coolness on my tongue.
I know not to bite or chew. I wait
for the thick melt,
our private green honey.

■ PATTERNS ■

AMY LOWELL

I walk down the garden-paths,
And all the daffodils
Are blowing, and the bright blue squills
I walk down the patterned garden-paths
In my stiff, brocaded gown
With my powdered hair and jeweled fan,
I too am a rare
Pattern. As I wander down
The garden-paths.

My dress is richly figured,
And the train
Makes a pink and silver stain
On the gravel, and the thrift
Of the borders.
Just a plate of current fashion,
Tripping by in high-heeled, ribboned shoes.

Not a softness anywhere about me,
Only whalebone and brocade,
And I sink on a seat in the shade
Of a lime-tree. For my passion
Wars against the stiff brocade.
The daffodils and squills
Flutter in the breeze
As they please.
And I weep;
For the lime-tree is in blossom
And one small flower has dropped upon my bosom.
And the plashing of waterdrops
In the marble fountain
Comes down the garden-paths.
The dripping never stops.
Underneath my stiffened gown

Is the softness of a woman bathing in a marble basin,
A basin in the midst of hedges grown
So thick, she cannot see her lover hiding,
But she guesses he is near,
And the sliding of the water
Seems the stroking of a dear
Hand upon her.
What is Summer in a fine brocaded gown!
I should like to see it lying in a heap upon the ground.

I would be the pink and silver as I ran along the paths,
And he would stumble after,
Bewildered by my laughter.
I should see the sun flashing from his sword-hilt and the buckles on his
      shoes.

I would choose
To lead him in a maze along the patterned paths,
A bright and laughing maze for my heavy-booted lover.
Till he caught me in the shade,
And the buttons of his waistcoat bruised my body as he clasped me,
Aching, melting, unafraid.
With the shadows of the leaves and the sundrops,
With the plopping of the waterdrops,
All about us in the open afternoon—
I am very like to swoon
With the weight of this brocade,
For the sun sifts through the shade.

Underneath the fallen blossom
In my bosom
Is a letter I have hid.
It was brought to me this morning by a rider from the Duke.
''Madam, we regret to inform you that Lord Hartwell
Died in action Thursday se'nnight.''*
As I read it in the white, morning sunlight,
The letters squirmed like snakes.
''Any answer, Madam?'' said my footman.
''No,'' I told him.
''See that the messenger takes some refreshment.
''No, no answer,''
And I walked into the garden,
Up and down the patterned paths,
In my stiff, correct brocade.
The blue and yellow flowers stood up proudly in the sun,
Each one.
I stood upright too,
Held rigid to the pattern
By the stiffness of my gown;
Up and down I walked,
Up and down.

In a month he would have been my husband.
In a month, here, underneath this lime,
We would have broke the pattern;
He for me, and I for him,

He as Colonel, I as Lady,
On this shady seat.
He had a whim
That sunlight carried blessing
And I answered, "It shall be as you have said."
Now he is dead.

In Summer and in Winter I shall walk
Up and down ·
The patterned garden-paths
In my stiff, brocaded gown.
The squills and daffodils
Will give place to pillared roses, and to asters, and to snow.
I shall go
Up and down
In my gown.
Gorgeously arrayed,
Boned and stayed.
And the softness of my body will be guarded from embrace
By each button, hook, and lace.
For the man who should loose me is dead,
Fighting with the Duke in Flanders,
In a pattern called a war.
Christ! What are patterns for?

*se'nnight: the space of seven nights and days.

■ SPRING AND FALL: ■
TO A YOUNG CHILD
GERARD MANLEY HOPKINS

Margaret, are you grieving
Over Goldengrove unleaving?
Leaves, like the things of man, you
With your fresh thoughts care for, can you?
Ah! as the heart grows older
It will come to such sights colder
By and by, nor spare a sigh
Though worlds of wanwood leafmeal lie;
And yet you will weep and know why.
Now no matter, child, the name:
Sorrow's springs are the same.
Nor mouth had, no nor mind, expressed
What heart heard of, ghost guessed:
It is the plight man was born for,
It is Margaret you mourn for.

■ DREAM DEFERRED ■
LANGSTON HUGHES

What happens to a dream deferred?
    Does it dry up
    like a raisin in the sun?
    Or fester like a sore—
    And then run?
    Does it stink like rotten meat?
    Or crust and sugar over—
    like a syrupy sweet?

    Maybe it just sags
    like a heavy load.

    Or does it explode?

■ STATUS SYMBOL ■

MARI EVANS

i
Have Arrived

i
am the
New Negro

i
am the result of
President Lincoln
World War I
and Paris
the
Red Ball Express
white drinking fountains
sitdowns and
sit-ins
Federal Troops
Marches on Washington
    and
prayer meetings . . .

today
They hired me
it
is a status
job . . .
along
with my papers
They
gave me my
Status Symbol
the
key
to the
White . . . Locked . . .
John

■ THERE WAS A CHILD ■
WENT FORTH

WALT WHITMAN

There was a child went forth every day,
And the first object he look'd upon, that object he became,
And that object became part of him for the day or a certain
     part of the day,
Or for many years or stretching cycles of years.

The early lilacs became part of this child,
And the grass and white and red morning-glories, and white
     and red clover, and the song of the phoebe-bird,
And the Third-month lambs and the sow's pink-faint litter,
     and the mare's foal and the cow's calf,
And the noisy brood of the barnyard or by the mire of the
     pond-side,
And the fish suspending themselves so curiously below there,
     and the beautiful curious liquid,
And the water-plants with their graceful flat heads, all became part of him.
The field-sprouts of Fourth-month and Fifth-month became
     part of him,
Water-grain sprouts and those of the light-yellow corn,
     and the esculent roots of the garden,
And the apple-trees cover'd with blossoms and the fruit
     afterward, and wood-berries, and the commonest weeds by the road,
And the old drunkard staggering home from the outhouse of
     the tavern whence he had lately risen,
And the schoolmistress that pass'd on her way to the school,
And the friendly boys that pass'd, and the quarrelsome boys,
And the tidy and fresh-cheek'd girls, and the barefoot negro
     boy and girl,
And all the changes of city and country wherever he went.

His own parents, he that had father'd him and she that had
     conceiv'd him in her womb and birth'd him,
They gave this child more of themselves than that,
They gave him afterward every day, they became part of him.

The mother at home quietly placing the dishes on the supper-
    table,
The mother with mild words, clean her cap and gown, a whole-
    some odor falling off her person and clothes as she
    walks by,
The father, strong, self-sufficient, manly, mean, anger'd, unjust,
The blow, the quick loud word, the tight bargain, the crafty
    lure,
The family usages, the language, the company, the furniture,
    the yearning and swelling heart,
Affection that will not be gainsay'd, the sense of what is
    real, the thought if after all it should prove unreal,
The doubts of day-time and the doubts of night-time, the
    curious whether and how,
Whether that which appears so is so, or is it all flashes
    and specks?
Men and women crowding fast in the streets, if they are not
    flashes and specks what are they?

The streets themselves and the facades of houses, and goods
    in the windows,
Vehicles, teams, the heavy-plank'd wharves, the huge crossing
    at the ferries,
The village on the highland seen from afar at sunset, the
    river between,
Shadows, aureola and mist, the light falling on roofs and
    gables of white or brown two miles off,
The schooner near by sleepily dropping down the tide, the
    little boat slack-tow'd astern,
The hurrying tumbling waves, quick-broken crests, slapping,
The strata of color'd clouds, the long bar of maroon-tint
    away solitary by itself, the spread of purity it lies
    motionless in,
The horizon's edge, the flying sea-crow, the fragrance of
    salt marsh and shore mud,
These became part of that child who went forth every day,
    and who now goes, and will always go forth every day.

■ NEXT TO OF COURSE GOD AMERICA I ■

e.e. cummings

''next to of course god america i
love you land of the pilgrims' and so forth oh
say can you see by the dawn's early my
country 'tis of centuries come and go
and are no more what of it we should worry
in every language even deafanddumb
thy sons acclaim your glorious name by gorry
by jingo by gee by gosh by gum
why talk of beauty what could be more beautiful than these heroic happy dead
who rushed like lions to the roaring slaughter
they did not stop to think they died instead
then shall the voice of liberty be mute?''

He spoke. And drank rapidly a glass of water

■ AFTER GREAT PAIN, A ■ FORMAL FEELING COMES

EMILY DICKINSON

After great pain, a formal feeling comes—
The Nerves sit ceremonious, like Tombs—
The stiff Heart questions was it He, that bore,
And Yesterday, or Centuries before?

The feet, mechanical, go round—
Of Ground, or Air, or Ought—
A Wooden way
Regardless grown,
A Quartz contentment, like a stone—

This is the Hour of Lead—
Remembered, if outlived,
As Freezing persons, recollect the Snow—
First—Chill—then Stupor—then the letting go—

■ PREFACE TO A TWENTY VOLUME ■ SUICIDE NOTE

LE ROI JONES

Lately, I've become accustomed to the way
The ground opens up and envelops me
Each time I go out to walk the dog.
Or the broad edged silly music the wind
Makes when I run for a bus—

Things have come to that.

And now, each night I count the stars,
And each night I get the same number.
And when they will not come to be counted
I count the hole they leave.

Nobody sings anymore.

And then last night, I tiptoes up
To my daughter's room and heard her
Talking to someone, and when I opened
The door, there was no one there . . .

Only she on her knees,
Peeking into her own cupped hands.

■ MOTHER TO SON ■

LANGSTON HUGHES

Well, Son, I'll tell you
Life for me ain't been no crystal stair
It's had tacks in it,
And splinters,
And boards torn up,
And places with no carpets on the floor,

Bare.
But all the time
I'se been climbin' on
And reachin' landin's
And turnin' corners
And sometimes goin' on in the dark
Where there ain't been no light.
So, Boy, don't you turn back.
Don't you set down on the steps
'Cause you find it's kinder hard.
Don't you fall now—
For I'se still goin', Honey,
I'se still climbin'
and life for me ain't been
             no crystal stair.

■ RICHARD CORY ■

EDWIN ARLINGTON ROBINSON

Whenever Richard Cory went down town,
We people on the pavement looked at him:
He was a gentleman from sole to crown,
Clean favored, and imperially slim.

And he was always quietly arrayed,
And he was always human when he talked;
But still he fluttered pulses when he said,
''Good-morning,'' and he glittered when he walked.

And he was rich—yes, richer than a king—
And admirably schooled in every grace:
In fine, we thought that he was everything
To make us wish that we were in his place.

So on we worked, and waited for the light,
And went without the meat, and cursed the bread;
And Richard Cory, one calm summer night,
Went home and put a bullet through his head.

■ WELCOME TO HIROSHIMA ■

MARY JO SALTER

is what you first see, stepping off the train:
a billboard brought to you in living English
by Toshiba Electric. While a channel
silent in the TV of the brain

projects those flickering re-runs of a cloud
that brims its risen columnful like beer
and, spilling over, hangs its foamy head,
you feel a thirst for history: what year

it started to be safe to breathe the air,
and when to drink the blood and scum afloat
on the Ohta River. But no, the water's clear,
they pour it for your morning cup of tea

in one of the countless sunny coffee shops
whose plastic dioramas advertise
mutations of cuisine behind the glass:
a pancake sandwich; a pizza someone tops

with a maraschino cherry. Passing by
the Peace Park's floral hypocenter (where
how bravely, or with what mistaken cheer,
humanity erased its own erasure),

you enter the memorial museum
and through more glass are served, as on a dish
of blistered grass, three mannequins. Like gloves
a mother clips to coatsleeves, strings of flesh

hang from their fingertips; or as if tied
to recall a duty for us, *Reverence*
the dead whose mourners too shall soon be dead,
but all commemoration's swallowed up

in questions of bad taste, how re-created
horror mocks the grim original,
and thinking at last *They should have left it all*
you stop. This is the wristwatch of a child.

Jammed on the moment's impact, resolute
to communicate some message, although mute,
it gestures with its hands at eight-fifteen
and eight-fifteen and eight-fifteen again

while tables of statistics on the wall
update the news by calling on a roll
of tape, death gummed on death, and in the case
adjacent, an exhibit under glass

is glass itself: a shard the bomb slammed in
a woman's arm at eight-fifteen, but some
three decades on—as if to make it plain
hope's only as renewable as pain,

and as if all the unsung
debasements of the past may one day come
rising to the surface once again—
worked its filthy way out like a tongue.

■ ALL THERE IS TO KNOW ■ ABOUT ADOLPH EICHMANN

LEONARD COHEN

EYES: . . . . Medium
HAIR: . . . . Medium
WEIGHT: . . . . Medium
HEIGHT: . . . . Medium
DISTINGUISHING FEATURES: . . . . None
NUMBER OF FINGERS: . . . . Ten
NUMBER OF TOES: . . . . Ten
INTELLIGENCE: . . . . Medium
What did you expect?
Talons?
Oversize incisors?
Green saliva?
Madness?

■ TO WOMEN, ■ AS FAR AS I'M CONCERNED

D. H. LAWRENCE

The feelings I don't have, I don't have.
The feelings I don't have, I won't say I have.
The feelings you say you have, you don't have.
The feelings you would like us both to have, we neither of us have.
The feelings people ought to have, they never have.
If people say they've got feelings, you may be pretty sure they haven't got
    them.
So if you want either of us to feel anything at all
You'd better abandon all idea of feelings altogether.

■ WAR IS KIND ■

STEPHEN CRANE

Do not weep, maiden, for war is kind.
Because your lover threw wild hands toward the sky
And the affrighted steed ran on alone,
Do not weep.
War is kind.

Hoarse, booming drums of the regiment,
Little souls who thirst for fight,
These men were born to drill and die.
The unexplained glory flies above them,
Great is the battle-god, great, and his kingdom—
A field where a thousand corpses lie.

Do not weep, babe, for war is kind.
Because your father tumbled in the yellow trenches,
Raged at his breast, gulped and died,
Do not weep.
War is kind.

Swift blazing flag of the regiment,
Eagle with crest of red and gold,
These men were born to drill and die.
Point for them the virtue of slaughter.
Make plain to them the excellence of killing
And a field where a thousand corpses lie.

Mother whose heart hung humble as a button
On the bright splendid shroud of your son,
Do not weep
War is kind.

■ MISS ROSIE ■

LUCILLE CLIFTON

When I watch you
wrapped up like garbage
sitting, surrounded by the smell
of too old potato peels
or
when I watch you
in your old man's shoes
with the little toe cut out
sitting, waiting for your mind
like next week's grocery
I say
when I watch you
you wet brown bag of a woman
who used to be the best looking gal in
    Georgia
used to be called the Georgia Rose
I stand up
through your destruction
I stand up

■ NEW MEXICAN MOUNTAIN ■

ROBINSON JEFFERS

I watch the Indians dancing to help the young corn at Taos
    pueblo. The old men squat in a ring
And make the song, the young women with fat bare arms, and
    a few shame-faced young men, shuffle the dance.

The lean-muscled young men are naked to the narrow loins,
    their breasts and backs daubed with white clay,
Two eagle-feathers plume the black heads. They dance with
    reluctance, they are growing civilized; the old men
    persuade them.

Only the drum is confident, it thinks the world has not
       changed; the beating heart, the simplest of rhythms,
It thinks the world has not changed at all; it is only a
       dreamer, a brainless heart, the drum has no eyes.

These tourists have eyes, the hundred watching the dance,
       white Americans, hungrily too, with reverence, not
       laughter;
Pilgrims from civilization, anxiously seeking beauty,
       religion, poetry; pilgrims from the vacuum.

People from cities, anxious to be human again. Poor show
       how they suck you empty! The Indians are emptied,
And certainly there was never religion enough, nor beauty
       nor poetry here . . . to fill Americans.

Only the drum is confident, it thinks the world has not
       changed. Apparently only myself and the strong
Tribal drum, and the rockhead of Taos mountain, remember
       that civilization is a transient sickness.

■ SOLILOQUY OF ■ THE SPANISH CLOISTER

ROBERT BROWNING

I

Gr-r-r—there go, my heart's abhorrence!
      Water your damned flower-pots, do!
If hate killed men, Brother Lawrence,
      God's blood, would not mine kill you!
What? your myrtle-bush wants trimming
      Oh, that rose has prior claims—
Needs its leaden vase filled brimming?
      Hell dry you up with its flames!

II

At the meal we sit together:
    Salve tibi! I must hear
Wise talk of the kind of weather,
    Sort of season, time of year:
Not a plenteous cork-crop: scarcely
    Dare we hope oak-galls, I doubt:
What's the Latin name for "parsley"?
    What's the Greek name for Swine's Snout?

III

Whew! We'll have our platter burnished,
    Laid with care on our own shelf!
With a fire-new spoon we're furnished,
    And a goblet for ourself,
Rinsed like something sacrificial
    Ere 'tis fit to touch our chaps—
Marked with L for our initial!

    (He-he! There his lily snaps!)

IV

Saint, forsooth! While brown Dolores
    Squats outside the Convent bank
With Sanchicha, telling stories,
    Steeping tresses in the tank,
Blue-black, lustrous, thick like horsehairs
    —Can't I see his dead eye glow,
Bright as 'twere a Barbary corsair's?
    (That is, if he'd let it show!)

V

When he finished reflection,
    Knife and fork he never lays
Cross-wise, to my recollection,
    As do I, in Jesu's praise.
I the Trinity illustrate,
    Drinking watered orange-pulp—
In three sips the Arian frustrate;
    While he drains his at one gulp.

VI

Oh, those melons! If he's able
    We're to have a feast! so nice!
One goes to the Abbot's table,
    All of us get each a slice.
How go on your flowers? None double?
    Not one fruit-sort can you spy?
Strange!—And I, too, at such trouble
    Keep them close-nipped on the sly!

VII

There's a great text in Galatians,
    Once you trip on it, entails
Twenty-nine distinct damnations,
    One sure, if another fails:
If I trip him just a-dying,
    Sure of heaven as sure can be,
Spin him round and send him flying
    Off to hell, a Manichee?

VIII

Or, my scrofulous French novel
    On grey paper with blunt type!
Simply glance at it, you grovel
    Hand and foot in Belial's gripe:
If I double down its pages
    At the woeful sixteenth print,
When he gathers his greengages,
    Ope a sieve and slip it in't?

IX

Or, there's Satan!—one might venture
    Pledge one's soul to him, yet leave
Such a flaw in the indenture
    As he'd miss till, past retrieve,
Blasted lay that rose-acacia
    We're so proud of! *Hy, Zy, Hine* . . .
'St, there's Vespers! *Plena gratiâ,*
    Ave, Virgo! Gr-r-r—you swine!

PART THREE

Widening the Art of Interpretation

- Performing Literature for Children
- Performing Literature from Around the World
- Using Documentary Material for Oral Interpretation
- Ensemble Approaches to Interpretation

CHAPTER EIGHT

Performing Literature for Children

The spirit of childhood, the playfulness and the sense of wonder required to tap the imaginative workings of the mind, are qualities you never want to be lost or stifled. Yet many of us do suppress these aspects of ourselves. Can your thoughts and reactions reflect those of a child? What, for example, is the figure below?

Do you see only a circle surrounding a smaller circle and three lines? If so, consider yourself "grown up." The essence of childhood, the spontaneity and creativity of youth, have escaped you for the moment. However, you can and should recapture those precious qualities.

Look at the figure again. Can you see an egg and three thin slices of bacon on a plate? Can you see a very neat person's small serving of spaghetti and a single meatball? Most children could see that there is more to this configuration than meets the eye. If you will work to keep the child alive in yourself, you will recapture a freshness and inventiveness that will serve you well as an interpreter of literature.

How, then, can someone become an adult without sacrificing those qualities? Doesn't gaining one necessitate losing the other? Although it is somewhat paradoxical, you can become a grownup and remain a child. You can do so by tending carefully the spark of childhood that burns within you. You will have to take time to remember growing pains, dragons and monsters, wonder and suspense, wild imaginings, and being afraid.

Chapter 8 will explore some techniques using literature to regain your childlike spirit. You will discover ways you can use children's literature both to reach children and to widen the scope of the interpretative performer. Reading children's literature to a young audience serves not only to enrich the children's lives, it is an enriching experience for the interpreter, as well.

Selecting Material for Children

How do you choose literature to interpret for a child audience? In order to answer this question, journey back to the days of your own childhood to examine a piece of literature that probably lived in it with you.

GETTING INVOLVED
A Childhood Visit

Read the following excerpt.

■ THE GLORIOUS WHITEWASHER ■
THE ADVENTURES OF TOM SAWYER
MARK TWAIN

Sunday morning was come, and all the summer world was bright and fresh, and brimming with life. There was a song in every heart; and if the heart was young the music issued at the lips. There was cheer in every face and a spring in every step. The locust trees were in bloom and the fragrance of the blossoms filled the air. Cardiff Hill, beyond the village and above it, was green with vegetation, and it lay just far enough away to seem a Delectable Land, dreamy, reposeful, and inviting.

Tom appeared on the sidewalk with a bucket of whitewash and a long-handled brush. He surveyed the fence, and all gladness left him and a deep melancholy settled down upon his spirit. Thirty yards of board fence nine feet high. Life to him seemed hollow, and existence but a burden. Sighing he dipped his brush and passed it along the topmost plank; repeated the operation, did it again; compared the insignificant whitewashed streak with the far-reaching continent of unwhitewashed fence, and sat down on a tree-box discouraged. Jim came skipping out at the gate with a tin pail, and singing ''Buffalo Gals.'' Bringing water from the town pump had always been hateful work in Tom's eyes, before, but now it did not strike him so. He remembered that there was company at the pump. White, mulatto, and negro boys and girls were always there waiting their turns, resting, trading playthings, quarreling, fighting, skylarking. And he remembered that although the pump was only a hundred and fifty yards off, Jim never got back with a bucket of water under an hour—and even then somebody generally had to go after him. Tom said:

"Say, Jim, I'll fetch the water if you'll whitewash some."

Jim shook his head and said:

"Can't, Mars Tom. Ole missis, she tole me I got to go an' git dis water an' not stop foolin' roun' wid anybody. She say she spec' Mars Tom gwine to ax me to whitewash, an' so she tole me go 'long an' 'tend to my own business—she 'lowed she'd 'tend to de whitewashin'."

"Oh, never you mind what she said, Jim. That's the way she always talks. Gimme the bucket—I won't be gone only a minute. *She* won't ever know."

"Oh, I dasn't, Mars Tom. Ole missis she'd take an' tar de head off'n me. 'Deed she would."

"*She!* She never licks anybody—whacks 'em over the head with her thimble—and who cares for that, I'd like to know. She talks awful, but talk don't hurt—anyways it don't if she don't cry. Jim, I'll give you a marvel. I'll give you a white alley!"

Jim began to waver.

"White alley, Jim! And it's a bully taw."

"My! Dat's a mighty gay marvel, I tell you! But Mars Tom, I's powerful 'fraid ole missis—"

"And besides, if you will I'll show you my sore toe."

Jim was only human—this attraction was too much for him. He put down his pail, took the white alley, and bent over the toe with absorbing interest while the bandage was being unwound. In another moment he was flying down the street with his pail and a tingling rear, Tom was whitewashing with vigor, and Aunt Polly was retiring from the field with a slipper in her hand and triumph in her eye.

But Tom's energy did not last. He began to think of the fun he had planned for this day, and his sorrows multiplied. Soon the free boys would come tripping along on all sorts of delicious expeditions, and they would make a world of fun of him for having to work—the very thought of it burnt him like fire. He got out his worldly wealth and examined it—bits of toys, marbles, and trash; enough to buy an exchange of *work*, maybe, but not half enough to buy so much as half an hour of pure freedom. So he returned his straitened means to his pocket, and gave up the idea of trying to buy the boys. At this dark and hopeless moment an inspiration burst upon him! Nothing less than a great, magnificent inspiration.

He took up his brush and went tranquilly to work. Ben Rogers hove in sight presently—the very boy, of all boys, whose ridicule he had been dreading. Ben's gait was the hop-skip-and-jump—proof enough that his heart was light and his anticipations high. He was eating an apple, and giving a long, melodious whoop, at intervals, followed by a deep-toned ding-dong-dong, ding-dong-dong, for he was personating a steamboat. As he drew near, he slackened speed, took the middle of the street, leaned far over to starboard and rounded to ponderously and with laborious pomp and circumstance—for he was personating the *Big Missouri*, and considered himself to be drawing nine feet of water. He was boat and captain and engine-bells combined, so he had to imagine himself standing on his own hurricane-deck giving the orders and executing them:

"Stop her, sir! Ting-a-ling-ling!" The headway ran almost out and he drew up slowly toward the sidewalk.

"Ship up to back! Ting-a-ling-ling!" His arms straightened and stiffened down his sides.

"Set her back on the stabboard! Ting-aling-ling! Chow! ch-chow-wow! Chow!" His right hand, meantime, describing stately circles—for it was representing a forty-foot wheel.

"Let her go back on the labboard! Ting-a-ling-ling! Chow-ch-chow-chow!" The left hand began to describe circles.

"Stop the stabboard! Ting-a-ling-ling! Stop the Labboard! Come ahead on the stabboard! Stop her! Let your outside turn over slow! Ting-a-ling-ling! Chow-ow-ow! Get out that headline—*Lively* now! Come—out with your spring-line—what're you about there! Take a turn round that stump with the bight of it! Stand by that stage, now—let her go! Done with the engines, sir! Ting-a-ling-ling! Sh't! s'h't! sh't!" (trying the gaugecocks).

Tom went on whitewashing—paid no attention to the steamboat. Ben stared a moment and then said:

"Hi-yi! *You're* up a stump, ain't you!"

No answer. Tom surveyed his last touch with the eye of an artist, then he gave his brush another gentle sweep and surveyed the result, as before. Ben ranged up alongside of him. Tom's mouth watered for the apple, but he stuck to his work. Ben said:

"Hello, old chap, you got to work, hey?"

Tom wheeled suddenly and said:

"Why, it's you, Ben! I warn't noticing."

"Say—I'm going in a-swimming, I am. Don't you wish you could? But of course you'd druther *work*—wouldn't you? Course you would!"

Tom contemplated the boy a bit, and said:

"What do you call work?"

"Why, ain't *that* work?"

Tom resumed his whitewashing, and answered carelessly:

"Well, maybe it is, and maybe it ain't. All I know is, it suits Tom Sawyer."

"Oh come now, you don't mean to let on that you *like* it?"

The brush continued to move.

"Like it? Well, I don't see why I oughtn't to like it. Does a boy get a chance to whitewash a fence every day?"

That put the thing in a new light. Ben stopped nibbling his apple. Tom swept his brush daintily back and forth—stepped back to note the effect—added a touch here and there—criticized the effect again—Ben watching every move and getting more and more interested, more and more absorbed. Presently he said:

"Say, Tom, let *me* whitewash a little."

Tom considered, was about to consent; but he altered his mind:

"No—no—I reckon it wouldn't hardly do, Ben. You see, Aunt Polly's awful particular about this fence—right here on the street, you know—but if it was the back fence I wouldn't mind and *she* wouldn't. Yes, she's awful particular; about this fence; it's got to be done very careful; I reckon there ain't one boy in a thousand, maybe two thousand, that can do it the way it's got to be done."

"No—is that so? Oh come, now—lemme just try. Only a little—I'd let *you*, if you was me, Tom."

"Ben, I'd like to, honest injun; but Aunt Polly—well, Jim wanted to do it, but she wouldn't let him; Sid wanted to do it, and she wouldn't let Sid. Now don't you see how I'm fixed? If you was to tackle this fence and anything was to happen to it—"

"Oh, shucks, I'll be just as careful. Now lemme try. Say—I'll give you the core of my apple."

"Well, here—No, Ben, now don't. I'm afeard—"

"I'll give you *all* of it!"

Tom gave up the brush with reluctance in his face, but alacrity in his heart. And while the late steamer *Big Missouri* worked and sweated in the sun, the retired artist sat on a barrel in the shade close by, dangled his legs, munched his apple, and planned the slaughter of more innocents. There was no lack of material; boys happened along every little while; they came to jeer, but remained to whitewash. By the time Ben was fagged out, Tom had traded the next chance to Billy Fisher for a kite, in good repair; and when *he* played out, Johnny Miller brought in for a dead rat and a string to swing it with—and so on, and so on, hour after hour. And when the middle of the afternoon came, from being a poor poverty-stricken boy in the morning, Tom was literally rolling in wealth. He had beside the things before mentioned, twelve marbles, part of a jews' harp, a piece of blue bottle-glass to look through, a spool cannon, a key that wouldn't unlock anything, a fragment of chalk, a glass stopper of a decanter, a tin soldier, a couple of tadpoles, six firecrackers, a kitten with only one eye, a brass door-knob, a dog collar—but no dog—the handle of a knife, four pieces of orange-peel, and a dilapidated old window-sash.

He had had a nice, good, idle time all the while—plenty of company— and the fence had three coats of whitewash on it! If he hadn't run out of whitewash, he would have bankrupted every boy in the village.

Tom said to himself that it was not such a hollow world, after all. He had discovered a great law of human action, without knowing it—namely, that in order to make a man or a boy covet a thing, it is only necessary to make the thing difficult to attain. If he had been a great and wise philosopher, like the writer of this book, he would now have comprehended that Work consists of whatever a body is *obliged* to do, and that Play consists of whatever a body is not obliged to do. And this would help him understand why constructing artificial flowers or performing on a treadmill is work, while rolling tenpins or climbing Mont Blanc is only amusement. There are wealthy gentlemen in England who drive four-horse passenger-coaches twenty or thirty miles on a daily line, in the summer, because the privilege costs them considerable money; but if they were offered wages for the service, that would turn it into work and then they would resign.

The boy mused awhile over the substantial change which had taken place in his worldly circumstances, and then wended toward headquarters to report.

Reflections

1. What is the plot of this story? Why is it effective for a child audience?

2. What is its theme?

3. What types of characters people the story?

4. What kind of language does the author use?

5. What uses are made of description?

6. In what ways would an adult audience respond differently from a group of children?

Effective literature for children is usually rich in imagery. It reaches out to children, as the previous piece by Mark Twain probably reached out to you. A good children's story exercises their sense of sight, smell, taste, touch, and hearing. In imaginative ways, it encourages them to participate in the selection as it appeals to their love of action and adventure.

In addition, a good children's story includes unique or memorable characters with whom the youngsters can identify. It doesn't matter whether the story's characters are people, animals, or objects. If the characters feed children's understanding of themselves and their curiosity about the world, then they fulfill an important function. Children become involved with the characters in a story; they watch and listen to the characters react to their world and attempt to solve problems. Struggles, successes, and needs of the characters are closely attended to by children. In fact, in an effective story the needs of the characters and the needs of the children often overlap.

As an interpreter of children's literature, remember that a child's needs are human needs: acceptance and belonging, control and achievement, love and affection. Stories that illustrate how these needs may be met help children adjust to their world. Accordingly, the world shown in children's literature need not continuously represent an ideal world. From time to time, even imaginary worlds are troubled by problems. Children need not be fed a steady diet of fantasies or fairy tales; realistic stories are also meaningful. The poet Yevgeni Yevtushenko reflects this in lines from his poem "Lies."

> Telling lies to the young is wrong.
> Proving to them that lies are true is wrong.
> Proving to them that God's in his heaven
> and all's well with the world is wrong.
> The young know what you mean.
> The young are people.

This is not to suggest that children's literature should be disturbing. But literature can do more than simply enrich the imaginary life of a child. Helping in the development of a child's social conscience can be another benefit of children's literature. Nightmares, as well as dreams, are part of life.

As an oral interpreter, respect the literary needs of children. Like adults, children relish the fanciful and delightful, the provoking and sometimes frightening. Thus, story selection for children is wide open. Keeping this in mind, would the following selection be appropriate for a child audience?

■ THE LITTLE PRINCE ■
ANTOINE DE SAINT-EXUPERY

It was then that the fox appeared.

"Good morning," said the fox.

"Good morning," the little prince responded politely, although when he turned around he saw nothing.

"I am right here," the voice said, "under the apple tree."

"Who are you?" asked the little prince, and added, "You are very pretty to look at."

"I am a fox," the fox said.

"Come and play with me," proposed the little prince. "I am so unhappy."

"I cannot play with you," the fox said. "I am not tamed."

"Ah! Please excuse me," said the little prince.

But after some thought, he added:

"What does that mean—'tame'?"

"You do not live here," said the fox. "What is it that you are looking for?"

"I am looking for men," said the little prince. "What does that mean—'tame'?"

"Men," said the fox. "They have guns, and they hunt. It is very disturbing. They also raise chickens. These are their only interests. Are you looking for chickens?"

"No," said the little prince. "I am looking for friends. What does that mean—'tame'?"

"It is an act too often neglected," said the fox. "It means to establish ties."

" 'To establish ties'?"

"Just that," said the fox. "To me, you are still nothing more than a little boy who is just like a hundred thousand other little boys. And I have no need of you. And you, on your part, have no need of me. To you, I am nothing more than a fox like a hundred thousand other foxes. But if you tame me, then we shall need each other. To me, you will be unique in all the world. To you, I shall be unique in all the world. . . ."

"I am beginning to understand," said the little prince. "There is a flower . . . I think that she has tamed me. . . ."

"It is possible," said the fox. "On the Earth one sees all sorts of things."

"Oh, but this is not on the Earth!" said the little prince.

The fox seemed perplexed, and very curious.

"On another planet?"

"Yes."

"Are there hunters on that planet?"

"No."

"Ah, that is interesting. . . ." But he came back to his idea.

"My life is very monotonous," he said. "I hunt chickens; men hunt me. All the chickens are just alike, and all the men are just alike. And, in consequence, I am a little bored. But if you tame me, it will be as if the sun came to shine on my life. I shall know the sound of a step that will be different from all the others. Other steps send me hurrying back underneath the ground. Yours will call me, like music, out of my burrow. And then look: you see the grain-fields down yonder? I do not eat bread. Wheat is of no use to me. The wheat fields have nothing to say to me. And that is sad.

"But you have hair that is the color of gold. Think how wonderful that will be when you have tamed me! The grain, which is also golden, will bring me back the thought of you. And I shall love to listen to the wind in the wheat. . . ."

The fox gazed at the little prince, for a long time.

"Please—tame me!" he said.

"I want to, very much," the little prince replied. "But I have not much time. I have friends to discover, and a great many things to understand."

"One only understands the things that one tames," said the fox. "Men have no more time to understand anything. They buy things all ready made at the shops. But there is no shop anywhere where one can buy friendship, and so men have no friends any more. If you want a friend, tame me. . . ."

"What must I do, to tame you?" asked the little prince.

"You must be very patient," replied the fox. "First you will sit down at a little distance from me—like that—in the grass. I shall look at you out of the corner of my eye, and you will say nothing. Words are the source of misunderstandings. But you will sit a little closer to me, every day. . . ."

The next day the little prince came back.

"It would have been better to come back at the same hour," said the fox. " . . . One must observe the proper rites. . . ."

"What is a rite?" asked the little prince.

"Those also are actions too often neglected," said the fox. "They are what make one day different from other days, one hour from other hours. . . ."

So the little prince tamed the fox. And when the hour of his departure drew near—

"Ah," said the fox, "I shall cry."

"It is your own fault," said the little prince. "I never wished you any sort of harm; but you wanted me to tame you. . . ."

"Yes, that is so," said the fox.

"But now you are going to cry!" said the little prince.

"Yes, that is so," said the fox.

"Then it has done you no good at all!"

"It has done me good," said the fox, "because of the color of the wheat fields."

Preparing to Read for Children

Think back to the literature you were exposed to as a child. What do you remember? Did most of your early exposure come from television? On Sesame Street, did Miss Piggy, Kermit, and the gang bring stories and ideas alive for you? In like fashion, you are certain to recall children's stories that were alive with animation. Which Disney classics were your favorites?

As you interpret literature for children, you will attempt to create the same involvement and excitement with the literature that Jim Henson and Walt Disney achieved through television and films. Of course, Henson had puppets and Disney had cartoon characters with which to attract and enchant children. How will you use your interpreter's skills to accomplish the same feat?

The methods of preparation you will use to interpret a selection for an audience of children are similar to those you use in preparing to read to your peers. For both types of audience, your aim is to have the individuals meet and merge their lives with the literature you present. However, the road you will travel to realize your goal when interpreting for young people differs from the peers' road. The road you will travel to prepare to effectively perform selections for children will have signposts to guide you. You will find, in many cases, that the signposts are familiar, as they are the same as those that prepared you for interpretative performance, in general.

Work to Understand Your Selection

As a performer of any type of literature, it is essential that you have a complete involvement with and understanding of the selections you hope to perform. Your job as an interpreter of children's literature is more than simply to pass on stories, of course; rather, your goal is to share experience.

Allow yourself vicariously and imaginatively to enter the child's literature. Experience it, process it, and then make it vivid and alive.

Show Emotion and Feeling

You will want to both physically and vocally illustrate the ways in which the words, events, and characters in the selection interact and affect each other. Present the literature in a manner that precipitates the desired emotional responses in your audiences. To determine what these desired responses are, you must identify with the feelings and attitudes expressed in the selection.

Make the Characters Believable

How can you make a crafty wolf, a scheming fox, or an impulsive little boy seem real? Begin by imagining yourself as each of the characters in the children's story. One at a time, re-create the image of each character during your performance before the audience of children. To succeed at this, you will need to empathize with each character.

Embody the Selection Vocally

As a children's performer, the demands you must make of your voice in performance are significant. You need to vary your rate, time, pitch, volume, quality, and emphasis as the literature requires. Children's literature will provide your voice with a real challenge. You may find that the vocal requirements called for in performing much adult literature seem negligible when compared to the vocal gymnastics the children's writer or the poet demand. Recall two characters from a familiar fable: a racing hare and a trudging tortoise. Children's characters do not move only from the neck up. Like the vocal challenges, literature for children offers unique physical challenges, as well. Of course facial expressions are important, but remember, too, the impact of posture and gesture.

Clearly, the signposts that apply to the interpreter of general literature apply, too, to the interpreter of children's literature—maybe even more so! Interpreting literature for audiences of children can be as fun and exciting for the performer as for the children who eagerly respond to the performances.

As you work, let your particular script serve as your guide. Emphasize the dynamic action in the story, the character's unique qualities, and the rhythm and description in the writing. Make the action of the story physical, using gestures that are overt rather than subtle. Broaden and exaggerate your facial expressions in response to the literature. And finally, make certain that each of the characters has a distinctive voice: shrill, gruff, singsong, rumbling—whatever suits the character.

In order to accept the world of the literature as both important and real, open yourself to a child's boundless world of imagination. In "The World of Imagination," an exhibit in Walt Disney's Epcot Center in Florida, an animated guide named "Figment" takes participants on an intriguing journey through the workings of the imagination. Open yourself to your own imaginative tour and you will doubtless develop appreciation for the magic that happens in children's literature.

GETTING INVOLVED
Imaginings: Motion and Voice

Read the following excerpt from *Alice's Adventures in Wonderland* by Lewis Carroll. Alice encounters some strange characters when she arrives at the "Mad Tea Party."

■ "A Mad Tea Party" ■
LEWIS CARROLL

There was a table set out under a tree in front of the house, and the March Hare and the Hatter were having tea at it: a Dormouse was sitting between them, fast asleep, and the other two were using it as a cushion, resting their elbows on it, and talking over its head. "Very uncomfortable for the Dormouse," thought Alice; "only, as it's asleep, I suppose it doesn't mind."

The table was a large one, but the three were all crowded together at one corner of it: "No room! No room!" they cried out when they saw Alice coming. "There's *plenty* of room!" said Alice indignantly, and she sat down in a large armchair at one end of the table.

"Have some wine," the March Hare said in an encouraging tone.

Alice looked all round the table, but there was nothing on it but tea. "I don't see any wine," she remarked.

"There isn't any," said the March Hare.

"Then it wasn't very civil of you to offer it," said Alice angrily.

"It wasn't very civil of you to sit down without being invited," said the March Hare.

"I didn't know it was *your* table," said Alice; "it's laid for a great many more than three."

"Your hair wants cutting," said the Hatter. He had been looking at Alice for some time with great curiosity, and this was his first speech.

"You should learn not to make personal remarks," Alice said with some severity: "It's very rude."

The Hatter opened his eyes very wide on hearing this; but all he *said* was, "Why is a raven like a writing-desk?"

"Come, we shall have some fun now!" thought Alice. "I'm glad they've begun asking riddles—I believe I can guess that," she added aloud.

"Do you mean that you think you can find out the answer to it?" said the March Hare.

"Exactly so," said Alice.

"Then you should say what you mean," the March Hare went on.

"I do," Alice hastily replied; "at least—at least I mean what I say— that's the same thing, you know."

"Not the same thing a bit!" said the Hatter. "Why, you might just as well say that 'I see what I eat' is the same thing as 'I eat what I see!' "

"You might just as well say," added the March Hare, "that 'I like what I get' is the same thing as 'I get what I like!' "

"You might just as well say," added the Dormouse, who seemed to be talking in his sleep, "that 'I breathe when I sleep' is the same thing as 'I sleep when I breathe!' "

"It is the same thing with you," said the Hatter, and here the conversation dropped, and the party sat silent for a minute, while Alice thought over all she could remember about ravens and writing-desks, which wasn't much.

The Hatter was the first to break the silence. "What day of the month is it?" he said, turning to Alice: he had taken his watch out of his pocket, and was looking at it uneasily, shaking it every now and then, and holding it to his ear.

Alice considered a little, and said, "The fourth."

"Two days wrong!" sighed the Hatter. "I told you butter wouldn't suit the works!" he added, looking angrily at the March Hare.

"It was the *best* butter," the March Hare meekly replied.

''Yes, but some crumbs must have got in as well,'' the Hatter grumbled: ''You shouldn't have put it in with the bread-knife.''

The March Hare took the watch and looked at it gloomily: then he dipped it into his cup of tea, and looked at it again: but he could think of nothing better to say than his first remark, ''It was the *best* butter, you know.''

Alice had been looking over his shoulder with some curiosity. ''What a funny watch!'' she remarked. ''It tells the day of the month, and doesn't tell what o'clock it is!''

''Why should it?'' muttered the Hatter. ''Does *your* watch tell you what year it is?''

''Of course not,'' Alice replied very readily: ''but that's because it stays the same year for such a long time together.''

''Which is just the case with *mine*,'' said the Hatter.

Alice felt dreadfully puzzled. The Hatter's remark seemed to her to have no sort of meaning in it, and yet it was certainly English. ''I don't quite understand you,'' she said, as politely as she could.

''The Dormouse is asleep again,'' said the Hatter, and he poured a little hot tea on to its nose.

The Dormouse shook its head impatiently, and said, without opening its eyes, ''Of course, of course: just what I was going to remark myself.''

''Have you guessed the riddle yet?'' the Hatter said, turning to Alice again.

''No, I give it up,'' Alice replied: ''what's the answer?''

''I haven't the slightest idea,'' said the Hatter.

''Nor I,'' said the March Hare.

Alice sighed wearily. ''I think you might do something better with the time,'' she said, ''than wasting it in asking riddles that have no answers.''

''If you knew Time as well as I do,'' said the Hatter, ''you wouldn't talk about wasting *it*! It's *him*.''

''I don't know what you mean,'' said Alice.

''Of course you don't!'' the Hatter said, tossing his head contemptuously. ''I dare say you never even spoke to Time!''

''Perhaps not,'' Alice cautiously replied: ''but I know I have to beat time when I learn music.''

''Ah! That accounts for it,'' said the Hatter. ''He won't stand beating. Now, if you only kept on good terms with him, he'd do almost anything you liked with the clock.''

''For instance, suppose it were nine o'clock in the morning, just time to begin lessons; you'd only have to whisper a hint to Time, and round goes the clock in a twinkling! Half-past one, time for dinner!''

("I only wish it was," the March Hare said to itself in a whisper.)

"That would be grand, certainly," said Alice thoughtfully; "but then—I shouldn't be hungry for it, you know."

"Not at first, perhaps," said the Hatter; "but you could keep it to half-past one as long as you liked."

"Is that the way *you* manage?" Alice asked.

The Hatter shook his head mournfully. "Not I!" he replied. "We quarreled last March—just before *he* went mad, you know—" (pointing with his teaspoon at the March Hare), "—it was at the great concert given by the Queen of Hearts, and I had to sing

'Twinkle, twinkle, little bat!

How I wonder what you're at!'

You know the song, perhaps?"

"I've heard something like it," said Alice. . . .

Here the Dormouse shook itself, and began singing in its sleep "*Twinkle, twinkle, twinkle, twinkle—*" and went on so long that they had to pinch it to make it stop.

"Well, I'd hardly finished the first verse," said the Hatter, "when the Queen bawled out 'He's murdering the time! Off with his head!'"

"How dreadfully savage!" exclaimed Alice.   .

"And ever since that," the Hatter went on in a mournful tone, "he won't do a thing I ask! It's always six o'clock now."

A bright idea came into Alice's head. "Is that the reason so many tea-things are put out here?" she asked.

"Yes, that's it," said the Hatter with a sigh: "It's always tea-time, and we've no time to wash the things between whiles."

"Then you keep moving round, I suppose?" said Alice.

"Exactly so," said the Hatter: "as the things get used up."

"But when you come to the beginning again?" Alice ventured to ask.

"Suppose we change the subject," the March Hare interrupted, yawning. "I'm getting tired of this. I vote the young lady tell us a story."

"I'm afraid I don't know one," said Alice, rather alarmed at the proposal.

"Then the Dormouse shall!" they both cried. "Wake up, Dormouse!" And they pinched it on both sides at once.

The Dormouse slowly opened his eyes. "I wasn't asleep," he said in a hoarse, feeble voice: "I heard every word you fellows were saying."

"Tell us a story!" said the March Hare.

"Yes, please do!" pleaded Alice.

"And be quick about it," added the Hatter, "or you'll be asleep again before it's done. . . ."

A. Imagine you are the March Hare. Move around the room as you believe the March Hare would move. Now, talk as you believe the March Hare would talk. Repeat this sequence for each of the characters in the selection.

B. Try sketching your conception of the world in which the characters operate. Your drawing may be realistic or abstract.

C. Now, prepare to read the selection aloud. Allow yourself to give full expression to the fictional world and to the characters that live in that world. Have fun with the material.

Reflections

1. Were your vocal tones and gestures appropriate to each of the characters? Did they serve to distinguish one character from another? How?

2. How was your drawing of the literary world expressed through your performance? In what ways might you actually share your drawing with a child audience? Via slides? Overhead projection transparencies? Crayon sketches on long sheets of shelf paper or wrapping paper? Might the children draw the environment for you after they experience your reading? Could they help by improvising the characters for a second reading?

You can see that the performance of children's literature opens up unexplored imaginative vistas for you to share with your audiences. Children love stories. They love to participate. They love to have fun. Have fun yourself, as your imagination takes you into the creative possibilities of children's literature.

GETTING INVOLVED
A Collage of Readings

Choose a selection to perform for a neighboring elementary school class or for the children's reading hour at your local library. In order to insure that no two students perform the same selection, clear your choice with your instructor.

Your goal, as always, is to encourage your audience to meet the literature. Let them feel the atmosphere, appreciate the action, meet and become acquainted with the characters. Take a look at the passages included in the "Story Box of Children's Literature"; those selections may give you some performance ideas. Do not, however, limit yourself to these suggestions.

A Story Box of Children's Literature

■ SICK ■

SHEL SILVERSTEIN

"I cannot go to school today,"
Said little Peggy Ann McKay.
"I have the measles and the mumps,
A gash, a rash and purple bumps.
My mouth is wet, my throat is dry,
I'm going blind in my right eye.
My tonsils are as big as rocks,
I've counted sixteen chicken pox
And there's one more—that's seventeen,
And don't you think my face looks green?
My leg is cut, my eyes are blue—
It might be instamatic flu.
I cough and sneeze and gasp and choke,
I'm sure that my left leg is broke—
My hip hurts when I move my chin,
My belly button's caving in,
My back is wrenched, my ankle's sprained,
My 'pendix pains each time it rains.
My nose is cold, my toes are numb,
I have a sliver in my thumb.
My neck is stiff, my spine is weak,
I hardly whisper when I speak.
My tongue is filling up my mouth,
I think my hair is falling out.
My elbow's bent, my spine ain't straight,
My temperature is one-o-eight.
My brain is shrunk, I cannot hear,
There is a hole inside my ear.
I have a hangnail, and my heart is—what?
What's that? What's that you say?
You say today is . . . Saturday?
G'bye, I'm going out to play!"

■ THE SECRET GARDEN ■

FRANCES HODGSON BURNETT

In each century since the beginning of the world, wonderful things have been discovered. In the last century more amazing things were found out than in any century before. In this new century, hundreds of things still more astounding will be brought to light. At first people refuse to believe that a strange new thing can be done, then they begin to hope it can be done, then they see it can be done—then it is done and all the world wonders why it was not done centuries ago. One of the new things people began to find out in the last century was that thoughts—just mere thoughts—are as powerful as electric batteries—as good for one as sunlight is, or as bad for one as poison. To let a sad thought or a bad one get into your mind is as dangerous as letting a scarlet fever germ get into your body. If you let it stay there after it has got in you, you never get over it as long as you live.

So long as Mistress Mary's mind was full of disagreeable thoughts about her dislikes and sour opinions of people and her determination not to be pleased by or interested in anything, she was a yellow-faced, sickly, bored and wretched child. Circumstances, however, were very kind to her, though she was not at all aware of it. They began to push her about for her own good. When her mind gradually filled itself with robins, and moorland cottages crowded with children, with queer crabbed old gardeners and common little Yorkshire housemaids, with springtime and with secret gardens coming alive day by day, and also with a boy and his ''creatures,'' there was no room left for the disagreeable thought which affected her liver and her digestion and made her yellow and tired.

So long as Colin shut himself up in his room and thought only of his fears and weakness and his detestation of people who looked at him and reflected hourly on humps and early death, he was a hysterical half-crazy little hypochondriac who knew nothing of the sunshine and the spring and also did not know that he could get well and could stand up on his feet if he tried to do it. When new beautiful thoughts began to push out the old hideous ones, life began to come back to him, his blood ran healthily through his veins and strength poured into him like a flood. His scientific experiment was quite practical and simple, and there was nothing weird about it at all. Much more surprising things can happen to anyone who, when a disagreeable or discouraged thought comes into his mind, just has the sense to remember in time and push it out by putting in an agreeable determinedly courageous one. Two things cannot be in one place.

''Where you tend a rose, my lad,
A thistle cannot grow.''

■ How the Camel ■
Got His Hump

RUDYARD KIPLING

Now this is the next tale, and it tells how the Camel got his big hump.

In the beginning of years, when the world was so new-and-all, and the Animals were just beginning to work for Man, there was a Camel, and he lived in the middle of a Howling Desert because he did not want to work; and besides, he was a Howler himself. So he ate sticks and thorns and tamarisks and milkweed and prickles, most 'scruciating idle; and when anybody spoke to him he said "Humph!" Just "Humph!" and no more.

Presently the Horse came to him on Monday morning, with a saddle on his back and a bit in his mouth, and said, "Camel, O Camel, come out and trot like the rest of us."

"Humph!" said the Camel; and the Horse went away and told the Man.

Presently the Dog came to him, with a stick in his mouth, and said, "Camel, O Camel, come and fetch and carry like the rest of us."

"Humph!" said the Camel; and the Dog went away and told the Man.

Presently the Ox came to him, with the yoke on his neck, and said, "Camel, O Camel, come and plough like the rest of us."

"Humph!" said the Camel; and the Ox went away and told the Man.

At the end of the day the Man called the Horse and the Dog and the Ox together, and said, "Three, O Three, I'm very sorry for you (with the world so new-and-all); but that Humph-thing in the Desert can't work, or he would have been here by now, so I am going to leave him alone, and you must work double-time to make up for it."

That made the Three very angry (with the world so new-and-all), and they held a palaver, and an *indaba*, and a *punchayet*, and a pow-wow on the edge of the Desert; and the Camel came chewing milkweed *most* 'scruciating idle, and laughed at them. Then he said "Humph!" and went away again.

Presently there came along the Djinn in charge of All Deserts, rolling in a cloud of dust (Djinns always travel that way because it is Magic), and he stopped to palaver and pow-wow with the Three.

"Djinn of All Deserts," said the Horse, "*is* it right for anyone to be idle, with the world so new-and-all?"

"Certainly not," said the Djinn.

"Well," said the Horse, "there's a thing in the middle of your Howling Desert (and he's a Howler himself) with a long neck and long legs, and he hasn't done a stroke of work since Monday morning. He won't trot."

"Whew!" said the Djinn, whistling, "that's my Camel, for all the gold in Arabia! What does he say about it?"

"He says 'Humph!' " said the Dog; "and he won't fetch and carry."

"Does he say anything else?"

"Only 'Humph!'; and he won't plough," said the Ox.

"Very good," said the Djinn. "I'll humph him if you will kindly wait a minute."

The Djinn rolled himself up in his dustcloak, and took a bearing across the desert, and found the Camel most 'scruciatingly idle, looking at his own reflection in a pool of water.

"My long and bubbling friend," said the Djinn, "what's this I hear of your doing no work, with the world so new-and-all?"

"Humph!" said the Camel.

The Djinn sat down, with his chin in his hand, and began to think a Great Magic, while the Camel looked at his own reflection in the pool of water.

"You've given the Three extra work ever since Monday morning, all on account of your 'scruciating idleness," said the Djinn; and he went on thinking Magics, with his chin in his hand.

"Humph!" said the Camel.

"I shouldn't say that again if I were you," said the Djinn; "you might say it once too often. Bubbles, I want you to work."

And the Camel said "Humph!" again; but no sooner had he said it than he saw his back, that he was so proud of, puffing up and puffing up into a great big lolloping humph.

"Do you see that?" said the Djinn. "That's your very own humph that you've brought upon your very own self by not working. Today is Thursday, and you've done no work since Monday, when the work began. Now you are going to work."

"How can I," said the Camel, "with this humph on my back?"

"That's made a-purpose," said the Djinn, "all because you missed those three days. You will be able to work now for three days without eating, because you can live on your humph; and don't you ever say I never did anything for you. Come out of the Desert and go to the Three, and behave. Humph yourself!"

And the Camel humphed himself, humph and all, and went away to join the Three. And from that day to this the Camel always wears a humph (we call it "hump" now, not to hurt his feelings); but he has never yet caught up with the three days that he missed at the beginning of the world, and he has never yet learned how to behave.

■ THE DEAD WIFE ■

NATIVE AMERICAN FOLKTALE

Once there was a man and his wife who lived on the edge of a large forest. They were Red Indians, but after they were married they chose to live apart from the rest of their tribe who had settled many miles away.

They lived in quiet harmony together. He would catch fish in the river nearby or hunt for food in the forest, while his wife worked at home cooking and sewing.

One day, when the man returned from his hunting, he found his wife had fallen ill with a violent fever. He nursed her as well as he knew how, but after a few days she died in her sleep.

The man wept for many weeks, he could not get used to being without his wife. In the end he felt so lonely he made a wooden doll of about the same height and size as his wife had been and then he dressed the doll with his wife's clothes. He carved a face out of the wood, and made-believe it was his wife come back to him. Night after night he would sit by the fire with the doll and talk gently to it as he used to talk to his wife. He looked after the doll carefully and would brush away any ashes that happened to fall on the doll from the fire.

He was always busy during the day now, as he had to cook and mend as well as go out hunting for food. But in the evenings he would sit quietly by the fire with the wooden doll and tell it of the day's happenings, and so a year passed by.

One evening he came back from hunting and found that some wood had been collected and left by his home, and he did not remember having done it himself. He thought he must have forgotten. But the next night when he returned home not only had there been wood gathered, but there was a merry fire burning, and by the fire sat not the doll, but his own dear wife. He was too astonished to speak, but simply gazed at his wife in wonder. After a short while she said to him: ''Dear husband, The Great Spirit took pity on you, because you could not be comforted after my death and you did not forget me. So he let me come back to you, but on one condition: you must not stretch out your hand and touch me till we have seen the rest of our people—if you do, I shall die.''

The man's heart was filled with tender happiness, and he said: ''Dear wife, we must go at once to our tribe.''

However, snow fell thick and fast all that night, and they were not able to travel for several days. The man longed to hold his wife, but he remembered her words and did not go near her.

At last they started on their journey, having prepared some deer's flesh to take with them. They traveled for five days, and they had one more day's journey to complete, when once again, a terrible snow blizzard started. They stopped to rest for the night and lay down on their skins to sleep. But the heart of the man was stirred by his wife lying so close to him and he stretched out his arms to her. She waved him away and said, "We haven't seen our people yet. It is too early." But this time he did not listen and he put his arms around her—and found he was clutching the wooden doll.

When he saw what had happened, he pushed it away from him in horror and anger and ran and ran until he finally came upon his tribe, where he lay down and wept and told them his story. Some people doubted, so he took them to the place where they had rested and there lay the doll. They saw footprints left in the snow by two people—but the prints of one were like that of a doll.

■ THE BREMEN TOWN MUSICIANS ■
THE BROTHERS GRIMM

A certain man owned a donkey who for many years helped him haul sacks to the mill without becoming fatigued. Finally, however, the donkey's strength was sapped and it was no longer able to work. Accordingly, its master began to think about how he could best reduce the amount of money he paid for the beast's keep. But the donkey, sensing there was mischief in the air, ran away and started on the road to Bremen. There he planned on becoming a town musician.

After he had been journeying a short while, he came upon a hound, who was lying panting on the road as though he was on his last leg.

"Well, what are you panting so for, Growler?" said the donkey.

"Ah," said the hound, "just because I am so old, and every day I get weaker. Also, since I can no longer keep up with the pack, my master decided to kill me, so I made my exit. But now how am I to earn my bread and stay alive?"

"Do you know what?" said the donkey. "I am going to Bremen and shall there become a town musician. Come and join me in making music. I shall play the lute, and you can beat the kettledrum."

The hound agreed and they traveled on.

After a while, they came upon a cat sitting in the road, with a face as long as a twenty foot scarf.

"Well, why are you so ornery, Whiskers?" asked the donkey.

"Who can be cheerful when he is in as much need as I?" said the cat. "I am getting on in years and my teeth are dull, and I prefer to sit by the stove and purr instead of hunting and chasing mice. Just because of this my mistress wanted to drown me. I made myself scarce, but now I don't know where to go."

"Come with us to Bremen," said the donkey. "You are a great hand at serenading, so you can also become a town musician."

The cat agreed and joined them.

Next the runaways passed by a yard where a barnyard rooster was sitting on the door, crowing with all its might.

"You crow so loud you make my ears ring and my skin get goosebumps," said the donkey. "What is wrong?"

"Since Sunday visitors are coming tomorrow, my owner has no pity, and she has ordered the cook to make me into soup. So I shall have my neck wrung tonight. Therefore, I am crowing with all my might while I still can."

"Come with us, Red-comb," said the donkey. "We are going to Bremen and you will find a much happier fate awaiting you there. You have a clear voice, and when we all make music together, you will add quality to our song."

The rooster allowed himself to be persuaded and all four friends went off together. They could not, however, reach the town in one day, and when evening came they were in a wood where they decided to spend the night. The donkey and the hound lay under a big tree. The cat and the rooster settled themselves in the branches, the rooster flying right up to the top, which he believed was the safest place for him. Before going to sleep he looked in every direction. Suddenly it seemed that he saw a light burning in the distance. He called out to his colleagues that there must be a house not far off, since he clearly saw a light.

"Okay," said the donkey. " 'let us set out and head for it; the entertainment here is very poor anyway."

The hound thought the house might contain some bones or meat, and that would please him, so they all set out in the direction of the light. They soon saw it shining more clearly and getting bigger and bigger, till they arrived at a brightly lit robbers' den. The donkey, being the tallest, approached the window and peered in.

"What do you see, old Jackass?" asked the rooster.

"What do I see?" answered the donkey. "Why, a table covered with luscious food and drink, and robbers seated at it enjoying themselves."

"That would just suit us," said the rooster.

"Yes, if we were only in there," responded the donkey.

Then the animals put their heads together in order to decide how to drive the robbers out. At last they hit upon a plan.

The donkey was to take up his position with his forefeet on the window sill, the hound was to jump on his back, the cat to climb up onto the hound, and finally, the rooster was to fly up and stand on the cat's head. When they were thus arranged, at a given signal they all began to perform their music. The donkey hee-hawed, the hound woofed, the cat meowed, and the rooster cock-a-doodle-dooed. They crashed through the window, splintering the panes. The robbers were startled by the horrendous noise. They thought that the devil was coming to join them; so they ran into the forest for fear of their lives. Then the four animals sat down at the table and had themselves a feast; they ate as though they had not eaten in weeks. When they had finished, they put out the light and looked for sleeping quarters.

The donkey lay down on a pile of straw, the hound in back of the door, the cat on the hearth near the warm ashes, and the rooster flew up to the rafters. Their long journey had tired them, so they all soon fell asleep.

When midnight had come and gone, the robbers noticed from afar that the light was no longer burning and that all seemed quiet. The chief robber said, "We should not have been scared by a false alarm." And he ordered one of his fellow robbers to go and examine the house.

Finding all quiet, the messenger went into the kitchen to light a candle. And mistaking the cat's glowing, fiery eyes for live coals, he held a match close to them in order to light it. But the cat would not put up with this—it flew at his face, clawed and scratched. The robber was startled and scared out of his wits; he quickly attempted to run away.

He tried first to get out of the back door, but the hound, who was lying there, jumped up and bit his leg. As he ran across the pile of straw in front of the house, the donkey gave him a good sound kick with his rear legs; while the rooster who had awakened at the uproar cried out from his rafter "Cock-a-doodle-doo."

At this, the robber ran back to his chief as quick as his legs would carry him. He said, "There is an awful witch in the house who breathed on me and then scratched me with her long fingers. Behind the door there stands a man with a knife, who stabbed me, while in the yard lies a black monster who hit me with a club. To top it off, upon the roof the judge is seated, and he called out, 'Bring the devil here!' So I ran away as fast as I could."

From that day on, the robbers did not dare approach the house; this pleased the four Bremen musicians so much that they decided never to leave *their* house again.

■ THE TRAVELS OF A FOX ■
ANONYMOUS

One day a fox was digging behind a stump and he found a bumblebee; and the fox put the bumblebee in a bag and took the bag over his shoulder and travelled.

At the first house he came to, he went in and said to the mistress of the house, "Can I leave my bag here while I go to Squintum's?"

"Yes," said the woman.

"Then be careful not to open the bag," said the fox.

But as soon as he was out of sight the woman said to herself, "Well, I wonder what the fellow has in his bag that he is so careful about. I will look and see. It can't do any harm, for I shall tie the bag right up again."

However, the moment she unloosed the string, out flew the bumblebee, and the rooster caught him and ate him all up.

After a while the fox came back. He took up his bag and knew at once that his bumblebee was gone, and he said to the woman, "Where is my bumblebee?"

And the woman said, "I untied the string just to take a little peep to find out what was in your bag, and the bumblebee flew out and the rooster ate him."

"Very well," said the fox; "I must have the rooster, then."

So he caught the rooster and put him in his bag and travelled.

At the next house he came to, he went in and said to the mistress of the house, "Can I leave my bag here while I go to Squintum's?"

"Yes," said the woman.

"Then be careful not to open the bag," said the fox.

But as soon as he was out of sight the woman said to herself, "Well, I wonder what the fellow has in his bag that he is so careful about. I will look and see. It can't do any harm, for I shall tie the bag right up again."

However, the moment she unloosed the string the rooster flew out and the pig caught him and ate him all up.

After a while the fox came back. He took up his bag and knew at once that his rooster was gone, and he said to the woman, ''Where is my rooster?''

And the woman said, ''I untied the string just to take a little peep to find out what was in your bag, and the rooster flew out and the pig ate him.''

''Very well,'' said the fox, ''I must have the pig, then.''

So he caught the pig and put him in his bag and travelled.

At the next house he came to, he went in and said to the mistress of the house, ''Can I leave my bag here while I go to Squintum's?''

''Yes,'' said the woman.

''Then be careful not to open the bag,'' said the fox.

But as soon as he was out of sight the woman said to herself, ''Well, I wonder what the fellow has in his bag that he is so careful about. I will look and see. It can't do any harm, for I shall tie the bag right up again.''

However, the moment she unloosed the string, the pig jumped out and the ox gored him.

After a while the fox came back. He took up his bag and knew at once that his pig was gone, and he said to the woman, ''Where is my pig?''

And the woman said, ''I untied the string just to take a little peep to find out what was in your bag, and the pig jumped out and the ox gored him.''

''Very well,'' said the fox. ''I must have the ox, then.''

So he caught the ox and put him in his bag and travelled.

At the next house he came to, he went in and said to the mistress of the house, ''Can I leave my bag here while I go to Squintum's?''

''Yes,'' said the woman.

''Then be careful not to open the bag,'' said the fox.

But as soon as he was out of sight the woman said to herself, ''Well, I wonder what the fellow has in his bag that he is so careful about. I will look and see. It can't do any harm, for I shall tie the bag right up again.''

However, the moment she unloosed the string, the ox got out, and the woman's little boy chased the ox out of the house and across a meadow and over a hill clear out of sight.

After a while the fox came back. He took up his bag and knew at once that his ox was gone, and he said to the woman, ''Where is my ox?''

And the woman said, ''I untied the string just to take a little peep to find out what was in your bag, and the ox got out and my little boy chased him out of the house and across a meadow and over a hill clear out of sight.''

''Very well,'' said the fox, ''I must have the little boy, then.''

So he caught the little boy and put him in his bag and travelled.

At the next house he came to, he went in and said to the mistress of the house, ''Can I leave my bag here while I go to Squintum's?''

''Yes,'' said the woman.

"Then be careful not to open the bag," said the fox.

The woman had been making cake, and when it was baked she took it from the oven, and her children gathered around her teasing for some of it.

"Oh, ma, give me a piece!" said one, and "Oh, ma, give me a piece!" said each of the others.

And the smell of the cake came to the little boy in the bag, and he heard the children beg for the cake, and he said, "Oh, mammy, give me a piece."

Then the woman opened the bag and took the little boy out; and she put the house-dog in the bag in the little boy's place, and the little boy joined the other children.

After a while the fox came back. He took up his bag and he saw that it was tied fast and he thought that the little boy was safe inside. "I have been all day on the road," said he, "without a thing to eat, and I am getting hungry. I will just step off into the woods now and see how this little boy I have in my bag tastes."

So he put the bag on his back and traveled deep into the woods. Then he sat down and untied the bag, and if the little boy had been in there things would have gone badly with him.

But the little boy was at the house of the woman who made the cake, and when the fox untied the bag the house-dog jumped out and killed him.

■ THE GOLDEN TOUCH ■

NATHANIEL HAWTHORNE

Once upon a time, there lived a very rich king whose name was Midas; and he had a little daughter, whom nobody but myself ever heard of, and whose name was Marygold.

This King Midas was fonder of gold than of anything else in the world. He valued his royal crown chiefly because it was composed of that precious metal. If he loved anything better, or half so well, it was the one little maiden who played so merrily around her father's footstool. But the more Midas loved his daughter, the more did he desire and seek for wealth. He thought, foolish man! that the best thing he could possibly do for this dear child would be to bequeath her the immensest pile of yellow, glistening coin that had ever been heaped together since the world was made. Thus, he gave all his thoughts and all his time to this one purpose. If ever he happened to gaze for an instant at the gold-tinted clouds of sunset, he wished that they were real gold, and that they could be squeezed safely into his strong box. When little Marygold ran to meet him, with a bunch of buttercups and dandelions, he used to say, ''Poh, poh, child! If these flowers were as golden as they look, they would be worth the plucking. . . .''

At length Midas had got to be so exceedingly unreasonable that he could scarcely bear to see or touch any object that was not gold. He made it his custom, therefore, to pass a large portion of every day in a dark and dreary apartment, underground, at the basement of his palace. It was here that he kept his wealth. . . . Here, after carefully locking the door, he would take a bag of gold coin, or a gold cup as big as a washbowl, or a heavy golden bar . . . and bring them from the obscure corners of the room into the one bright and narrow sunbeam that fell from the dungeon-like window. He valued the sunbeam for no other reason but that his treasure would not shine without its help. . . .

Midas was enjoying himself in his treasure-room, one day, as usual, when he perceived a shadow fall over the heaps of gold; and, looking suddenly up, what should he behold but the figure of a stranger, standing in the bright and narrow sunbeam! It was a young man, with a cheerful and ruddy face. Whether it was that the imagination of King Midas threw a yellow tinge over everything, or whatever the cause might be, he could not help fancying that the smile with which the stranger regarded him had a kind of golden radiance in it. . . .

As Midas knew that he had carefully turned the key in the lock, and that no mortal strength could possibly break into his treasure-room, he, of course, concluded that his visitor must be something more than mortal. . . .

The stranger gazed about the room; and when his lustrous smile had glistened upon all the golden objects that were there, he turned again to Midas.

''You are a wealthy man, friend Midas!'' he observed. ''I doubt whether any other four walls, on earth, contain so much gold as you have contrived to pile up in this room.''

''I have done pretty well—pretty well,'' answered Midas, in a discontented tone. ''But, after all, it is but a trifle, when you consider that it has taken me my whole life to get it together. If one could live a thousand years, he might have time to grow rich!''

''What!'' exclaimed the stranger. ''Then you are not satisfied?''

Midas shook his head.

''And pray what would satisfy you?'' asked the stranger. . . .

Midas paused and meditated. . . . At last, a bright idea occurred to him. It seemed really as bright as the glistening metal which he loved so much. . . .

"Well, Midas," observed his visitor, "I see that you have at length hit upon something that will satisfy you. Tell me your wish."

"It is only this," replied Midas. "I am weary of collecting my treasures with so much trouble, and beholding the heap so diminutive, after I have done my best. I wish everything that I touch be changed to gold!"

The stranger's smile grew so very broad, that it seemed to fill the room like an outburst of the sun, gleaming into a shadowy dell, where the yellow autumnal leaves—for so looked the lumps and particles of gold—lie strewn in the glow of light.

"The Golden Touch!" exclaimed he. "You certainly deserve credit, friend Midas, for striking out so brilliant a conception. But are you quite sure that this will satisfy you?"

"How could it fail?" said Midas.

"And will you never regret the possession of it?"

"What could induce me?" asked Midas. "I ask nothing else to render me perfectly happy."

"Be it as you wish, then," replied the stranger, waving his hand in token of farewell. "Tomorrow, at sunrise, you will find yourself gifted with the Golden Touch."

The figure of the stranger then became exceedingly bright, and Midas involuntarily closed his eyes. . . .

Whether Midas slept as usual that night, the story does not say. At any rate, day had hardly peeped over the hills when King Midas was broad awake, and stretching his arms out of bed, began to touch the objects that were within reach. He was anxious to prove whether the Golden Touch had really come, according to the stranger's promise. . . . The Golden Touch had come to him with the first sunbeam!

Midas started up, in a kind of joyful frenzy, and ran about the room, grasping at everything that happened to be in his way. He seized one of the bed-posts, and it became immediately a fluted golden pillar. He pulled aside a window-curtain in order to admit a clear spectacle of the wonders which he was performing; and the tassel grew heavy in his hand—a mass of gold. He took up a book from the table. At his first touch, it assumed the appearance of such a splendidly bound and gilt-edged volume as one often meets with, nowadays; but, on running his fingers through the leaves, behold! It was a bundle of thin golden plates, in which all the wisdom of the book had grown illegible. He hurriedly put on his clothes, and was enraptured to see himself in a magnificent suit of gold cloth, which retained its flexibility and softness, although it burdened him a little with its weight. . . .

Midas now took his spectacles from his pocket, and put them on his nose, in order that he might see more distinctly what he was about. . . . To his great perplexity, however, excellent as the glasses were, he discovered that he could not possibly see through them. But this was the most natural thing in the world; for, on taking them off, the transparent crystals turned out to be plates of yellow metal, and, of course, were worthless as spectacles, though valuable as gold. It struck Midas as rather inconvenient that, with all his wealth, he could never again be rich enough to own a pair of serviceable spectacles.

"It is no great matter, nevertheless," said he to himself, very philosophically. "We cannot expect any great good, without its being accompanied with some small inconvenience. The Golden Touch is worth the sacrifice of a pair of spectacles, at least, if not of one's very eyesight. My own eyes will serve for ordinary purposes, and little Marygold will soon be old enough to read to me. . . ."

By the time this good work was completed, King Midas was summoned to breakfast; and as the morning air had given him an excellent appetite, he made haste back to the palace.

On this particular morning, the breakfast consisted of hot cakes, some nice little brook-trout, roasted potatoes, fresh boiled eggs, and coffee, for King Midas himself, and a bowl of bread and milk for his daughter Marygold.

Little Marygold had not yet made her appearance. Her father ordered her to be called, and, seating himself at table, awaited the child's coming, in order to begin his own breakfast. To do Midas justice, he really loved his daughter, and loved her so much the more this morning, on account of the good fortune which had befallen him. It was not a great while before he heard her coming along the passageway crying bitterly. This circumstance surprised him, because Marygold was one of the cheerfullest little people whom you would see in a summer's day, and hardly shed a thimbleful of tears in a twelve-month. When Midas heard her sobs, he determined to put little Marygold in better spirits, by an agreeable surprise; so, leaning across the table, he touched his daughter's bowl . . . and transmuted it to gleaming gold.

Meanwhile, Marygold slowly and disconsolately opened the door, and showed herself with her apron at her eyes, still sobbing as if her heart would break. . . . Marygold, without taking the apron from her eyes, held out her hand, in which was one of the roses which Midas had so recently transmuted.

"Beautiful!" exclaimed her father. "And what is there in this magnificent golden rose to make you cry?"

"Ah, dear father!" answered the child, as well as her sobs would let her; "It is not beautiful, but the ugliest flower that ever grew! As soon as I was dressed I ran into the garden to gather some roses for you. . . . But, oh dear, dear me! What do think has happened? . . . All the beautiful roses, that smelled so sweetly and had so many lovely blushes, are blighted and spoilt! They are grown quite yellow, as you see this one, and have no longer any fragrance! What can have been the matter with them?"

"Poh, my dear little girl,—pray don't cry about it!" said Midas, who was ashamed to confess that he himself had wrought the change which so greatly afflicted her. . . .

Midas, meanwhile, had poured out a cup of coffee, and, as a matter of course, the coffee-pot, whatever metal it may have been when he took it up, was gold when he set it down. He thought to himself, that it was rather an extravagant style of splendor. . . .

Amid these thoughts, he lifted a spoonful of coffee to his lips, and, sipping it, was astonished to perceive that, the instant his lips touched the liquid, it became molten gold, and, the next moment, hardened into a lump!

"Ha!" exclaimed Midas, rather aghast.

"What is the matter, father?" asked little Marygold, gazing at him, with the tears still standing in her eyes.

"Nothing, child, nothing!" said Midas. . . .

"I don't quite see," thought he to himself, "how I am to get any breakfast!"

He took one of the smoking-hot cakes, and had scarcely broken it, when, to his cruel mortification, though, a moment before, it had been of the whitest wheat, it assumed the yellow hue of Indian meal. Almost in despair, he helped himself to a boiled egg, which immediately underwent a change similar to those of the trout and the cake. . . .

"Well, this is a quandary!" thought he, leaning back in his chair, and looking quite enviously at little Marygold, who was now eating her bread and milk with great satisfaction: "Such a costly breakfast before me, and nothing that can be eaten."

Hoping that, by dint of great dispatch, he might avoid what he now felt to be a considerable inconvenience, King Midas next snatched a hot potato, and attempted to cram it into his mouth, and swallow it in a hurry. But the Golden Touch was too nimble for him. He found his mouth full, not of mealy potato, but of solid metal, which so burnt his tongue that he roared aloud, and, jumping up from the table, began to dance and stamp about the room, both with pain and affright.

"Father, dear father!" cried little Marygold, who was a very affectionate child, "pray what is the matter? Have you burnt your mouth?"

"Ah, dear child," groaned Midas, dolefully, "I don't know what is to become of your poor father. . . ."

Our pretty Marygold could endure it no longer. She sat a moment, gazing at her father, and trying, with all the might of her little wits, to find out what was the matter with him. Then, with a sweet and sorrowful impulse to comfort him, she started from her chair, and, running to Midas, threw her arms affectionately about his knees. He bent down and kissed her. He felt that his little daughter's love was worth a thousand times more than he had gained by the Golden Touch.

"My precious, precious Marygold!" cried he.

But Marygold made no answer.

Alas, what had he done? The moment the lips of Midas touched Marygold's forehead, a change had taken place. Her sweet, rosy face, so full of affection as it had been, assumed a glittering yellow color, with yellow teardrops, congealing on her cheeks. . . . Oh, terrible misfortune! The victim of his insatiable desire for wealth, little Marygold was a human child no longer, but a golden statue!

Yes, there she was, with the questioning look of love, grief, and pity, hardened into her face. It was the prettiest and most woeful sight that ever mortal saw. . . .

Midas, in the fullness of all his gratified desires, began to wring his hands and bemoan himself; and how he could neither bear to look at Marygold, nor yet to look away from her. . . .

While Midas was in this tumult of despair, he suddenly beheld a stranger standing near the door. Midas bent down his head, without speaking; for he recognized the same figure which had appeared to him, the day before, in the treasure-room and had bestowed on him this disastrous faculty of the Golden Touch. . . .

"Well, friend Midas," said the stranger, "pray how do you succeed with the Golden Touch?"

Midas shook his head.

"I am very miserable," said he. . . .

"Gold is not everything . . . and I have lost all that my heart really cared for."

"Ah! So you have made a discovery, since yesterday?" observed the stranger. "Let us see, then. Which of these two things do you think is really worth the most—the gift of the Golden Touch, or one cup of clear cold water?"

"O blessed water!" exclaimed Midas. . . .

"The Golden Touch," asked the stranger, "or your own little Marygold, warm, soft, and loving as she was an hour ago?"

"Oh, my child, my dear child!" cried poor Midas, wringing his hands. "I would not have given that one small dimple in her chin for the power of changing this whole big earth into a solid lump of gold!"

"You are wiser than you were, King Midas!" said the stranger, looking seriously at him. "Your own heart, I perceive, has not been entirely changed from flesh to gold. . . . Tell me now do you sincerely desire to rid yourself of this Golden Touch?"

"It is hateful to me!" replied Midas.

"Go, then," said the stranger, "and plunge into the river that glides past the bottom of your garden. Take likewise a vase of the same water, and sprinkle it over any object that you may desire to change back again from gold into its former substance. If you do this in earnestness and sincerity, it may possibly repair the mischief which your avarice has occasioned."

King Midas bowed low; and when he lifted his head, the lustrous stranger had vanished. . . .

On reaching the river's brink, he plunged headlong in, without waiting so much as to pull off his shoes.

"Poof! poof! poof!" snorted King Midas, as his head emerged out of the water. "Well, this is really a refreshing bath, and I think it must have quite washed away the Golden Touch. And now for filling my pitcher!"

As he dipped the pitcher into the water, it gladdened his very heart to see it change from gold into the same good, honest earthen vessel which it had been before he touched it. He was conscious, also, of a change within himself. . . . The curse of the Golden Touch had . . . really been removed from him. . . .

King Midas hastened back to the palace. . . . The first thing he did, as you need hardly be told, was to sprinkle it by handfuls over the golden figure of little Marygold.

No sooner did it fall on her than you would have laughed to see how the rosy color came back to the dear child's cheek!

. . . Her father did not think it necessary to tell his beloved child how very foolish he had been, but contented himself with showing how much wiser he had now grown. . . .

When King Midas had grown quite an old man, and used to trot Marygold's children on his knee, he was fond of telling them this marvelous story, pretty much as I have now told it to you. . . .

"And to tell you the truth, my precious little folks," quoth King Midas, diligently trotting the children all the while, "ever since that morning, I have hated the very sight of all other gold. . . ."

■ THE RICH MAN ■
AND THE POOR MAN
ANONYMOUS

A poor man went to his rich friend,
And said, with gracious smile:
"I've come to ask if you would lend
Your ass to me awhile."

"My ass, alas, is out today,"
The rich man made reply.
"At nine o'clock it went away,
I don't know where or why."

"Too bad, too bad," the poor man said,
"I'll bid you, then, good day,"
But at that moment, in the shed,
An ass began to bray.

"You lied to me!" the poor man cried.
" 'My ass is out' forsooth!
But even if its master lied,
The ass has told the truth."

"I lied?!"—the rich man's face grew red—
"I cannot let that pass!
It's me you should believe, instead
Of trusting a mere ass!"

The poor man turned without a word
And climbed the pathway steep.
On coming to a grove he heard
The bleating of a sheep.

The thirsty sheep had left the flock
In search of water cool
It now was standing by a rock,
And drinking at a pool.

The poor man caught it, tied its feet,
And put it on his back.
He then continued in the heat
To climb the rugged track.

The rich man came that afternoon:
"You stole my sheep, they say.
I want it back and want it soon,
I want it straightaway."

"No sheep of yours is in my shed,
Go search another place,"
The poor man to the rich one said,
And turned away his face.

The rich man was about to go,
When from behind a wall,
He heard a bleat he seemed to know—
A most familiar call.

"My sheep is here!" he roared in rage.
"I hear it calling me.
It's a disgrace for one your age
To lie so shamelessly!"

"You trust that foolish sheep in there?"
The poor man calmly said.
"Far better would it be, I swear,
To trust your friend instead."

■ THE EMPEROR'S NEW CLOTHES ■

HANS CHRISTIAN ANDERSEN

Many years ago there was an Emperor who was so excessively fond of new clothes that he spent all his money on them. He cared nothing about his soldiers, nor for the theatre, nor for driving in the woods except for the sake of showing off his new clothes. He had a costume for every hour in the day, and instead of saying as one does about any other King or Emperor, "He is in his council chamber," here one always said, "The Emperor is in his dressing-room."

Life was very gay in the great town where he lived; hosts of strangers came to visit it every day, and among them one day two swindlers. They gave themselves out as weavers, and said that they knew how to weave the most beautiful stuffs imaginable. Not only were the colors and patterns unusually fine, but the clothes that were made of these stuffs had the peculiar quality of becoming invisible to every person who was not fit for the office he held, or if he was impossibly dull.

"Those must be splendid clothes," thought the Emperor. "By wearing them I should be able to discover which men in my kingdom are unfitted for their posts. I shall distinguish the wise men from the fools. Yes, I certainly must order some of that stuff to be woven for me.

He paid the two swindlers a lot of money in advance so that they might begin their work at once.

They did put up two looms and pretended to weave, but they had nothing whatever upon their shuttles. At the outset they asked for a quantity of the finest silk and the purest gold thread, all of which they put into their own bags while they worked away at the empty looms far into the night.

"I should like to know how these weavers are getting on with the stuff," thought the Emperor; but he felt a little queer when he reflected that anyone who was stupid or unfit for his post would not be able to see it. He certainly thought that he need have no fears for himself, but still he thought he would send somebody else first to see how it was getting on. Everybody in the town knew what wonderful power the stuff possessed, and everyone was anxious to see how stupid his neighbor was.

"I will send my faithful old minister to the weavers," thought the Emperor. "He will be best able to see how the stuff looks, for he is a clever man and no one fulfills his duties better than he does!"

So the good old minister went into the room where the two swindlers sat working at the empty loom.

"Heaven preserve us!" thought the old minister, opening his eyes very wide. "Why, I can't see a thing!" But he took care not to say so.

Both the swindlers begged him to be good enough to step a little nearer, and asked if he did not think it a good pattern and beautiful coloring. They pointed to the empty loom, and the poor old minister stared as hard as he could but he could not see anything, for of course there was nothing to see.

"Good heavens!" thought he, "it is possible that I am a fool? I have never thought so and nobody must know it. Am I not fit for my post? It will never do to say that I cannot see the stuffs."

"Well, sir, you don't say anything about the stuff," said the one who was pretending to weave.

"Oh, it is beautiful! quite charming!" said the old minister looking through his spectacles; "this pattern and these colors! I will certainly tell the Emperor that the stuff pleases me very much."

"We are delighted to hear you say so," said the swindlers, and then they named all the colors and described the peculiar pattern. The old minister paid great attention to what they said, so as to be able to repeat it when he got home to the Emperor.

Then the swindlers went on to demand more money, more silk, and more gold, to be able to proceed with the weaving; but they put it all into their own pockets—not a single strand was ever put into the loom, but they went on as before weaving at the empty loom.

The Emperor soon sent another faithful official to see how the stuff was getting on, and if it would soon be ready. The same thing happened to him as to the minister; he looked and looked, but as there was only the empty loom, he could see nothing at all.

"Is not this a beautiful piece of stuff?" said both the swindlers, showing and explaining the beautiful pattern and colors which were not there to be seen.

"I know I am not a fool!" thought the man, "so it must be that I am unfit for my good post! It is very strange though! however, one must not let it appear!" So he praised the stuff he did not see, and assured them of his delight in the beautiful colors and the originality of the design. "It is absolutely charming!" he said to the Emperor. Everybody in the town was talking about this splendid stuff.

Now the Emperor thought he would like to see it while it was still on the loom. So accompanied by a number of selected courtiers, among whom were the two faithful officials who had already seen the imaginary stuff, he went to visit the crafty imposters, who were working away as hard as ever they could at the empty loom.

"It is magnificent!" said both the honest officials. "Only see, Your Majesty, what a design! What colors!" And they pointed to the empty loom, for they thought no doubt the others could see the stuff.

"What!" thought the Emperor; "I see nothing at all! This is terrible! Am I a fool? Am I not fit to be Emperor? Why, nothing worse could happen to me!"

"Oh, it is beautiful!" said the Emperor. "It has my highest approval!" and he nodded his satisfaction as he gazed at the empty loom. Nothing would induce him to say that he could not see anything.

The whole suite gazed and gazed, but saw nothing more than all the others. However, they all exclaimed with His Majesty, "It is very beautiful!" and they advised him to wear a suit made of this wonderful cloth on the occasion of a great procession which was just about to take place. "It is magnificent! gorgeous! excellent!" went from mouth to mouth; they were all equally delighted with it. The Emperor gave each of the rogues an order of knighthood to be worn in their buttonholes and the title of "Gentlemen Weavers."

The swindlers sat up the whole night, before the day on which the procession was to take place, burning sixteen candles, so that people might see how anxious they were to get the Emperor's new clothes ready. They pretended to take the stuff off the loom. They cut it out in the air with a huge pair of scissors, and they stitched away with needles without any thread in them. At last they said, "Now the Emperor's new clothes are ready!"

The Emperor, with his grandest courtiers, went to them himself, and both the swindlers raised one arm in the air, as if they were holding something, and said, "See, these are the trousers, this is the coat, here is the mantle!" and so on. "It is as light as a spider's web. One might think one had nothing on, but that is the very beauty of it!"

"Yes!" said all the courtiers, but they could not see anything, for there was nothing to see.

"Will Your Imperial Majesty be graciously pleased to take off your clothes," said the imposters, "so that we may put on the new ones, along here before the great mirror?"

The Emperor took off all his clothes, and the imposters pretended to give him one article of dress after the other, of the new ones which they had pretended to make. They pretended to fasten something around his waist and to tie on something; this was the train, and the Emperor turned round and round in front of the mirror.

"How well His Majesty looks in the new clothes! How becoming they are!" cried all the people round. "What a design, and what colors! They are most gorgeous robes!"

"The canopy is waiting outside which is to be carried over Your Majesty in the procession," said the master of the ceremonies.

"Well, I am quite ready," said the Emperor. "Don't the clothes fit well?" and then he turned round again in front of the mirror, so that he would seem to be looking at his grand things.

The chamberlains who were to carry the train stooped and pretended to lift it from the ground with both hands, and they walked along with their hands in the air. They dared not let it appear that they could not see anything.

Then the Emperor walked along in the procession under the gorgeous canopy, and everybody in the streets and at the windows exclaimed, "How beautiful the Emperor's new clothes are! What a splendid train! And they fit to perfection!" Nobody would let it appear that he could see nothing, for then he would not be fit for his post, or else he was a fool.

None of the Emperor's clothes had been so successful before.

"But he has got nothing on," said a little child.

"Oh, listen to the innocent," said its father; and one person whispered to the other what the child had said. "He has nothing on; a child says he has nothing on!"

"But he has nothing on!" at last cried all the people.

The Emperor writhed, for he knew it was true, but he thought "the procession must go on now," so he held himself stiffer than ever, and the chamberlains held up the invisible train.

■ MACAVITY, THE MYSTERY CAT ■

T. S. ELIOT

Macavity's a Mystery Cat: he's called the Hidden Paw—
For he's the master criminal who can defy the Law.
He's the bafflement of Scotland Yard, the Flying Squad's
    despair:
For when they reach the scene of crime—*Macavity's not there!*

Macavity, Macavity, there's no one like Macavity,
He's broken every human law, he breaks the law of gravity.
His powers of levitation would make a fakir stare,
And when you reach the scene of crime—*Macavity's not there!*
You may seek him in the basement, you may look up in the air—
But I tell you once and once again, *Macavity's not there!*

Macavity's a ginger cat, he's very tall and thin;
You would know him if you saw him, for his eyes are sunken in.
His brow is deeply lined with thought, his head is highly
        domed;
His coat is dusty from neglect, his whiskers are uncombed.
He sways his head from side to side, with movements like a
        snake;
And when you think he's half asleep, he's always wide awake.

Macavity, Macavity, there's no one like Macavity,
For he's a fiend in feline shape, a monster of depravity.
You may meet him in a by-street, you may see him in the square—
But when a crime's discovered, then *Macavity's not there!*

He's outwardly respectable. (They say he cheats at cards.)
And his footprints are not found in any file of Scotland Yard's.
And when the larder's looted, or the jewel-case is rifled,
Or when the milk is missing, or another Peke's been stifled,
Or the greenhouse glass is broken, and the trellis past repair—
Ay, there's the wonder of the thing! *Macavity's not there!*

And when the Foreign Office find a Treaty's gone astray,
Or the Admiralty lose some plans and drawings by the way,
There may be a scrap of paper in the hall or on the stair—
But it's useless to investigate—*Macavity's not there!*
And when the loss has been disclosed, the Secret Service say:
''It *must* have been Macavity!''—but he's a mile away.
You'll be sure to find him resting, or a-licking of his thumbs,
Or engaged in doing complicated long division sums.

Macavity, Macavity, there's no one like Macavity,
There never was a Cat of such deceitfulness and suavity.
He always has an alibi, and one or two to spare:
At whatever time the deed took place—MACAVITY WASN'T THERE!
And they say that all the Cats whose wicked deeds are widely
    known,
(I might mention Mungojerrie, I might mention Griddlebone)
Are nothing more than agents for the Cat who all the time
Just controls their operations: the Napoleon of Crime!

■ THE RAT'S DAUGHTER ■
A JAPANESE FABLE

There lived once in Japan a rat and his wife who came from an old and noble family. They had one beautiful and clever daughter of whom they were very proud. She could gnaw through the hardest wood and run like the wind. Her coat was a lovely soft silky brown and her pointed teeth shone like pearls. Many of the other young female rats envied her good looks.

Her proud parents expected her to marry well. Her father was a rat through and through and happily dreamed of his daughter marrying a handsome young rat from their own group. There was a particularly fine specimen that he thought would be suitable: a young rat with long moustaches that touched the ground and whose family was even nobler and older than his own.

The rat's mother had very different ideas, however. She despised all rats outside her own family and could not consider that any of them would be good enough for her own darling daughter.

"My daughter shall never marry a mere rat," she declared, holding her head high. "With her beauty and talents she has a right to marry someone better than *that*."

So the husband and wife quarreled day and night about who would make a suitable husband for their child. But they never even thought to ask their daughter what she herself thought.

At last the wife said:

"I think only the mighty and powerful Sun is good enough for my child—let us pay him a visit."

The husband reluctantly agreed and they set off with their daughter to visit the Sun in his golden palace. Once there the wife looked up at the Sun and said bravely:

"Noble king, here is our precious daughter and we are offering her to you in marriage as we know that you are the most powerful being on earth, and only you will be worthy of her."

Now the Sun was amused at this proposal but he hadn't the slightest intention of marrying anybody, least of all a rat, so he said carefully:

"It is very kind of you to offer your beautiful daughter to me, but I really cannot accept—after all I am not really the most powerful being on earth: the Cloud is. He can pass over me and stop my light whenever he wishes." At that moment the Cloud did indeed cover the Sun and he was blocked from view.

The husband and wife agreed to ask the Cloud immediately. Certainly, they thought, the Cloud was more powerful than the Sun, as at any time he could cover the Sun whether the Sun wanted this or not.

The Cloud was rather taken aback when the rats offered their daughter to him in marriage. He did not want to offend the couple, but he did not want to marry a rat—even a very beautiful one—and so he said:

"It is kind of the Sun to describe me as the most powerful being in the world, but he really isn't right. The Wind is far more powerful than I am, watch this—" and at that moment a great gust of Wind blew the Cloud across the sky.

The husband and wife saw that the Wind was more powerful than the Cloud and asked him if he would like to marry their darling daughter. The Wind was secretly appalled at the idea—he was far too busy traveling around the world to be stuck in one place and married to a rat. So he said in a great booming voice:

"The Cloud is quite right—I am more powerful than he is but I am not more powerful than that Wall over there. He has the power to stop me in my flight. Ask him to marry your daughter."

The three rats all stared at the huge brick wall looming over them.

The wife said:

"Well, Wall, as you are the most powerful being, we can offer you the hand of our beautiful daughter in marriage."

The Wall was considering this proposal when all at once there was a terrible wailing noise. It was the young female rat.

"I don't want to marry a *Wall*!" she cried. "How can you all be so cruel and not consider my feelings? I would have married the Sun, or the Cloud or the Wind, because that was what you wished, but *not* an ugly old Wall!"

The Wall was somewhat hurt at this outburst and declared that he had no wish to marry a rat anyway.

"It is quite true," he said, "that I can stop the Wind, but there is someone who is more powerful than I—that is the rat who lives under me. He can reduce me to powder, simply by gnawing with his teeth. A fine young male rat would surely make the best companion for your daughter."

The young female rat was delighted at this suggestion and said she would love to marry the handsome young rat with the moustaches that touched the ground, whom her father had suggested in the first place. Her mother was happy to agree now that she knew how powerful rats really were.

So they all returned home. The lady rat married the handsome rat with the moustaches and a wonderful wedding celebration was enjoyed by all.

Performer's Journal

Consider these questions both before and after your performance of your children's literature. Note your responses in your journal.

1. Why did you select this piece of literature for interpretation?

2. What did you do to adapt the material to the requirements of oral performance?

3. Describe your work techniques as you rehearsed the material. How do they differ from the way you have rehearsed material for adult audiences?

4. Describe the response you received from your peers as you shared the material with them.

5. Were you able to locate a child audience?

6. How did you feel when approaching the audience? Were you nervous? Confident?

7. How did they respond to the material? In what ways was the reaction similar to that of adults? In what ways was the reaction different?

8. What changes would you make if you were to present the material for another group of children?

9. Do you find working for children a fulfilling experience? Would you consider doing it again? Why or why not?

CHAPTER NINE

Performing Literature from Around the World

Technology—telecommunications, communication satellite systems, the fax—has made our lives easier. Have you also considered how this technology has shrunk our world? We can get in touch almost instantly with people in all but the remotest corners of the world. The concept of our being part of a global community is becoming a reality. We are discovering that we have things in common with people of different countries and cultures.

And yet, we are different from one another, as well. Recall the Vulcan greeting in the television series *Star Trek*: "Greetings! I am pleased to see that we are different. May we together become greater than the sum of both of us." In order to live harmoniously in today's global village, we must make a huge leap from suspicion to mutual respect and understanding for others. As an interpreter of literature, you are in an enviable position both to increase your understanding of the various cultures that make up our world and to share that understanding with audiences.

Nearly three hundred years ago, the poet Basho wrote:

> Nearing Autumn's close.
> My neighbor—
> How does he live, I wonder?

People have always been curious about how other people live and think. Experiencing the literature of America as an interpreter makes it possible for you to share the feelings of the people of your native land. Your interpretation is a key to gain entry into the minds and emotions of people of different nations, too.

Use your interpretative art to examine literature from around the world. In studying a variety of works, you can come to appreciate the ideas, beliefs, customs, and attitudes that characterize each group of people. In this way you can come to know something about the people and to understand that people in other societies view themselves differently. Consequently, sometimes their behavior is unlike that in our society. For example, different cultures exhibit different attitudes toward the concepts of time and nature. Such attitudes, as well as the behaviors through which these attitudes are manifested, reveal themselves in the literature of that culture.

A Confucian saying tells us, "Human beings draw close to one another by their common nature, but habits and customs keep them apart." The interpretation of literature gives you the opportunity to explore those habits and customs and to find ways to help your audience understand and identify with them. As theorist Edward T. Hall pointed out, "There is not one aspect of human life that is not touched and altered by culture. This means personality, how people express themselves, the way they think, how they move, how problems are solved . . . as well as how economic and government systems are put together and function." Culture teaches you how to act, feel, and believe, as it helps you to distinguish proper from improper behavior.

Remember, oral interpretation is a social art. Widening your literary maps will allow your audiences to experience the commonality of all humanity through a variety of cultures.

The literary selections included in the preceding chapters of *Literature Alive!* are, for the most part, by authors from the United States. In this chapter, you will have the opportunity to explore the literature of other countries and learn about their diverse cultures, discovering what is different and what we have in common. Through analyzing and interpreting literature from around the world, you will learn that we share basic emotions— joy, fear, sorrow, love, anger. Performing the literature of other countries will help you understand your place in the global community as well as the cultures and peoples in other parts of the world.

GETTING INVOLVED
A World's Fair of Literature

Divide the class into small groups. Each group should select a foreign country to explore in terms of literature and culture. Each member of your group should select a piece of literature from that part of the world. To begin your search for your individual selection for performance, you may first consider the sampling of cuttings from world literature in this chapter. However, be encouraged to explore other possibilities in a world literature anthology, do research at the library, or check with your foreign language department for recommendations on literature available in translation. In addition to sharing your interpretation of literature with your class, your group may also consider bringing in samples of your chosen country's culture—foods, clothing, or recordings of music representative of that country.

As you analyze the following literature and rehearse your performance, consider the questions in the following "Performer's Journal," writing your responses in your notebook.

Performer's Journal

1. What type of experience is being described in the literature?

2. What theme is treated?

3. What types of characters, if any, are revealed in the literature? What attitudes, beliefs, and ideas do these characters express?

4. What moods are highlighted in your interpretation?

5. What does the literature tell you about the foreign country, its culture, and its inhabitants?

6. What feelings do you want your audience to experience as you share your interpretation of the literature with them?

■ OUT OF DARKNESS ■
ALEX LA GUMA

The smell of unwashed bodies and sweaty blankets was sharp, and the heat in the cell hung as thick as cotton wool. The man on the rope mat beside me turned, grunted, and flung a long arm across my face.

'How do you do?' he said, waking up and giggling.

'Very well,' I replied soothingly, for he was a little mad.

In the dark the other bodies turned, cursed, and tried to settle back into perspiring sleep.

'Did Joey bring the eggs?'

I could make out the dim shapeless bulge of his body curled up on the mat. He had entered the seventh year of his ten-year sentence for culpable homicide, and being shut up so long had unhinged him somewhat. He was neither staring mad nor violent. His insanity was of a gentle quality that came in spells. It was then that he would talk. Otherwise he was clamped up tight and retired, like a snail withdrawn into its shell. He was friendly enough but it was the friendliness of a man on the other side of a peephole.

To the rest of the inmates he was known as Ou Kakkelak, Old Cockroach, and was either the butt of their depraved humour or was completely ignored. He took everything with a gentle smile. From parts of his conversations during his spells I gained the impression that he was an educated man and might have been a schoolmaster before he had committed his crime. . . .

'Is the heat troubling you?' I asked, as kindly as I could make it. 'It's damn hot, isn't it?' He did not reply. I decided to do a little probing. 'You speak of Cora now and then. Who is she?' But he turned on his side and was asleep again.

In the morning there was the usual shouting and clanging of doors. Blankets were folded; the long line of convicts streamed down to the yards. The guards stood by, lashing out with their leather belts. . . .

We squatted, packed into the cement yard, and breakfasted on the mealie meal and black, bitter coffee. Old Cockroach sat near me, smiling his gentle, vacant smile and wolfing his food.

I saw him again when we were locked up after supper. He sank down in his place beside me. Around us secret cigarettes were emerging. . . . Figures in washed-out red shirts and canvas shirts packed the floor of the cell.

'Here we are,' Old Cockroach said and giggled at me. 'The wreckage which mankind, on its onward march, left behind.'

'Well,' I answered, smiling at him. 'Perhaps it's better to say that we are the results of mankind's imperfections.'

'Perhaps. Perhaps. I wonder where Joey is tonight?' He sat with his knees drawn up and his long arms clasped about his shins, gazing vacantly about at the faces around him. 'Ah, there he is now.'

I looked and said, 'That's Smiley Abrams. Remember? That's not Joey. That's Smiley Abrams.'

'Oh, *ja.* He's here for murder. I believe he's killed three people in his lifetime. They got him for the last one. An ape-man roaming a jungle. Here he is king. In a cave the cave man is king.'

He fell silent again. . . . I sat with my back against the concrete wall and looked at Old Cockroach. He was tall and thin and bony, folded up now like a carpenter's ruler. His skin was as dark as burnt leather, and he had slightly negroid features and kinky hair going gray, close to his skull, like a tight-fitting cap. . . .

'Cora,' he rambled. 'I think. . . .'

'She'll turn up on visiting day,' I told him, although I knew she would not . . . because nobody had ever visited him for as long as I had been in. I began to wish I could learn more about him. . . .

The sun faded beyond the barred windows like lights being dimmed in a theatre. It had become hot again in the casern, and from the bucket latrine came the sharp, acrid smell of ammonia. Old Cockroach lay back on his mat and pulled the thin blanket up to his waist. He did not seem to feel the heat, but just lay there. . . . It was as if he had drawn an invisible armour around himself. . . .

The next night started much the same. The heat was overpowering, and the stench of bodies increased quickly. Men fought and clawed around the water buckets, snarling like jackals around their carrion. The cave man, Smiley Abrams, hurled men from the centre of the turmoil, growling and snapping at his cringing subjects. . . .

'A slave has revolted,' Old Cockroach observed in a voice as gentle as the fall of dust. 'Do you know that the whole of mankind's history consists of a series of revolutions?'

'You're an educated man, Old Cockroach,' I said. 'You don't belong here. How did you come to kill anybody? If you don't mind me asking.'

'I used to be a schoolmaster,' he replied, confirming my old suspicion. Then his mind wandered again, and he murmured, 'I hope Joey brings that book he borrowed last week. *Treasure Island.* Have you ever read *Treasure Island?*'

. . . The brawl around the water buckets had subsided, since they both had been emptied. . . . Men sat around, hunched stark naked under the light, exploring their clothes and blankets for lice. . . .

Old Cockroach had settled down on his blankets and I could hear him scratching himself. . . . From all around us grunts, curses, and tiny cries came like suppressed voices out of hell.

'. . . Cora,' Old Cockroach's voice came out of the dark, quiet as the trickle of sweat. 'Cora.'

'Take it easy, old man,' I murmured. . . .

I decided to probe a little more. 'By the way, who is Cora?'

Silence. Then he said, 'Hullo, Joey. I'm glad you've come. I'll tell you a story. Would you like to listen to a story?'

'Okay. That would be fine.'

'All right, then, it was a long time ago. A very long time ago, I think. I was in love with her. You don't think this is going to be a silly story, do you?'

'Certainly not.'

'I was a teacher at a junior school and was doing a varsity course in my spare time. And I was in love with Cora. She was beautiful. . . . Her skin was soft and smooth and the colour of rich cream. She was almost white you see. I was in love with her. . . .'

He was silent again while the sounds of sleep went on around us. When he went on his voice had taken on a dullness. 'Then she began to find that she could pass as white, and I was black. She begun to go to the white places . . . Places where I couldn't take her. . . . She drifted away from me, but I kept on loving her.

'I talked to her, pleaded with her. But she wouldn't take any notice of what I said. I became angry. I wept. I raved . . . I grovelled. . . . But it wasn't of any use. She said I was selfish and trying to deny her the good things of life. . . .

'In the end she turned on me. She told me to go to hell. She slapped my face and called me a black nigger. . . .'

'Then you lost your head and killed her,' I said quietly. 'That's why you're here now.'

'Oh no,' Old Cockroach answered. 'I could never have done that to Cora. I did lose my head, but it was Joey whom I killed. He said I was a damn fool for going off over a damn play-white. . . . So I hit him, and he cracked his skull on something. Ah, here's Joey now. Hullo, Joey. I hope you've brought my book. . . .'

NIGERIA

■ TELEPHONE CONVERSATION ■
WOLE SOYINKA

The price seemed reasonable, location
Indifferent. The landlady swore she lived
Off premises. Nothing remained
But self-confession. 'Madam,' I warned,
'I hate a wasted journey—I am African.'
Silence. Silenced transmission of
Pressurized good-breeding. Voice, when it came,
Lipstick-coated, long gold-rolled
Cigarette-holder pipped. Caught I was, foully.
'HOW DARK?' . . . I had not misheard . . . 'ARE YOU LIGHT
OR VERY DARK?' Button B. Button A. Stench
of rancid breath of public hide-and-speak.
Red booth. Red pillar box. Red double-tiered
Omnibus squelching tar. It *was* real! Shamed
By ill-mannered silence, surrender
Pushed dumbfounded to beg simplication.
Considerate she was, varying the emphasis—
'ARE YOU DARK? OR VERY LIGHT?' Revelation came.
'You mean—like plain or milk chocolate?'
Her assent was clinical, crushing in its light
Impersonality. Rapidly, wave-length adjusted,
I chose. 'West African sepia'—and as afterthought,
'Down in my passport.' Silence for spectroscopic

Flight of fancy, till truthfulness clanged her accent
Hard on the mouthpiece. 'WHAT'S THAT?' conceding
'DON'T KNOW WHAT THAT IS.' 'Like brunette.'
'THAT'S DARK, ISN'T IT?' 'Not altogether.
Facially, I am brunette, but madam, you should see
the rest of me. Palm of my hand, soles of my feet
Are a peroxide blonde. Friction, caused—
Foolishly madam—by sitting down, has turned
My bottom raven black—One moment, madam!''—sensing
Her receiver rearing on the thunderclap
About my ears—'Madam,' I pleaded, 'wouldn't you rather
See for yourself?'

KENYA

■ LEARNING ONE'S PLACE ■
MUGA GICARU

The European manager was a keen hunter, and it was not long before he discovered that my father knew more than he did about wild life, as well as being a good shot with a rifle. When my father was not working away from home, he used to call for him every Friday for an evening's hunting. It was here that I met my first employer. We children used to look forward eagerly to the visits of 'Karanga,' as we called him, mainly because he was a curiosity to us in the same way as I myself was later to become a curiosity to children in Britain, and also because his way of hunting was different from ours; we fought with the animals, he just stood and killed them.

One afternoon my father came home and told us he had got me a job with Karanga. I was to help amuse his young son, a white boy just a year younger than myself, and stay at Karanga's until the child went back to school.

This was a great day for me and I thought about it all night after I had been forcibly sent to bed for asking too many questions. Very early next morning . . . I had my best clothes on and was ready to leave my friends and the world I knew . . . I was ready to leave the world where I was somebody for a world where, as I afterwards discovered, I was at best something; ready to go into a world where I was to discover that I and my race were instruments for supplying the white man with everything congenial to his earthly leisure and enjoyment. . . . This came to me a few years later, and has been a cause of bitterness to me. At the same time, it has inspired in me the determination to find a way of living for our community which will enable us all, irrespective of colour or creed, to develop our personalities to the fullest extent in an atmosphere of complete equality of opportunity, when all our talents can be used not for the exploitation of fellow human beings but for attaining the maximum happiness for all in accordance with the will of the Creator.

I waited for my father to get up and take his breakfast; and that morning hour, waiting to go off to my first job, was the longest in my life. I knew where the farmhouse was, so my father had only to tell me to ask for his friend, the head cook.

On arrival I asked for the cook, who was already well known to me, and was sent into the kitchen. He gave me the first day to get cleaned up and broken in the ways of the house and receive instructions as to what I was expected to do. . . . Not only did I pay no attention, I was not in the least interested in what he was saying, for the cook explained everything in these words— *'Urutage Kaana ihoru'*—'Help the boy (Karanga Junior) not to feel lonely.' Although I was ready to start work immediately, I was going to do it my own way and not in the way he was instructing me in a long and monotonous speech explaining the numerous toys, emphasizing how expensive they were and how important it was for me to be careful of them. I was not going to touch them. I was ready to ask the other boy to join me in exploring the world that I knew and loved. The natural world. The world that we both loved, as we found afterwards. . . .

INDIA

■ THE BLIND DOG ■

R. K. NARAYAN

It was not a very impressive or high-class dog; it was one of those commonplace dogs one sees everywhere—color of white and dust, tail mutilated at a young age by God knows whom, born in the street, and bred on the leavings and garbage of the marketplace. He had spotty eyes and undistinguished carriage and needless pugnacity. Before he was two years old he had earned the scars of a hundred fights on his body. When he needed rest on hot afternoons he lay curled up under the culvert at the Eastern gate of the market. In the evenings he set out on his daily rounds, loafed in the surrounding streets and lanes, engaged himself in skirmishes, picked up edibles on the roadside, and was back at the market gate by nightfall.

This life went on for three years. And then occurred a change in his life. A beggar, blind of both eyes, appeared at the market gate. An old woman led him up there early in the morning, seated him at the gate, and came up again at midday with some food, gathered his coins, and took him home at night.

The dog was sleeping near by. He was stirred by the smell of food. He got up, came out of his shelter, and stood before the blind man, wagging his tail and gazing expectantly at the bowl, as he was eating his sparse meal. The blind man swept his arms about and asked: ''Who is there?'' At which the dog went up and licked his hand. The blind man stroked its coat gently tail to ear and said: ''What a beauty you are. Come with me—'' He threw a handful of food which the dog ate gratefully. It was perhaps an auspicious moment for starting a friendship. They met every day there, and the dog cut off much of its rambling to sit up beside the blind man and watch him receive alms morning to evening. In course of time observing him, the dog understood that the passersby must give a coin, and whoever went away without dropping a coin was chased by the dog; he tugged the edge of their clothes by his teeth and pulled them back to the old man at the gate and let go only after something was dropped in his bowl. . . .

RUSSIA

Babiy Yar

YEVGENI YEVTUSHENKO

Over Babiy Yar
there are no memorials.
The steep hillside like a rough inscription.
I am frightened.
Today I am as old as the Jewish race.
I seem to myself a Jew at this moment.

I, wandering in Egypt.
I, crucified. I perishing.
Even today the mark of the nails.
I think also of Dreyfus. I am he.
The Philistine my judge and my accuser.
Cut off by bars and cornered,
ringed round, spat at, lied about;
the screaming ladies with the Brussels lace
poke me in the face with parasols.
I am also a boy in Belostok,
the dropping blood spreads across the floor,
the public-bar heroes are rioting
in an equal stench of garlic and of drink.
I have no strength, go spinning from a boot,
shriek useless prayers that they don't listen to;
with a cackle of 'Thrash the kikes and save Russia!'
the corn-chandler is beating up my mother.
I seem to myself like Anna Frank
to be transparent as an April twig
and am in love, I have no need for words,
I need for us to look at one another.
How little we have to see or to smell
separated from foliage and the sky,
how much, how much in the dark room
gently embracing each other.
They're coming. Don't be afraid.
The booming and banging of the spring.
It's coming this way. Come to me.
Quickly, give me your lips.
They're battering in the door. Roar of the ice.
Over Babiy Yar
rustle of the wild grass.
The trees look threatening, look like judges.
And everything is one silent cry.
Taking my hat off
I feel myself slowly going grey.
And I am one silent cry
over the many thousands of the buried;
am every old man killed here,
every child killed here.

O my Russian people, I know you.
Your nature is international.
Foul hands rattle your clean name.
I know the goodness of my country.
How horrible it is that pompous title
the anti-semites calmly call themselves,
Society of the Russian People.
No part of me can ever forget it.
When the last anti-semite on the earth
is buried for ever
let the International ring out.
No Jewish blood runs among my blood,
but I am as bitterly and hardly hated
by every anti-semite
as if I were a Jew. By this
I am a Russian.

■ INVASION ■

ROMAN PODOLNY

One fine spring day in the year 2074, She and He sat on a bench in the midst of a tropical forest, preserved as a sanctuary. Their little go-everywhere plane dozed quietly under a nearby palm.

Even the wind was still, not to disturb them. And there was not another living soul for a hundred kilometers around. But at the moment when His lips came close to Hers, there was a strange hiss, some unknown force thrust them apart, and on the bench between them appeared, from heaven knows where, a bearded little old man.

Instantly grasping the situation, the stranger said in a frightened voice:

"Forgive me, I had no intention. . . ." But he quickly recovered his self-possession and changed from apologetic to solemn tones. "You will, of course, forgive my intrusion when you learn that I am a visitor from the distant past. . . ."

He had not finished his sentence when the young man crossed his arms and clasped his own shoulders, whispering in despair:

"I must be cursed! Another one!" He turned to the girl. "I swear I had nothing to do with it."

"I understand," she said coldly.

"But I don't!" protested the visitor. "Why don't you welcome me?"

The young man mastered himself sufficiently to answer:

"For the six millionth time? It's enough that we welcomed the first one."

"But I have invented a machine for traveling into the future! I was the first to test it!"

"Congratulations," he said drily. "We studied you at school. . . . But your machine . . . well . . . I mean, those who left later came earlier. It happens. Don't upset yourself. Better tell me something," and the young man's gloomy face brightened. "Why is it that visitors from the past always appear in the most inconvenient times? After all, this sends the whole theory of probability into the antiworld. Even the Council of the Wise cannot make head or tail of it. Couldn't something be done about it?"

"It's the fourth time he was interrupted just as he was going to say he loves me," She sighed resentfully.

"Again, forgive me. . . . As for your question . . . If you studied me at school, you know that the time machine does not travel with the passenger. It merely shoots him forward, across so many years—approximately, of course. And the properties of space-time are such that a man who travels in time also moves in space, and it's impossible to foresee. . . ." The great inventor was now speaking in the manner of a lecturer.

"We know it without you," said the young man, evidently losing all interest in his neighbor.

"Um . . . excuse me, but what about me now? I'm sure you have already invented a machine for traveling back into the past? I would like to go home."

"Ah, if we had! All the six million of you only wanted to take a peek at the future and then go home. If they didn't would so many have come? Every one of them was desperately eager to go back to his relatives and friends as soon as possible. Eight years ago, after the first visits, the Council of the Wise transferred forty million physicists and mathematicians to work on this problem. True, some of them felt that such a machine was impossible because it would violate the law of cause and effect, but we're used to manipulating natural laws. And meantime, until the problem is solved, the great Nurden suggested sending our guests further into the future—into a time when people have learned to travel back and forth in time. We've sent on nearly four million. But then a poet suddenly asked a question: 'If travel into the past is possible, how is it that no one has come to us from the future?' And so we had to liquidate the whole project. And we stopped sending our visitors into the future: that would have meant merely shoving our own problems onto someone else's shoulders.''

''What problems?''

''What problems? Don't we have to console you, and give you medical care, and spend decades retraining you? . . .''

The great Nurden stepped onto the podium and looked at the audience with his kindly eyes.

''I think,'' he began, ''that I can bring you good news. According to our calculations, the last of the six million, twenty-four thousand, five hundred and thirty-three persons sent into our era from the year 1974 has just arrived. The second invasion will take place about two centuries hence. We must accept those who have been sent three hundred years into the future. But in the next two centuries we shall have time to prepare. . . .''

The podium on which Nurden stood rocked violently. And the physicist received a most painful jab in the side as a badly embarrassed young man appeared next to him.

''You, Nikolay?'' the great man gasped. ''But you were the first to arrive from the past, eight years ago, and we immediately dispatched you into the future. . . .''

''Forgive me, they must have miscalculated,'' the uninvited guest whispered miserably. ''I never meant. . . .''

JAPAN

> I sit like Buddha
>   but the mosquitoes
>   keep biting.
>   —Oemaru

> Clouds come from time to time—
>   and bring to men a chance to rest
>   from looking at the moon.
>   —Basho

The piercing chill I feel:
   my dead wife's comb, in our bedroom,
     under my heel . . .
         —Buson

At the butterflies
   the caged bird gazes, envying—
     just watch its eyes!
         —Issa

Brown discarded leaf
   clinging tightly
     to this green mushroom.
         —Basho

Tremble o tomb!
   as from my wailing throat
     this wind of autumn.
            —Composed by Basho at the grave of
              a poet friend.

Even the sparrows
   can hardly lift their feet
     in the hot sand.
         —Chibo

CHINA

FROM
■ SERVES YOU RIGHT, ■
BEGGAR
HSU CHIH-MO

"Kindhearted ladies, charitable sirs,"
>The northwest wind slashes his face like a sharp
>>knife.

"Give me a little bit of your leftovers, just a little bit!"
>A patch of dark shadow curls up near the gate.

"Have pity, my wealthy lord, I'm dying of hunger,"
>Inside the gate there are jade cups, warm fire and
>>laughter.

"Have pity, my lord of good fortunes, I'm dying of cold."
>Outside the gate the northwest wind chuckles,
>>"Serves you right, beggar!"

I am but a pile of black shadows, trembling,
Lying like a worm on the frontage road of humanity;
I wish only a bit of the warmth of sympathy
To shelter what's left of me, after repeated carving . . . .

■ A WITHERED TREE ■
HAN YÜ

Not a twig or a leaf on the old tree,
Wind and frost harm it no more.
A man could pass through the hole in its belly,
Ants crawl searching under its peeling bark.
Its only lodger, the toadstool which dies in a morning,
The birds no longer visit in the twilight.
But its wood can still spark tinder.
It does not care yet to be only the void at its heart.

■ "The Pawnshop" ■
CHU HSIANG

Beauty runs a pawnshop,
Accepting only the hearts of men.
When the time comes for them to redeem their
    belongings,
She has already closed the door.

FROM
■ To Hiroshima ■
AI CH'ING

You should be a beautiful harbor
With mountains on three sides, and one side open to a plain.
Embraced by the hills, your city
Spreads like a fan southward.
Seven streams feed the bay,
Warm and moist sea breezes come from the south
To cheer the blossoms blanketing the seashore,
Where seaweeds drape their tassels and ribbons.
Hiroshima, you are an ancient city
Scented with sandalwood.
Over the years your thousands of residents
Have worked diligently, like bees.
The noise of berthing boats filled the days,
And songs and music accompanied the long nights.

None of them ever wanted war—
These common Japanese workers and farmers,
Of Nagasaki or Hiroshima,
None of them ever wanted war.
They nursed no hatred
Against the Chinese or the Malayans.
The Japanese never sought a rubber plant in Ceylon,
Or a coconut plantation in Java,
Or a colony on the Mekong River,
To support any claim to a conqueror's fame.
These people gained nothing from the war;

The war fattened other people,
Not them.
Yet, one morning
When sirens had just stirred people awake,
A sudden flash, without any noise,
Slashed the sky from the east westward.
Everyone knew disaster had arrived.

The survivors
Have become deformed, mostly—
As if meant to tell the world
Of their experience of horror . . . .

Hiroshima, you are the eyewitness,
You must rise from the disaster.
Your existence itself is a declaration,
For you have recorded the cruelty of war.
You must speak in defense of peace,
And tell the world,
How the dead died,
And how the survivors live.

Today—Silence, please, everybody,
Let Hiroshima speak.

THAILAND

■ ON MY SHORT-SIGHTEDNESS ■
PREM CHAYA

> To my short-sighted eyes,
> The world seems better far
> Than artificial aid
> To sight would warrant it:
> The earth is just as green,
> The sky a paler blue;
> Many a blurred outline
> Of overlapping hue;

Shapes, forms are indistinct;
Distance a mystery;
Often a common scene
Conceals a new beauty;
Ugliness is hidden
In a curtain of mist;
And hard, cruel faces
Lose their malignity.
So do not pity me
For my short-sighted eyes;
They see an unknown world
Of wonder and surprise.

IRELAND

■ THE WEARIN' O' THE GREEN ■

ANONYMOUS

Oh, Paddy dear! and did ye hear the news that's goin' round?
The shamrock is forbid by law to grow on Irish ground!
No more St. Patrick's day we'll keep; his color can't be seen,
For there's a cruel law ag'in' the Wearin' o' the Green!

I met with Napper Tandy, and he took me by the hand,
And he said, "How's poor ould Ireland, and how does she stand?"
"She's the most distressful country that ever yet was seen,
For they're hanging men and women there for the Wearin' o' the Green."

An' if the color we must wear is England's cruel red,
Let it remind us of the blood that Ireland has shed;
Then pull the shamrock from your hat, and throw it on the sod,
An' never fear, 'twill take root there, though under foot 'tis trod.

When law can stop the blades of grass from growin' as they grow,
An' when the leaves in summer time their color dare not show.
Then I will change the color, too, I wear in my caubeen;
But till that day, praise God, I'll stick to the Wearin' o'
     the Green.

SPAIN

FROM
■ THEY CLOSED HER EYES ■
GUSTAVO ADOLFO BECQUER

They closed her eyes
That were still open;
They hid her face
With a white linen,
And, some sobbing,
Others in silence,
From the sad bedroom
All came away.

The night light in a dish
Burned on the floor;
It threw on the wall
The bed's shadow,
And in the shadow
One saw sometime
Drawn in sharp line
The body's shape.

The dawn appeared.
At its first whiteness
With its thousand noises
The town awoke.
Before that contrast
Of light and darkness,
Of life and strangeness
I thought a moment.
My God, how lonely
The dead are!

FRANCE

■ THE OTHER WIFE ■
COLETTE

"TABLE FOR TWO? THIS WAY, MONSIEUR, MADAME, THERE IS STILL A TABLE next to the window, if Madame and Monsieur would like a view of the bay."

Alice followed the maître d'.

"Oh, yes. Come on, Marc, it'll be like having lunch on a boat on the water . . .''

Her husband caught her by passing his arm under hers. "We'll be more comfortable over there."

"There? In the middle of all those people? I'd much rather . . .''

"Alice, please."

He tightened his grip in such a meaningful way that she turned around. "What's the matter?"

"Shh . . ." he said softly, looking at her intently, and led her toward the table in the middle.

"What is it, Marc?"

"I'll tell you, darling. Let me order lunch first. Would you like the shrimp? Or the eggs in aspic?"

"Whatever you like, you know that."

They smiled at one another, wasting the previous time of an overworked maître d', stricken with a kind of nervous dance, who was standing next to them, perspiring.

"The shrimp," said Marc. "Then the eggs and bacon. And the cold chicken with a romaine salad. *Fromage blanc?* The house specialty? We'll go with the specialty. Two strong coffees. My chauffeur will be having lunch also, we'll be leaving again at two o'clock. Some cider? No, I don't trust it . . . Dry champagne."

He sighed as if he had just moved an armoire, gazed at the colorless midday sea, at the pearly white sky, then at his wife, whom he found lovely in her little Mercury hat with its large, hanging veil.

"You're looking well, darling. And all this blue water makes your eyes look green, imagine that! And you've put on weight since you've been traveling . . . It's nice up to a point, but only up to a point!"

Her firm, round breasts rose proudly as she leaned over the table.

"Why did you keep me from taking that place next to the window?"

Marc Seguy never considered lying. ''Because you were about to sit next to someone I know.''

''Someone I don't know?''

''My ex-wife.''

She couldn't think of anything to say and opened her blue eyes wider.

''So what, darling? It'll happen again. It's not important.''

The words came back to Alice and she asked, in order, the inevitable questions. ''Did she see you? Could she see that you saw her? Will you point her out to me?''

''Don't look now, please, she must be watching us. . . . The lady with brown hair, no hat, she must be staying in this hotel. By herself, behind those children in red . . .''

''Yes, I see.''

Hidden behind some broad-brimmed beach hats, Alice was able to look at the woman who, fifteen months ago, had still been her husband's wife.

''Incompatibility,'' Marc said. ''Oh, I mean . . . total incompatibility! We divorced like well-bred people, almost like friends, quietly, quickly. And then I fell in love with you, and you really wanted to be happy with me. How lucky we are that our happiness doesn't involve any guilty parties or victims!''

The woman in white, whose smooth, lustrous hair reflected the light from the sea in azure patches, was smoking a cigarette with her eyes half closed. Alice turned back toward her husband, took some shrimp and butter, and ate calmly. After a moment's silence she asked: ''Why didn't you ever tell me that she had blue eyes, too?''

''Well, I never thought about it!''

He kissed the hand she was extending toward the bread basket and she blushed with pleasure. Dusky and ample, she might have seemed somewhat coarse, but the changeable blue of her eyes and her wavy, golden hair made her look like a frail and sentimental blonde. She vowed overwhelming gratitude to her husband. Immodest without knowing it, everything about her bore the overly conspicuous marks of extreme happiness.

They ate and drank heartily, and each thought the other had forgotten the woman in white. Now and then, however, Alice laughed too loudly, and Marc was careful about his posture, holding his shoulders back, his head up. They waited quite a long time for their coffee, in silence. An incandescent river, the straggled reflection of the invisible sun overhead, shifted slowly across the sea and shone with a blinding brilliance.

''She's still there, you know,'' Alice whispered.

''Is she making you uncomfortable? Would you like to have coffee somewhere else?''

''No, not at all! She's the one who must be uncomfortable! Besides, she doesn't exactly seem to having a wild time, if you could see her . . .''

''I don't have to. I know that look of hers.''

''Oh, was she like that?''

He exhaled his cigarette smoke through his nostrils and knitted his eyebrows. ''Like that? No. To tell you honestly, she wasn't happy with me.''

''Oh, really now!''

''The way you indulge me is so charming, darling . . . It's crazy . . . You're an angel . . . You love me . . . I'm so proud when I see those eyes of yours. Yes, those eyes . . . She . . . I just didn't know how to make her happy, that's all. I didn't know how.''

''She's just difficult!''

Alice fanned herself irritably, and cast brief glances at the woman in white, who was smoking, her head resting against the back of the cane chair, her eyes closed with an air of satisfied lassitude.

March shrugged his shoulders modestly.

''That's the right word,'' he admitted. ''What can you do? You have to feel sorry for people who are never satisfied. But we're satisfied . . . Aren't we, darling?''

She did not answer. She was looking furtively, and closely, at her husband's face, ruddy and regular; at his thick hair, threaded here and there with white silk; at his short, well-cared-for hands; and doubtful for the first time, she asked herself, ''What more did she want from him?''

And as they were leaving, while Marc was paying the bill and asking for the chauffeur and about the route, she kept looking, with envy and curiosity, at the woman in white, this dissatisfied, this difficult, this superior . . .

NORWAY

■ LOCKED IN ■

INGEMAR GUSTAFSON

All my life I lived in a cocoanut.
It was cramped and dark.
Especially in the morning when I had to shave.
But what pained me most was that I had no way
to get into touch with the outside world.
If no one out there happened to find the cocoanut,
if no one cracked it, then I was doomed
to live all my life in the nut, and maybe even die there.
   I died in the cocoanut.
   A couple of years later they found the cocoanut,
cracked it and found me shrunk and crumbled inside.
   "What an accident!"
   "If only we had found it earlier . . ."
   "Then maybe we could have saved him."
   "Maybe there are more of them locked in like that . . ."
   "Whom we might be able to save,"
they said, and started knocking to pieces every cocoanut
within reach.
   No use! Meaningless! A waste of time!
A person who chooses to live in a cocoanut!
Such a nut is one in a million!
   But I have a brother-in-law who
lives in an
acorn.

CHAPTER TEN

Using Documentary Material for Oral Interpretation

Would you like to stand beside Abraham Lincoln as he delivers the Gettysburg Address? To walk beside Helen Keller as she conquers the darkness? To rise with William Faulkner to accept the Nobel Prize for literature? Nonfictional prose allows you to share compelling moments in history—the thoughts, cares, and hopes of men and women in real-life drama. In effect, nonfictional prose holds a mirror up to life, reflecting personal visions of the past, the present, and even the future.

By including selections of nonfictional prose in your literary storehouse, you will widen your experience as an interpreter. Experience is reflected not only in fictional prose, poetry, and drama, but also in speeches, letters, diaries, essays, newspapers, magazines, recorded radio and television news broadcasts, trial transcripts, interviews, biographies, and autobiographies.

The experiences detailed in such works are as intriguing and interesting as the experiences detailed in short stories, novels, poems, and plays. Indeed, it has been said many times that fact is often stranger than fiction. Thus, documentary materials may contain as much intensity as fictional prose, as much immediacy as drama, and as much personal revelation as lyric poetry.

Let us briefly sample some of the documentary materials available to you as an interpreter. Remember, the writers of these documentary materials unwittingly served as historians, reflecting in their many writings the fears, concerns, hopes, values, and mores of their ages. Regardless of when these authors lived, their comments on and responses to life may help us in understanding ourselves and our times.

The Interpreter Meets the Public Speech

A great speech lives on after its delivery and often deals with significant movements that change the course of history. A public speech is neither created nor delivered in a vacuum; thus, it cannot be fully understood unless one understands the individual who wrote it and the circumstances that provoked it, as well. Every speaker reflects the age in which he or she lives. Memorable speakers, however, also affect the beliefs and patterns of life to come, usually making universal appeals and usually reflecting universal concerns.

GETTING INVOLVED

Analyzing the Speech

Read all of the following speeches carefully. Then, working with classmates in small groups, select one speech for further study. After discussing the selected speech as a group, answer the following questions.

Reflections

1. How does this speech contribute to your understanding of the period in which it was written?

2. How does this speech contribute to your understanding of the speaker?

3. What message does the speech have for today?

This speech was delivered by a Native American warrior after a white missionary had addressed a council of chiefs.

■ To the Council ■

RED JACKET
(1805)

Friend and Brother:—It was the will of the Great Spirit that we should meet together this day. He orders all things and has given us a fine day for our council. He has taken His garment from before the sun and caused it to shine with brightness upon us. Our eyes are opened that we see clearly; our ears are unstopped that we have been able to hear distinctly the words you have spoken. . . .

Brother, this council fire was kindled by you. It was at your request that we came together at this time. We have listened with attention to what you have said. You requested us to speak our minds freely. This gives us great joy; for we now consider that we stand upright before you and can speak what we think. All have heard your voice and all speak to you now as one man. Our minds are agreed. . . .

Brother, listen to what we say. There was a time when our forefathers owned this great island. Their seats extended from the rising to the setting sun. The Great Spirit had made it for the use of Indians. He had created the buffalo, the deer, and other animals for food. He had made the bear and the beaver. Their skins served us for clothing. He had scattered them over the country and taught us how to take them. He had caused the earth to produce corn for bread. All this He had done for His red children because He loved them. If we had some disputes about our hunting-ground they were generally settled without the shedding of much blood.

But an evil day came upon us. Your forefathers crossed the great water and landed on this island. Their numbers were small. They found friends and not enemies. They told us they had fled from their own country for fear of wicked men and had come here to enjoy their religion. They asked for a small seat. We took pity on them, granted their request, and they sat down among us. We gave them corn and meat; they gave us poison in return.

The white people, brother, had now found our country. Tidings were carried back and more came among us. Yet we did not fear them. We took them to be friends. They called us brother. We believed them and gave them a larger seat. At length their numbers had greatly increased. They wanted more land; they wanted our country. Our eyes were opened and our minds became uneasy. Wars took place. Indians were hired to fight against Indians, and many of our people were destroyed. They also brought liquor among us. It was strong and powerful, and has slain thousands.

Brother, our seats were once large and yours were small. You have now become a great people, and we have scarcely a place left to spread our blankets. You have got our country, but are not satisfied; you want to force your religion upon us. . . .

Brother, you say there is but one way to worship and serve the Great Spirit. If there is but one religion, why do you white people differ so much about it? . . .

Brother, we do not understand these things. We are told that your religion was given to your forefathers and has been handed down from father to son. We also have a religion which was given to our forefathers and has been handed down to us, their children. We worship in that way. It teaches us to be thankful for all the favors we receive, to love each other, and to be united. We never quarrel about religion.

Brother, the Great Spirit has made us all, but He has made a great difference between His white and His red children. He has given us different complexions and different customs. To you He has given the arts. To these He has not opened our eyes. We know these things to be true. Since He has made so great a difference between us in other things, why may we not conclude that He has given us a different religion according to our understanding? The Great Spirit does right. He knows what is best for His children; we are satisfied.

Brother, we do not wish to destroy your religion or take it from you. We only want to enjoy our own. . . .

Brother, you have now heard our answer to your talk, and this is all we have to say at present. As we are going to part, we will come and take you by the hand, and hope the Great Spirit will protect you on your journey and return you safe to your friends.

■ ACCEPTANCE OF THE NOBEL PRIZE ■
WILLIAM FAULKNER
(1950)

I feel that this award was not made to me as a man, but to my work—a life's work in the agony and sweat of the human spirit, not for glory and least of all for profit, but to create out of the materials of the human spirit something which did not exist before. So this award is only mine in trust. It will not be difficult to find a dedication for the money part of it commensurate with the purpose and significance of its origin. But I would like to do the same with the acclaim too, by using this moment as a pinnacle from which I might be listened to by the young men and women already dedicated to the same anguish and travail, among whom is already that one who will some day stand where I am standing.

Our tragedy today is a general and universal physical fear so long sustained by now that we can even bear it. There are no longer problems of the spirit. There is only one question: When will I be blown up? Because of this, the young man or woman writing today has forgotten the problems of the human heart in conflict with itself which alone can make good writing because only that is worth writing about, worth the agony and the sweat.

He must learn them again. He must teach himself that the basest of all things is to be afraid; and, teaching himself that, forget it forever, leaving no room in his workshop for anything but the old verities and truths of the heart, the universal truths lacking which any story is ephemeral and doomed—love and honor and pity and pride and compassion and sacrifice. Until he does so, he labors under a curse. He writes not of love but of lust, of defeats in which nobody loses anything of value, and victories without hope and worst of all, without pity or compassion. His griefs grieve on no universal bones, leaving no scars. He writes not of the heart but of the glands.

Until he learns these things, he will write as though he stood among and watched the end of man. I decline to accept the end of man. It is easy enough to say that man is immortal simply because he will endure: that when the last ding-dong of doom has clanged and faded from the last worthless rock hanging tideless in the last red and dying evening, that even then there will still be one more sound: that of his puny inexhaustible voice, still talking. I refuse to accept this. I believe that man will not merely endure: he will prevail. He is immortal, not because he alone among creatures has an inexhaustible voice, but because he has a soul, a spirit capable of compassion and sacrifice and endurance. The poet's, the writer's, duty is to write about these things. It is his privilege to help man endure by lifting his heart, by reminding him of the courage and honor and hope and pride and compassion and pity and sacrifice which have been the glory of his past. The poet's voice need not merely be the record of man, it can be one of the props, the pillars to help him endure and prevail.

■ Tribute to the Crew of the ■ Space Shuttle *Challenger*
PRESIDENT RONALD REAGAN
(1986)

We come together today to mourn the loss of seven brave Americans, to share the grief that we all feel, and perhaps in that sharing, to find the strength to bear our sorrow and the courage to look for the seeds of hope.

Our nation's loss is first a profound personal loss to the family and the friends and the loved ones of our shuttle astronauts. To those they left behind—the mothers, the fathers, the husbands and wives, brothers and sisters, yes, and especially the children—all of America stands beside you in your time of sorrow.

What we say today is only an inadequate expression of what we carry in our hearts. Words pale in the shadow of grief; they seem insufficient even to measure the brave sacrifice of those you loved and we so admired. Their truest testimony will not be in the words we speak, but in the way they led their lives and in the way they lost their lives—with dedication, honor, and an unquenchable desire to explore this mysterious and beautiful universe.

The best we can do is remember our seven astronauts, our *Challenger* Seven, remember them as they lived, bringing life and love and joy to those who knew them and pride to a nation.

They came from all parts of this great country—from South Carolina to Washington State; Ohio to Mohawk, New York; Hawaii to North Carolina to Concord, New Hampshire. They were so different; yet in their mission, their quest, they held so much in common.

We remember Dick Scobee, the commander who spoke the last words we heard from the space shuttle *Challenger.* He served as a fighter pilot in Vietnam earning many medals for bravery and later as a test pilot of advanced aircraft before joining the space program. Danger was a familiar companion to Commander Scobee.

We remember Michael Smith, who earned enough medals as a combat pilot to cover his chest, including the Navy Distinguished Flying Cross, three Air Medals, and the Vietnamese Cross of Gallantry with Silver Star in gratitude from a nation he fought to keep free.

We remember Judith Resnik, known as J.R. to her friends, always smiling, always eager to make a contribution, finding beauty in the music she played on her piano in her off-hours.

We remember Ellison Onizuka, who as a child running barefoot through the coffee fields and macadamia groves of Hawaii dreamed of someday traveling to the Moon. Being an Eagle Scout, he said, had helped him soar to the impressive achievements of his career.

We remember Ronald McNair, who said that he learned perseverance in the cottonfields of South Carolina. His dream was to live aboard the space station, performing experiments and playing his saxophone in the weightlessness of space. Well, Ron, we will miss your saxophone; and we *will* build your space station.

We remember Gregory Jarvis. On that ill-fated flight he was carrying with him a flag of his university in Buffalo, New York—a small token, he said, to the people who unlocked his future.

We remember Christa McAuliffe, who captured the imagination of the entire nation; inspiring us with her pluck, her restless spirit of discovery; a teacher, not just to her students, but to an entire people, instilling us all with the excitement of this journey we ride into the future.

We will always remember them, these skilled professionals, scientists, and adventurers, these artists and teachers and family men and women; and we will cherish each of their stories, stories of triumph and bravery, stories of true American heroes.

On the day of the disaster, our nation held a vigil by our television sets. In one cruel moment our exhilaration turned to horror; we waited and watched and tried to make sense of what we had seen. That night I listened to a call-in program on the radio; people of every age spoke of their sadness and the pride they felt in our astronauts. Across America we are reaching out, holding hands, and finding comfort in one another.

The sacrifice of your loved ones has stirred the soul of our nation and through the pain our hearts have been opened to a profound truth: The future is not free; the story of all human progress is one of a struggle against all odds. We learned again that this America, which Abraham Lincoln called the last, best hope of man on Earth, was built on heroism and noble sacrifice. It was built by men and women like our seven star voyagers, who answered a call beyond duty, who gave more than was expected or required, and who gave little thought to worldly reward.

We think back to the pioneers of an earlier century, the sturdy souls who took their families and their belongings and set out into the frontier of the American West. Often they met with terrible hardship. Along the Oregon

Trail, you could still see the gravemarkers of those who fell on the way. But grief only steeled them to the journey ahead.

Today the frontier is space and the boundaries of human knowledge. Sometimes when we reach for the stars, we fall short. But we must pick ourselves up again and press on despite the pain. Our nation is indeed fortunate that we can still draw on immense reservoirs of courage, character, and fortitude; that we're still blessed with heroes like those of the space shuttle *Challenger*.

Dick Scobee knew that every launching of a space shuttle is a technological miracle. And he said, ''If something ever does go wrong, I hope that doesn't mean the end to the space shuttle program.'' Every family member I talked to asked specifically that we continue the program, that that is what their departed loved one would want above all else. We will not disappoint them.

Today we promise Dick Scobee and his crew that their dream lives on, that the future they worked so hard to build will become reality. The dedicated men and women of NASA have lost seven members of their family. Still, they, too, must forge ahead with a space program that is effective, safe, and efficient, but bold and committed.

Man will continue his conquest of space. To reach out for new goals and ever greater achievements—that is the way we shall commemorate our seven *Challenger* heroes.

Dick, Mike, Judy, El, Ron, Greg, and Christa—your families and your country mourn your passing. We bid you goodbye; we will never forget you. For those who knew you well and loved you, the pain will be deep and enduring. A nation, too, will long feel the loss of her seven sons and daughters, her seven good friends. We can find consolation only in faith, for we know in our hearts that you who flew so high and so proud now make your home beyond the stars, safe in God's promise of eternal life.

May God bless you all and give you comfort in this difficult time.

■ ADVICE TO YOUTH ■

MARK TWAIN

(1882)

Being told I would be expected to talk here, I inquired what sort of a talk I ought to make. They said it should be something suitable to youth— something didactic, instructive; or something in the nature of good advice. Very well; I have a few things in my mind which I have often longed to say for the instruction of the young; for it is in one's tender early years that such things will best take root and be most enduring and most valuable. First, then, I will say to you, my young friends—and say it beseechingly, urgingly—

Always obey your parents, when they are present. This is the best policy in the long run; because if you don't, they will make you. Most parents think they know better than you do; and you can generally make more by humoring that superstition than you can by acting on your own better judgment.

Be respectful of your superiors, if you have any; also to strangers, and sometimes to others. If a person offends you, and you are in doubt as to whether it was intentional or not, do not resort to extreme measures; simply watch your chance and hit him with a brick. That will be sufficient. If you shall find that he had not intended any offense, come out frankly and confess yourself in the wrong when you struck him; acknowledge it like a man, and say you didn't mean to. Yes, always avoid violence; in this age of charity and kindness, the time has gone by for such things. Leave dynamite to the low and unrefined.

Go to bed early, get up early—this is wise. Some authorities say get up with one thing, some with another. But a lark is really the best thing to get up with. It gives you a splendid reputation with everybody to know that you get up with the lark; and if you get the right kind of a lark, and work at him right, you can easily train him to get up at half-past nine, every time— it is no trick at all.

Now as to the matter of lying. You want to be very careful about lying; otherwise you are nearly sure to get caught. Once caught, you can never again be, in the eyes of the good and the pure, what you were before. Many a young person has injured himself permanently through a singly clumsy and ill-finished lie, the result of carelessness born of incomplete training. Some authorities hold that the young ought not to lie at all. That, of course, is putting it rather stronger than necessary; still, while I cannot go quite so far as that, I do maintain, and I believe I am right, that the young ought to be temperate in the use of this great art until practice and experience shall give them that confidence, elegance, and precision which alone can make the accomplishment graceful and profitable. Patience, diligence, painstaking attention to detail—these are the requirements; these, in time, will make the student perfect; upon these, and upon these only, may he rely as the sure foundation for future eminence. Think what tedious years of study, thought, practice, experience went to the equipment of that peerless old master who was able to impose upon the whole world the lofty and sounding maxim that, ''Truth is mighty and will prevail''—the most majestic compound fracture of fact which any of woman born has yet achieved. For the history of our race, and each individual's experience, are sown thick with evidences that a truth is not hard to kill, and that a lie well told is immortal. There in Boston is a monument to the man who discovered anesthesia; many people are aware, in these latter days, that that man didn't discover it at all, but stole the discovery from another man. Is this truth mighty, and will it prevail? Ah, no, my hearers, the monument is made of hardy material, but the lie it tells will outlast it a million years. An awkward, feeble, leaky lie is a thing which you ought to make it your unceasing study to avoid; such a lie as that has no more real permanence than an average truth. Why, you might as well tell the truth at once and be done with it. A feeble, stupid, preposterous lie will not live two years—except it be a slander upon somebody. It is indestructible, then, of course, but that is no merit of yours. A final word: begin your practice of this gracious and beautiful art early—begin now. If I had begun earlier, I could have learned how.

Never handle firearms carelessly. The sorrow and suffering that have been caused through the innocent but heedless handling of firearms by the young! Only four days ago, right in the next farmhouse to the one where I am spending the summer, a mother, old and gray and sweet, one of the loveliest spirits in the land, was sitting at her work, when her young son crept in and got down an old, battered, rusty gun which had not been touched for many years, and was supposed not to be loaded, and pointed it at her, laughing and threatening to shoot. In her fright she ran screaming and pleading toward the door on the other side of the room; but as she passed him he placed the gun almost against her very breast and pulled the trigger! He had supposed it was not loaded. And he was right: it wasn't. So there wasn't any harm done. It is the only case of the kind I ever heard of. Therefore, just the same, don't you meddle with old unloaded firearms; they are the most deadly and unerring things that have ever been created by man. You don't have to take any pains at all, with them; you don't have to have a rest, you don't have to have any sights on the gun, you don't have to take aim, even. No, you just pick out a relative and bang away, and you are sure to get him. A youth who can't hit a cathedral at thirty yards with a Gatling gun in three-quarters of an hour, can take up an old empty musket and bang his mother every time, at a hundred. Think what Waterloo would have been if one of the armies had been boys armed with old rusty muskets supposed not to be loaded, and the other army had been composed of their female relations. The very thought of it makes me shudder.

There are many sorts of books; but good ones are the sort for the young to read. Remember that. They are a great, an inestimable, an unspeakable means of improvement. Therefore be careful in your selection, my young friends; be very careful; confine yourself exclusively to Roberson's *Sermons,* Baxter's *Saint's Rest, The Innocents Abroad,* and works of that kind.

But I have said enough. I hope you will treasure the instructions which I have given you, and make them a guide to your feet and a light to your understanding. Build your character thoughtfully and painstakingly upon these precepts; and by and by, when you have got it built, you will be surprised and gratified to see how nicely and sharply it resembles everybody else's.

■ The "Monument" at ■
Wounded Knee
CECILE LARSON
(1980)

We Americans are big on monuments. We build monuments in memory of our heroes. Washington, Jefferson, and Lincoln live on in our nation's capital. We erect monuments to honor our martyrs. The Minute Man still stands guard at Concord. The flag is ever raised over Iwo Jima. Sometimes we even construct monuments to commemorate victims. In Ashburn Park downtown there is a monument to those who died in the yellow fever epidemics. However, there are some things in our history that we don't memorialize. Perhaps we would just as soon forget what happened. Last summer I visited such a place—the massacre site at Wounded Knee.

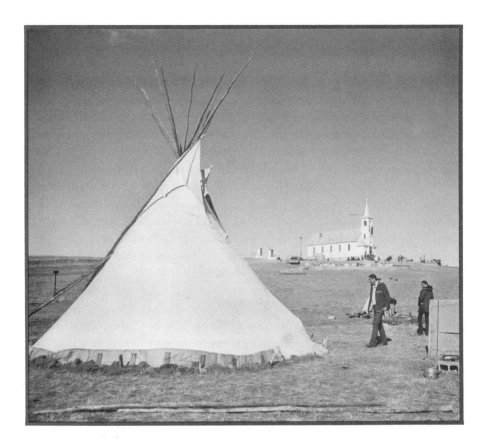

In case you have forgotten what happened at Wounded Knee, let me refresh your memory. On December 29, 1890, shortly after Sitting Bull had been murdered by the authorities, about 400 half-frozen, starving, and frightened Indians who had fled the nearby reservation were attacked by the Seventh Cavalry. When the fighting ended, between 200 and 300 Sioux had died—two-thirds of them women and children. Their remains are buried in a common grave at the site of the massacre.

Wounded Knee is located in the Pine Ridge Reservation in southwestern South Dakota—about a three-hour drive from where Presidents Washington, Jefferson, Theodore Roosevelt, and Lincoln are enshrined in the granite face of Mount Rushmore. The reservation is directly south of the Badlands National Park, a magnificently desolate area of wind-eroded buttes and multicolored spires.

We entered the reservation driving south from the Badlands Visitor's Center. The landscape of the Pine Ridge Reservation retains much of the desolation of the Badlands but lacks its magnificence. Flat, sun-baked fields and an occasional eroded gully stretch as far as the eye can see. There are no signs or highway markers to lead the curious tourist to Wounded Knee. Even the *Rand-McNally Atlas* doesn't help you find your way. We got lost three times and had to stop and ask directions.

When we finally arrived at Wounded Knee, there was no official historic marker to tell us what had happened there. Instead there was a large, hand-made wooden sign—crudely lettered in white on black. The sign first directed our attention to our left—to the gully where the massacre took place. The mass grave site was to our right—across the road and up a small hill.

Two red-brick columns topped with a wrought-iron arch and a small metal cross form the entrance to the grave site. The column to the right is in bad shape: cinder blocks from the base are missing; the brickwork near the top has deteriorated and tumbled to the ground; graffiti on the columns proclaim an attitude we found repeatedly expressed about the Bureau of Indian Affairs—''The BIA sucks!''

Crumbling concrete steps lead you up to the mass grave. The top of the grave is covered with gravel, punctuated by unruly patches of chickweed and crabgrass. These same weeds also grow along the base of the broken chain-link fence that surrounds the grave, the ''monument,'' and a small cemetery.

The ''monument'' itself rests on a concrete slab to the right of the grave. It's a typical, large, old-fashioned granite cemetery marker, a pillar about six feet high topped with an urn—the kind of gravestone you might see in any cemetery with graves from the turn of the century. The inscription tells us that it was erected by the families of those who were killed at Wounded Knee. Weeds grow through the cracks in the concrete at its base.

There are no granite headstones in the adjacent cemetery, only simple white wooden crosses that tell a story of people who died young. There is no neatly manicured grass. There are no flowers. Only the unrelenting and unforgiving weeds.

Yes, Americans are big on monuments. We build them to memorialize our heroes, to honor our martyrs, and sometimes, even to commemorate victims. But only when it makes us feel good.

■ WOMEN IN POLITICS ■

LADY ASTOR

(1922)

My entrance into the House of Commons was not, as some thought, in the nature of a revolution. It was an evolution. My husband was the one who started me off on this downward path—from the fireside to public life. If I have helped the cause of women, he is the one to thank, not me.

A woman in the House of Commons! It was almost enough to have broken up the House. I don't blame them—it was equally hard on the woman as it was on them. A pioneer may be a picturesque figure, but they are often rather lonely ones. I must say for the House of Commons, they bore their shock with dauntless decency. No body of men could have been kinder and fairer to a "pirate" than they were. When you hear people over here trying to run down England, please remember that England was the first large country to give the vote to women and that the men of England welcomed an American born woman in the House with a fairness and a justice which, at least, this woman never will forget. . . .

Now, why are we in politics? What is it all about? Something much bigger than ourselves. Schopenhauer was wrong in nearly everything he wrote about women—and he wrote a lot, but he was right in one thing. He said, in speaking of women, "the race is to her more than the individual," and I believe that it is true. I feel somehow we do care about the race as a whole, our very nature makes us take a forward vision; there is no reason why women should look back; mercifully we have no political past; we have all the mistakes of sex legislation with its appealing failures to guide us.

We should know what to avoid, it is no use blaming the men—we made them what they are—and now it is up to us to try and make ourselves—the makers of men—a little more responsible in the future. We realize that no one sex can govern alone. I believe that one of the reasons why civilization has failed so lamentably is that it has had a one-sided government. Don't let us make the mistake of ever allowing that to happen again.

I can conceive of nothing worse than a man-governed world except a woman-governed world—but I can see the combination of the two going forward and making civilization more worthy of the name of civilization based on Christianity, not force. A civilization based on justice and mercy. I feel men have a greater sense of justice and we of mercy. They must borrow our mercy and we must use their justice. We are new brooms; let us see that we sweep the right rooms.

FROM

■ On Woman's Right ■
to Suffrage
SUSAN B. ANTHONY
(1873)

Friends and Fellow Citizens—I stand before you to-night under indictment for the alleged crime of having voted at the last presidential election, without having a lawful right to vote. It shall be my work this evening to prove to you that in thus voting, I not only committed no crime, but, instead, simply exercised my *citizen's rights,* guaranteed to me and all United States citizens by the National Constitution, beyond the power of any State to deny.

The preamble of the Federal Constitution says:

"We, the people of the United States, in order to form a more perfect union, establish justice, insure *domestic* tranquility, provide for the common defense, promote the general welfare, and secure the blessings of liberty to ourselves and our posterity, do ordain and establish this Constitution for the United States of America."

It was we, the people; not we, the white male citizens; nor yet we, the male citizens; but we, the whole people, who formed the Union. And we formed it, not to give the blessings of liberty, but to secure them; not to the half of ourselves and the half of our posterity, but to the whole people—women as well as men. And it is a downright mockery to talk to women of their enjoyment of the blessings of liberty while they are denied the use of the only means of securing them provided by this democratic-republican government—the ballot. . . .

Webster, Worcester and Bouvier all define a citizen to be a person in the United States, entitled to vote and hold office.

The only question left to be settled now is: Are women persons? And I hardly believe any of our opponents will have the hardihood to say they are not. Being persons, then, women are citizens; and no State has a right to make any law that shall abridge their privileges or immunities. Hence, every discrimination against women in the constitutions and laws of the several States is to-day null and void, precisely as is every one against negroes.

■ THE GETTYSBURG ADDRESS ■

ABRAHAM LINCOLN

(1863)

Four score and seven years ago our fathers brought forth on this continent, a new nation, conceived in Liberty, and dedicated to the proposition that all men are created equal.

Now we are engaged in a great civil war, testing whether that nation or any nation so conceived and so dedicated, can long endure. We are met on a great battle-field of that war. We have come to dedicate a portion of that field, as a final resting place for those who here gave their lives that that nation might live. It is altogether fitting and proper that we should do this.

But, in a larger sense, we can not dedicate—we can not consecrate—we can not hallow—this ground. The brave men, living and dead, who struggled here, have consecrated it, far above our poor power to add or detract. The world will little note, nor long remember what we say here, but it can never forget what they did here. It is for us the living, rather, to be dedicated here to the unfinished work which they who fought here have thus far so nobly advanced. It is rather for us to be here dedicated to the great task remaining before us—that from these honored dead we take increased devotion—that we here highly resolve that these dead shall not have died in vain—that this nation, under God, shall have a new birth of freedom—and that government of the people, by the people, for the people, shall not perish from the earth.

FROM

■ I HAVE A DREAM ■

MARTIN LUTHER KING, JR.

(1963)

I am not unmindful that some of you have come here out of great trials and tribulations. Some of you have come fresh from jail cells. Some of you have come from areas where your quest for freedom left you battered by the storms of persecution and staggered by the winds of police brutality. . . .

Go back to Mississippi; go back to Alabama; go back to South Carolina; go back to Georgia; go back to Louisiana; go back to the slums and ghettoes of our Northern cities, knowing that somehow this situation can, and will be changed. Let us not wallow in the valley of despair.

I say to you today, my friends, so even though we face the difficulties of today and tomorrow, I still have a dream. It is a dream deeply rooted in the American dream. I have a dream that one day this nation will rise up . . . live out the true meaning of its creed—we hold these truths to be self-evident, that all men are created equal. . . .

I have a dream that my four little children will one day live in a nation where they will not be judged by the color of their skin but by the content of their character. I have a dream today! . . .

I have a dream that one day every valley shall be exalted, and every hill and mountain shall be made low, the rough places shall be made plain, and the crooked places shall be made straight and the glory of the Lord will be revealed and all flesh shall see it together.

This is our hope. This is the faith that I go back to the South with.

With this faith we will be able to hew out of the mountain of despair a stone of hope. With this faith we will be able to transform the jangle and discords of our nation into a beautiful symphony of brotherhood.

With this faith we will be able to work together, to pray together, to struggle together, to go to jail together, to stand up for freedom together, knowing that we will be free one day. This will be the day when all of God's children will be able to sing with new meaning—''my country 'tis of thee; sweet land of liberty; of thee I sing; land where my fathers died, land of the pilgrim's pride; from every mountainside, let freedom ring''—and if America is to be a great nation, this must come true.

So let freedom ring from the prodigious hilltops of New Hampshire.

Let freedom ring from the mighty mountains of New York.

Let freedom ring from the heightening Alleghenies of Pennsylvania.

Let freedom ring from the snow-capped Rockies of Colorado.

Let freedom ring from the curvaceous slopes of California.

But not only there.

Let freedom ring from Stone Mountain of Georgia.

Let freedom ring from Lookout Mountain of Tennessee.

Let freedom ring from every hill and molehill of Mississippi, from every mountainside, let freedom ring.

And when this happens, when we allow freedom to ring, when we let it ring from every village and every hamlet, from every state and every city, we will be able to speed up that day when all of God's children—black men and white men, Jews and Gentiles, Protestants and Catholics—will be able to join hands and sing in the words of the old Negro spiritual. ''Free at last, free at last, thank God Almighty, we are free at last.''

Presenting the Speech

How do you perform a public speech? As an interpreter of public speeches, aim to make your audience one with the original audience of your chosen speaker. To do this you must directly address and include your listeners in the world of your literature as you share with them the logical and emotional content of the manuscript. Your voice and body will help you re-create the speech and will suggest the bearing of the original speaker, as well. Work hard to reflect visibly and vocally the emotions, attitudes, and images inherent in the work you chose, because in history, as in performance, much depends upon not only what is said, but on how it is said.

Approach the performance of the public speech as you have approached the performance of literature in general. Decide which words to emphasize, at what points to change your rate, at what points to increase or decrease your volume, and when to pause for effect. When will you incorporate gesture, how should you move, and how might your face reflect the material you are interpreting? If it is appropriate, use suggestive bits of costuming, visual aids, and/or music from the era of your speech maker to set the stage for sharing your documentary script with the audience.

GETTING INVOLVED
Recreating the Speech

Select one person from your small group to perform your group's assigned speech for the class. Help prepare him or her to successfully re-create the speech by rehearsing with group members as a team.

Reflections

1. What audience moods did each interpreter try to evoke?

2. What did the interpreters do to transfer the intellectual and emotional meanings of their speeches to the audience?

3. What did they do that hindered or impeded the communication of meaning?

4. How did each of the speakers reflect the period in which the speech was originally presented?

The Interpreter Meets the Essay

Like a public speech, an essay also reflects the mood and spirit of the time in which it was written. Through essays, writers share their ideas, their experiences, and their impressions of events, places, or people. In this way, you can experience the life-style and attitudes of individuals you do not know personally. Just as a speech reveals the speaker, so an essay reveals its author.

The focus of an essay is not on make-believe happenings, though fictional devices sometimes help authors develop and communicate a philosophy or statement. Although the writers of essays may not have intended for their works to be read aloud, oral performance certainly provides a viable avenue to appreciation.

When interpreting an essay, consider your responsibility to be threefold. First, determine how the essay mirrors the appropriate time and setting. Second, determine the central idea and mood of the work. And third, determine what the essay says about people and their values. In addition, before you "behave" the work, ask yourself how much of the writer's personality you should reflect in your re-creation of his or her work.

Participate in the next exercise to develop your essay-reading skills.

GETTING INVOLVED
Analyzing the Essay

A. Read each of the following essays carefully.

■ A Modest Proposal ■

JONATHAN SWIFT

(1729)

For Preventing the Children of Poor People in Ireland From Being a Burden to Their Parents or Country, and For Making Them Beneficial to the Public

It is a melancholy object to those who walk through this great town or travel in the country, when they see the streets, the roads, and cabin doors, crowded with beggars of the female sex, followed by three, four, or six children, all in rags and importuning every passenger for an alms. These mothers, instead of being able to work for their honest livelihood, are forced to employ all their time in strolling to beg sustenance for their helpless infants, who, as they grow up, either turn thieves for want of work, or leave their dear native country to fight for the Pretender in Spain, or sell themselves to the Barbadoes.

I think it is agreed by all parties that this prodigious number of children in the arms, or on the backs, or at the heels of their mothers, and frequently of their fathers, is in the present deplorable state of the kingdom a very great additional grievance; and therefore whoever could find out a fair, cheap, and easy method of making these children sound, useful members of the commonwealth would deserve so well of the public as to have his statue set up for a preserver of the nation.

But my intention is very far from being confined to provide only for the children of professed beggars; it is of a much greater extent, and shall take in the whole number of infants at a certain age who are born of parents in effect as little able to support them as those who demand our charity in the streets.

As to my own part, having turned my thoughts for many years upon this important subject, and maturely weighed the several schemes of other projectors, I have always found them grossly mistaken in their computation. It is true, a child just dropped from its dam may be supported by her milk for a solar year, with little other nourishment; at most not above the value of two shillings, which the mother may certainly get, or the value in scraps, by her lawful occupation of begging; and it is exactly at one year old that I propose to provide for them in such a manner as instead of being a charge upon their parents or parish, or wanting food and raiment for the rest of their lives, they shall on the contrary contribute to the feeding, and partly to the clothing of many thousands.

There is likewise another great advantage in my scheme, that it will prevent those voluntary abortions, and that horrid practice of women murdering their bastard children, alas, too frequent among us, sacrificing the poor innocent babes, I doubt, more to avoid the expense than the shame, which would move tears and pity in the most savage and inhuman breast.

The number of souls in this kingdom being usually reckoned one million one and a half, of these I calculate there may be about two hundred thousand couples whose wives are breeders; from which number I subtract thirty thousand couples who are able to maintain their own children, although I apprehend there cannot be so many under the present distresses of the kingdom; but this being granted, there will remain a hundred and seventy thousand breeders. I again subtract fifty thousand for those women who miscarry, or whose children die by accident or disease within the year. There only remain a hundred and twenty thousand children of poor parents annually born. The question therefore is, how this number shall be reared and provided for, which as I have already said, under the present situation of affairs, is utterly impossible by all the methods hitherto proposed. For we can neither employ them in handicraft or agriculture; we neither build houses (I mean in the country) nor cultivate land. They can very seldom pick up a livelihood by stealing till they arrive at six years old, except where they are of towardly parts; although I confess they learn the rudiments much earlier, during which time they can however be looked upon only as probationers, as I have been informed by a principal gentleman in the county of Cavan, who protested to me that he never knew above one or two instances under the age of six, even in a part of the kingdom so renowned for the quickest proficiency in that art.

I am assured by our merchants that a boy or girl before twelve years old is no salable commodity; and even when they come to this age they will not yield above three pounds, or three pounds and half a crown at most on the exchange; which cannot turn to account either to the parents or the kingdom, the charge of nutriment and rags having been at least four times that value.

I shall now therefore humbly propose my own thoughts, which I hope will not be liable to the least objection.

I have been assured by a very knowing American of my acquaintance in London, that a young healthy child well nursed is at a year old a most delicious, nourishing, and wholesome food, whether stewed, roasted, baked, or boiled; and I make no doubt that it will equally serve in a fricassee or a ragout.

I do therefore humbly offer it to public consideration that of the hundred and twenty thousand children, already computed, twenty thousand may be reserved for breed, whereof only one fourth part to be males, which is more than we allow to sheep, black cattle, or swine; and my reason is that these children are seldom the fruits of marriage, a circumstance not much regarded by our savages, therefore one male will be sufficient to serve four females. That the remaining hundred thousand may at a year old be offered in sale to persons of quality and fortune through the kingdom, always advising the mother to let them suck plentifully in the last month, so as to render them plump and fat for a good table. A child will make two dishes at an entertainment for friends; and when the family dines alone, the fore or hind quarter will make a reasonable dish, and seasoned with a little pepper or salt will be very good boiled on the fourth day, especially in winter.

I have reckoned upon a medium that a child just born will weigh twelve pounds, and in a solar year if tolerably nursed increaseth to twenty-eight pounds.

I grant this food will be somewhat dear, and therefore very proper for landlords, who, as they have already devoured most of the parents, seem to have the best title to the children. . . .

■ THREE DAYS TO SEE ■

HELEN KELLER

I have often thought it would be a blessing if each human being were stricken blind and deaf for a few days at sometime during his early adult life. Darkness would make him more appreciative of sight; silence would teach him the joys of sound.

Now and then I have tested my seeing friends to discover what they see. Recently I was visited by a good friend who had just returned from a long walk in the woods, and I asked her what she had observed. ''Nothing in particular,'' she replied. I might have been incredulous had I not been accustomed to such responses, for long ago I became convinced that the seeing see little.

How was it possible, I asked myself, to walk for an hour through woods and see nothing worthy of note? I who cannot see find hundreds of things to interest me through mere touch. I feel the delicate symmetry of a leaf. I pass my hands lovingly about the smooth skin of a silver birch, or the rough shaggy bark of a pine. In spring I touch the branches of trees hopefully in search of a bud, the first sign of awakening Nature after her winter's sleep. I feel the delightful velvety texture of a flower, and discover its remarkable convolutions; and something of the miracle of Nature is revealed to me. . . .

Perhaps I can best illustrate by imagining what I should most like to see if I were given the use of my eyes, say, for just three days. . . . If, by some miracle, I were granted three seeing days, to be followed by a relapse into darkness, I should divide the period into three parts.

On the first day, I should want to see the people whose kindness and gentleness and companionship have made my life worth living. First I should like to gaze long upon the face of my dear teacher, Mrs. Anne Sullivan Macy, who came to me when I was a child and opened the outer world to me. I should want not merely to see the outline of her face, so that I could cherish it in my memory, but to study that face and find in it the living evidence of the sympathetic tenderness and patience with which she accomplished the difficult task of my education. . . .

The first day would be a busy one. I would call to me all my dear friends and look long into their faces, imprinting upon my mind the outward evidences of beauty that is within them. I should let my eyes rest, too, on the face of a baby, so that I could catch a vision of the eager, innocent beauty which precedes the individual's consciousness of the conflicts which life develops. . . .

When dusk had fallen, I should experience the double delight of being able to see by artificial light, which the genius of man has created to extend the power of his sight when Nature decrees darkness.

The next day—the second day of sight—I should arise with the dawn and see the thrilling miracle by which night is transformed into day. I should behold with awe the magnificent panorama of light with which the sun awakens the sleeping earth.

This day I should devote to a hasty glimpse of the world, past and present. I should want to see the pageant of man's progress, the kaleidoscope of the ages. How can so much be compressed into one day? Through museums. . . .

The evening of my second day of sight I should spend at a theatre or at the movies. Even now I often attend theatrical performances of all sorts, but the action of the play must be spelled into my hand by a companion. But how I should like to see with my own eyes the fascinating figure of Hamlet, or the gusty Falstaff amid colorful Elizabethan trappings!

The following morning, I should again greet the dawn . . . this according to the terms of my imagined miracle, is to be my third and last day of light. I shall have no time to waste in regrets or longings; there is too much to see. The first day I devoted to my friends, animate and inanimate. The second revealed to me the history of man and Nature. Today I shall spend in the workaday world of the present, amid the haunts of men going about the business of life . . . on the evening of that last day, I should again run away to the theatre, to a hilariously funny play, so that I might appreciate the overtones of comedy in the human spirit.

At midnight my temporary respite from blindness would cease, and permanent night would close in on me again.

I who am blind can give one hint to those who see: use your eyes as if tomorrow you would be stricken blind. And the same method can be applied to the other senses. . . . But of all the senses, I am sure that sight must be the most delightful.

■ ATOMIC BOMBING OF NAGASAKI ■
WILLIAM L. LAURENCE

With the atomic-bomb mission to Japan, August 9 (Delayed)—We are on our way to bomb the mainland of Japan. Our flying contingent consists of three specially designed B-29 Superforts, and two of these carry no bombs. But our lead plane is on its way with another atomic bomb, the second in three days, concentrating in its active substance an explosive energy equivalent to twenty thousand and, under favorable conditions, forty thousand tons of TNT.

We have several chosen targets. One of these is the great industrial and shipping center of Nagasaki . . . one of the main islands of the Japanese homeland. . . .

I watched the assembly of this man-made meteor during the past two days and was among the small group of scientists and Army and Navy representatives privileged to be present at the ritual of its loading in the Superfort last night, against a background of threatening black skies torn open at intervals by great lightning flashes.

It is a thing of beauty to behold, this "gadget." Into its design went millions of man-hours of what is without doubt the most concentrated intellectual effort in history. Never before had so much brain power been focused on a single problem.

This atomic bomb is different from the bomb used three days ago with such devastating results on Hiroshima.

I saw the atomic substance before it was placed inside the bomb. By itself it is not at all dangerous to handle. . . .

The briefing at midnight revealed the extreme care and the tremendous amount of preparation that had been made to take care of every detail of the mission, to make certain that the atomic bomb fully served the purpose for which it was intended. . . .

The briefing period ended with a moving prayer by the chaplain. We then proceeded to the mess hall for the traditional early-morning breakfast before departure on a bombing mission. . . .

We took off at 3:50 this morning and headed northwest on a straight line for the Empire. . . . On we went through the night. . . . The first signs of dawn came shortly after five o'clock. Sergeant Curry, of Hoopeston, Illinois, who had been listening steadily on his earphones for radio reports, while maintaining a strict radio silence himself, greeted it by rising to his feet and gazing out the window. . . .

"Think this atomic bomb will end the war?" he asks hopefully.

"There is a very good chance that this one may do the trick," I assured him, "but if not, then the next one or two surely will. . . ."

By 5:50 it was really light outside. . . .

Our genial bombardier, Lieutenant Levy, comes over to invite me to take his front-row seat in the transparent nose of the ship, and I accept eagerly. . . . At that height the vast ocean below and the sky above seem to merge into one great sphere. . . .

My mind soon returns to the mission I am on. Somewhere beyond these vast mountains of white clouds ahead of me there lies Japan, the land of our enemy. In about four hours from now one of its cities, making weapons of war for use against us, will be wiped off the map by the greatest weapon ever made by men. In one tenth of a millionth of a second, a fraction of time immeasurable by any clock, a whirlwind from the skies will pulverize thousands of its buildings and tens of thousands of its inhabitants. . . .

Captain Bock informs me that we are about to start our climb to bombing altitude. . . . We reached our altitude at nine o'clock. . . .

We reached Yakushima at 9:12 and there, about four thousand feet ahead of us, was *The Great Artiste* with its precious load. . . .

We started circling. We saw little towns on the coastline, heedless of our presence. We kept on circling, waiting for the third ship in our formation. . . .

We flew southward down the channel and at 11:33 crossed the coastline and headed straight for Nagasaki, about one hundred miles to the west.

Here again we circled until we found an opening in the clouds. It was 12:01 and the goal of our mission had arrived.

We heard the prearranged signal on our radio, put on our arc welder's glasses and watched tensely the maneuverings of the strike ship about half a mile in front of us.

"There she goes!" someone said.

Out of the belly of *The Great Artiste* what looked like a black object went downward.

Captain Bock swung around to get out of range; but even though we were turning away in the opposite direction, and despite the fact that it was broad daylight in our cabin, all of us became aware of a giant flash that broke through the dark barrier of our arc welder's lenses and flooded our cabin with intense light.

We removed our glasses after the first flash, but the light still lingered on. . . . A tremendous blast wave struck our ship and made it tremble from nose to tail. . . .

Observers in the tail of our ship saw a giant ball of fire rise as though from the bowels of the earth, belching forth enormous white smoke rings. Next they saw a giant pillar of purple fire, ten thousand feet high, shooting skyward with enormous speed.

By the time our ship had made another turn in the direction of the atomic explosion the pillar of purple fire had reached the level of our altitude. Only about forty-five seconds had passed. Awestruck, we watched it shoot upward like a meteor coming from the earth instead of from outer space, becoming ever more alive as it climbed skyward through the white clouds. It was no longer smoke, or dust, or even a cloud of fire. It was a living thing, a new species being born right before our incredulous eyes.

At one stage of its evolution, covering millions of years in terms of seconds, the entity assumed the form of a giant square totem pole, with its base about three miles long, tapering off to about a mile at the top. Its bottom was brown, its center was amber, its top white. But it was a living totem pole, carved with many grotesque masks grimacing at the earth.

Then, just when it appeared as though the thing had settled down into a state of permanence, there came shooting out of the top a giant mushroom that increased the height of the pillar to a total of forty-five thousand feet. The mushroom top was even more alive than the pillar, seething and boiling in a white fury of creamy foam, sizzling upward and then descending earthward, a thousand Old Faithful geysers rolled into one.

It kept struggling in an elementary fury, like a creature in the act of breaking the bonds that held it down. In a few seconds it had freed itself from its gigantic stem and floated upward with tremendous speed, its momentum carrying it into the stratosphere to a height of about sixty thousand feet.

But no sooner did this happen when another mushroom, smaller in size than the first one, began emerging out of the pillar. It was as though the decapitated monster was growing a new head.

As the first mushroom floated off into the blue it changed its shape into a flower-like form, its giant petals curving downward, creamy white outside, rose-colored inside. . . . Much living substance had gone into those rainbows. The quivering top of the pillar was protruding to a great height through the white clouds, giving the appearance of a monstrous prehistoric creature with a ruff around its neck, a fleecy ruff extending in all directions, as far as the eye could see.

Reprinted by permission from *The New York Times,* September 9, 1945.

■ SELF-ESTEEM IS SELF-DISCOVERY ■

from *Revolution From Within*

GLORIA STEINEM

When I was living in India on a fellowship after college, a kind Indian friend took me aside and suggested I might consider saying "South Asia," "Southeast Asia," and the like, instead of the "Near" and "Far East." It was the first time I'd ever realized that "Near" and "Far" assumed Europe as the center of the world.

Ever since then, I've noticed that the process of discovering and esteeming a true self is remarkably similar for a person or a race, a group or a nation. When women began to call themselves "Mary Jones" instead of "Mrs. John Smith," for example, they were doing the same thing as formerly colonized countries that stopped identifying themselves in relation to Europe. When India and England continued their Commonwealth and other relationships after India's independence, one might say that, as George Sand once suggested men and women do, they had broken the marriage bond and reformed it as an equal partnership. When "Negroes" became "blacks" and then "African Americans" in the United States, it was part of a long journey from the humiliation of slavery to a pride of heritage.

When I myself started to say "we" instead of "they" when speaking of women, it was a step toward self-esteem that was at least as important as identifying with one's true ethnic heritage. It was also my Declaration of Interdependence.

No matter who we are, the journey toward recovering the self-esteem that should have been our birthright follows similar steps: a first experience of seeing through our own eyes instead of through the eyes of others (for instance, the moment when an Algerian first looked in defiance at a French soldier, or when a woman stops being defined by the male gaze); telling what seemed to be shameful secrets, and discovering they are neither shameful nor secret (from the woman who has survived childhood sexual abuse to the man whose bottomless need for power hides weakness); giving names to problems that have been treated as normal and thus have no names (think of new terms like *homophobia, battered women,* or *Eurocentrism*); bonding with others who share similar experiences (from groups of variously abled people to conferences of indigenous nations); achieving empowerment and self-government (from the woman who has a room and income of her own to the nation that declares its independence); bonding with others in shared power (think of democratic families, rainbow coalitions, or the principles of the United Nations); and finally, achieving a balance of independence and interdependence, and taking one's place in a circle of true selves.

B. Divide the class into small groups and select one of the preceding essays to consider and perform. Choose a member of your group to present the chosen essay and work as a team to help that individual prepare adequately.

Reflections

1. What is the central idea of the chosen essay?

2. What is its mood-tone?

3. How does the language of the essay reflect its tone?

4. How might the oral reader use the techniques of interpretation to make the essay live for the audience?

5. How does the work reflect the concerns of both the author and the times in which it was written?

The Interpreter Meets
Biography and Autobiography

Although both the *biography* and the *autobiography* document the life and history of one man or woman, they do so in very different ways. Before examining them in detail, take a few moments to read the samples that follow.

GETTING INVOLVED
Character Portraits

Read the following passages carefully, giving special attention to point of view.

■ DOWN THESE MEAN STREETS ■
PIRI THOMAS

I had been walking around since 9 P.M. My thoughts were boiling. *Poppa ain't ever gonna hit me again. I'm his kid, too, just like James, Jose, Paulie, and Sis. But I'm the one that always gets the blame for everything. I'm sorry Momma's gotta worry, but she gotta understand that it wasn't my fault.*

"*Caramba,*" I muttered aloud, "I'm getting hungry."

The streets of Harlem make an unreal scene of frightened silence at 2 A.M. Like everything got a layoff from noise and hassling. Only the rumbling of a stray car passing by or the shy foraging of a cat or dog make the quietness bearable—especially to a twelve-year-old kid whose ability to make noise had got him a whipping from his poppa.

I could see Poppa's face, tired and sleepy. . . .

I could feel my mouth making the motions of wanting to say something in my defense. Of how it wasn't my fault that Jose had almost knocked the toaster off the table, and how I had tried to save it from falling, and in trying had finished knocking it to the floor along with a large jar of black coffee. But I just couldn't get the words out. Poppa just stood there, eyes swollen and hurting from too much work, looking at a river of black coffee. He didn't give me a chance. Even before the first burning slap of his belt awakened tears of pain, I was still trying to get words out that would make everything all right again. The second whap of the belt brought words of pain to my lips, and my blind running retreat was a mixture of tears and ''I hate you.''

■ THE OLD GENTLEMAN ■
GILBERT HIGHET

The old gentleman was riding round his land. He had retired several years ago, after a busy career; but farming was what he liked, and he knew that the best way to keep farms prosperous was to supervise them in person. So, although he was approaching seventy, he rode round his property for four or five hours, several days each week. It was not easy for him, but it was not difficult either. He never thought whether a thing was easy or difficult. If it ought to be done, it would be done. Besides, he had always been strong. Although his hair was white and his eyes were dimming, he stood a good six feet and weighed 210 pounds. He rose at four every morning. It was December now, Christmas was approaching, snow was in the air, frost and snow on the ground. This month he had been away from home on a toilsome but necessary trip, and in the hard weather he had been able to ride over his farms very seldom. Still, he liked to see them whenever he could. The land was quiet; yet a great deal of work remained to be done.

There was much on the old gentleman's mind. His son had come home from college in some kind of disturbance and uneasiness, unwilling to go back again. Perhaps he should be sent elsewhere—to Harvard, or William and Mary? Perhaps he should have a private tutor? . . . Meanwhile, in order to teach him habits of quiet and undistracted industry, ''I can (the old gentleman wrote to a friend), and I believe I do, keep him in his room a certain portion of the twenty-four hours.'' But even so, nothing would substitute for the boy's own will power, which was apparently defective. The grandchildren, too, were sometimes sick, because they were spoiled. Not by their grandmother, but by their mother. The old gentleman's wife never spoiled anyone: indeed, she wrote to Fanny to warn her, saying emphatically, "I am sure there is nothing so pernicious as over charging the stomack of a child."

He thought hard and long about the state of the nation. Although he had retired from politics, he was often consulted, and he kept closely in touch. One advantage of retirement was that it gave him time to think over general principles. Never an optimist, he could usually see important dangers some time before they appeared to others. This December, as he rode over the stiff clods under the pale sky, he was thinking over two constant threats to his country. One was the danger of disputes between the separate States and the central government. (Congress had just passed a law designed to combat sedition, and two of the States had immediately denounced it as unconstitutional. This could lead only to disaster.) The other problem was that respectable men were not entering public life. They seemed to prefer to pursue riches, to seek their private happiness, as though such a thing were possible if the nation declined. The old gentleman decided to write to Mr. Henry, whom he considered a sound man, and urge him to reenter politics: he would surely be elected if he would consent to stand; and then, with his experience, he could do much to bridge the gap between the federal government and the States.

The old gentleman stopped his horse. With that large, cool, comprehensive gaze which every visitor always remembered, he looked round the land. It was doing better. Five years ago his farms had been almost ruined by neglect and greed. During his long absence the foremen had cropped them too hard and omitted to cultivate and fertilize, looking for quick and easy profits. Still, even before retiring, he had set about restoring the ground to health and vigor: first, by feeding the soil as much as possible, all year round; second by "a judicious succession of crops"; and third, most important of all, by careful regularity and constant application. As he put it in a letter, "To establish good rules, and a regular system, is the life and the soul of every kind of business." Now the land was improving every year. It was always a mistake to expect rapid returns. To build up a nation and to make a farm out of the wilderness, both needed long, steady, thoughtful, determined application; both were the work of the will.

Long ago, when he was only a boy, he had copied out a set of rules to help in forming his manners and his character—in the same careful way as he would lay out a new estate or survey a recently purchased tract of land. The last of the rules he still remembered. *Keep alive in your breast that little spark of celestial fire called Conscience.* Some of the philosophers said that the spark from heaven was reason, the power of the intellect, which we share with God. The old gentleman did not quarrel with them, but he did not believe them. He knew that the divine fire in the spirit was the sense of duty, the lawfulness which orders the whole universe, the power of which a young poet then alive was soon to write:

> Thou dost preserve the stars from wrong;
> And the most ancient heavens, through Thee,
>   are fresh and strong.

His mind turned back over his long and busy life. He never dreamed or brooded, but he liked to note things down, to plan them and record them. Now, on this cold December day, he could recall nearly every Christmas he had ever spent: sixty at least. Some were peaceful, some were passed in deadly danger, many in war, some in strange lonely places, some in great assemblies, some in happiness and some in anguish of soul, none in despair.

One of the worst was Christmas Day of twenty-one years before. That was early in the war, a bad time. It snowed four inches on Christmas. His men were out in the open, with no proper quarters. Although he started them on building shelters, an aggressive move by the enemy made them stand to arms and interrupt all other work for nearly a week. And they had no decent uniforms, no warm coats, no strong shoes, no regular supplies, two days without meat, three days without bread, almost a quarter of his entire force unfit for duty. He was receiving no supplies from the government, and he was actually meeting opposition from the locals. They had sent up a protest against keeping the troops in service during the winter. Apparently they thought you could raise an army whenever you needed one—not understanding that this little force was the only permanent barrier between them and foreign domination. He had replied with crushing energy to that protest. In a letter to the President of Congress, he wrote:

> I can assure those gentlemen that it is a much easier and less distressing thing to draw remonstrances in a comfortable room by a good fireside than to occupy a cold, bleak hill, and sleep under frost and snow without clothes or blankets. However, although they seem to have little feeling for the naked and distressed soldiers, I feel superabundantly for them, and from my soul I pity those miseries which it is neither in my power to relieve or prevent.

He ended with his well-known, strongly and gracefully written signature, G. WASHINGTON.

Reflections

1. What is the dominant point of view in each passage?

2. Who is the speaker of each passage?

3. What is being described in each of the selections?

4. How can you as an interpreter re-create these passages for an audience? How do you alter your performance when you change from autobiographical to biographical material?

An autobiography presents a literary self-portrait in which the writer describes his or her own life and times. Thus, in the excerpt from *Down These Mean Streets*, the autobiographical point of view is almost always first person, rather than third person, as is usual in biographical works. In addition, the author of an autobiography writes from a dual perspective: his or her words are reflective of both past and present attitudes. This duality complicates the task of the interpreter who seeks to re-create such works. Consequently, when interpreting autobiographical literature, your goal is to suggest your author-subject's outlooks and behaviors at various points in his or her lifetime. How does the author-subject experience himself or herself and others? How does your author-subject react to various events and people helpful to him or her? Share details such as these with your audience.

Like the autobiography, the biography also presents a literary portrait of an individual; in the biography, though, that portrait has been carefully sketched in the words of another individual who came to know the subject well through interviews and/or research. How does an interpreter approach the task of re-creating biographical material for an audience? First, realize that just as two artists will paint portraits of the same subject in contrasting ways, so will "word sketches" of a subject differ. How much can they differ? Take a new look at a familiar personality by reading the following opinion.

GETTING INVOLVED
Little Miss Muffet

As you read the following passage from an editorial carefully, consider what it tells you about this famous Miss.

■ An Opinion: An Analysis of ■ Miss Muffet

Russell Baker

Little Miss Muffet, as everyone knows, sat on a tuffet eating her curds and whey when along came a spider who sat down beside her and frightened Miss Muffet away. While everyone knows it, the significance of the event had never been analyzed until a conference of thinkers recently brought their special insights to bear upon it. Following are excerpts from the transcript of their discussion:

SOCIOLOGIST: Miss Muffet is nutritionally underprivileged, as evidenced by the subminimal diet of curds and whey upon which she is forced to subsist, while the spider's cultural disadvantage is evidenced by such phenomena as legs exceeding standard norms, odd mating habits and so forth.

In this instance, spider expectations lead the culturally disadvantaged to assert demands to share the tuffet with the nutritionally underprivileged. Due to a communications failure, Miss Muffet assumes without evidence that the spider will not be satisfied to share her tuffet, but will also insist on eating her curds and whey. . . .

MILITARIST: Second-strike capability, sir! That's what was lacking. If Miss Muffet had developed a second-strike capability instead of squandering her resources on curds and whey, no spider on earth would have dared launch a first strike capable of carrying him right to the heart of her tuffet. I am confident that Miss Muffet had adequate notice from experts that she could not afford both curds and whey and at the same time support an early-spider-warning system. . . .

BOOK REVIEWER: Written on several levels, this searing, sensitive exploration of the arachnid heart illuminates the agony and splendor of Jewish family life with a candor that is at once breathtaking in its simplicity and soul-shattering in its implied ambiguity. Some will doubtless be shocked to see such subjects as tuffets and whey discussed without flinching, but hereafter writers too timid to call a tuffet a tuffet will no longer. . . .

EDITORIALIST: Why has the Government not seen fit to tell the public all it knows about the so-called curds-and-whey affair? It is not enough to suggest that this was merely a random incident involving a lonely spider and a young diner. . . .

PSYCHIATRIST: Little Miss Muffet is, of course, neither little, nor a miss. These are obviously the self she has created in her own fantasies to escape the reality that she is a . . . divorcee whose superego makes it impossible for her to sustain a normal relationship with any man, symbolized by the spider. . . .

STUDENT: Little Miss Muffet, tuffets, curds, whey and spiders are what's wrong with education today. They're all irrelevant. Tuffets are irrelevant. Curds are irrelevant. Whey is irrelevant. . . .

CHILD: This is about a little girl who gets scared by a spider.

(The child was sent home when the conference broke for lunch. It was agreed that the child was too immature to add anything to the sum of human understanding and should not return until he had grown up.)

Reprinted by permission from *The New York Times*, April 14, 1969.

Reflections

1. What do the respondents' comments concerning Miss Muffet tell you about themselves?

2. How do the respondents reveal their own biases?

Although the conference on Miss Muffet never actually occurred (so far as we know), the imagined results are probably only slightly exaggerated. The purpose for reading the Miss Muffet piece is to emphasize that in reality there simply is no such thing as a completely objective human being. Thus, when re-creating a portion of a biography, be certain that your own preconceptions of the person or subject do not blind or hinder you in internalizing the impressions of your author. In other words, when re-creating a selection from a biography, share your author's concept—not your own—of his or her subject. Be accurate in determining the writer's perspective or frame of reference; you want to reflect faithfully the author's attitude toward the subject in order to embody the tensions, feelings, qualities, and events the author chose to emphasize. Consider the author's orientation and biases regarding the subject of the following biographies.

GETTING INVOLVED
Biographies

Read the following selections written about the assassination of President John F. Kennedy.

■ THROUGH RUSSIAN EYES: ■
PRESIDENT KENNEDY'S 1036 DAYS
ANATOLII ANDREIEVICH GROMYKO

It was late autumn in Texas. The sky was filled with threatening greyish clouds, and it drizzled. The sun, it seemed, would not hearten Texans on the morning of November 22, 1963. But later that morning the weather began to clear, and by eleven a bright southern sun was sparkling over Dallas.

Air Force Two landed at the Dallas airport at 11:35 A.M. Lyndon Johnson, Vice-President of the United States of America, was aboard. Five minutes later the shadow of a second plane, Air Force One, appeared on the runway. That aircraft carried the 45-year-old President of the United States, John Fitzgerald Kennedy. . . .

The President's airplane slowly taxied to the airport terminal. It is hard to say what Kennedy was thinking as he prepared to leave the aircraft, in front of which a large welcoming crowd had already gathered. There is every reason to believe, however, that at the bottom of his heart he felt an ominous foreboding about his journey. . . .

Kennedy's wife, Jacqueline, and Kenneth O'Donnell, his close friend, shared his apprehension. It was no accident that the three, while having breakfast at their hotel before flying to Dallas on the morning of November 22, discussed a highly unusual topic: the personal risks Kennedy was taking during his public appearances. Kennedy remarked that "if somebody really wanted to shoot the President of the United States of America, it would not be a very difficult task. All he would have to do is to climb a tall building, have a telescopic rifle, and nobody could do anything to prevent such an attempt. . . ."

The President did not realize how close he came to the truth.

The main reason for Kennedy's journey to Texas was his desire to bolster his prestige in this southern state, the birthplace of Vice-President Johnson, on the eve of the 1964 presidential elections. In the 1960 election, Kennedy almost lost Texas to Richard Nixon, the Republican party candidate. . . .

Now Kennedy was in Dallas. At 11:50 A.M., local time, the motorcade set out from the airport for the city. Kennedy and his wife were seated in the back of the first car; in the jump-seats were Governor Connally and his wife. In the front seat were two Secret Service agents to protect the President. Immediately behind Kennedy's car was another which held eight additional security agents. . . .

The suburbs were behind them. The President's motorcade entered Main Street, the principal artery of Dallas' business district, which crosses it from east to west. The welcoming crowds had swollen in number. Squinting in the sunlight, Kennedy gazed with curiosity at the spectators lining the sidewalks who had come—if not to welcome him—at least to look at the President of the United States. Nothing appeared to foreshadow danger.

At the end of Main, the presidential procession turned right on Houston Street. Ahead, at the intersection of Houston and Elm Streets, stood a seven-floor red brick building, a book depository. The clock on one building now showed the time as 12:30 P.M. The President's car slowly turned left onto Elm Street.

Seconds later, sharp shots rang out in quick succession. Eyewitnesses to Kennedy's assassination later maintained that the shots had been fired from the book depository as well as from the railroad viaduct. . . . John Kennedy was fatally wounded in the neck and head. . . .

Naturally, since Kennedy's assassination, the question of who actually murdered the President has preoccupied everyone. And to this day the question remains essentially unanswered. It appears as though all traces of the crime have vanished.

It is generally known that Lee Harvey Oswald, the person charged with Kennedy's assassination, was shot within the Dallas police station by the owner of a night club, one Jack Ruby, who later died in a prison hospital. . . . How could it happen that the only American apprehended as the apparent perpetrator of the crime was liquidated literally before the eyes of everyone, and, naturally, can no longer furnish any evidence. . . ?

■ THE DEATH OF A PRESIDENT ■

WILLIAM MANCHESTER

12:22. *Main and Ervay.*

A dozen young people surged into the street; from his curbside command post Dallas' husky Inspector Herbert Sawyer gave a signal and a clutch of patrolmen closed in, pressing them back. The Secret Service showed signs of activity. . . .

On the left loomed the Mercantile Building and the Neiman Marcus department store. The seventh floor of the Mercantile Building was the headquarters of H. L. Hunt, Dallas' billionaire. Flanked by two secretaries, Hunt stared down as the President gaily saluted the mob in front of Walgreen's.

12:23. *Main and Akward.*

Forrest Sorrels, in the lead car, heard shouts of ''The President's coming!''
He craned his neck and muttered to Lawson, ''My God, look at the people
hanging out the windows!''

Clint Hill was watching the windows. So was Yarborough, and he
didn't like them. The Senator was delighted by the throngs on the sidewalks. Next to the President, he was the most exuberant campaigner in
the motorcade. . . .

12:24. *Main and Field.*

Jim Hosty, the local FBI agent in charge of Lee Oswald's file, had his wish.
He saw Kennedy from the curb and then stepped into the Alamo Grill for
lunch. His day, he felt, was made.

12:26. *Main and Poydras.*

. . . Liz Carpenter, listening to the echoing roars, crowed, ''Well, this
pulls the rug out from under . . . Barry Goldwater!''

12:28. *Main and Market.*

The neighborhood began to deteriorate. They were entering a seamy section of bail-bond shops, bars, a public gym. It occurred to Yarborough that
anyone could drop a pot of flowers on Kennedy from an upper story. *It will
be good to have the President out of this*, he thought, and then he saw that they
were nearly at the end. . . .

12:29. *Main and Houston.*

. . . Nellie, surprised and delighted at Dallas' showing, twisted in her jump
seat. ''You sure can't say Dallas doesn't love you, Mr. President,'' she said
jubilantly. Kennedy smiled and answered, ''No, you can't.''

12:30.   *Houston and Elm.*

. . . Sorrels was saying to Curry, ''Five more minutes and we'll have him
there.'' Noting that there was only a handful of spectators ahead, Lawson
alerted the four-to-twelve shift. He radioed the Trade Mart that they would
reach there in five minutes. Then he automatically scanned the
overpass. . . .

The pool car was approaching it. Kilduff, misreading the sign on the
front of the warehouse, said to Merriman Smith, ''What the hell is a Book
Repository?''

Back on Main Street Evelyn Lincoln was saying, ''Just think—we've
come through all of Dallas and there hasn't been a single demonstration.''
One of Liz Carpenter's local friends laughed. ''That's Dallas,'' she
said. . . .

The Lincoln moved ahead at 11.2 miles an hour. It passed the tree. . . . Momentarily the entire car was obscured. But it was no longer hidden from the sixth-floor corner window. It had passed the last branch.

Brend's five-year-old boy timidly raised his hand. The President smiled warmly. He raised his hand to wave back.

There was a sudden, sharp, shattering sound. . . .

The President was wounded, but not fatally. A 6.5 millimeter bullet had entered the back of his neck, bruised his right lung, ripped his windpipe, and exited at his throat, nicking the knot of his tie. . . .

And now it was too late. Howard Brennan, open-mouthed, saw Oswald take deliberate aim for his final shot. . . . Crooking his arm, Oswald drew a fresh bead with his Italian rifle. *Ready on the left, ready on the right, all ready on the firing line*, his Marine Corps instructors had shouted on the San Diego range, signaling the appearance of rapid-fire targets. He was ready now. They had also told him to hold his front sight at six o'clock on an imaginary clock dial. It was there, and steady. His target, startlingly clear in the cross hairs of his telescopic sight, was eighty-eight yards away.

He squeezed the trigger.

The First Lady, in her last act as First Lady, leaned solicitously toward the President. His face was quizzical. She had seen that expression so often, when he was puzzling over a difficult press conference question. Now, in a gesture of infinite grace, he raised his right hand, as though to brush back his tousled chestnut hair. But the motion faltered. The hand fell back limply. He had been reaching for the top of his head. But it wasn't there any more.

■ Plausible Denial ■

MARK LANE

The radio reports continued to assert that the president had been injured and was alive.

I suddenly realized that for the first time in my life I was late for an appearance in court. The trial was to have been continued five minutes earlier. I rushed to the courtroom not sure of what I would encounter there, but certain that the trial would not go forth that day. I explained to the judge that the president had been shot and that he had died. He was unmoved. He had heard about it; the case would go forward. "Let's move along with this trial," he said.

I hesitated. "Call your next witness, Mr. Lane. We have work to do." My client testified. The jury apparently was satisfied with his explanation, for at the close of the day he was acquitted.

I hurried from the courthouse aware that I was, several hours after the assassination, one of the least knowledgeable persons in the country about the details of the historic event that had transpired earlier that day. I was eager to rush to my office to a television set and telephone.

With a briefcase in one hand and a topcoat in the other, I ran down the massive stone steps, stepping around an elderly gentleman who was walking slowly in the same direction. He turned and said, "Well, Lane, do you think he did it alone?" I recognized a judge of my acquaintance, a distinguished though somewhat irascible jurist for whom I had great respect and at least a modicum of fondness. Identifying with Rip van Winkle as he rose, I responded, "Who, sir? Did what?"

"Do you think Oswald killed the president?" he asked.

I explained that I had just tried a case and had heard nothing about the details of the assassination. The judge waved away my response, clearly ruling it to be irrelevant. He stopped walking, looked at me, and said:

"He couldn't very well shoot him from the back and cause an entrance wound in his throat, could he?"

The rhetorical question required no response. He continued:

"The doctors said the throat wound was an entrance wound. It'll be an interesting trial. I want to see how they answer that question."

More than a quarter of a century later, the question—how could Oswald shoot Kennedy from the back from the front?—remains without adequate response.

▪ KENNEDY ▪

THEODORE C. SORENSEN

I must ask to be excused from repeating the details of that tragedy. How and why it happened are of little consequence compared to what it stopped. No amount of argument or investigation can alter the fact that Jack Kennedy was assassinated. His assassin was assassinated. His assassin's assassin, as of this writing, has been condemned to be executed. Some blame leftists, some blame rightists, some blame Dallas or the security forces, some blame us all. John Kennedy would have said it is too late to be blaming anyone—and he would have had compassion for his assassin and compassion for us all.

He would not have condemned the entire city of Dallas. Certainly the warmth of its welcome that day was genuine and impressive. . . .

Personally I accept the conclusion that no plot or political motive was involved, despite the fact that this makes the deed all the more difficult to accept. For a man as controversial yet beloved as John Kennedy to be killed for no real reason or cause denies us even the slight satisfaction of drawing some meaning or moral from his death. . . .

He had traveled to Dallas to tell its citizens that ''ignorance . . . can handicap . . . this country's security,'' and that ''the righteousness of our cause must always underlie our strength. For as was written long ago: 'Except the Lord keep the city, the watchman waketh but in vain.' '' On November 22, 1963, in the city of Dallas, Texas, the watchman woke but in vain.

Reflections

1. What do the preceding excerpts tell you about each author's orientation toward John F. Kennedy?

2. What occurrences has each writer chosen to emphasize? Why do you believe these choices were made?

3. How do each of the writers' comments reveal their biases?

4. How would a careful analysis of each work help you to re-create the material during a performance?

The Interpreter Meets the Diary and the Letter

Diaries and letters allow intimate glimpses into the lives and times of interesting individuals, providing an interpreter of literature with stimulating performance material. In a diary, a writer speaks to himself or herself; in a letter, he or she speaks to another person. Consequently, both forms of literature reflect differences in communication processes—differences an interpreter must mirror in performance.

When re-creating a diary entry, you seek to suggest an *intra*personal transaction is taking place; in effect, the person is talking within himself or herself. You allow your audience to overhear your speaker's meditations; however, be certain you don't sound as if you are engaging in subvocal musings. Adequate voice projection is a necessity for the audience to hear and understand the speaker. Although it is thoughts you are communicating, remember that you are thinking *aloud*.

On the other hand, when re-creating a letter or a series of letters, you want to suggest an *inter*personal communication transaction is occurring. Place your scene out front and speak to your recipient as if he or she were seated in your audience. When interpreting letters, be certain you determine the kind of relationship the writer shared with the letter's recipient. Often, the style and content of the letter will offer clues, but you will probably find it both interesting and beneficial to research the relationship.

When interpreting either a diary entry or a letter, be certain you comprehend how these documents reflect their author's daily life and concerns. Interpreting material of such a personal nature necessitates an empathic understanding of the author and his or her environmental influences.

GETTING INVOLVED

Intimate Glimpses

Read the following passages carefully. Think about what the content of each selection reveals about its author.

■ LETTERS TO A BLACK BOY ■

BOB TEAGUE

Dear Adam,

> Question the mysteries that you
>> do not understand
> Question the answers that
>> quickly come to hand
> Question your teachers, yourself
>> and what you see
> Question him, question her
> Question me.

Despite your daddy's desire simply to guide you through the maze, there will be times when I am guilty of pushing and preaching. My excuse is that I cannot forget that the black skin you got from me will force you to waste a kingsize slice of your lifetime climbing invisible barriers, imagining other barriers where none exist, fending off affronts—real and imagined—to your dignity, proving that you are human, disproving that you are inferior, living down stereotypes, protesting injustice, choking down helpless rage, waiting for freedom, and adjusting to the knowledge that you will still be waiting when you die.

All those distractions, of course, will rob you of more time and energy than any man can afford to lose from his search for personal fulfillment, from learning to help, to share, to build, to laugh, to dream, to love.

And that is why with a sense of desperation I pound away, trying to instill in you the notion that the real concerns of living have no relation to the color of your skin; that besides learning to cope with the distractions that come with being black in this society, you must also face the more fundamental distractions that plague all men. . . .

Dear Adam,

We have just lived through the longest night of our lives. The black patron saint, the Rev. Dr. Martin Luther King, Jr., was assassinated, mourned and buried. We also survived the violent aftermath of black brothers by the thousands blindly searching for revenge.

Dr. King's passage from living symbol to entombed martyr required only six unaccountably sunny days. The passage of black vigilantes from stunned mourners to bitter marauders and finally back to men required a week of accountably ugly nights. . . .

My main impression is that we watched the complete horror from beginning to end, sitting slumped in front of our television screen. . . . The four of us in the living room sob openly. There is no attempt to comfort one another. There is no attempt to hide our tears. . . .

Eventually, we are swept by the screen into the mournful trek to the cemetery. His coffin lies on the bed of a creaking mule-drawn cart. A symbol of his commitment to the poor. . . .

At last they lower his body—and a part of us—into the grave. We will weep yet again upon reading the epitaph engraved on his white marble tomb:

> "Free at last, free at last
> Thank God Almighty
> I'm free at last."

■ ANNE FRANK: ■
DIARY OF A YOUNG GIRL

Saturday, July 15, 1944

"For in its innermost depths youth is lonelier than old age." I read this saying in some book and I've always remembered it, and found it to be true. Is it true then that grownups have a more difficult time here than we do? No. I know it isn't. Older people have formed their opinions about everything, and don't waver before they act. It's twice as hard for us young ones to hold our ground, and maintain our opinions, in a time when all ideals are being shattered and destroyed, when people are showing their worst side, and do not know whether to believe in truth and right and God.

Anyone who claims that the older ones have a more difficult time here certainly doesn't realize to what extent our problems weigh down on us, problems for which we are probably much too young, but which thrust themselves upon us continually, until, after a long time, we think we've found a solution, but the solution doesn't seem able to resist the facts which reduce it to nothing again. That's the difficulty in these times: ideals, dreams, and cherished hopes rise within us, only to meet the horrible truth and be shattered.

It's really a wonder that I haven't dropped all my ideals, because they seem so absurd and impossible to carry out. Yet I keep them, because in spite of everything I still believe that people are really good at heart. I simply can't build up my hopes on a foundation consisting of confusion, misery, and death. I see the world gradually being turned into a wilderness, I hear the ever approaching thunder, which will destroy us too, I can feel the sufferings of millions and yet, if I look up into the heavens, I think that it will all come right, that this cruelty too will end, and that peace and tranquility will return again.

In the meantime, I must uphold my ideals, for perhaps the time will come when I shall be able to carry them out.

Yours, Anne

Reflections

1. What do the preceding passages tell you about the individuals who wrote them? What personal traits or qualities were revealed?

2. What performance techniques would help to re-create these materials for an audience?

Remember, your aim as interpreter is to match the style of your performance to the style and content of the literature. Use your rehearsal period to decide the vocal and physical gestures you will adopt to indicate the author's attitudes and feelings. Select facial expressions, gestures, movements, and voice qualities carefully to exhibit the essence and personality of the work.

The Interpreter Meets Video and Audio Tape

Today, taped interviews, news broadcasts, and radio and television documentaries store important events of our age. Interpreters should not neglect these materials, as the public or private monologues and dialogues recorded on them are, in fact, drama in our time. In re-creating these materials, interpreters help others see with clarity the times in which they live and know the individuals who have affected their society. Once again, the oral reader's task is to bring alive "stored" speech and experience.

GETTING INVOLVED
The Drama of Our Times

Read the following excerpts. Think about how they reflect the drama and conflicts of our century.

■ Plain Speaking: ■
An Oral Biography of
Harry S. Truman
MERLE MILLER

. . . Mr. President, can you tell me about the day Franklin Roosevelt died?

"It is a day . . . it's a time I can even now not think about without feeling very deep emotion.

"It was an ordinary day in the Senate, and I presided. I usually presided most of the time when I was Vice President. Senator Wiley . . . was making a speech about something. I forget what it was about; it didn't make any difference with Wiley. He could go on forever about nothing. And so I wrote a letter to Mamma. . . .

Dear Mamma and Mary:

I am trying to write you a letter from the desk of the President of the Senate while a windy Senator is making a speech on a subject with which he is in no way familiar. . . .

. . . Turn on your radio tomorrow night at 9:30 your time, and you'll hear Harry make a Jefferson Day address to the nation. . . . It will be followed by the President, whom I'll introduce.

"Along about, oh I guess it was probably half past four or a quarter of five, Sam Rayburn called. He'd been in Texas, and he called and said there was a meeting of the Board of Education."

The Board of Education was the name of a group of legislators who dropped into Rayburn's private office from time to time after a legislative session to share stories and drink a little bourbon and tap water. Rayburn, a bachelor from Texas, was Speaker of the House.

". . . and so I went over, and before I could sit down . . . Sam told me that Steve Early (Roosevelt's press secretary) had called and wanted me to call right back. I did, and Early said to come right over to the White House and to come to the front entrance, and he said to come up to Mrs. Roosevelt's suite on the second floor. I didn't think much about it. I just supposed that the President had come back from Georgia (Roosevelt died at Warm Springs, Georgia) and was going to be at Bishop Atwood's funeral. . . . Roosevelt was an honorary pallbearer, and I just supposed that was what had happened.

"And so I went over to the White House, and Mrs. Roosevelt . . . Mrs. Roosevelt . . . she told me that . . . the President . . . was dead."

For a moment Mr. Truman was unable to continue.

When he could, he said, "I was able . . . I told Steve Early to call the Cabinet, and they started phoning for the Chief Justice (Harlan F. Stone) and members of Congress.

"I went over to the office of the President in the West End of the White House and tried to call my wife and daughter. I had a hard time getting them, but I finally did, and they came, and the Chief Justice was there, and all the others, including the Cabinet, and everybody was crying.

"They had just an awful time finding a Bible. I'm sure there were plenty of them in the family living quarters of the White House, but down in the executive wing they had a terrible time finding one, and the Chief Justice was waiting to swear me in.

"Finally, they found one in the office I believe it was of Bill Hassett, who was Roosevelt's secretary. . . .

". . . Anyway, that's the one I was sworn in on . . . I was sworn in—there was a clock on the mantel—and I was sworn in at 7:09. Exactly at 7:09 on April 12, 1945, and that's all the time it took for me to become President of the United States. . . ."

■ In Search of Light, ■
a Broadcast of
Edward R. Murrow
EDITED BY EDWARD BLISS, JR.

April 15, 1945

. . . Permit me to tell you what you would have seen, and heard, had you been with me on Thursday. It will not be pleasant listening. If you are at lunch, or if you have no appetite to hear what Germans have done, now is a good time to switch off the radio, for I propose to tell you of Buchenwald. It is on a small hill about four miles outside Weimar, and it was one of the largest concentration camps in Germany, and it was built to last. As we approached it, we saw about a hundred men in civilian clothes with rifles advancing in open order across the fields. There were a few shops; we stopped to inquire. We were told that some of the prisoners had a couple of SS men cornered in there. We drove on, reached the main gate. The prisoners crowded up behind the wire. We entered.

And now, let me tell this in the first person, for I was the least important person there, as you shall hear. There surged around me an evil-smelling horde. Men and boys reached out to touch me; they were in rags and the remnants of uniform. Death had already marked many of them, but they were smiling with their eyes. I looked out over that mass of men to the green fields beyond where well-fed Germans were ploughing.

A German, Fritz Kersheimer, came up and said, "May I show you round the camp? I've been here ten years." An Englishman stood to attention, saying, "May I introduce myself, delighted to see you, and can you tell me when some of our blokes will be along?" I told him soon and asked to see one of the barracks. It happened to be occupied by Czechoslovakians. When I entered, men crowded around, tried to lift me to their shoulders. They were too weak. Many of them could not get out of bed. I was told that this building had once stabled eighty horses. There were twelve hundred men in it, five to a bunk. The stink was beyond all description.

When I reached the center of the barracks, a man came up and said, "You remember me. I'm Peter Zenkl, one-time mayor of Prague." I remembered him, but did not recognize him. . . .

As I walked down to the end of the barracks, there was applause from the men too weak to get out of bed. It sounded like the hand clapping of babies;

they were so weak. The doctor's name was Paul Heller. He had been there since 1938.

As we walked out into the courtyard, a man fell dead. Two others—they must have been over sixty—were crawling toward the latrine. I saw it but will not describe it.

In another part of the camp they showed me the children, hundreds of them. Some were only six. One rolled up his sleeve, showed me his number. It was tatooed on his arm. D-6030, it was. The others showed me their numbers; they will carry them till they die.

An elderly man standing beside me said, ''The children, enemies of the state.'' I could see their ribs through their thin shirts. The old man said, ''I am Professor Charles Richer of the Sorbonne.'' The children clung to my hands and stared. We crossed to the courtyard. Men kept coming up to speak to me and touch me, professors from Poland, doctors from Vienna, men from all Europe. Men from the countries that made America.

We went to the hospital; it was full. The doctor told me that two hundred had died the day before. . . . Dr. Heller pulled back the blankets from a man's feet to show me how swollen they were. The man was dead. Most of the patients could not move. . . .

I asked to see the kitchen; it was clean. The German in charge had been a Communist, had been at Buchenwald for nine years, had a picture of his daughter in Hamburg. He hadn't seen her for almost twelve years, and if I got to Hamburg, would I look her up? He showed me the daily ration—one piece of brown bread about as thick as your thumb, on top of it a piece of margarine as big as three sticks of chewing gum. That, and a little stew, was what they received every twenty-four hours. . . .

Dr. Heller, the Czech, asked if I would care to see the crematorium. He said it wouldn't be very interesting because the Germans had run out of coke some days ago and had taken to dumping the bodies into a great hole nearby. Professor Richer said perhaps I would care to see the small courtyard. I said yes. . . . The wall was about eight feet high; it adjoined what had been a stable or garage. We entered. It was floored with concrete. There were two rows of bodies stacked up like cordwood. They were thin and very white. Some of the bodies were terribly bruised, though there seemed to be little flesh to bruise. . . . I tried to count them as best I could and arrived at the conclusion that all that was mortal of more than five hundred men and boys lay there in two neat piles.

There was a German trailer which must have contained another fifty, but it wasn't possible to count them. . . . It appeared that most of the men and boys had died of starvation. . . . But the manner of death seemed unimportant. Murder had been done at Buchenwald. God alone knows how many men and boys have died there during the last twelve years. . . .

As I left that camp, a Frenchman who used to work for Havas in Paris came up to me and said, "You will write something about this, perhaps?" And he added, "To write about this you must have been here at least two years, and after that—you don't want to write any more."

I pray you to believe what I have said about Buchenwald; I have reported what I saw and heard, but only part of it. For most of it I have no words. . . .

■ LIFE AT "JEFF": ■
TOUGH STUDENTS WONDER WHERE CHILDHOOD WENT

from *The New York Times*, March 7, 1992

New Yorkers and indeed the nation were shocked when two students were gunned down in the hallway of Thomas Jefferson High School in East New York, Brooklyn, on Feb. 26. Khalil Sumpter, a 15-year-old student, was arrested and charged with the slayings of Tyrone Sinkler, 16, and Ian Moore, 17.

For the 1,800 students who attend "Jeff," in one of the poorest and most violent sections of the city, murder and mayhem are as much a feature of teen-age life as pep rallies and proms.

To learn more about the lives, hopes and fears of these "children of war," as their principal calls them, The New York Times invited Thomas Jefferson students to a discussion this week.

Even as city officials called for such measures as more metal detectors in the schools, many of the students said the problems went far beyond guns, ultimately to a kind of erosion of the spirit.

MARIANA BRYANT   Last night we was looking through my junior high school yearbook and my friend pointed out a number of people in that book that was dead.

Q.   About how many would you estimate?

MARIANA   Ten, all guys from eighth and ninth grade.

CAROLINE GRIFFITH   There was a shooting around my building over this girl. I was on my way to school. Two guys were going with one girl, so after one found out then he just pulled out his gun and shot him. . . . The one that got shot was 17.

SEAN WILLIAMS   One of the guys that died from this school was Wesley. . . . He got shot in a barbershop right across the street on Pennsylvania. . . . I think he was 16.

He was caught on the wrong side of Pennsylvania Avenue, the demarcation line in long-running guerrilla warfare between those who live in the Linden housing project and those who live "on the other side."

NEREIDA TORRES   I had a boyfriend that recently died. He got killed right there across the street at a party over an argument and they decided, well, if they couldn't get him to fight . . . He wasn't a punk. Why you gone fight over an argument, something stupid? So they just decided just to come up and kill him. . . . They shot him in the neck.

NORVEN CHARLES   A couple of months ago there was a drive-by shooting and one of my friends died.

KAREEM SMITH   I already got shot. . . . I ran into this kid that I had a little problem with.

Q.   Larry, how many do you know who have been shot?

LARRY BUGETT   A lot. That's all I can say is a lot of people I know.

Q.   More than five?

LARRY   More than 20. People that's 18 and under. Cause we used to be in a posse called V.I.P.: Vanderveer International Posse.

Q.   Over what period of time were these people shot?

LARRY   Like two years, three years. Some is dead. Some crippled. Some of them is still selling. Some of them is in jail now.

The students, boys and girls, say they have to walk the streets ever mindful that there are certain blocks that are unsafe for them because of ongoing gang rivalries and "beef" that someone may have with them personally.

Q.   How do you know what the rules are, that you can walk on one side of a street and not the other side?

EUGENE ROBICHAUX   Examples. They make examples of people. They catch somebody and kill 'em and then you know: don't be over on this side.

Q. Are you afraid that you could be the next victim?

MARIANA   I'm afraid. Right now it's a dispute between these two guys, a
rivalry over two gangs. My brother said he was sitting in a barbershop
and they came in there and shot through the window. . . . It gets to
the point where I don't walk up that block no more because I heard
the guys that cut hair there, they've got to wear bulletproof vests.

SHAWN   I got one.

Q. Where did you get a bulletproof vest?

SHAWN   My uncle.

*Kareem said that he also has a bulletproof vest that he bought for "a buck fifty"—
that is, $150—after telling his mother he needed the money for new sneakers.*

KAREEM   I wear it on Fridays and Saturdays. . . . Sometimes I wear it
when I'm going off my block, out my projects. Like if I'm going to
Bed-Stuy to see this other chick, I wear my vest.

Q. Isn't that an awful way to have to live, to have to wear a bulletproof
vest when you leave home for parties or dates?

KAREEM   No, if you want to be safe.

Q. Why don't you carry a gun?

KAREEM   Cause you'll get arrested for carrying a gun, not for wearing a
bulletproof vest.

Q. What about a knife?

KAREEM   I don't carry no knife. What am I going to do: stab the bullet?

*But there is a more deeply-rooted anger that seems to lead to an ever escalating level
of violence.*

Q. Why are people so angry, angry enough to kill?

SHAWN   The main reason is somebody in their family probably got shot or
got murdered, and they just go out and have revenge on everybody
they don't like.

RETISHA   I think it's peer pressure. It's a lot of guys that hang around
other people just to be in the crowd. . . . Some people just got guns to
have them and then a lot of them use them. Then the ones that do use
them don't know how to use them. That's how a lot of innocent by-
standers get killed, too.

*Everyone wants some kind of "rep" or reputation—and one way to earn one for
being tough is to carry a gun, the teen-agers said. No one wants to be seen as a
"herb" or wimp.*

SEAN   If a guy steps on your foot, it's one of your peers says, 'Oh, you gone let that happen to you? He stepped on your foot.' You know, you have the right mind that's like, 'I'm gone ignore that.' But your friend says, 'You ain't gone do nothing about that?' That puts you to the limit. You be like 'Ahh, what I'm gone do?' It gets you thinking and you say something: 'Yo, what the hell are you doing?' or something like that. You start, you know, to break.

NATHANIEL EDWARDS   Say I was walking in the hallway and somebody bumped me and they meant to bump me. And now, me, I'm the herb. I will turn and I will walk away from them. Next day, he gone bump me again. Now it's a Friday, right? And he comes and bump me and he says, 'Yo, what's up, man? If you keep walking away, we'll keep bothering you.' . . . You can fight right there, but a gun gone come in sooner or later.

Disputes can start over what the teenagers acknowledge to be "the stupidest things." Kareem Smith said he almost fought a friend who tried to grab his cheeseburger.

Some Thomas Jefferson students cope with the violence around them by staying indoors as much as possible, whether home or school. Others say they try to suppress their feelings altogether. Nathaniel Edwards has a different way.

NATHANIEL   It hurts me, but I hardly cry because I take everything as a joke. That's how I protect myself. I can't be taking nothing too seriously because that's when you sit down and sob and you mope. That's what makes you commit suicide, too, you know? So I just make jokes.

Reprinted by permission from *The New York Times*, March 7, 1992.

High-school student Jennifer Swartout felt that she had to help get the AIDS message to her classmates.

■ DEATH OF INNOCENCE ■

FRANK BRUNI

Listening to the wild stories her classmates brought back from the beaches of spring break last year, Jennifer Swartout feared some of them were true.

She wasn't jealous.

She was panicky.

The boys who counted their sexual conquests, the girls who gulped birth control pills, didn't they know?

Swartout did.

She had watched AIDS lay waste to her favorite uncle, her godfather, left emaciated and addlebrained by the disease at age 35.

He died last September.

In November, Swartout made an appointment with her school principal, Rodney Hosman, at Livonia Churchill High.

"This is going to sound strange," she told him. "But please, just listen."

She told Hosman that this year, the week before spring break, there should be a senior class assembly about AIDS.

It should be blunt and forceful, because she didn't want any of her friends ever to get the gruesome disease. They should learn a little fear, a lot of caution.

Swartout offered to coordinate the project. That night, she phoned the president of the school's Parent, Teacher, and Student Association, a woman she had never met.

In subsequent days, she talked to health teachers. She told them that whatever AIDS education she had gotten in the 10th grade wasn't gripping enough—she couldn't even remember it. How could the assembly go further?

She got answers and help. Next month, just before school lets out for a week's recess, most of the 388 seniors will gather in the auditorium, listen to guest speakers infected with the virus that causes AIDS, and be told how to save themselves.

They also will hear Swartout's story. The 17-year-old girl will stand up before her classmates and talk about losing her uncle to AIDS, an experience she felt compelled to keep secret while it was happening because some people view the disease as a shameful curse.

"I don't know—maybe 98 percent of the seniors won't listen," Swartout said. "But that's OK. When you've seen the kind of pain I've seen, you just feel that if you can save one person or make a few people think, 'I better be careful,' that's great."

Before the assembly, a note will go to the parents of every senior, letting them know their children can be excused, said Hosman. He said some parents don't want their kids hearing candid talk about AIDS and sexual behavior.

But Hosman believes the assembly is important. He said that while most teenagers have a good scientific grasp of what AIDS is, they don't feel its threat or impact in any direct way.

For Swartout, it was particularly important for teenagers to know. They seemed oblivious to AIDS.

"They hear about it so much it becomes part of the background noise," she said. "It blends in with all the other crises in the world.

"But if you've watched a person die this way, it just becomes so urgent that people understand how serious it is."

Reprinted by permission of the Knight Ridder News Service, March 8, 1992.

Reflections

1. What challenges must you meet in order to effectively re-create each of the preceding excerpts?

2. How does the tone of each passage reflect the times it describes?

3. What can an interpreter bring to these passages that simply replaying a videotape cannot bring? How might you combine videotape segments with your performance to heighten the impact of the speeches?

Performer's Journal

Choose an individual, living or dead, whose attitudes, thoughts, and personality you would enjoy sharing with the rest of the class. In your journal, write how you would present that person through the performance of documentary materials reflecting that character's life experiences and ideals.

Make certain that the person you choose is prominent enough so that there is a fairly wide range of documentary material—published material by and/or about that person—from which to draw for purposes of interpretation. Just a few of the individuals whom you might consider for performance are: Frederick Douglass, Winston Churchill, Anne Frank, Malcolm X, Helen Gurley Brown, Oliver North, Terry Anderson, or current media celebrities.

CHAPTER ELEVEN

Ensemble Approaches to Interpretation

Ensemble interpretation may be defined as group interpretation. When two or more performers set out to bring a literary selection alive, what advantages would the group have over an individual interpretation? Would you anticipate any limitations in interpreting as a group? To prepare you for working as a group, try the following exercises.

GETTING INVOLVED
On the Move in Groups

Divide into groups of six to eight members and clear all obstacles from the center of the classroom. In turn, each performing unit will stand in a group against one wall and, as a unit, move to the opposite side of the room. The object is to move as if all the group's members were part of a single organism. As you do so, you must adhere to the following three conditions:

Condition 1: The first time your group crosses the room, it should move to a slow, regular beat provided by your instructor.

Condition 2: When your group recrosses the room, move to the fairly rapid beat provided by your instructor.

Condition 3: In the final trip across the room, assume a crouched position and move cautiously to an irregular beat provided by your instructor.

Listen carefully to the rhythm your instructor beats. You must all freeze when the beat stops and start as a unit when it continues. Work interdependently to sustain an element of suspense.

Reflections

1. What challenges did you experience personally in this series of exercises?

2. What challenges did you experience as a group member?

Now that you have started thinking and working as part of a performing team, try the following challenge.

GETTING INVOLVED
Ensemble Machines

Working in small groups of five or six members, choose one of the following objects or organisms to create together. Work as a unit, but each group member must play a unique part in your group's creation. You may use both voice and movement to help you suggest to the audience your group creation of one of the items listed:

a washing machine

a people-eating machine

a computer

an air hammer

a typewriter

a telephone

a car

a wheel

Reflections

1. How were you able to coordinate your efforts to create a machine?

2. What were the barriers that had to be overcome?

In each of the preceding exercises you operated as part of an *ensemble*—a group of individuals who work together to produce an effect or achieve a mutual goal. An ensemble of interpreters is, in fact, a literary performing team. Their team goal is to re-create literature. In doing so, the group must share or effectively communicate to audiences all the experiences that exist in selected pieces of literature.

Ensemble performers are expected to utilize the skills they acquired as solo readers and to apply them to the needs of the group. In ensemble interpretation, the emphasis must be on the *interdependence* of the group members rather than on the independence of any individual interpreter. It is the performing effects that the group is able to create—not an individual's expertise—that must be the focus of ensemble interpretation.

The Nature of Ensemble Reading

Many of the aesthetic principles and techniques that characterize the art of solo interpretation also characterize the art of ensemble reading. For example, both forms of interpretation use *presentational staging approaches*; that is, in neither form is there the attempt to create the illusion of reality. In fact, a presentational style of staging serves to distinguish the ensemble interpreter from the actor. The goal of the interpreter, unlike the goal of the actor, is to present or to suggest literary experience to an audience. It is not to represent that experience for the audience, as the actor is charged to do. Thus, the techniques and the devices of both ensemble and solo interpretation remind the audience that art, rather than life, is being portrayed on the stage; in both forms of interpretation the emphasis is placed on suggestion—not explicitness.

The interpreter's task, whether he or she works alone or in an ensemble, is to help make the literature live for the audience. This is not accomplished by acting out an event or experience on stage, in an atmosphere created by lifelike sets and elaborate costumes. Whether working singly or in an ensemble, interpreters use the body and the voice to make literature real for an audience. And, as is true for an interpreter working alone, ensemble interpretation requires both reading and performing abilities and careful analysis of a selection for its effect.

Members of your performing ensemble should agree on the dominant ideas, moods, and attitudes of the literature to be presented. Agree on specifics, such as the ways that timing, volume, and pitch may be used to support the meaning of the literature. Discuss and agree on ways that visible action will be used to reinforce the content of the literature. Finally, reach a consensus regarding the effect the ensemble wants its presentation to have on the audience. You must satisfy these conditions as a group in order to work together well to suggest the sensory, emotional, and cognitive experiences in the chosen selection or selections.

Performers who belong to an ensemble may be compared to musicians who belong to orchestras. A musician's responsibility broadens when he or she joins an orchestra. The same is true for the performers who join an ensemble. No longer are the performers responsible only for themselves; rather, they work together with and for their group. Orchestra members learn to blend their instruments to create a unified sound. Performers must learn to blend their performing efforts as well. Work together with group members to do the following exercises.

GETTING INVOLVED
Word Combos

Working in small groups, each unit should select one of the following words to express. Voice and choreographed movement are your group's communication instruments.

jealousy

gossip

war

strength

weakness

sympathy

Combine your efforts with other group members' so the experiences represented in the chosen word are fully realized through your performance. Your group may be able to create your presentation by speaking the word only once, or you may decide to repeat the word many times in different ways to bring it alive for your audience.

Reflections

1. How did your group work to physicalize and vocalize your word image?

2. How does this exercise help you realize your role as a member of a performing ensemble?

Type of Focus

The ensemble group also needs to decide upon the kind of eye interaction in performance that the script's readers will have with each other and with the audience. Interactional choices include total out-front focus, total onstage focus, and a mixture of out-front and onstage focus.

The **out-front focus**, also known as *indirect interaction*, is the type of focus usually employed by solo interpreters when they read from works involving numerous characters. This same convention is applicable to ensemble performance. An out-front focus simply requires that each of the reader/characters speak to or address the other reader/characters as if they were situated out front, or in the audience, rather than on the stage. Using this type of focus technique, reader/characters establish an indirect interactional contact with each other. Off-stage or out-front focus does not mean the reader/characters establish eye contact with the members of the audience, however. It indicates only that the reader/characters are placing the imagined scene and the imagined characters of that scene in the realm of the audience. On the other hand, the reader who functions as narrator may look directly into the eyes of the audience members at certain points in the performance.

Onstage focus requires that the reader/characters relate to each other on the stage. This type of focus makes the interactions or conversations among the reader/characters more natural and direct.

A mixture of onstage and out-front focus can be used in works that seem to call for a combination of approaches. A change of focus can be used to achieve variety in staging techniques and to heighten various effects of the literature. For example, some scenes—especially those containing descriptions of the environment or descriptions of the characters' inner thoughts—work best with an out-front focus. With this technique the scene is actually directed physically closer to the audience members reaching out to draw them into the literature. Some scenes, however, may be more effective if performed with an onstage focus. This focus allows the audience members to appreciate the script's forward movements, since they can both see and hear the relations and interactions among the reader/characters.

Accordingly, the members of a performing ensemble should freely vary and mix the types of focus they use. Keep in mind that directorial decisions regarding focus should be made only after a careful and thorough textual analysis. Consider the following analogy.

Imagine that your interpretative ensemble is a giant pair of eyes. These eyes must wear eyeglasses to perfect their vision. The prescription for the eyeglass lenses changes according to the observational situation the eyes are placed in. Thus, sometimes the eyes need to wear lenses designed for nearsighted people, so the scene they are to observe receives onstage focus. When the eyes need lenses designed for farsighted people, the scene they are to observe is placed in the midst of the audience. In some situations, however, the eyes need to wear bifocals—lenses that allow a rapid switch from a nearsighted correction to a farsighted correction; that is, the ensemble of readers moves from an onstage focus to an out-front or indirect focus. The type of lens (focus) prescribed by the doctor (director) for the eyes (ensemble of readers) depends on the situation (the literature) the eyes are observing (staging). Check your understanding of the concept of focus with this exercise.

GETTING INVOLVED
Bifocus

Read the following selection carefully. How does this excerpt lend itself to a mixed focus or bifocus approach? Determine where you would focus in each segment of the selection.

■ THE GOOD WOMAN OF SETZUAN ■
BERTOLT BRECHT

WONG   I sell water here in the city of Setzuan. It isn't easy. When water is scarce, I have long distances to go in search of it, and when it is plentiful, I have no income. But in our part of the world there is nothing unusual about poverty. Many people think only the gods can save the situation. And I hear from a cattle merchant—who travels a lot—that some of the highest gods are on their way here at this very moment. Informed sources have it that heaven is quite disturbed at all the complaining. I've been coming out here to the city gates for three days now to bid these gods welcome. I want to be the first to greet them. What about those fellows over there? No, no they *work*. And that one there has ink on his fingers, he's no god, he must be a clerk from the cement factory. *Those* two are another story. They look as though they'd like to beat you. But gods don't need to beat you, do they? (THREE GODS *appear*.) What about those three? Old-fashioned clothes—dust on their feet—they must be gods! (*He throws himself at their feet*.) Do with me what you will, illustrious ones!

FIRST GOD   (*with an ear trumpet*) Ah! (*He is pleased*.) So we were expected?

WONG   (*giving them water*) Oh, yes. And I *knew* you'd come.

FIRST GOD   We need somewhere to stay the night. You know of a place?

WONG   The whole town is at your service, illustrious ones! What sort of a place would you like?
(*The* GODS *eye each other*.)

FIRST GOD   Just try the first house you come to, my son.

WONG   That would be Mr. Fo's place.

FIRST GOD   Mr. Fo.

WONG   One moment! (*He knocks at the first house.*)

VOICE FROM MR. FO'S   *No!*

(*WONG returns a little nervously.*)

WONG   It's too bad. Mr. Fo isn't in. And his servants don't dare do a thing without his consent. He'll have a fit when he finds out who they turned away, won't he?

FIRST GOD   (*smiling*) He will, won't he?

Reflections

1. At what points in the preceding selection would you employ an onstage focus? Where would you employ an out-front focus? Why?

2. Why does this work lend itself to a mixed-focus approach?

Action, Movement, and Physical Arrangement

In general, movement or overt action in ensemble interpretation is kept to a minimum. This is not to say that the readers do not use their bodies to help them communicate—of course they do—but the movement is selective rather than literal. Avoid movement for the sake of movement. Ensemble interpreters should deliberate before deciding upon the appropriate gestures and movements. They should select only those physical actions that will help to illustrate emotions and intellectual meanings inherent in their script. Besides understanding the ways that muscle tonicity and facial expressions aid in communication as a member of an ensemble, you need to appreciate the ways that combinations involving body position, levels, and stage areas can be combined to help display the literature.

Body position is an important source of emphasis in performance. Facing audiences signifies one thing, turning your back to them indicates something else. Ensemble readers often use these two basic body positions to represent their entrances and exits. Rather than actually turning their backs to their audience, the readers sometimes indicate their exit simply by lowering their heads. Using another technique, readers may freeze their positions to indicate that they have temporarily withdrawn from the developments on the stage.

Varying the head levels or heights of the readers is a means to provide emphasis and contrast in a performance. As an interpreter, you may sit, stand, kneel, or lie on the floor or on artificial levels such as chairs or stools. Arranging characters on levels helps the audience in its perceptions of the literary text.

GETTING INVOLVED
The Chair

Explore all the different parts of this exercise.

A. On your own, try to determine all the different body positions you can assume when working with a single, sturdy chair whose four feet remain on the floor at all times. You may want to photograph the various positions for this and the following exercises.

B. Now, with a partner explore all the different ways the two of you can vary your body positions and/or levels using the same chair. Again, the four feet of the chair must remain firmly planted on the floor at all times. Perform and photograph (optional) this as you performed the previous part of this exercise.

C. Finally, explore the different group pictorial arrangements that can be created with two or three chairs and six to eight people. Hint: Do not hesitate to use more than the central portion of the performing area. Again, you may wish to photograph the different arrangements for further study.

Reflections

1. Did you sit on the chair? stand on it? lean against it? sit with your back against it? lie under it? crouch on it? hide behind it? straddle it?

2. What messages were sent by each of the different positions you assumed? How did the addition of one other person affect the possibilities? How did the addition of the group affect the possibilities?

3. How could these different positions or levels have been used to clarify the actions, character attitudes, or general meaning of selected scripts?

4. If you chose to take photographs, did the resulting pictures send the message you thought you were sending? Do the photographs give you ideas for additional ways to structure the physical arrangements for ensemble performance? How?

Although ensemble interpreters do not engage in a great deal of overt movement in performance, the number of group arrangements that can be created to illustrate and refine the script is almost infinite. Stools, orange crates, barrels, and other simple platform devices provide instant level variety.

How would the addition of facial expressions and gestures alter the possibilities available to your group? Find out by exploring the next exercise.

GETTING INVOLVED
Refining Group Pictures

Repeat each section of the preceding chair exercise. This time, add facial expressions and body gestures to the pictures created by your various arrangements. Again, you may want to photograph your efforts for future examination.

Reflections

1. How do the pictures change in meaning when physical gestures and facial expressions are added to them?

2. How would you title the pictures resulting from your group's arrangements? Would any depict an emotion such as anger? friendship? jealousy? jubilance?

Adding appropriate facial expressions and gestures to group members helps to define or suggest the meaning of the created picture. Rather than evolving moods spontaneously or randomly, as in the previous two exercises, the performing group will look to the literature to precipitate the mood intensities and psychological relations they seek to re-create.

Multimedia Devices

Ensemble interpreters sometimes employ multimedia devices to help them share meaning with their audience. Film, slides, recordings, and live music may be incorporated into their performances. Such embellishments, however, should never be employed as gimmicks. Use them only when they will enhance the literary experience.

A simple, but effective, technique is to use an overhead projector, 8½-by-11-inch transparencies, and magic markers. Create some abstract images on the transparencies and project them on the wall. Experiment with people moving around and through the image. Standard black-and-white copiers make transparencies of photographs and drawings that can be used by performers. Color copiers also provide transparencies of paintings and photographs.

Thirty-five-millimeter slides can be used when it is possible to darken the room. Or, make a photograph of an object that can become the backdrop for your presentation. Pictures from books (prepared as overhead transparencies) can prove to be effective additions, as well. For example, a picture of the writer could serve as part of the environment for a reading of some of his or her works. Photographs of the performers taken in other locations may also be used to help emphasize the message in the literature.

In addition, audio recordings can set the mood for a reading. Use sound to support your presentation by suggesting the appropriate environment: a noisy crowd, applause, wind in the trees, or even the voice of the writer.

Selective use of videotape enhances performances as well. Select video excerpts that make a point early. Then turn them off or pause them in freeze frame. This allows the audience to focus clearly on the literature and the message the interpreters are presenting. Some performers have also experimented with large-screen projections as a part of an ensemble performance.

Of course, the risks with technology are that it can break down or become too obtrusive and obscure the actual performance. Employing the technology requires both time and effort; gathering and effectively integrating such materials into a presentation is challenging. If time and technical expertise among group members allow it, experiment with multimedia devices. Otherwise, focus on the presentation itself. Media could be incorporated later in the presentation development process, if desired.

Choral Speaking and Chamber Theatre

Turn your attention now to two basic styles of ensemble performance: **choral speaking** and **chamber theatre**. Each style provides the group reader with a unique performing experience. Both styles use the techniques discussed earlier in this chapter.

Ensemble Performance of Poetry: Choral Speaking

Choral speaking is group interpretation of poetry. In choral speaking, individuals in the ensemble understand and express, sometimes collectively, the ideas, emotions, and moods inherent in their poetic selection.

Choral speakers help to illustrate a poem by dividing the poetic material into various voices or phrases. This division, if applied to appropriate literary material, usually works to illuminate the work. When choosing literature for choral interpretation, the interpreters should adhere to the following guidelines.

1. The material should allow for the possibility of organized mass effects.

2. The material should be enhanced by the addition of an ensemble.

Once these two conditions are met, the main tasks of the ensemble are to decide how the lines of the poem can best be divided and assigned for reading. There are a number of traditional choral-speaking structures to guide you as you make these decisions. One approach is to divide the ensemble group into solo speaker(s) and a chorus. This type of structure lends itself to poems that include a refrain or repetitive passage. The goal of the chorus when reading a refrain is to reinforce the moods that exist in the poem. Try this exercise to check your understanding.

GETTING INVOLVED
Refrain Work

Read the following ballad.

■ THERE WAS A FROG ■
ANONYMOUS

There was a frog lived in a well,
Whipsee diddle-dee dandy dee;
There was a frog lived in a well,
And a merry mouse in a mill,
With a harum, scarum, diddle dum darum,
Whipsee diddle-dee dandy dee.

This frog he would a-wooing ride,
Whipsee diddle-dee dandy dee;
This frog he would a-wooing ride,
And on a snail he got astride,
With a harum, scarum, diddle dum darum,
Whipsee diddle-dee dandy dee.

He rode till he came to my Lady Mouse Hall,
Whipsee diddle-dee dandy dee;
He rode till he came to my Lady Mouse Hall,
And there he did both knock and call,
With a harum, scarum, diddle dum darum,
Whipsee diddle-dee dandy dee.

''Miss Mouse, Miss Mouse, I'm come to thee,''
Whipsee diddle-dee dandy dee;
''Miss Mouse, Miss Mouse, I'm come to thee,
To see if thou canst fancy me,''
With a harum, scarum, diddle dum darum,
Whipsee diddle-dee dandy dee.

''Oh answer I will give you none,''
Whipsee diddle-dee dandy dee;
''Oh answer I will give you none
Until my Uncle Rat comes home,''
With a harum, scarum, diddle dum darum,
Whipsee diddle-dee dandy dee.

And when her Uncle Rat came home,
Whipsee diddle-dee dandy dee;
And when her Uncle Rat came home,
''Who's been here since I've been gone?''
With a harum, scarum, diddle dum darum,
Whipsee diddle-dee dandy dee.

''There's been a worthy gentleman,''
Whipsee diddle-dee dandy dee;
''There's been a worthy gentleman,
That's been here since you've been gone.''
With a harum, scarum, diddle dum darum,
Whipsee diddle-dee dandy dee.

The frog he came whistling through the brook,
Whipsee diddle-dee dandy dee;
The frog he came whistling through the brook,
And there he met with a dainty duck.
With a harum, scarum, diddle dum darum,
Whipsee diddle-dee dandy dee.

The duck she swallowed him up with a quack,
Whipsee diddle-dee dandy dee;
The duck she swallowed him up with a quack,
So there's an end of my history book.
With a harum, scarum, diddle dum darum,
Whipsee diddle-dee dandy dee.

Reflections

1. How would you divide the poem for the group and the individual reader?

2. What mood or moods will you suggest as you interpret each refrain?

3. How can you use time and emphasis to help establish the tone and share the ideas?

The ensemble group reading "There Was a Frog" may be divided into two parts, with the speaker reading the lines and the group reading the refrain. This arrangement is commonly employed in religious services, in poems that contain questions or answers, or when a balance between two groups of voices is desired. This vocal balance may be attained by contrasting male and female voices, by contrasting pitch levels, or by contrasting vocal levels. You can see that the choral speaking ensemble is very much like a singing ensemble or chorus. In fact, in early rehearsals it may be prudent to have a member of the group actually "conduct" the reading as a choral conductor would direct a musical performance. As your group becomes more proficient with the material, the conductor will no longer be necessary. Practice more choral reading using the following poem.

GETTING INVOLVED
Two-Part Chorus Ensemble

Here is another ballad that works well when the ensemble group is divided into two parts. Rehearse and perform it with your group.

■ LORD RANDALL ■

ANONYMOUS

O, where have you been, Lord Randall, my son?
O, where have you been, my handsome young man?
I have been to the wild wood, mother make my bed soon,
For I'm weary with hunting, and fain would lie doon.

Where got ye your dinner, Lord Randall, my son,
Where got ye your dinner, my handsome young man?
I dined with my true love; mother make my bed soon,
For I'm weary with hunting and fain would lie doon.
What got you to your dinner, Lord Randall, my son?
What got you to your dinner, my handsome young man?
I got eels boiled in brew; mother make my bed soon,
For I'm weary with hunting, and fain would lie doon.
What became of your bloodhounds, Lord Randall, my son?
What became of your bloodhounds, my handsome young man?
They swelled and they died; mother make my bed soon,
For I'm weary with hunting, and fain would lie doon.
O, I fear you are poisoned, Lord Randall, my son!
O, I fear you are poisoned, my handsome young man!
O, yes, I am poisoned, mother make my bed soon,
For I'm sick at the heart a-n-d- f-a-i-n w-o-u—

Reflections

1. What effect is achieved by a two-part division?

2. How does this structure help to communicate the literature? Did you decide to divide the voices for high and low pitches?

Sometimes it enhances the literature if the choral group is divided into three or more parts. This type of division allows for finer discriminations in pitch and quality. Work as a group or as an entire class to bring the following poem to life.

GETTING INVOLVED
The Trio

Your group will need a conductor to help you work three groups into this poem. This is a much more advanced experience that will require the concentration of everyone in the group.

■ TRIO ■

TOBIE LURIE

```
1  This is a poem for three voices
2                        This is a poem
3

1  that asks each voice          to listen
2              for three voices
3

1                              to create silence
2            that asks each voice
3  This is a poem

1
2            to listen
3  for three voices      that asks each voice

1  and to feel.
2              to create silence
3        to listen

1  That shows by doing
2                        and to feel.
3              to create silence

1  that poems        can be read
2        That shows        by doing
3

1  together        to enhance meaning.
2
3        and to feel.            That shows

1                              This is a poem
2  that poems        can be read together
3            by doing
```

1   that become three poems
2 to enhance meaning.
3   that poems

1   when given to
2   This is a poem
3 can be read   together

1 three voices
2   that becomes three poems
3   to enhance meaning.

1 each voice bringing   its quality
2
3   this is   a poem

1 into the whole   and adding
2   when given   to three voices
3

1   to poetry
2   each voice
3 that becomes   three poems

1   the dimension
2   bringing its
3 when given to three voices

1   of dialogue.
2 quality   into the whole
3   each voice

1   This is a poem   that says
2   and adding
3 bringing its quality

1   we
2 to poetry   the dimension   of dialogue.
3   into the whole

1 should come together
2
3   and adding to poetry

1   celebrate together
2 This is a poem
3   the dimension

1   create together
2   that says
3 of dialogue   This is a poem

1   and understand
2 we should come together
3   that says

1 together.
2   celebrate together
3   we should come together

1   This is a poem
2 create together
3   celebrate together

1   a simple poem
2 and understand together.
3   create together

1   which I hope
2 This is a poem
3   and understand together.

1   succeeds in expressing
2 a simple poem
3   This is a poem

1   the idea
2 which I hope   succeeds in expressing
3   a simple poem

1	that the human voice is an instrument
2 the idea	
3	which I hope

1	
2 that the human voice	
3	succeeds in expressing the idea

1 of infinite possibilities.	
2	is an instrument
3	that the human voice

1	is an instrument of infinite possibilities
2 of infinite possibilities.	is an instrument of infinite possibilities
3	is an instrument of infinite possibilities

Reflections

1. How does dividing the poem into three sections help to communicate its meaning?

2. What special skills does the interpreter need to develop in order to function as an effective member of the ''Trio'' ensemble?

3. How would you stage this reading? Where would you position the three groups?

Of course, choral speaking teams could be divided into four or even more groups to accommodate other pieces of literature. The groups could position themselves in the four corners of the room or in an area that includes multilevels, such as balconies or stairs. In such instances, the choral speaking group members could place themselves in a wide variety of areas for the presentation. Keep in mind, however, that the divisions and locations of the readers must spring from the literature. They should not be pasted in place arbitrarily.

Often a poem calls for a **sequential speaking structure**. This type of structure allows an individual from the ensemble to interpret a single line or a stanza. As you might imagine, it is a difficult structure to utilize effectively, for the individuals of the performing team must be sure when delivering their lines that they do not break the continuity or destroy the flow of the work. Try sequential speaking with some classmates in the exercise that follows.

GETTING INVOLVED
Sequential Work

A. Divide the class into groups of seven or eight members. In consecutive order, each member will select a single syllable from the following sentence:

I am part of an ensemble.

Each person will speak aloud the syllable he or she is assigned as it occurs in the sentence. Try to express clearly the meaning of the sentence as your group maintains vocal continuity. As much as possible, make the sentence sound as if it is being spoken by one person.

I

am

part

of

an

en-

sem-

ble.

B. Now, prepare as a group to use the sequential approach to read aloud the following poem, actually a verse from the Bible. That is, divide the words and syllables and assign them to each group member, as was done in the first part of this exercise. Note that each of the lines in the poem carries a specific image that relates to the main idea of the poem.

■ ECCLESIASTES ■
3:1

To everything there is a season, and a time to every
    purpose under the heaven
A time to be born, and a time to die;
A time to plant, and a time to pluck that which is planted;
A time to kill, and a time to heal;
A time to break down and a time to build up;

A time to weep, and a time to laugh;
A time to mourn, and a time to dance;
A time to cast away stones, and a time to gather stones
    together;
A time to embrace, and a time to refrain from embracing;
A time to get, and a time to lose;
A time to keep, and a time to cast away;
A time to rend, and a time to sew;
A time to keep silence, and a time to speak;
A time to love, and a time to hate;
A time of peace, and a time of war;
To everything there is a season, and a time to every purpose
    under the heaven.

Reflections

1. What forms of behavior did you have to use in order to give the impression that a single individual was speaking?

2. What challenges did these exercises present to you as an interpreter?

3. How does a sequential approach support the tone and meaning of the poem?

4. What gestures could a group use to enhance the poetic statements?

An entire poem may also be spoken in unison. When adopting this structure, the ensemble again aims for the effect of a single voice. Thoughts and feelings need to be perfectly blended as timing, tone, and volume are carefully controlled. Work as a group to realize the dominant mood and ideas within the selection. The Japanese haiku, or short lyric poem, lends itself to this approach.

GETTING INVOLVED
Unison Work

Divide the class into two groups. Each group should select one of the following two short poems to perform using a unison approach.

■ UNTITLED HAIKU ■

ISSA

The old, plump bullfrog
held his ground and stared at me—
what a sour face!

■ BUFFALO DUSK ■

CARL SANDBURG

The buffaloes are gone.
And those who say the buffaloes are gone.
Those who saw the buffaloes by thousands and how
    they pawed the prairie sod into dust with their
    hoofs, their great heads down, pawing on in a
    great pageant of dusk,
Those who saw the buffaloes are gone,
And the buffaloes are gone.

Reflections

1. What mood did your group work to create?

2. How were timing, phrasing, stress, and movement coordinated?

   You should recognize that the five preceding structures —solo/chorus,
two-part chorus, trio, sequential, and unison—do not tell the whole story of
choral speaking. As an ensemble performer, experiment with these structures, using them in various combinations or patterns. Create a new speaking structure for use by your own ensemble to match and enhance a literary
selection. Check your understanding of choral speaking by participating in
the following exercise.

GETTING INVOLVED
A Choral Ensemble

Divide the class into five or six groups and choose one of the following poems to perform. Each group is to adapt its selection for choral presentation. You should also be familiar with the remaining literature selections so you can analyze strengths and weaknesses of the other groups' presentations.

■ WHAT'S THAT SMELL IN THE ■ KITCHEN?

MARGE PIERCY

All over America women are burning dinners.
It's lambchops in Peoria; it's haddock
in Providence; it's steak in Chicago;
tofu delight in Big Sur; red
rice and beans in Dallas.
All over America women are burning
food they're supposed to bring with calico
smile on platters glittering like wax.
Anger sputters in her brainpan, confined
but spewing out missiles of hot fat.
Carbonized despair presses like a clinker
from a barbecue against the back of her eyes.
If she wants to grill anything, it's
her husband spitted over a slow fire.
If she wants to serve him anything
it's a dead rat with a bomb in its belly
ticking like the heart of an insomniac.
Her life is cooked and digested,
nothing but leftovers in Tupperware.
Look, she says, once I was roast duck
on your platter with parsley but now I am Spam.
Burning dinner is not incompetence but war.

■ LOVE YOUR ENEMY ■

YUSEF IMAN

Brought here in slave ships and pitched overboard
Love your enemy
Language taken away, culture taken away
Love your enemy
Work from sun up to sun down
Love your enemy
Last hired, first fired
Love your enemy
Rape your mother
Love your enemy
Lynch your father
Love your enemy
Bomb your churches
Love your enemy
Forced to fight his wars
Love your enemy
Pay the highest rent
Love your enemy
Sell you rotten food
Love your enemy
Dilapidated schools
Love your enemy
Puts you in jail
Love your enemy
Bitten by dogs
Love your enemy
Water hose you down
Love your enemy
Love,
Love,
Love,
Love,
Love, for everyone else,
    but when will we love ourselves?

◼ THE WALRUS AND ◼
THE CARPENTER
LEWIS CARROLL

The sun was shining on the sea,
Shining with all his might;
He did his very best to make
The billows smooth and bright—
And this was odd, because it was
The middle of the night.

The moon was shining sulkily,
Because she thought the sun
Had got no business to be there
After the day was done—
"It's very rude of him," she said,
"To come and spoil the fun!"

The sea was wet as wet could be,
The sands were dry as dry.
You could not see a cloud, because
No cloud was in the sky:
No birds were flying overhead—
There were no birds to fly.

The Walrus and the Carpenter
Were walking close at hand:
They wept like anything to see
Such quantities of sand:
"If this were only cleared away,"
They said, "It would be grand!"

"If seven maids with seven mops
Swept it for half a year,
Do you suppose," the Walrus said,
"That they could get it clear?"
"I doubt it," said the Carpenter,
And shed a bitter tear.

"Oysters, come and walk with us!"
The Walrus did beseech.
"A pleasant walk, a pleasant talk,
Along the briny beach:
We cannot do with more than four,
To give a hand to each."

The eldest Oyster looked at him,
But never a word he said:
The eldest Oyster winked his eye,
And shook his heavy head—
Meaning to say he did not choose
To leave the oyster-bed.

■ DEATH SNIPS PROUD MEN ■

CARL SANDBURG

Death is stronger than all the governments because the
    governments are men, and men die, and then death laughs:
    "Now you see 'em, now you don't."

Death is stronger than all proud men and so death snips
    proud men on the nose, throws a pair of dice and says:
    "Read 'em and weep."

Death sends a radiogram every day: "When I want you I'll
    drop in"—and then one day he comes with a master-
    key and lets himself in and says: "We'll go now."

Death is a nurse mother with big arms: " 'Twon't hurt you
    at all; it's your time now; you just need a long sleep,
    child; what have you had anyhow better than sleep?"

■ I Hear America Singing ■

WALT WHITMAN

I hear America singing the varied carols I hear;
Those of mechanics—each one singing his, as it should be,
    blithe and strong;
The carpenter singing his as he measures his plane or beam,
The mason singing his, as he makes ready for work, or
    leaves off work;
The boatman singing what belongs to him in his boat—
The deck-hand singing on the steam-boat deck,
The shoemaker singing as he sits at his bench,
The hatter singing as he stands;
The wood-cutter's song—
The ploughboy's on his way in the morning or at noon
    intermission, or at sundown;
The delicious singing of the mother—or the young wife at
    work—or the girl sewing or washing—
Each singing what belongs to her, and to none else;
The day what belongs to the day—at night, the party of
    young fellows, robust, friendly,
Singing with open mouths, their strong melodious songs.

■ Cool Tombs ■

CARL SANDBURG

When Abraham Lincoln was shoveled into the tombs, he forgot
    the copperheads and the assassin . . . in the dust, in the
    cool tombs.

And Ulysses Grant lost all thought of con men and Wall Street;
    cash and collateral turned ashes . . . in the dust, in the
    cool tombs.

Pocahontas' body, lovely as a poplar, sweet as a red haw in
    November or a pawpaw in May, did she wonder? does
    she remember? . . . in the dust, in the cool tombs?

Take any streetful of people buying clothes and groceries,
cheering a hero or throwing confetti and blowing tin
horns . . . tell me if the lovers are losers . . . tell me
if any get more than the lovers . . . in the dust . . . in
the cool tombs.

Reflections

1. What was there about the selection that led your group to develop a specific speaking structure?

2. How did your group choose to use rhythm, volume, and pitch to support the meaning of the poem?

3. What visible action, if any, did your ensemble employ to enhance the performance?

4. How could you change your presentation to increase its effectiveness?

Concrete Poetry for Choral Speaking

Choral speaking techniques may also be used to aid in the recreation of a nontraditional kind of literature termed concrete poetry.

Concrete poems are visual structures that work to create a sensory experience in the perceiver. They are intended to affect the minds, eyes, ears, and bodies of their readers. Thus, concrete poems are not merely read, they are felt. In fact, they are not merely felt, they are played with.

Take some time to explore the concrete poems displayed here. In what ways could an ensemble group make the concepts inherent in the poems live for an audience? For which poems would movement be appropriate? How could eye and head movements be used to reflect poem content? For example, in one poem you might work with a group to "watch" a ping pong game. In another poem, you could use movement to illustrate the effects of wind on the performers. In another, your repetition of the word "silencio" or silence could suddenly cease—as it does in the poem.

Take some time and work with others to bring your ideas alive for an audience using both sound and movement as your tools. You can see that concrete poetry encourages you to play with or experiment with an image until you discover an original and exciting interpretation. Have fun!

```
ping   pong
       ping   pong   ping
       pong   ping   pong
                     ping    pong
```

—Eugen Gomringer

```
silencio   silencio   silencio
silencio   silencio   silencio
silencio              silencio
silencio   silencio   silencio
silencio   silencio   silencio
```

—Eugen Gomringer

```
        w       w
    d       i
  n     n       n
  i   d   i       d
w           w
```

—Eugen Gomringer

```
VVVVVVVVV
VVVVVVVVVE
VVVVVVVVEL
VVVVVVVELO
VVVVVVELOC
VVVVVELOCI
VVVVELOCID
VVVELOCIDA
VVELOCIDAD
VELOCIDADE
```

—Ronaldo Azeredo

Ensemble Interpretation of Narrative Prose: Chamber Theatre

A style of ensemble performance known as **chamber theatre** is group interpretation of narrative prose. The text of the narrative tale is maintained, but the scenes of the story often are located onstage, rather than out front. This adds the impact and immediacy of drama to the performance, while leaving the original narrative form intact. In chamber theatre, the narrator of the written story is the narrator of the staged version, as well. His or her point of view is manifested in the presentation onstage. The narrator thus assumes a major role in a chamber theatre production.

A chamber theatre performance style usually works best with stories in which the narrator functions as a liaison between the characters and their world. This performing style does not work as well in stories told mostly in scene—where there is little, if any, narration. In chamber theatre the narrator usually delivers his or her lines with an out-front focus. This kind of focus is also shared by the story's characters as they express their own unspoken thoughts or engage in *indirect discourse*.

A scene from the short story ''Louis,'' by Saki (the pen name of British-born writer H. H. Munro), one of four authors whose works are performed in QUARTET!™, a production of Chamber Repertory Theatre featuring Joseph Costa, Melanie Johnson, and Jerry Snee. Photo by Michael Romanos, courtesy of Chamber Theatre Productions Inc., Boston, Massachusetts.

The characters will probably shift to an onstage focus when interacting directly with each other. Thus, chamber theatre does more than simply dramatize a narrative text; rather, it preserves the epic mode of narrative writing and combines it with a theatre performance style. Consequently, in chamber theatre the narrator continues to serve descriptive and reflective functions, summarizing and clarifying events in the world of the literature.

In addition, chamber theatre actually provides the narrator with the opportunity to physicalize his or her relationship to the characters. For example, the narrator can work physically near a specific character—in effect, moving in for a close-up. Or the narrator can freely roam about the stage, stopping at a particular vantage point in order to identify with a number of characters. The narrator can operate objectively and can physically separate himself or herself from the scene of the action. In these ways the audience feels and understands the presence and the point of view of the narrator, so that his or her proper function is served.

The following excerpt from a chamber theatre adaptation of ''The Cat and the Mouse Together'' by the Brothers Grimm will colorfully illustrate these concepts.

■ THE CAT AND THE MOUSE ■ TOGETHER

ADAPTED BY TERI AND MICHAEL GAMBLE

Cast of Characters:

NARRATOR *a skillful storyteller, male or female*
CAT *a proud, adventuresome animal*
MOUSE *a meek, loyal friend*

Setting:

A chair is placed to the right of the performing area at the front of the classroom. The chair represents a chosen hiding place in a church. The NARRATOR sits on a stool to the left of the stage; the mouse and the cat when at home perform up center-stage.

NARRATOR A cat met a mouse (*while* NARRATOR *speaks, action described is pantomimed by the characters*); after getting to know the mouse a bit, the cat professed such great love and affection for the mouse that the mouse consented to live and keep house with him. (MOUSE *puts on an apron.*) The cat was a wise animal and always thought ahead.

CAT "We must prepare our food for the winter," said the cat, "or we shall go hungry. (*Adamant*) And you, little mouse, are not to leave the house or you'll be caught in a trap."

NARRATOR So they put their heads together (CAT *and* MOUSE *do this*) and they decided to make a pot of food to store for the winter. (*Pantomime filling the pot*) Then, they debated for a long while about where to place the pot for safety. (*An argument between the* CAT *and the* MOUSE *is pantomimed.*)

CAT Finally, the cat suggested that the church was probably the safest site to store their pot.

NARRATOR So they agreed to put the pot under the church's altar. (*While the* NARRATOR *speaks, the* CAT *and the* MOUSE *pantomime carrying their pot to the church. They walk around in a large circle three times until they finally arrive at the chair.*) They also agreed not to touch it until they were really in need. When the pot was safely hidden, they traveled back home again (*we see them retracing their steps*), pleased that they had made a wise decision. However, before long the cat was seized with a great desire to eat from that giant pot of food.

CAT (*brightly*) "Listen to me, dear mouse," said he. "My cousin has asked me to act as godfather to her newborn son. The little feller is white with brown spots, and the christening is set for this afternoon. So, let me go to it, if you will, while you stay at home and keep house."

MOUSE (*kindly*) "Why, of course," answered the mouse. "By all means you can go. And when you're eating and drinking all the refreshments, think a bit of me. I would really enjoy a drop of sweet, red wine."

NARRATOR But there was not a bit of truth in all of this. The cat had no cousin, and certainly, he had not, therefore, been asked to serve as godfather. (*As the* NARRATOR *starts to speak, the* MOUSE, *out of the scene, turns her back to the audience: the* CAT, *however, skips around in a large circle and finishes at the chair. He pantomimes the action described by the* NARRATOR.) Instead, he went to the church, dragged out the hidden pot, and licked all the tasty morsels off the top. (*After eating, the* CAT *starts to leisurely retrace his steps, pantomiming as the* NARRATOR *indicates.*) The cat took a stroll over the rooftops of the town, saw some of his friends, relaxed in the sun and licked his whiskers whenever he thought of the pot of food. And, when evening came, he arrived home.

MOUSE (*indulgently*) "Here you are at last," said the mouse. "I hope you've had a great time!"

CAT   "Not bad," answered the cat.

MOUSE   "And what did your cousin choose to name the child?"

CAT   "Top-off," said the cat quite dryly.

MOUSE   "Top-off!" cried the mouse. "What an odd name! Is it widely used in your family?"

CAT   "Does it matter? It's not any worse than Crumbpicker, like your godchild."

NARRATOR   They laughed together. However, it was not long before the cat was again seized with a yearning for the pot of food.

CAT   "I'm afraid I'm going to have to ask you to do me a favor," intoned the cat sweetly to the mouse. "Will you keep house alone again for a day? I have once more been asked to serve as godfather, and this new child has a white ring about its neck. In all good conscience, I cannot refuse."

NARRATOR   So the innocent little mouse agreed. (*As the* NARRATOR *speaks the next lines, the* CAT *creeps around the stage in a circle three times, until he once again reaches the chair.*) The cat departed and crept along by the town wall, until he reached the church where . . . he went directly to the pot of food and proceeded to eat half of it. (*The* CAT *pantomimes this.*)

CAT   "Nothing tastes so good as what one keeps to oneself." (*The* CAT *contentedly pats his tummy, and starts to retrace his steps home.*)

NARRATOR   When the cat reached home . . .

MOUSE   . . . the mouse asked him what name had been given to the child.

CAT   "Half-Gone," answered the cat.

MOUSE   "Half-Gone!" screeched the mouse. "What a strange, strange name."

NARRATOR   Events returned to normal. (*The* CAT *and* MOUSE *are cleaning.*) However, within a few days, the cat's mouth again began to water for the hidden pot of food.

CAT   (*He approaches the* MOUSE *happily.*) "Good things always come in threes," he said to her. "Believe it or not, I once again have to act as godfather. This new little one is jet-black with white feet. Such an event doesn't happen every day. You will permit me to go and serve, won't you?"

MOUSE   "Top-Off, Half-Gone!" murmured the mouse. "They're such odd names, I cannot help but ponder them."

CAT (*firmly*) "That's because you always stay at home in your grey dress and hairy tail, never journeying the world."

NARRATOR (*As the* NARRATOR *starts to speak, the* CAT *starts to run in a circle as before, only this time his manner is quite exaggerated; he stops when he reaches the chair.*) So once again the mouse stayed home alone and cleaned the house while the greedy cat ran to the church to finish downing the pot of food.

CAT (*After eating*) "Now all is completed, and my mind is at rest." (*The* CAT *slinks back home; he looks quite full, quite content, and displays a self-satisfied smile.*)

MOUSE When he arrived the mouse asked what name had been given to the third child.

CAT "It won't please you any more than any of the other names. It's called All-Gone."

MOUSE "All-Gone! What an unheard of name! I never met anyone named that. All-Gone! What in heavens can it mean?" And shaking her head, she curled herself up and went to sleep.

CAT After that the cat was not again asked to act as godfather.

NARRATOR When the winter arrived (*the* CAT *and the* MOUSE *pantomime putting on coats, scarves and hats*), and there was no more food to be found outdoors . . .

MOUSE . . . the mouse began to think of their hidden treasure. "Come cat, we'll go get our pot of food. I'm sure it will just hit the spot!"

CAT "Of course it will," said the cat bravely. "Let's go."

NARRATOR So they set out. (*The* CAT *and the* MOUSE *shiver through the streets, walking together in a circle as before, until they reach the chair.*) When they reached the church, they went behind the altar, and they found the pot. . . .

MOUSE . . . But it was standing empty. (*Very deliberately*) "Oh, now I know what it all meant. Some partner and friend you have been. Instead of acting as a godfather, you have acted as a diner. First, Top-Off! Then Half-Gone! Then—"

CAT "Hold your tongue!" screamed the cat. "One more word and I'll eat you, too!"

MOUSE The poor little mouse couldn't help it. (*Quickly*) Out came the words "All-Gone—"

CAT —and the cat leaped upon her and made an end of her.

NARRATOR (*casually*) And that is the way of the world.

Chamber theatre techniques are effective before adult audiences, as well. *Zapp!* is a business management novel written by William C. Byham, Ph.D., and Jeff Cox. In their tale, which is directed at business managers and supervisors, Byham and Cox tell the story of Ralph Rosco and his supervisor Joe Mode who get "zapped" into a new way of looking at corporate excellence. The cutting that follows was adapted for chamber theatre.

■ Zapp! ■

WILLIAM C. BYHAM AND JEFF COX

NARRATOR 1   Once upon a time, in a magic land called America, there lived a normal guy named Ralph Rosco.

NARRATOR 2   Ralph worked in Department N of the Normal Company in Normalburg, USA. For years, Normal had been a leading manufacturer of normalators, those amazing devices which are so fundamental to society as we know it.

NARRATOR 3   As you might expect, just about everything was normal at Normal, including the understanding of who was normally supposed to do what:

NARRATOR 1   Managers did the thinking.

NARRATOR 2   Supervisors did the talking.

NARRATOR 3   And employees did the doing.

NARRATOR 1   That was the way it had always been—ever since Norman Normal had invented the normalator and founded the company— and so everybody just assumed that was the way it should always be.

NARRATOR 2   Ralph was your normal type of employee. He came to work. He did the jobs his supervisor told him to do. At the end of the day he dragged himself home to get ready to do it all again.

NARRATOR 3   When friends or family asked him how he liked his work, Ralph would say:

RALPH   Oh, it's all right, I guess. Not very exciting, but I guess that's normal. Anyway, it's a job, and the pay is OK.

NARRATOR 1   Ralph worked on a subsystem of what was technically termed the *guts* of the Normal normalator.

NARRATOR 2   One day on his way back from lunch, Ralph happened to be thinking about the guts of the normalator, and, well, he was simply (*lightning-like cracking sound*)

ZAPPED!

by an idea so original and so full of promise that his head nearly exploded with excitement!

RALPH   Wowee! Zowee!! Yeah!!!

NARRATOR 3   The Normal employees around him were shocked!

NARRATOR 1   In his excitement, Ralph totally forgot that probably nobody would listen, and he ran down the hall to explain his idea to his supervisor, Joe Mode.

JOE   It doesn't sound to me like the Normal way to do things. Don't you think if that idea is good, the Normal Research and Development people would have thought of it? But, tell you what, when I get time, I'll kick it upstairs and we'll see what happens. Maybe they'll form a task force to look into it.

NARRATOR 2   How do you feel about that, Ralph?

NARRATOR 3   Ralph was tempted to tell Joe that he didn't want his idea to be kicked anywhere by anybody. . . .

NARRATOR 1   But being normal, Ralph didn't tell Joe anything. He just nodded and went back to work.

NARRATOR 2   Of course, Joe Mode soon forgot about Ralph's idea. But Ralph did not. And because of that, something very abnormal began to take place. Weeks passed, but little by little, from an old normalator evolved a new device, one that Ralph proudly called: RALPH: THE RALPHOLATOR!

NARRATOR 3   Naturally, Ralph just had to try it out. He typed a command on his desktop computer.

NARRATORS 1, 2, 3   (*A whining sound is heard*) A high-pitched whine began to emanate from the strange machine. Ralph gripped the arms of the chair, grinned, and vanished as he was ZAPPED in a powerful flash!

NARRATOR 1   A few hours later, Joe Mode was looking for Ralph, but Ralph was not around. He entered Ralph's work area and was astounded at the tangles of wires running everywhere.

JOE   What's all this?

NARRATORS 1, 2, 3   He sat down in Ralph's chair, and in doing so, his elbow hit the return key on the computer. There was a high-pitched whine, a blinding flash of light, and Joe Mode was ZAPPED into the 12th Dimension!

Ensemble Interpretation of Drama: Reader's Theatre

Another style of ensemble interpretation, **reader's theatre** is group interpretation of drama or dramatic poetry. This mode is similar to the other ensemble modes examined thus far in that it is nonrepresentational. It relies on the physical and vocal abilities of the readers for its effects. The role of the audience members is to picture and complete the dramatic presentation in their imaginations.

As with the other ensemble forms, there is no single way to stage reader's theatre. The group should work at finding the staging techniques that best illustrate and express the nature of their selection. For example, a reader's theatre group may adopt an onstage focus (the type of focus usually used in a fully staged production, an out-front focus (the type of focus usually used in solo-interpretation events), or a combination of off-stage and on-stage focus (the type of focus usually used in chamber theatre). The ensemble should investigate all performance possibilities before settling on the most effective manner of staging and re-creating the literature.

Reader's theatre groups must also be concerned with the narrator's role. What stage directions must he or she reveal to the audience? Should the individual performers function as characters and as narrators? Demonstrate your own creativity by adapting the following material for reader's theatre.

GETTING INVOLVED
Experiencing Reader's Theatre

The following selections from *You're a Good Man, Charlie Brown* and *The Rivals* have been successfully staged for reader's theatre. Read them carefully.

■ You're a Good Man, ■ Charlie Brown
CLARK GESNER

Based on the comic strip *Peanuts*
CHARLES M. SCHULZ

CHARLIE BROWN   I think lunchtime is about the worst time of the day for me. Always having to sit here alone. Of course, sometimes mornings aren't so pleasant, either—waking up and wondering if anyone would really miss me if I never got out of bed. Then there's the night, too—lying there and thinking about all the stupid things I've done during the day. And all those hours in between—when I do all those stupid things. Well, lunchtime is *among* the worst times of the day for me.

Well, I guess I'd better see what I've got. (*He opens the bag, unwraps a sandwich, and looks inside.*) Peanut butter. (*He bites and chews.*) Some psychiatrists say that people who eat peanut butter sandwiches are lonely. I guess they're right. And if you're really lonely, the peanut butter sticks to the roof of your mouth. (*He munches quietly, idly fingering the bench.*) Boy, the PTA sure did a good job of painting these benches. (*He looks off to one side.*) There's that cute little red-headed girl eating her lunch over there. I wonder what she'd do if I went over and asked her if I could sit and have lunch with her. She'd probably laugh right in my face. It's hard on a face when it gets laughed in. There's an empty place next to her on the bench. There's no reason why I couldn't just go over and sit there. I could do that right now. All I have to do is stand up. (*He stands.*) I'm standing up. (*He sits.*) I'm sitting down. I'm a coward. I'm so much of a coward she wouldn't even think of looking at me. She hardly ever *does* look at me. In fact, I can't remember her ever looking at me. Why shouldn't she look at me? Is there any reason in the world why she shouldn't look at me? Is she so great and am I so small that she couldn't spare one little moment just to . . . (*He freezes.*) She's looking at me. (*In terror he looks one way, then another.*) She's *looking* at me.

(*His head looks all around, frantically trying to find something else to notice. His teeth clench. Tension builds. Then, with one motion, he pops the paper bag over his head.* LUCY *and* PATTY *enter.*)

LUCY No, Patty, you're thinking of that other dress, the one I wore to Lucinda's party. The one I'm talking about was this very light blue one and had a design embroidered around the waist.

PATTY I don't remember that dress.

LUCY (*Takes a pencil and draws matter-of-factly on the bottom of the paper bag*) Something like this. The skirt went out like this and it had these puffy sleeves and a sash like this.

PATTY Oh, yes, I remember.

LUCY Yes, well *that* was the dress I was wearing last week when I met Frieda and she told me she'd seen one just like it over at . . . (*The girls have exited.* CHARLIE BROWN *sits immobile as their voices fade.*)

CHARLIE BROWN (*The paper bag still pulled over his head.*) Lunchtime is among the worst times of the day for me. . . .

In *The Rivals*, Captain Absolute, posing as Ensign Beverley, woos Lydia Languish, a sentimental heiress. Lydia is guarded by her Aunt, Mrs. Malaprop—a woman renowned for using long words incorrectly. She is unaware that Absolute and Beverley are one and the same.

■ THE RIVALS ■
RICHARD BRINSLEY SHERIDAN

MRS. MALAPROP, *with a letter in her hand, and* CAPTAIN ABSOLUTE

MRS. MALAPROP   Your being Sir Anthony's son, Captain, would itself be a sufficient accommodation; but from the ingenuity of your appearance, I am convinced you deserve the character here given of you.

CAPTAIN ABSOLUTE   Permit me to say, Madam, that as I never yet have had the pleasure of seeing Miss Languish, my principal inducement in this affair at present is the honour of being allied to Mrs. Malaprop; of whose intellectual accomplishments, elegant manners, and unaffected learning, no tongue is silent.

MALAPROP   Sir, you do me infinite honour! I beg, Captain, you'll be seated. (*sit*) Ah! few gentlemen now-a-days know how to value the ineffectual qualities in a woman! Men have no sense now but for the worthless flower of beauty!

ABSOLUTE   It is but too true, indeed, Ma'am. Yet I fear our ladies should share the blame—they think our admiration of *beauty* so great, that *knowledge* in *them* would be superfluous. Thus, like garden-trees, they seldom show fruit till time has robbed them of the more specious blossom. Few, like Mrs. Malaprop and the orange-tree, are rich in both at once!

MALAPROP   Sir—you overpower me with good breeding. (*aside*) He is the very pineapple of politeness!—you are not ignorant, Captain, that this giddy girl has somehow contrived to fix her affections on a beggarly, strolling, eavesdropping Ensign, whom none of us have seen, and nobody knows anything of.

ABSOLUTE   Oh, I have heard the silly affair before. I'm not at all prejudiced against her on *that* account.

MALAPROP   You are very good, and very considerate, Captain. I am sure I have done everything in my power since I exploded the affair! Long ago I laid my positive conjunctions on her never to think on the fellow again; I have since laid Sir Anthony's proposition before her; but I'm sorry to say, she seems resolved to decline every particle that I enjoin her.

ABSOLUTE   It must be very distressing, indeed, Ma'am.

MALAPROP   Oh! it gives me the hydrostatics to such a degree! I thought she had persisted from corresponding with him; but behold this very day I have interceded another letter from the fellow! I believe I have it in my pocket.

ABSOLUTE   (*aside*) Oh the devil! my last note.

MALAPROP   Aye, here it is.

ABSOLUTE   (*aside*) Aye, my note, indeed! Oh the little traitress Lucy!

MALAPROP   There, perhaps you may know the writing. (*gives him the letter*)

ABSOLUTE   I think I have seen the hand before—yes, I certainly must have seen this hand before—

MALAPROP   Nay, but read it, Captain.

ABSOLUTE   (*reads*) "*My soul's idol, my adored Lydia!*"—Very tender, indeed!

MALAPROP   Tender! aye, and profane, too, o' my conscience!

ABSOLUTE   "*I am excessively alarmed at the intelligence you send me, the more so as my new rival*"—

MALAPROP   That's *you*, Sir.

ABSOLUTE   "*has universally the character of being an accomplished gentleman, and a man of honour.*"—Well, that's handsome enough.

MALAPROP   Oh, the fellow had some design in writing so.

ABSOLUTE   That he had, I'll answer for him, Ma'am.

MALAPROP   But go on, Sir—you'll see presently.

ABSOLUTE   "*As for the old weather-beaten she-dragon who guards you*"—Who can he mean by that?

MALAPROP   Me! Sir—*me!*—he means *me!* There—what do you think now? But go on a little further.

ABSOLUTE   Impudent scoundrel!—"*it shall go hard but I will elude her vigilance, as I am told that the same ridiculous vanity which makes her dress up her coarse features, and deck her dull chat with hard words which she don't understand*"—

MALAPROP   There, Sir! an attack on my language! What do you think of that?—an aspersion upon my parts of speech! Was ever such a brute!

Sure if I reprehend anything in this world, it is the use of my oracular tongue, and a nice derangement of epitaphs!

ABSOLUTE   He deserves to be hanged and quartered! Let me see—*"same ridiculous vanity—"*

MALAPROP   You need not read it again, Sir.

ABSOLUTE   I beg pardon, Ma'am— *"does also lay her open to the grossest deceptions from flattery and pretended admiration"*—an impudent coxcomb!—*so that I have a scheme to see you shortly with the old harridan's consent, and even to make her a go-between in our interviews."*—Was ever such assurance!

MALAPROP   Did you ever hear anything like it? He'll elude my vigilance, will he? Yes, yes! ha! ha! He's very likely to enter these doors! We'll try who can plot best!

ABSOLUTE   So we will, Ma'am—so we will. Ha! ha! ha! A conceited puppy, ha! ha! ha! Well, but Mrs. Malaprop, as the girl seems so infatuated by this fellow, suppose you were to wink at her corresponding with him for a little time—let her even plot an elopement with him—then do you connive at her escape—while *I*, just in the nick, will have the fellow laid by the heels, and fairly contrive to carry her off in his stead.

MALAPROP   I am delighted with the scheme; never was anything better perpetrated!

ABSOLUTE   But, pray, could not I see the lady for a few minutes now? I should like to try her temper a little.

MALAPROP   Why, I don't know—I doubt she is not prepared for a visit of this kind. There is a decorum in these matters.

ABSOLUTE   O Lord! she won't mind *me*—only tell her Beverley—

MALAPROP   Sir!—

ABSOLUTE   (*aside*) Gently, good tongue.

MALAPROP   What did you say of Beverley?

ABSOLUTE   Oh, I was going to propose that you should tell her, by way of jest, that it was Beverley who was below—she'd come down fast enough then—ha! ha! ha!

MALAPROP   'Twould be a trick she well deserves. Besides, you know the fellow tells her he'll get my consent to see her—ha! ha! ha! Let him if he can, I say again. (*calling*) Lydia, come down here!—He'll make me a *go-between in their interviews!*—ha! ha! ha!—Come down, I say, Lydia!—I don't wonder at your laughing, ha! ha! ha!—his impudence is truly ridiculous. . . .

Reflections

1. How would you physically set the stage for each production?

2. What kind of focus would you employ if you were to stage each excerpt?

3. What type of costuming would you suggest?

4. What kind of movement and how much of it would you have the characters use in each scene?

Ensembles for Children

The wealth of literature for children and young people provides another source for ensemble performers. Libraries and bookstores house an extensive variety of materials for the interpretative group. Children's poetry is great fun to perform. Short stories can be produced as children's chamber theatre and plays can be staged in a reader's theatre style for young audiences. A well-rehearsed, well-performed program for children is rewarding for both performers and audience. Try this. Work with your group to choose some piece of literature you all enjoyed when you were young. Next, stage it for an audience of children.

Performer's Journal

Working with group members, select one of the following options to perform for children.

Option 1: Choose a number of poems to stage and present chorally for a young audience.

Option 2: Choose an appropriate short story to present in chamber theatre style for a young audience.

Option 3: Choose a scene or scenes from a play. Using reader's theatre techniques, stage that portion of the play for a young audience.

If possible, arrange for an audience of appropriate age to visit your classroom and watch your performances. Or, take your performances on tour to nearby schools. In your journal, make notes on the audience's reactions to your performance, as well as your assessment of your interpretation.

You can see that ensemble performances of literature have much to offer both the performers and their audiences. Working with others to bring literature alive is both challenging and satisfying. Because it takes time, effort, and commitment to develop effective presentations, ensemble performance is for mature, motivated performers who truly want to explore themselves and their chosen literature. And in the process, they often have fun!

Final Word

Throughout *Literature Alive!* you have explored the art of oral performance. In doing so, you probably have come to know yourself in new ways. Experiencing literature brought this about. You have used your body, voice, and senses to bring literature to life—both for yourself and for others. In prose, poetry, drama, literature for children, literature from diverse cultures, and even documentary materials you have found fuel for oral interpretation.

We hope your journeys into literature have been fruitful and worthwhile, both for you and for your audiences. Oral interpretation is entertaining as well as challenging. Continue to use the techniques you learned in this class to reach yourself and others through literature.

AUTHOR/TITLE INDEX

SUBJECT INDEX

ACKNOWLEDGMENTS

Grateful acknowledgment is given authors, publishers, and agents for permission to reprint or reproduce the following copyrighted literary selections and cuttings.

"My Mother Pieced Quilts" by Teresa Paloma Acosta from *Festival de Flor Y Conte*. Originally published by the University of Southern California Press, El Centro Chicano, Los Angeles. From "The Sandbox" by Edward Albee. Reprinted by permission of the Putnam Publishing Group. Copyright © 1960 by Edward Albee. "For My People" by Margaret Walker Alexander from *This Is My Century, New and Collected Poems* by Margaret Walker. Copyright © 1942, 1989 by Margaret Walker. Published by University of Georgia Press. From *Death in the Woods* by Sherwood Anderson. Reprinted by permission of Harold Ober Associates Incorporated. Copyright 1926 by The American Mercury, Inc. Copyright renewed 1953 by Eleanor Copenhaver Anderson. From *The Lark* by Jean Anouilh, translated and adapted by Lillian Hellman. Copyright © 1955 as an unpublished work. Copyright © 1956 by Lillian Hellman. Reprinted by permission of Random House, Inc. "Money" by Richard Armour. Copyright 1964 by permission of Branden Press, Inc. Reprinted by permission of Branden Publishing. "The Unknown Citizen" from W. H. Auden: COLLECTED POEMS by W. H. Auden, edited by Edward Mendelson. Copyright 1940 and renewed 1968 by W. H. Auden. Reprinted by permission of Random House, Inc. "An Analysis of Miss Muffet" from *Growing Up* by Russell Baker. Copyright © 1982. Used with permission of Congdon & Weed, Chicago. "Growing Up" by Russell Baker. Copyright 1969 by The New York Times Company. Reprinted by permission. From *Go Tell It on the Mountain* by James Baldwin. Copyright 1952, 1953 by James Baldwin. Used with permission of The Dial Press. "The Lesson" from *Gorilla, My Love* by Toni Cade Bambara. Copyright © 1972 by Toni Cade Bambara. Reprinted by permission of Random House, Inc. "Preface to a Twenty-Volume Suicide Note" by Amini Baraka. Reprinted by permission of Sterling Lord Literistic, Inc. Copyright © 1961 by LeRoi Jones (Amini Baraka). "They Closed Her Eyes" by Gustavo Adolfo Becquer, trans. by John Masefield in *Story of a Roundhouse and Other Poems* by John Masefield. Copyright 1912 by Macmillan Publishing Co., Inc. Reprinted by permission of the Society of Authors as the literary representatives of the Estate of John Masefield. From "Family Life in America" by Robert Benchley from *The Benchley Roundup* edited by Nathaniel Benchley. Copyright 1954 by Nathaniel Benchley. Reprinted by permission of HarperCollins Publishers, Inc. "Tears, Idle Tears" by Elizabeth Bowen. Copyright 1941 by Elizabeth Bowen. Reprinted by permission of Alfred A. Knopf, Inc. From "The Good Woman of Setzuan" by Bertolt Brecht, translated by Eric Bentley, edited by Eric Bentley. Copyright © 1947, 1956, 1961 by Eric Bentley. "Death of Innocence" by Frank Bruni. Reprinted by permission of Knight-Ridder/Tribune News Service. From *ZAPP! The Lightning of Empowerment* by William Byham, Ph.D. Copyright © 1988 by Development Dimensions, International. Reprinted by Harmony Books, a division of Crown Publishers, Inc. "On My Short-Sightedness" by Prem Chaya. Originally published in the Cheshire (Australia) Publication *Span—An Adventure in Asian and Australian Writing*, edited by Lionel Wigmore. Reprinted by permission of Prem Chaya and the Chatra Press. From "A Wicked Boy" by Anton Chekhov. Translated by Helen Reeve; copyright © 1961 by Bantam, a division of Bantam Doubleday Dell Publishing Group, Inc. From *75 Short Masterpieces* edited by Roger Goodman. Used by permission of Bantam Books, a division of Bantam Doubleday Dell Publishing Group, Inc. "To Hiroshima" by Ai Ch'ing, "Serves You Right, Begger" by Hsu Chih-mo, "The Pawnshop" by Chu Hsiang, from *Twentieth Century Chinese Poetry* by Kai-yu Hsu, translated by Kai-yu Hsu, translation copyright © 1963 by Kai-yu Hsu. Used by permission of Doubleday, a division of Bantam Doubleday Dell Publishing Group, Inc. "Miss Rosie" by Lucille Clifton © 1987. Reprinted from *Good Woman: Poems and a Memoir, 1969–1980* by Lucille Clifton with the permission of BOA Editions, Ltd. 92 Park Avenue, Brockport, NY 14420. "All There Is to Know about Adolph Eichmann" by Leonard Cohen. Copyright © 1964 by Leonard Cohen. Used by permission. All rights reserved. "The Other Wife" from *The Stories of Colette*, edited by Robert Phelps. Translation copyright © 1983 by Farrar, Straus & Giroux, Inc. Reprinted by permission of Farrar, Straus & Giroux. From "The Heart of Darkness" by Joseph Conrad. Reprinted by permission of J. M. Dent & Sons Ltd. "The Hat Act" from *Pricksongs and Descants* by Robert Coover. Copyright © 1969 by Robert Coover. Used by permission of the publisher, Dutton, an imprint of New American Library, a division of Penguin Books USA Inc. "Childhood" from *Collected Poems* and "The Guitarist Tunes Up" from *On a Calm Shore* by Frances Cornford, published by Cresset Press. Reprinted by permission of Random Century Group, London. "Incident" from *Color* by Countee Cullen. Copyright 1925 by Harper & Brothers; copyright renewed by Ida M. Cullen. Reprinted by permission of GRM Associates, Inc., Agents for the Estate of Ida M. Cullen. "next to of course god america i" is reprinted from *Complete Poems, 1913–1962*, by E. E. Cummings, by permission of Liveright Publishing Corporation. Copyright © 1923, 1925, 1931, 1935, 1938, 1939, 1940, 1944, 1945, 1946, 1947, 1948, 1949, 1950, 1951, 1952, 1953, 1954, 1955, 1956, 1957, 1958, 1959, 1960, 1961, 1962 by the Trustees for the E. E. Cummings Trust. Copyright © 1961, 1963, 1968 by Marion Morehouse Cummings. "Silver" by Walter de la Mare. Reprinted by permission of The Literary Trustees of Walter de la Mare, the Society of Authors as their representative. From *The Little Prince* by Antoine de Saint-Exupéry, copyright 1943 and renewed 1971, by Harcourt Brace Jovanovich, Inc. and reprinted with their permission. "The Hunters" by Harris Downey. Reprinted by permission of the author. From *The Visit* by Friedrich Duerrenmatt as adapted and translated by Maurice Valency. Copyright 1956, 1958 by Maurice Valency. Reprinted by permission of Random House, Inc. "Macavity the Mystery Cat" from *Old Possum's Book of Practical Cats* by T. S. Eliot, copyright 1939, by T. S. Eliot; copyright, 1967, by Esme Valerie Eliot. Reprinted by permission of Harcourt Brace Jovanovich, Inc. "Status Symbol" by Mari Evans from *I Am a Black Woman*, published by William Morrow & Co., 1970. Reprinted by permission of the author. "Snake Dance" by Corey Ford. Copyright 1934 by Liberty Publishing Company. Copyright renewed 1961 by Corey Ford. Reprinted by permission of Harold Ober Associates Incorporated. From *Anne Frank: The Diary of a Young Girl* by Anne Frank. Copyright 1952 by Otto H. Frank. Used by permission of Doubleday, a division of Bantam Doubleday Dell Publishing Group, Inc. From *The Grapes of Wrath* (Stage Adaptation) by John Steinbeck adapted by Frank Galati. Copyright 1939 by John Steinbeck. Copyright © renewed 1967 by John Steinbeck. Stage adaptation copyright © 1990 by Frank Galati. Used by permission of Viking Penguin, a division of Penguin Books USA Inc. "Consoling Meditation on the Great Majority: Fathers" by Don Geiger. Reprinted by Don Geiger. Reprinted by permission of the author. "The Test" by Angelica Gibbs. Reprinted by permission; © 1940, 1968 The New Yorker Magazine, Inc. Excerpt from *Learning One's Place* by Muga Gicaru. Copyright by Muga Gicaru and Lawrence and Wishart Ltd. Reprinted by permission. "Knoxville, Tennessee" by Nikki Giovanni from *Natural Process* edited by Ted Wilentz and Tom Weatherly. Copyright © 1970 by Hill & Wang, Inc. Reprinted by permission of Hill and Wang, a division of Farrar, Straus & Giroux, Inc. From *Through Russian Eyes: President Kennedy's 1036 Days* by Anatolii Andreievich Gromyko. Copyright 1973 by International Library, Inc., Washington, D.C. Excerpt is from the Authorized Translation edited by Philip A. Garon. "Locked In" by Ingemar Gustafson translated by May Swenson © 1967. Used with the permission of the Estate of May Swenson. From *Roots* by Alex Haley. Copyright © 1976 by Alex Haley. Used by permission of Doubleday, a division of Bantam Doubleday Dell Publishing Group, Inc. From *A Raisin in the Sun* by Lorraine Hansberry. Copyright © 1958 by Robert Nemiroff. Copyright © 1959, 1966, 1984 by Robert Nemiroff. Reprinted by permission of Random House, Inc. From "Hills Like White Elephants" by Ernest Hemingway from *Men Without Women*. Copyright 1927 Charles Scribner's Sons. Renewal Copyright © 1955 by Ernest Hemingway. Reprinted by permission of Charles Scribner's Sons, an imprint of Macmillan Publishing Company. From *The Old Man and the Sea* by Ernest Hemingway. Copyright 1952 by Ernest Hemingway; renewal copyright © 1980 by Mary Hemingway. Reprinted by permission of Charles Scribner's Sons, an imprint of Macmillan Publishing Company. "Eight Haiku" from *An Introduction to Haiku* by Harold G. Henderson. Copyright © 1958 by Harold G. Henderson. Used by permission of Doubleday, a division of Bantam Doubleday Dell Publishing Group, Inc. From *The Old Gentleman* by Gilbert Highet. Copyright © 1952 by Oxford University Press, Inc.; renewed 1980 by Helen MacInnes Highet. Reprinted by permission of the publisher. "Dream Boogie" by Langston Hughes. Copyright 1951 by Langston Hughes. Copyright 1979 by George Houston Bass. "A Dream Deferred" from *The Panther and the Lash* by Langston Hughes. Copyright © 1951 by Langston Hughes. Reprinted by permission of Alfred A. Knopf, Inc. "Mother to Son" from *Selected Poems of Langston Hughes* by Langston Hughes. Copyright 1926 by Alfred A. Knopf, Inc., and renewed 1954 by Langston Hughes. Reprinted by permission of Alfred A. Knopf, Inc. "Charles" by Shirley Jackson in *The Lottery*. Copyright © 1948, 1949 by Shirley Jackson. Reprinted by permission of Farrar, Straus & Giroux, Inc. "New Mexican Mountain" from *The Selected Poetry of Robinson Jeffers* by Robinson Jeffers. Copyright 1932 and renewed 1960 by Robinson Jeffers. Reprinted by permission of Random House, Inc. "In Black and White" by Ann Jones. Reprinted by permission of the author. From *The Metamorphosis* by Franz Kafka, trans. by Willa and Edwin Muir. Copyright 1946, 1948 by Schocken Books, Inc. Reprinted by permission of Schocken Books, published by Pantheon Books, a division of Random House, Inc. From "The Hopeland" by K. Kam from *Making Waves* by Asian Women United of California. Copyright © 1989 by Asian Women United of California. Reprinted by permission of Beacon Press. "Lines for an Album" reprinted from *The Collected Poems of Weldon Kees*, edited by Donald Justice, by permission of University of Nebraska Press. Copyright © 1975 by the University of Nebraska Press. From *One Flew Over the Cuckoo's Nest* by Ken Kesey. Copyright © 1962, 1990 by Ken Kesey. Used by permission of Viking Penguin, a division of Penguin Books USA Inc. From "I Have a Dream" by Martin Luther King, Jr., reprinted by arrangement with the heirs of the Estate of Martin Luther King, Jr., c/o Joan Daves Agency as agent for the proprietor. From *A Separate Peace* by John Knowles. © 1959 by John Knowles. Reprinted by permission of Curtis Brown, Ltd. "Out of Darkness" by Alex La Guma from *Quartet: New Voices from South Africa* edited by Richard Rive. Copyright © 1963 by Crown Publishers, Inc. Reprinted by permission of Crown Publishers, Inc. From the book, *Plausible Denial: Was the CIA Involved in the Assassination of JFK?* by Mark Lane. Copyright © 1991 by Mark Lane. Used by permission of the publisher, Thunder's Mouth Press. "The Monument at Wounded Knee" by Cecile Larson. From Osborn, Michael